OXFORD INDIA STUDIES IN CONTEMPORARY SOCIETY

SERIES EDITOR
SUJATA PATEL

OXFORD INDIA STUDIES IN CONTEMPORARY SOCIETY is a new series of interdisciplinary compilations on issues and problems shaping our lives in twenty-first century India. The Series appears at an opportune time, when the boundaries of social science disciplines are being redefined, and theories and perspectives are being critically interrogated. Using the frameworks developed by social science interdisciplinarity, this Series captures, assesses, and situates social trends in contemporary India. It affirms the necessity of analysing issues and themes that have a direct bearing on our daily lives, and in doing so, brings fresh perspectives into play, integrating knowledge from a variety of unexplored sources in conventional social science practice in India. The Series aims to introduce to a wider audience the central importance of interdisciplinarity in contemporary social sciences. It presents novel themes of investigation and builds a fresh approach towards the longstanding debates on methodologies and methods. With its emphasis on the debates on and about 'society' rather than 'social sciences', this Series should find an audience not only among the students and scholars of conventional social sciences, but also among the students, researchers, and practitioners of fields such as law, media, environment, medicine, policy studies, and business studies.

Sujata Patel is National Fellow at the Indian Institute of Advanced Study, Shimla.

T0344552

OXFORD INDIA STUDIES IN CONTEMPORARY SOCIETY

MINORITY
STUDIES

edited by
Rowena Robinson

OXFORD
UNIVERSITY PRESS

OXFORD
UNIVERSITY PRESS

Oxford University Press is a department of the University of Oxford.
It furthers the University's objective of excellence in research, scholarship,
and education by publishing worldwide. Oxford is a registered trademark of
Oxford University Press in the UK and in certain other countries

Published in India by
Oxford University Press
22 Workspace, 2nd Floor, 1/22 Asaf Ali Road, New Delhi 110002, India

First Edition published in 2012
Oxford India Paperbacks 2020

ISBN-13: 978-0-19-948728-8
ISBN-10: 0-19-948728-6

Typeset in 10.5/12.5 Adobe Garamond Pro
by Excellent Laser Typesetters, Pitampura, Delhi 110 034
Printed in India by Replika Press Pvt. Ltd

Contents

Acknowledgements

When the Series Editor, Professor Sujata Patel, invited me to join the Oxford India Studies in Contemporary Society series with a volume on Minority Studies, I was both nervous and excited. I know from experience that editing a book, especially when one has to commission a fresh set of papers, tends to be a long project and involves a great deal of work—finding authors, working around their schedules and your own, sending reminders, revisions of the works. At the same time, it was stimulating and I thank Sujata for this opportunity, for it gave me the chance to do what had not yet been done in Indian social science, which is to reflect on what minority studies means in the Indian context. What might it look like? What questions could it ask? What materials should it explore? Certainly, my own work so far—in the areas of conversion, Christianity, and ethnic violence—could well be said to lead logically into this area and towards such questions. There is a degree of natural progression involved.

Moreover, the idea appealed to me because as with a lot of my earlier research, it lies on the boundaries of disciplines and cannot be confined to any one academic field of study. One would need to bring together political scientists, historians, sociologists, and anthropologists among others, and to think about the ways in which they could contribute and bring depth to this idea of 'Minority Studies'. I would like, therefore, to thank all the contributing authors for the time they spent and the deep reflection and novel ideas they brought to this project. Though each author was given an outline and possible lines of thought that they could follow, they developed their chapters along self-directed trajectories, throwing up new questions and raising issues that had not been conceived of in the initial stages. At the same time, they reflected on other contributors' chapters, thus giving the volume a coherence it might else not have achieved. I need to also thank them for their patience. This volume has been several years in the making, and yet they have stayed the course without complaint.

I would like to thank Oxford University Press's anonymous referees for their very insightful and useful comments, which helped us make this a much better book than it might have been otherwise. It was indeed a pleasure to work with OUP. Though the persons I interacted with changed over time, the whole team worked very hard to make this volume a success. They were exacting and rigorous, but always in a gentle manner. I would especially like to mention Nitasha Devasar, Neha Kohli, and the editorial team at OUP, who were patient with all my queries and never lost their enthusiasm despite several hurdles and delays, which inevitably accompany such a project along the way.

One of my doctoral students, Sai Thakur, who is now a faculty member at the Tata Institute of Social Sciences, went out of her way to help me procure certain research materials, for which I am very grateful. Nilika Mehrotra and Soumendra Patnaik, Sudha Shastri, Omita Goyal, Zarin Ahmad, Sharit Bhowmik, Virginius Xaxa, Huma Kidwai, and, especially, Dhruba Saikia, were always there to reassure me when things looked tough or simply to provide a listening ear. I am deeply indebted to all of them, and most certainly not just in connection with this volume.

Abbreviations

AICC	All-India Christian Council
BJP	Bharatiya Janata Party
CAD	*Constituent Assembly Debates*
CBI	Central Bureau of Investigation
CHHEM	Caste Hill Hindu Elite Males
CIDCO	City and Industrial Development Corporation
CMS	Church Missionary Society
CNI	Church of North India
CrPC	Criminal Procedure Code
CSI	Church of South India
DPI	Director of Public Instructions
DSP	Deputy Superintendent of Police
GFA	Gospel for Asia
HUDCO	Housing Urban Development Corporation
IAS	Indian Administrative Service
IIJ	International Initiative for Justice
IISc	Indian Institute of Science
KSCC	Kandha Kui Samaj Coordination Committee
LTTE	Liberation Tigers of Tamil Eelam
LSD	*Lok Sabha Debates*
MLA	Member of Legislative Assembly
MP	Member of Parliament
MPLB	Muslim Personal Law Board
MWA	Muslim Women (Protection of Rights on Divorce) Act

MWB	Muslim Women (Protection of Rights on Divorce) Bill
NGO	Non-governmental Organization
NSSO	National Sample Survey Organisation
NWGEL	North West Gossner Evangelical Lutheran
OBC	Other Backward Class
PIL	Public Interest Litigation
PPS	People's Power Sanghatana
RCC	Roman Catholic Church
RPI	Republican Party of India
RSS	Rashtriya Swayamsevak Sangh
SC	Scheduled Caste
SCF	Scheduled Caste Federation
SDO	Sub-divisional Officer
SGPC	Shiromani Gurdwara Prabandhak Committee
SNDP	Sri Narayana Dharma Paripalana
ST	Scheduled Tribe
UCC	Uniform Civil Code
UPA	United Progressive Alliance
UK	United Kingdom
US	United States
VHP	Vishva Hindu Parishad

Introduction

Rowena Robinson

In several parts of the world, 'minority studies' or 'ethnic and minority studies' is established as a field of study and offered as a university programme. In India, this has not been the case. While 'minorities' in India are largely thought of as 'religious' minorities, the field of 'religious' or 'minority studies' is not established anywhere.[1] This may be due in part to the modernist stance of India's early leadership, particularly that of Jawaharlal Nehru, who perceived the sway of religion in the lives of ordinary Indians, but saw it more as future India's problem, and not its solution. It would also be a reflection of the opposition of this early leadership to the British colonial policy of using religion to divide the people. In the post-independence period, as we shall examine later, this led to sensitivity to the position of Indian minorities. At the same time, it impeded the generation of a field of the historical or comparative study of religion, ethnicity, or minorities.

There is greater interest today in the study of minorities, and there are several reasons for this change. As we shall see, this is so because of recent shifts in Western academic discourses as well as in interrogations of scholarship on India and changes in political discourses. In Western political philosophy scholarship, the period of the 1990s saw an immense interest in ideas of citizenship, multiculturalism, and the rights of minority groups in the democratic nation state. This was the period when the United Nations prepared the draft Declaration of the Rights of Indigenous Peoples. The framing of this Declaration was itself probably influenced by the rise of ethnic nationalist movements in countries coming out of communism in Eastern Europe as well as the increasing strength of anti-immigration movements in countries such as Britain, the United States (US), and France for instance (Kymlicka and Norman 2000: 3). The result of such ferment was increased attention to minorities and their relationship to the nation state.

I begin by looking at these more recent arguments which have highlighted the idea of the minority in academic discourse and then working my way back to the Indian context and the debates waged on this site, and thence to the historical–colonial interventions which have so crucially shaped our thinking as well as the Indian state's policymaking with regard to minorities. This will necessitate a brief review of *Constituent Assembly Debates* (*CAD*), the question of reservations, as well as much more recent state interventions with respect to minorities. The Introduction then looks at the studies of minority religion across several disciplines, and returns to a consideration of Hindutva or Hindu nationalism, without reference to which minorities in India today cannot be discussed. A wider perspective on all these issues is introduced through a brief excursion into South and Southeast Asian waters. The Introduction then turns to a delineation of some of the volume's critical and cross-cutting themes. The chapters are then introduced and linked back to these earlier discussions before some final remarks are made regarding the field's future.

MINORITIES AND MULTICULTURALISM

The Western debate on minorities in the 1990s was conducted largely in the context of the idea of multiculturalism and focused on minority rights.[2] Who constituted the minorities in these debates and how was the question of rights framed? The groups referred to as minorities largely included immigrant groups, but there was also reference to indigenous peoples and racial and ethno-religious sects. In the debates in Western democracies, the term 'minority rights' largely referred to the cultural rights of minorities, which they lay claim to on the basis of their separate ethnic, racial, religio-cultural, or national identity.

The homogenizing nation state disadvantages minorities. As it attempts to unite the heterogeneous groups within its territory, it emphasizes some form of national culture. This is objectified, for instance, in language, a certain interpretation of history, the selection of national heroes, and the adoption of particular symbols of national identity. The national culture may be projected as neutral or secular, but it usually reflects the culture and symbols of the dominant ethno-religious or ethno-linguistic community (Bhargava 2002; Kymlicka 1992; Sheth 1999). Thus, minorities argued that the 'national' culture of the state devalues and erodes their cultural identity. Immigrants felt that the requirement to conform to the 'national norm' discriminates against them and leads to inter-generational conflicts as the younger generation is alienated from the culture of its elders (Mahajan and Sheth 1999). Groups insisted on at least a certain degree of public endorsement of and respect for their language, cultural practices, and identities (Kymlicka 2001; Taylor 1994).

Discussions, thus, focused on the 'value' and 'equal worth' to be accorded to all human cultures. Culture defines the self and constitutes one's personal identity. Indeed, identity is itself unattainable without signifiers of distinction, for these alone can fulfil the condition of relevance, which is constitutive of identity. Respect for other persons must, therefore, include respect for other cultures. Thus, even a liberal–democratic state might be justified in intervening to protect or maintain the integrity of endangered cultures and forms of life. A further defence of the protection of minority cultures emerges from the liberal theory that diverse cultures provide individuals with real alternatives in the form of different ways of life from among which they can effectively choose (Bhargava 2002; Mahajan and Sheth 1999; Taylor 1994).

At some point, the discussions of citizenship intersected with these debates, for certainly the affirmation of separate minority group rights has crucial implications for an understanding of what constitutes the idea of a 'citizen' (Kymlicka and Norman 2000: 5). Clearly, it was now accepted that a common set of civil and political rights for all citizens is insufficient because the needs of minority groups are not addressed by this. Young (1989) called for a concept of 'group differentiated citizenship', thereby acknowledging that certain groups have both individual and group rights. A notion of citizenship based singularly on individual rights, without reference to group identities, would be unjust because it marginalizes and further disadvantages groups with histories of oppression.[3]

In Europe, the idea of multiculturalism came to contend quite quickly with discussions about whether the liberal–democratic state could effectively integrate other peoples, in particular, Muslim immigrants. In France, for instance, the model of *laïcité* strongly discouraged the emergence of religion or ethnicity in politics. The issues which modern France has contended with—headscarves, turbans, the wearing of religious symbols, covering of the face, and so on—bring out its consistently different struggle with the manifestation of minority identities (Jaffrelot 2004). In other countries of Europe, too, there have been heated discussions regarding the hijab, the necessity of halal food for Muslim school children, the construction of mosques, or the demand for Islamic schools (Joppke 2004).

The rise of the Right and of a nativist reaction against immigrants in some of these societies has been compounded by the defensiveness of particular state legislation. France recently passed a law banning the covering of the face in public; there is the Integration of Newcomers Act (1998) in the Netherlands which makes it necessary for non-European newcomers to learn and be tested in Dutch language and in social and civic orientation, and there are similar programmes framed to ensure that the non-European communities accept and engage with national institutions in countries such as Austria, Germany, Belguim, and Norway. The renewed affirmation of a majoritarian national ethos and a greater demand for civic engagement, interaction, and integration manifest the growing assertiveness of some European states with regard to their liberal principles, and perhaps their increasing lack of willingness to tolerate dissensions from these in the name of multiculturalism (Alam 2004). In other words, among countries even in the West, there are varying degrees of acceptance of the idea of multiculturalism. In large part (as in this Introduction), it is Anglo-American ideas that are referred to when one discusses Western discourses of multiculturalism. Kymlicka (2001), in fact, examines the limits of the applicability of these notions in discussions of nation state formation in East Europe.

On the other hand, criticisms have emerged from within of the idea of the 'minority' and of the 'multiculturalist' framework as well. Kukathas (1998) asserts an idea of liberalism that maintains law and order, but is indifferent to the identities of groups—minorities or majorities—or of individuals within society and certainly does nothing to preserve or support these. He claims that liberal political society of this kind is not united by common culture or collective goals, and the pursuit of these lie beyond the capacity of state institutions. This comes close to the description of what Bhargava (1998) in the Indian context calls 'political secularism', though he feels that it is a rather 'minimalist' understanding of the state, in which it keeps a principled distance from religious communities in order to ensure minimal standards of living to ordinary citizens and prevent the degradation of life. He contrasts this with ethical secularism, which is more demanding in that it necessitates not merely living together in a political association, but living together well. Ethical secularism, he argues, is more difficult, but worth striving for.

Beyond the critique of the notion of multiculturalism lies that of the idea of the 'minority' and of the majority–minority framework itself. Writing from an African-American perspective, Wilkinson (2000: 115) launches a scathing critique of the idea of the minority, which she regrets has been given credibility in matters of policy even though it is 'nonscientific and devoid of conceptual clarity and empirical validity'. As she points out, the term bears a stigma and is steeped in negative associations. Groups defined as minorities are seen as 'lacking': culturally devalued or not having political and economic power. On the other hand, so weak is the conceptualization that many of the characteristics used to understand minorities—that they have a sense of shared identity or possess inherited status—may well be used to describe all groups, including the majority. Size alone is not enough to demarcate minorities; usually, discrimination or disadvantage is part of the definition. However, groups defined as minorities may share few attributes in common, with respect to class, gender, or culture.

Wilkinson argues further that the term 'minority' lacks historical specificity. Asserting that 'specificity is imperative in policy formulation' (2000: 125), she insists on precision in ethnic and race consciousness for policymaking, which should not be based on obfuscating ideas like that of the 'minorities'. As we shall see later, in the Indian context, the 'majority' and the 'minorities' are almost too deeply historically contextualized, such that Bhargava (1999) speaks of a 'majority–minority syndrome' that precedes the 'majority–minority' framework. Bajpai (2000) corroborates that colonial policies for the safeguard of minorities had led by the time of constitutional debates, to the almost routine association of the idea of the minority with special claims or protective privileges of some sort. The 'legitimating vocabulary' for minority rights had been established (Bajpai 2000: 1837). Mayaram (1999) further argues precisely against the kind of 'exactness' of cultural identity that Western models of multiculturalism appear to impose on their bearers, which cannot grasp the possibility of fluid identities. This deficiency would hardly be corrected by Wilkinson's argument which replaces her 'minorities' (an unclear conceptualization in her view) with the greater precision of racial and ethnic categories.

THE INDIAN CONTEXT

There are several issues to be pursued here. While it is true that recent conversations on multiculturalism in India have tended to begin with references to Western discourses discussed earlier (see Bhargava 2002), actually, the Indian practice of multiculturalism and attention to minority rights has been in place for long. In fact, the Indian experience not only constitutes a critique of the central concerns of Western discourses, but also offers a critique of their theoretical underpinnings. On the other hand, as mentioned at the start, as an academic discipline, the study of religion itself has been subsumed under other subject heads and has not come into its own. Moreover, the focus—when such research did take place—was, for a long time, largely on Hinduism. At first, the usual route through which minority religions entered the discussion was through the exploration of 'communal' conflict.

An exploration of the historical context may be integrated with discussions of minority rights and multiculturalism today. The understanding of India in terms of the 'majority–minority' dichotomy was introduced by British colonial rulers, who viewed particularly the Hindus and Muslims essentially through the lens of religion and saw them as bounded and undifferentiated communities. The employment of the decennial census cemented this process by presenting its demographic evidence. With the Morley–Minto Reforms, separate electorates were created for Muslims, and the Government of India Acts of 1919 and 1935 extended privileges of reserved seats and separate electorates to other sections of the population, including the Sikhs, the Indian Christians, and the Depressed Classes.

The application of such categories and of the rigid notion of cultural/communal identity that accompanied them is, as we know, far from the localized, criss-crossing, and overlapping nature of identities that existed prior to British interventions. Rina Verma Williams (see Chapter 2 in this volume) argues further that the constitution of Muslims as a minority proceeded cumulatively rather than being accomplished in an instant. The creation of separate electorates and, later (in the 1930s), the codification of Muslim Personal Law were crucial steps in the process. In other words, she argues that the minority identity needs to be remade and reconstructed over time.

Nevertheless, official categorization has its own consequences. In India, by the time of Independence and the *CAD*, the categories of 'majority' and 'minority' were pretty much entrenched. The politics of the Muslim League leading to the violent and bloody Partition of India on the basis of the 'two-nation' theory had ensured most certainly that framers of the Constitution were well aware of the potential for divisiveness of religion. On the other hand, they were also aware of the need to assuage the fears of the Muslims and other minorities in divided India.

The institutionalization of minority rights in India was coeval with the Constitution of the nation state. A discussion of these rights as framed by the Indian Constitution makes us aware of the differences between the Western and the Indian experiences in configuring the relationship of minorities with the state. As Mahajan (1999) argues, in Western democracies, group rights are being justified just as community life has to a large extent weakened, and they deal largely with the cultural rights of communities. The plea for community rights is put forward, for the most part, by indigenous peoples or by immigrants, and so, it has to be constantly justified against the dominant political culture.

Certainly, contemporary Western states have to factor in religious communities and their different histories, beliefs, and expectations, if only to ensure, minimally, that in the struggle with terrorism, whole groups—particularly large immigrant populations—are not targeted. As an extension of this concern, it becomes important to ensure that the benefits of public policy reach all communities, particularly, groups with a potential for disaffection—marginalized groups with histories of deprivation and difference from the mainstream in terms of language, culture, and religion (see Mahajan 2010: 17).

On the other hand, in India, social and political representation has always been a crucial component of minority demands, rather than only cultural 'recognition'. Further, there is wide consensus in India about community rights within the state, and these are extended not just to marginalized groups, but to all groups in society. Again, while in Western societies minorities claimed community rights against the homogenizing tendencies of the nation state, in India, these rights were granted precisely to pre-empt the overwhelming of minority cultures by the majority. Further, in the West, the granting of minority rights as part of the affirmation of equality introduces the category of the 'cultural' into legitimate political discourse. In India, the concern with equality and cultural diversity was simultaneous, and what emerged was cultural autonomy for communities. This empowered groups, but held the state back from being able to legislate for equal rights, particularly equal gender rights (Mahajan 1999; Mahajan and Sheth 1999).

MINORITIES IN THE INDIAN CONSTITUTION

The history of British colonial policy and the Communal Award, the Partition and Hindu–Muslim politics on the threshold of Independence, and the work of the Constituent Assembly have all ensured that reference to minorities in the Indian context is invariably a reference to religious minorities. The Constitution speaks of the rights of linguistic and religious minorities (Articles 29 and 30), but as Mahajan (1999: 61) points out, the Advisory Committee on Fundamental Rights of Citizens and Minorities had representatives of religious minorities alone. The Assembly, too, had representatives of religious communities that were culturally different from and numerically smaller than the Hindus. These included representatives from among the Muslim, Christian, Sikh, Parsi, and Anglo-Indian communities. It is not surprising, therefore, that the views about community rights at the time of the framing of the Constitution were shaped by the requirements and anxieties of the religious minorities. On account of their numbers, Indian minorities perceived themselves as 'permanent minorities' and on the basis of this, sought constitutional privileges that could not be revoked.

When finally laid down in the Constitution, the cultural rights of communities were as follows. Article 25 ensures all citizens the right to freely profess, practice, and propagate their religion. Article 26 gives every religious denomination the right to establish and maintain institutions for religious and charitable purposes, to manage its own affairs in matters of religion, to own and acquire movable and immovable property, and to administer such property in accordance with the law. Article 29 ensures the right of any section of citizens with a distinct language, script, or culture of its own to conserve the same. Article 29(2) prohibits any citizen from being denied admission into any educational institution maintained by or receiving aid from the state on the grounds of religion, race, caste, or language.

Article 30 is one of the most important constitutional provisions from the point of view of minority rights. It refers to educational rights of the minorities. It gives to all minorities, whether religious or linguistic, the right to establish and administer educational institutions of their choice. It lays down, further, that with respect to the granting of aid, the state shall not discriminate against any educational institution on the ground that it is under the management of a minority, whether based on language or religion.

Some of the rights conferred on citizens by the Constitution refer to all religious communities, while some are meant particularly for the minorities. All religious communities, for instance, have the right to be governed by their personal laws in areas of marriage, inheritance, succession, and the like. They have the right to practice their religion in any way they wish, as well as the right to run and manage organizations for the purposes of religion or charity. Minorities are further extended the right to manage educational institutions, to provide for religious education in such institutions, and to receive aid from the state to run these institutions.

The extension of such rights at the time of Independence affirms that the framers of the Constitution took seriously the place of religion in the lives of the people and accepted the importance of religious and cultural identity. On the other hand, as Mahajan (1999: 62) argues, the granting of specific cultural rights to minorities was considered essential to secure their commitment and loyalty to the emerging nation state. Still, there are particular problems that several scholars have pointed out in the constitutional framing of minority rights.

It is true that minority and majority cultural and religious rights were instituted simultaneously in the Constitution and were, thus, not framed, as it were, against each other. Rather, both are original, equal, and valid claims made on the nation state, which it accedes to, thus, protecting—from the start—the autonomy of religion from the state. In this way, the Constitution acts on the principle of equality rather than on the idea of the majority versus the minority. Further, it is also true that special regard was shown to particular minority needs. For instance, concern was shown towards Indian Christians by the inclusion of the word 'propagate' in the rights of religious communities, for they laid special emphasis on it.

On the other hand, initially, constitutional debates had discussed the issue of disadvantage in terms of three sections of Indians: religious minorities, Scheduled Castes (SCs), and Scheduled Tribes (STs). All through these initial discussions, the rights to political and administrative representation as well as the need for a special office to investigate and report on matters relating to minority safeguards—for all these three groups defined as minorities—were on the table. These were written into the early 1948 draft of the Constitution (Ansari 1999; Bajpai 2000; Jha 2003). By the time of the final draft of the Constitution, however, a split had emerged: minorities based on language, culture, and religion were pulled together and given the 'cultural' rights that have been outlined earlier; and SCs and STs alone were given 'political' rights, that is, reserved seats in legislatures and quotas in government employment (to be reassessed after a period of ten years).

It has been argued that the communal holocaust that the Partition plunged the country into changed the conditions for the framers of the Constitution who now set themselves firmly against narrow communal and separatist demands in the name of secular democracy and national unity. Minorities themselves gave up their demands for the provision of separate seats in legislatures, though Ansari (1999) argues that such a view was not unanimous. Bajpai (2000) holds that the Partition had less to do with the changed stance of the Indian nationalists for whom minority claims for representation were from the outset illegitimate from the point of view of liberal secular democracy. When they were acceded to at all—with respect to SCs and STs—their legitimacy came less from the argument of representation than that of systematic disadvantage, which could be obliterated by access to political and economic power, thus, enabling the 'integration' of these groups with the mainstream.

In other words, in this view, cultural rights appear as compensation for more substantive political rights that remained unachieved. Indeed, it is argued that the trade-off for the Indian Christian consent to the proposal to eliminate special representation for minorities was the agreement by the Hindu 'majority' to the inclusion of the word 'propagate' in Article 25 of the Constitution. Further problems have been noted in the cultural rights themselves. For instance, Article 29(2) appears to put limits on the ambit of Article 30. Thus, in 1989, the judges in *Sheetansu Srivastava v. Allahabad Agricultural Institute* ruled that a minority institution cannot insist on reserving seats for students of its own community (Ansari 1999). In 1991, though, the Supreme Court argued differently in the St. Stephen's case, allowing minority institutions to act on preference for community candidates, up to the limit of 50 per cent.

Ansari (1999: 131), however, points out that the judgement reserves 50 per cent of seats in minority institutions for non-minority candidates in the name of national integration, as schools 'are said to be the melting pot for a nation in the making'. A similar logic is not applied to reserve seats for minorities in non-minority institutions. According to him, this amounts to placing the entire burden of national integration on the minorities. Though it remains unimplemented, in fact, the Ranganath Misra Report (2007), to be discussed later, recommended that 15 per cent of seats in non-minority educational institutions should be earmarked by law for the minorities (10 per cent for Muslims and 5 per cent for other minorities).

From a different point of view, despite the acknowledgement and protection of the welfare-related functions of religious communities, such as the running of schools or charities, the state does not view these communities as central to the concerns of national development and social change (Mahajan 2010: 11). Indeed, with their potential for mobilization and assertion, they have been perceived as possible impediments to change. This was a major concern with respect to religious communities and personal laws. The Indian state managed to push through legislation reforming and rendering more gender-just Hindu personal laws with respect to marriage, divorce, inheritance, and succession, but, for a long while, held back from any intervention in the personal laws of other communities. The provision for the cultural autonomy of communities, according to Mahajan (1999: 60), has curtailed the processes of democratization and the ability of the state to institute equal rights, has reified communities, and legitimized the politics of majoritarianism and minoritarianism.

There are also concerns with the definition of the majority in the Constitution. The definition of Hindu in Article 25 of the Constitution and its ratification in the Hindu Code Bill, the Untouchability Abolition Act, and other legislation treats Sikhs, Jains, and Buddhists as a part of the Hindu community, refusing to recognize their distinctive identities or accord to them minority privileges. This certainly compromises the multicultural posture of the state. From the point of view of the state, further, conversion would imply a change of religion to Islam, Christianity, Judaism, or Zoroastrianism, but not to one of the three religions subsumed under Hinduism.

There are wide-ranging ramifications to this. As part of the Hindu Code Bill, the definition of a Hindu acts as a disincentive to conversion. For instance, one of the grounds for divorce in the Hindu Marriage Act is conversion by one party to another religion and his/her ceasing to be a Hindu. While this provision is understandable from the perspective of the Hindu marriage as a religious sacrament, it is nonetheless surprising that there should not be any need for proof that conversion interferes in other ways with the marital bond or the religious life of the other party (Vijapur 1999).

Under the Hindu Adoptions and Maintenance Act, a separated Hindu wife is entitled to maintenance, but only if she is not unchaste or does not convert to another religion. The conjunction of the two conditions is telling. As Vijapur (1999: 257) puts it, even if a woman was treated cruelly or if her husband maintained a concubine in the same house where she resided, she would not be entitled to maintenance if she separated from him had she converted to another religion.

The Hindu Succession Act disinherits the children of converts or their descendants unless these were Hindus at the time of the succession. Several scholars have pointed out that the sum of these provisions is to create a powerful disincentive for Hindus to convert to another religion. Those who decide to convert can do so only at severe financial cost (Conrad 1995; Smith 1963; Vijapur 1999). These legal provisions constitute a barrier to conversion and compromise the freedom to choose or to change one's belief or religion. Needless to say, these legal disabilities do not arise in the case of conversion between the Hindu religion (narrowly defined) and Jainism, Buddhism, and Sikhism.

The law appears to target conversion to religions—Islam, Christianity, or Judaism—that came from outside India. Its provisions seem intent on protecting Hinduism—extended to include other indigenous religions such as Sikhism, Buddhism, or Jainism—from the effect of conversions. This constitutes a clear example of discrimination based on religion, and the existence of such legal disabilities throws the secular identity of the state in doubt. The law heightens the differences between religious groups and increases religious divides. It privileges the indigenous religions and treats them, in effect, as a community (Conrad 1995).

Despite the constitutional protection of the right to propagate one's faith, there have been attempts to pass laws restricting the conversion, particularly of Dalits and tribals, to other religions, especially Islam and Christianity. Orissa and Arunachal Pradesh, for instance, passed such acts in 1969 and 1978, respectively. Other states recently began to get into the act of bringing in legislation against conversion. There were experiments in Tamil Nadu and in Gujarat. While the constitutional validity of such bills has been questioned, the Supreme Court has declared that states have the right to bring in protective legislation. The Gujarat 'Freedom of Religion Bill' actually stifles the freedom of religious expression selectively in that it attempts to limit conversions among the majority Hindus. The Bill declared that Hindus may convert to Jainism and Buddhism, but not to any other faith without explicit permission from the authorities. The implication is that Jainism and Buddhism have been treated as Hindu sects. Islam and Christianity, two 'outside' minority religions, are more clearly the targets of this kind of legislation.

Such issues are central to debates among those who study minority rights in the Constitution or the legal framework in India and they constitute an important part of what might be included under a potential 'minority studies' rubric. On the other hand, as we shall discuss further, rather than isolating minority questions the more by labelling them under a different category (as, for instance, occurred with women's studies), a case may be made for using the issues raised by the study of minorities to reframe the paradigms of the basic social science disciplines themselves in order to make them comprehensive and comparative in approach.

MINORITIES AND RESERVATIONS

The Constitution has provided positive discrimination mechanisms for the former Untouchables who have been oppressed by the caste system and its legitimating ideologies in our society for centuries. The Constitutional Order of 1950 listed SCs and STs using the list employed by the Government of India (Scheduled Castes) Order of 1936. This Order excluded minorities from being counted among the SCs because at the time, they were covered by the Communal Award. The 1950 Order again specifies that no person professing a religion other than Hinduism may be deemed a member of an SC. However, at this time, as we have discussed earlier, special representation for the minorities was rejected.

The limitation in the 1950 Order has been understood and defended in terms of the logic that religions such as Islam or Christianity claimed the principle of human equality and therefore, there could strictly not be any 'SCs' in these communities. However, the Order was amended in 1956 to include Sikh Dalits, and again in 1990 to include Buddhist Dalits, despite the fact that these are also religions that espouse the idea of equality. Thus, it is principally the Dalits of Christian and of Muslim origin that are affected by the exclusion clause of the Order at present. In the states, Dalit Muslim or Christian converts are usually classified as Other Backward Classes (OBCs), but the benefits they receive are limited and they are competing with larger numbers and with those perhaps having access to greater resources. However, no such discrimination exists with respect to Christians of tribal origin, to whom the category of STs applies.

Thus, while in India religion was acknowledged to have a public presence of a sort and religious institutions were guaranteed protection and autonomy, it was virtually impossible to talk about the pervasive, but also complicated, links between religion and regional, social, and economic inequalities. The Constitution was silent on the subject; it only permitted the state to create and implement policies to benefit 'socially and educationally backward' communities (apart from the separate quotas for SCs and STs). For the most part, the question of positive discrimination in the form of reservation—in legislature, educational institutions, and state employment—was framed in the language of caste. One could speak of and address the questions of the marginalization and socioeconomic disparity of SCs and STs; one could not do so with regard to any other kind of community, particularly one defined by religion.

There has been a shift in recent times, however, and political discourses are more inclined towards a 'communitarian understanding of society' (Mahajan 2010: 15). In particular, the present United Progressive Alliance (UPA) government at the centre, now in its second term, inaugurated this shift. This government made it clear from the outset that it wished to begin a new relationship with minorities, particularly with Muslims (Mahajan 2010). The 2001 Census, taken during the first term of the UPA government, provided systematic data on social and economic inequalities by religion for the country as a whole for the first time since Independence. The UPA set up a committee under Justice Rajinder Sachar in 2005 to report on the social, economic, and educational position of Muslims.

The case for extending reverse discrimination to Dalit Christians and Muslims could also find a more sympathetic ear in the present government. The government set up a Ministry of Minority Affairs and a National Commission for Religious and Linguistic Minorities to recommend practical measures for the welfare of socially and economically backward sections among religious and linguistic minorities. In 2007, in fact, the Report of the National Commission for Religious and Linguistic Minorities, also known as the Justice Ranganath Misra Report after the chairperson of the Commission, advocated that the restriction should be removed and SC status should be delinked completely from religion, as it is in the case of STs. The Report has not so far been implemented, but a Public Interest Litigation (PIL) with regard to extending reservations to Indian Christians is being considered by the Supreme Court.

In June 2006, the prime minister came out with a new 15-point programme for the welfare of minorities. It instituted special measures for the provision of employment, improved educational opportunities, and better living conditions for the minorities. The Sachar Committee

Report was also tabled in 2006, and it showed the extent of disadvantage and even discrimination faced by Muslims in terms of access to political, economic, and educational resources. Muslims showed up consistently as more backward on all indices in relation to other socio-religious communities. The Report made it possible for the first time since Independence to confront—with the help of hard data—the gap in Muslim achievement and advantage.

Apart from provisions for reservations and certain economic benefits, the legislation on SCs and STs includes the Scheduled Caste and Scheduled Tribe (Prevention of Atrocities) Act, 1989. This law contains sanctions to protect Dalits, in particular, from violence by caste Hindus. The law which refuses to recognize SC Christians or Muslims is blind to the fact that conversion has by no means secured them from discrimination or violence by caste Hindus. Violence against Christian Dalits and tribals, for instance, has been recorded in many parts of the country. In some areas, as in Andhra Pradesh, Dalit Christians record their identity legally as Hindu. This is not merely to obtain the economic benefit that goes with SC status, but, crucially, to ensure themselves the protection of the Prevention of Atrocities Act. In a state such as Andhra Pradesh, caste is a grim reality and violence against Dalits is routine.

OVERVIEW OF THE STUDY OF MINORITIES

As mentioned earlier, religious or minority studies did not establish itself in India. For the most part, religion has been studied by historians, anthropologists, and sociologists. With the manifestation of religion as an ethnic identity, political scientists also began to look at religion more seriously. The modern study of religion initiated by Indological scholars and colonial administrators constructed pan-Indian civilization in terms of Brahmanic Hinduism, best studied through its Sanskrit textual tradition. Islam was seen to have come from outside in the medieval period and to have wrought havoc on ancient Hindu civilization. This became the route through which modern communal conflict was understood and formed the basis of the colonial view that Hindus and Muslims were completely separate entities, which could not live in peace together.

The idea that Hinduism synthesized India and was the basis of its civilization paved the way for the academic focus on Hinduism and its characteristic marker—caste. This was particularly true of sociological and anthropological studies. In the post-Independence period, village and caste studies, inspired by the structural–functionalist approach and the folk–civilization continuum model, products of British and American anthropological traditions respectively, took centrality. The Indological emphasis on the 'text' was replaced by a stress on 'context' or the field. Even so, there is a merging of anthropological and Indological traditions. Anthropologists and sociologists linked field data with textual tradition: one had the 'great' and the 'little' traditions; the 'civilizational' and the 'folk'; the 'universal' and the 'parochial'; and the 'text' and 'context'.

It was difficult to understand Christianity or Islam from such a perspective for where was the great Indian tradition to which these could be linked? The major shift from the fieldwork tradition came with the structuralist perspective of Louis Dumont, who saw the study of India as lying at the confluence of Indology and sociology and turned again to the text as the source of indigenous categories of meaning. Dumont's work did influence scholars and lead to an upper-caste, essentialized, and ahistorical understanding of Hinduism and of religion per se; at the same time, the critique of Dumont also played a significant role in throwing open the field of the study of religion and even of minorities. His idea that there was lasting social heterogeneity between the Muslim and Hindu communities and his questioning whether caste could exist in non-Hindu communities, for instance, perhaps initiated both investigation as well as counter-investigations.

Thus, in the initial stages of research into Muslim and other communities, one of the first questions to be raised was: Is there caste in non-Hindu communities? (Ahmad 1973). Ahmad pioneered studies into the world of Muslim communities arguing that greater attention must be paid to non-Hindu communities to build a comprehensive sociology of India. The understanding of Muslims and others as undifferentiated monolithic communities, an idea bequeathed by British constructions of Hindu–Muslim communalism, and its insertion into colonial–legal categories, was contested. Communities, particularly minority communities, were shown to be regionally, culturally, and even linguistically distinct.

Certainly, the paradigms of the debate did not immediately alter, but the shift had already begun. At first, rituals such as life-crisis rituals came in for considerable attention, perhaps because they could be more easily captured by the conceptual category of 'syncretism' (Ahmad 1978). This perspective allowed for the idea that Islam (or Christianity) in India was somehow not fully authentic. It appeared that the most important feature of these religions was their syncretic character, marked by the 'adoption' of Hindu practices—in the first instance, obviously, caste.

Again, in the initial stages, interest in Muslims, Christians, or Sikhs developed in relation to their importance vis-à-vis Hindu society, due to conflict. Hence, studies of Muslims, especially among historians, figured for a long while in the area of the politics of separatism, the Partition, and the history of Hindu–Muslim communalism. Studies on Sikhism emerged prominently in the context of the politics of identity in Punjab. Christianity was viewed through the lens of conversion (*from* Hinduism), as Sikhism and Islam were through the lens of communalism or fundamentalism (*in opposition to* Hinduism). Interest in conversion has risen sharply in recent decades, possibly in relation to the heightening politics of identity in the region as a whole.

An important aspect of recent studies that arose in part out of the critique of Dumont, but is also linked with trying to understand the reworking of Hinduism under the influence of fundamentalist and nationalist ideas, has been an interest in looking at the modern 'representation' or construction of Hindutva. The literature also began to raise serious questions regarding the insertion and assertion of women in the Hindu Right's project of cultural nationalism. The effects of religious fundamentalism on the freedoms of women were also the focus of sustained analysis. In the context of the *Shah Bano* controversy, scholarship looked at the status of women and women's rights under Islamic law in the 1980s in India. This was a critical moment in Hindu–Muslim relations in the post-Independence period. There was violence over the *Shah Bano* issue and the Bharatiya Janata Party (BJP) raised the question of why the state did not implement the directive principle regarding the formulation of a Uniform Civil Code (UCC). This posed difficulties for feminists who did not want to be seen to support the Hindu Right, but who also promoted the idea of the UCC on grounds of gender justice.

We shall discuss ahead the relationship between changing ideas of the nation state, Hindu nationalism, and the minorities. As a result of the tumult of ethnic conflicts during recent decades (Sikh separatism, Babri Masjid, the Gujarat violence, attacks on Christians), certainly, the interest in the study of minorities, in relation to conversion, conflict, and interactions across religious boundaries, has grown tremendously. In recent years, studies of Muslims and Christians in particular have begun to increase. They have challenged several received notions in the study of religion in South Asia. In particular, terms such as 'syncretism' and 'composite culture', which have been freely employed, have been shown to have their limitations. It has been shown that it is facile to view the retention of Hindu elements among converts as a sign of the lack of authenticity of their faith or to assume that they always have a harmonious ('syncretic') relationship with all strands of Hinduism.

As a result, a whole new range of themes have now entered the field: the study of Christianity has certainly benefited from this opening up. Studies have focused on the dynamics of interaction between converters and social groups in different regions, the forms this interplay of cultures and discourses takes, and the modes through which converts challenge and contest elite or priestly authority. Scholarship has begun to look critically at the complex relationship between evangelical discourses and the culture of colonialism and the ways in which converts might subvert missionary agendas.

Work on Islam and Muslim communities has similarly seen enormous shifts. Several taken-for-granted understandings about Muslim identity and relationship to the state have been queried. Mayaram's work on the Meos of north-west India problematized received notions about Muslims, their relationship with other communities and with the modern state. Categories of cultural memory, identity, and tradition were now treated in a historical perspective and one that was by no means secure against conflict and control (Mayaram 1997). The transgressive culture of the Meos survives, but increasingly precariously on liminal terrain, neither absolutely Hindu nor wholly Islamic. The current political shifts and concerns have further given rise to a specific focus on Muslims, an increased interest in the socio-economic and developmental profiles of different religious communities, and a deeper attention to the micro-level processes of dislocation and disruption that impact men and women as a result of religious violence and strife.

HINDUTVA AND THE MINORITIES

The ideology of Hindu nationalism (referred to as Hindutva) understands minorities, particularly Muslims and Christians, as second-class citizens who live in India at the sufferance of the descendants of the ancient Hindus. It is Hindu civilization that defines India and though this civilization has taken in and given shelter, over the centuries, to many foreign elements, these—such as Muslims and Christians—remain alien to the land. This ideology achieved its coherence in the mission of the Rashtriya Swayamsevak Sangh (RSS) founded in 1925 to unite and organize Hindu society and protect it from the influence of foreign missionaries out to convert Indians to these alien religions. Hindus alone were native to the land because they considered Bharat to be both their *pitrbhumi* (ancestral land) and *punyabhumi* (land of dharma or religion); for both Christians and Muslims, the source of religious authority lay elsewhere.

Christians and Muslims have been perceived as a threat to Hinduism because they reduced and weakened the Hindu majority. They have faced the charge of bringing about 'forced conversions', through the offering of incentives or coercion. Either through undisciplined breeding or through forced conversions, these groups threaten Hindu numbers and, hence, its demographic position as India's majority religious group. This view feeds, for instance, the focus of the RSS on reconverting adivasis. At the same time, the strength and aggression of Islam and Christianity historically, which enabled these religions to spread on a worldwide scale, is implicitly esteemed. It is considered necessary for Hinduism—enfeebled by long years of Muslim and British rule—to learn from and emulate these practices, in order to emerge again as a rejuvenated force not only in the form of the Hindu *Rashtra*, but also on a global scale.

Soon after Independence, the RSS was banned following Gandhi's assassination by one of its ideologues. It emerged as a potent force in the 1980s, together with a host of other organizations such as the Vishva Hindu Parishad (VHP) and the Bajrang Dal as well as the political arm of the 'family', the BJP, to assert anew Hindu nationalist politics around the issue of the Babri Masjid–Ram Janmabhoomi in Ayodhya. The battle for Ayodhya saw the magnification of ethnic violence on an unprecedented scale, the brunt of it borne by the Muslims. The violence against Muslims in Gujarat in 2002, following the Godhra incident, has been described by many as a pogrom. What has been noticed increasingly in recent decades is the connivance or the passive concurrence of police and paramilitary forces with Hindu rioters. The soaring violence in recent times has been characterized by carefully executed attacks against Muslims across different states, and the attacks have involved increasingly heavier losses to Muslim life and property.

Politically, the Hindu Right, through the voice of the BJP, rejects the secular nationalism of the Indian Constitution, which it labels as 'pseudo-secularism'. It believes that the articles in the Constitution protecting minority rights are a form of pandering to or pampering the minorities. What is sought is a robust Hindu nationalism in which minorities give up their special rights and accept the supremacy of Hindu culture. As we have seen, however, Muslims are not the only enemies of Hinduism, which also include Christians (and communists). In fact, the RSS has been active in several tribal districts, as—through *ghar vapasi* (home-coming) or *shuddhi* (purification) programmes—it seeks to undo the perceived influence of Christian missionaries on the adivasis. In recent years, Hindu–Christian violence, especially on the adivasi terrain, has been on the increase in several states. Even here, the extent of the fatalities suffered by Christians and Christian missionaries has been particularly severe.

The activities of Hindutva organizations have also had important implications for reducing religious and cultural diversity on the ground. Their schools, publishing units, and youth and women's groups function throughout the country. Hindu revivalist groups work actively to stream-line and split shared religious traditions through their interventions in places of religious worship at local levels. Public gatherings, speeches, and pilgrimages are used to unify diverse groups under the Hindu umbrella. In the process, Hindutva not only attacks the Muslims and Christians, it also underplays the differences among Hindus themselves.

Even so, the construction of a homogenous Hindu culture is not easily achievable. Though its backbone is made up of the higher Hindu castes, the Hindu Right seeks to include Dalits, adivasis, and others through various processes of co-option. However, as Mayaram (2004) argues, despite the fact that they portray themselves as tolerant, organizations such as the RSS or the VHP are unable to accept the cultural practices and identities of a whole host of castes, including Rajputs, Jats, Ahirs, adivasis, and Dalits. As she argues, when these organizations enter local contexts, they capture local associations and reduce cultural diversity even if they open up possibilities of mobility and the enhancement of capabilities for their participants.

The politics of Hindu nationalism spurred studies of secularism and multiculturalism in the context of India. The idea of a Hindu Rashtra strongly challenges the notion of the secular democratic nation state that is enshrined by the Indian Constitution. The discomfort expressed by the Hindu Right with regard to minority protections in the Constitution erupted in the 1980s into a raging controversy over the rights of women under Muslim Personal Law. The political and public questioning of the idea of secularism, or of its value for the Indian nation by the BJP and its allies, has contributed to a growing sense of unease among the minorities. This, combined with the increasing collective violence of the last decades—at separate times against Sikhs, Muslims, and Christians—has spread fear and uncertainty among many groups, especially the minorities.

Recent debates in the literature, therefore, have sought to address the challenge posed by these political arguments to the idea of secularism. While all scholars do not concur on the framework of multiculturalism, they agree that the future of the Indian nation state lies in the ratification of its plural and diverse character, as understood and recognized by its Constitution. The tumult of the recent decades has further opened up other interconnected questions with regard to conversion, the application of personal laws to different communities, and as mentioned earlier, the issue of reservations for minorities. In particular, the controversy over the *Shah Bano* verdict in the 1980s brought out the complicated and not always congruent concerns of minorities, women, and the state. This is a theme that is taken up for further discussion later.

MINORITIES IN SOUTH AND SOUTHEAST ASIA

Other countries in South and Southeast Asia share some of India's predicaments with respect to minorities. In contrast to many Western countries, in this region of the world, plurality and diversity is not a product just of the twentieth century, but of longer-term migrations and settlement patterns that have created complex societies and interconnected states. In fact, for most of these countries, plurality was already in existence at the moment of decolonization or state formation itself; it was not simply injected by later immigrations. For the most part, therefore, it was nascent rather than long-established states that had to work out the position of different groups relative to each other and to the state itself. Moreover, these were largely developing states with fewer resources and greater internal inequalities.

In most of these countries, therefore, unlike in the West, the questions vexing minorities have to do not only with cultural rights or recognition, but also with unequal access to economic and political resources, and social exclusion. On the whole, minorities throughout Asia experience real clashes with nation states on the basis of these differences. Indeed, the provision of special benefits in some of these states for minorities may well have led to greater ethnic consciousness and assertion. Minorities in several of these countries are backward and impoverished; in all, they suffer from considerable disadvantages in comparison to the majority.

In South Asia, moreover, the linkages of history and separations produced of a majority in one state, a minority in the other, thus knotting minority issues with cross-border political relations (Manchanda 2010). This has fashioned complex engagements with diasporic populations that further complicate the manufacture of nationhood as well as the production of community within a rapidly changing political and cultural space. In some Southeast Asian countries, such as Indonesia, Singapore, and Malaysia, a further pattern of enforced heterogeneity was introduced under colonial rule through the influx of migrant workers. Colonial rule also led to the bringing of ethnic and religious politics to the forefront in several of these countries.

In many Asian countries—India, Pakistan, Bangladesh, Nepal, Sri Lanka, and even Malaysia or Indonesia—one sees the rise of 'majority' fundamentalism. The dominant ethno-religious group has shown a tendency in recent times to develop a 'minority complex'. Several of these countries are nominally secular. At the same time, in each of them, the majority religio-ethnic community has expanded its sphere of influence in the realm of politics and governance at the cost of the minority groups. These countries emerging out of colonialism have had diverse experiences of governance, from completely authoritarian rule to the institutionalization of democracy in weak or stronger forms. Countries such as Nepal, Sri Lanka, India, Indonesia, Singapore, and even Pakistan made commitments of different kind to protect minorities; these commitments have altered over the decades and have, in any case, been honoured in varying degrees.

The Indonesian Constitution of 1945 was based on the principle of one people, one language, one Indonesia. The military-backed Suharto regime constructed Indonesia as a highly centralized and tightly controlled country. Islam was not the religion of state, though the country was based on belief in one supreme god. Hence, it was nominally secular, but there were no legal religious minorities since the law recognized no religious majority. Since the Suharto regime, fundamentalist Islam has been rising in Indonesia, but the country has also been moving to a more liberal, democratic system. Constitutional amendments protect the right of the individual to be free from discrimination and the right to practice or not practice religion. Respect for cultural identities and the rights of traditional communities are established. However, regional autonomy in a situation where provinces are created on ethnic lines might lead to minorities being discriminated in these regions, their being displaced or forced to live in fear of being hounded out (Bell 2001).

In Malaysia, the three main ethnic groups are: the Bumiputras (sons of the soil), largely Muslim Malays, who constitute around 61 per cent of the population; the Chinese, who constitute around 30 per cent of the population; and largely Tamil-speaking Indians, who constitute

8 per cent of the population. Others account for the remaining 1 per cent. Two policies of the 1970s have shaped the pro-Muslim Malay character of the polity. First, Malay was required to be adopted as the medium of instruction by all primary schools. While Chinese and Tamil primary schools were allowed to function, Malay became a compulsory language and the language of official government correspondence. Second, the government's National Culture Policy based itself on the culture of the indigenous people, while proposing that suitable elements from non-indigenous cultures would be incorporated into the national culture. It also isolated Islam as an important ingredient of the national culture.

A far greater cause for ethnic discontent was the bundle of state proposals designed to promote the economic advancement of the Malays. Muslims as a community are privileged in the economy and polity. Under the Bumiputra policy of the 1970s, efforts were made to restructure urban employment and corporate ownership by increasing the share of the Muslim Malays in these areas. As a result, a Malay bourgeoisie dependent on the patronage of the state came into being, while Chinese business grew more vulnerable to state discrimination (Hedman 2001). While on the whole, the state claimed 'secularism' and tried to keep in check radical Islamic elements, it also experimented with these forms of official Islamization.

Malaysia's pluralistic model has been under stress both because of the official patronage given to Islam and Muslim Malays as well as because of the perception by more conservative Muslims that Islamization needs to be brought even more to the centre of the political agenda. Malaysia has developed a general civil code of law as well as an Islamic code, which is applied only to Muslims in personal and family matters. Cases relating to conversion are becoming increasingly controversial. Today, every Malaysian must declare a religious affiliation, which is registered with the government. This makes it difficult for Muslims to leave Islam without formalizing the change of status through the legal process. There have been several controversial cases as a result, some involving Hindu migrants from India (Mohamad 2006).

Another interesting country in the Southeast Asian region is Singapore. Singapore's three largest ethnic groups are the dominant Chinese, the Malays, and the Indians. The country's Constitution recognizes Malays as indigenous and, therefore, occupying a special position. It also states that the government must care for the interests of the racial and religious minorities. This strictly organized society has given rise to what has been called the 'Singapore model' of the management of race/ethnic relations. While English is the main government language, officially, Tamil, Mandarin, and Malay are also recognized and employed. Muslim, Hindu, and Christian religious festivals are celebrated and are designated as public holidays. Each political party must have at least one—Malay, Indian, or other—ethnic minority candidate in a multi-seat constituency.

There is a Presidential Council for Minority Rights which examines draft legislation to ensure that it is not discriminatory towards minorities, and also reports on ethnic issues or investigates complaints. A somewhat more controversial 1989 Ethnic Integration Policy decides the maximum proportions in which each of the main ethnic groups can be represented in state housing. The state's tolerance does not extend to smaller minorities. The Jehovah's Witnesses, for instance, were banned some decades ago. Further, in more recent times, the headscarf has been banned for Muslim girls in public schools. The government has certainly not shown any inclination to improve the presence of Malay and Indian minorities in upper-level employment. Malays, certainly, remain underrepresented in the army, the judiciary, and even the cabinet.

The South Asian context provides further instances of the diversity of state–minority relationships. In Bangladesh, the non-Bengali hill and plains tribes as well as the Hindus, Christians, and Buddhists constitute the main minority groups. The Bangladeshi Constitution established Bengali as the state language and accepted nationalism and secularism as state principles. However, the Pakistan Enemy Property Order of 1965, which allowed the state appropriation of 'enemy' (that is, Indian) properties, became, in 1972, the Bangladesh Vesting of Property and Assets Order. This Order has been used to dispossess many Hindus of their property, turning them into second-class citizens. In the case of the hill communities, forced settlement of Bengalis in their midst has led to their eviction or further impoverishment.

Bengali nationalism was replaced by Bangladeshi nationalism under Ziaur Rahman in 1975. Islamic ideals were incorporated into the Constitution and secularism as a state principle was dropped. In 1988, by the Eighth Amendment, Islam was declared the state religion. These moves strengthened the feelings of insecurity of the minorities. The first protests of minorities began to be organized under the banner of Hindu, Boudha, Christian Oikya Parishad. The movement began as a protest against the Eighth Amendment, but later demanded the abolition of all discriminatory laws, such as the Vesting of Property Act. Outmigration to India has been a long-standing response of Bangladeshi minorities to discrimination by the state. This has only reinforced the idea among Muslim Bangladeshis that Hindus have no loyalty to the country. Attacks against Hindus and their places of worship have increased after the Babri Masjid demolition. National parties, for the most part, have sought to consolidate the majority and have failed to incorporate minority needs in party agendas (Mohsin 1999).

In Pakistan, though the 1956 Constitution incorporated fundamental rights for all citizens and special rights for minorities (including the right to be governed by their own personal laws) reminiscent of the rights instituted in the Indian Constitution, these were effectively rendered problematic when placed alongside the Objective Resolution, which opened the way for the incorporation of Islamic provisions. In particular, the foundation of Pakistan on Islamic principles and the requirement that the head of state had to be Muslim decisively neutralized any provision of equality for minorities. Later provisions (1973) ensured that both the president and the prime minister had to be Muslim. The stipulation that no law was to be enacted that went against Islamic injunction and that existing laws would be brought into conformity with such injunctions further weakened the legal position of the minorities.

The Islamic provisions outlined here were reiterated by the 1973 Constitution, which also declared Islam as the state religion of Pakistan. Though it was stated that these provisions would not affect the personal law of non-Muslims or their status as citizens, the Islamization of the Constitution had been effectively set in place. President Zia introduced the Hudood Ordinances prescribing Islamic law punishments for different offences. The incorporation in the 1980s of the blasphemy laws in the Pakistan Penal Code radically widened the scope for the targeting of minorities, including Ahmedis who were prohibited from calling themselves Muslim, from describing their places of worship as mosques, and from preaching or propagating their faith (Zia 2010). The Pakistan judiciary has not effectively protected minority rights and the electoral system successfully denies the minorities meaningful political representation.

Hindus, particularly, are viewed in Pakistan as a fifth column and become a target whenever there is violence against Muslims in India. Christians, too, have suffered several attacks following the US-led war in Afghanistan. The smallest communities such as the Bahais or Parsis are affluent and well-connected and so are protected to a degree against the majority. However, Ahmedis are severely restricted in enjoyment of religious and political rights (Hussain 2010).

In Sri Lanka, the Tamil conflict has dominated all discussions of minority groups and their relationship with the state. However, the Tamils of the northern and eastern provinces considered themselves a nationality rather than a minority. Sri Lanka has a dubious record when it comes to institutionalizing minority rights. There is no affirmative action for the ethnic and social minorities. The Sinhala majority has an almost exclusive monopoly on state power and Sri Lanka is, in effect, a majoritarian democracy. The Constitution does ensure that no citizen shall be discriminated against on grounds of race, religion, language, caste, sex, and other grounds. Further, though Sinhalese is the official language of the state, both Sinhalese and Tamil are designated national languages and persons can be educated in either of these languages (Uyangoda 2010). An Official Languages Commission was set up in 1991 to provide institutional support for the implementation of language legislation. However, officials of the state rarely transact in Tamil and the Commission is only a recommendatory body.

The protracted civil war in Sri Lanka between the Liberation Tigers of Tamil Eelam (LTTE), fighting for a Tamil nation, and the state has altered the discussion on minority rights considerably. The authoritarian Tamil Tigers, unwilling to concede internal democracy, brought into focus the limits for emancipation of projects of self-determination. Moreover, Muslims and Upcountry Tamils, considered as Tamils of recent Indian origin, among other minorities, have kept away from the LTTE. They have tried more pragmatically to enter into coalition alliances with the main parties. The military defeat of the LTTE throws doubt on the political survival of minority rights campaigns. If regional autonomy is considered at all, it would involve only minimum devolution. Minority political parties appear to have accepted their second-class status on the grounds that war with the state has brought them nothing (Uyangoda 2010).

Nepal is a fledgling democracy with continuing difficulties of power sharing and overcentralization. The political sphere sees the domination of the Caste Hill Hindu Elite Males (CHHEM) composed mainly of the Chhetri, Bahun, Thakuri, and Sanyasi castes, and other ethnic and caste groups are disadvantaged and marginalized. Linguistically, too, the policy of instruction in Khas Nepali in schools has disadvantaged non-native Nepali speakers (Lawoti 2010: 282). Protection of the rights of minorities has yet to become a part of the Constitution, and judicial rulings in the recent past have tended to go against the interests of marginalized groups.

In all states just examined, the 'minority' is defined in relation to the nation state, and depending on their past experiences or patterns of colonial intervention, different bases—religion, language, caste, or region—become relevant to its identification. In various countries, religion combines with region or ethnic/linguistic identity to constitute the category of the minority. India's particular trajectory before and after Independence, and the history of Partition, has led to the term minority being associated principally with the religious minorities.

Even more specific contemporary concerns link the countries of this region. As Pfaff–Czarnecka and Rajasingham–Senanayake (1999: 9) argue, while there has been an increasing ethnicization of politics in the South and Southeast Asian region as a whole, what seems to be 'new about recent culture clashes is the scale on which processes of nation-state building and globalization appear to have unleashed local conflicts in ethnic terms, as well as the extent to which dominant ethno-religious groups have developed minority complexes in countries like Sri Lanka, India, Malaysia and Nepal'. Again, global terror discourses have constituted the minorities of some of these states as suspect, including, for instance, Tamils of Sri Lanka or Muslims of India (Manchanda 2010: 1).

Further considerations interconnect the countries of South Asia: often, minorities in one country are related by ethnicity or religion to neighbouring states. As we have seen, this affects—usually adversely— the situation of minorities in these states. On the other hand, if in some states, minorities are considered a 'fifth column' or if security considerations rather than the concerns of liberal democracy appear to affect the ways in which several of these states treat or deal with particular minorities (Kymlicka 2001), this only emphasizes their difference from the West and underlines the need to bring them together for analysis in a comparative perspective.

When it comes to the literature, we see that studies of minorities have been influenced by the 'ethnicization' or even 'nationalization' of minority identities. However, when it comes to religious or ethnic and minority studies, the regions discussed here have not institutionalized these academically. This again marks something of a difference from Western countries. On the whole, with respect to religious minorities, in Southeast Asia, Hinduism and Christianity have found a place in the literature. On the other hand, Islam, Chinese religion, and Buddhism occupy a larger part of the terrain. Relations between minorities and the state, conversion to Christianity, strains between textual and popular religion, and the working of religion within the framework of the urban, secular context have all been discussed. The Singapore model is discussed as one that may be applicable in other countries.

South Asian studies of minority religions also show up many gaps. For a long time, as discussed earlier, minorities were almost invisible in literature on India. As with Hinduism in India, in Sri Lanka, Buddhism, the 'majority' religion, has been the subject of most studies, whereas Islam has been almost completely ignored. Both Hinduism and Christianity have received only passing attention. In Nepal, there have been studies of Hinduism and Buddhism but not of other ethnic/religious groups.

Conflict rendered minorities more visible and significant, whether in Sri Lanka, India, or Pakistan. Certainly, in states such as Bangladesh, Pakistan, and even Sri Lanka, the academic study of minorities is marked by many deficiencies. Pakistan and Bangladesh do not provide a great deal by way of secular studies on religion as a whole. The relationship between state and religion in these countries—the fact that in both the countries Islam is the state religion—has made this a difficult theme for scholars. In Pakistan, social analysis as a whole, whether of religion or other issues, has often employed the technique of absolving the country of its problems by pointing to those of neighbouring countries such as India.

As an introductory volume, the aim of this volume has been limited to defining what 'minority studies' might mean in the context of India. As such, except for Michel Seymour's and perhaps Jal's chapters, the chapters do not enter into comparative analyses across the region. However, this Introduction has sought to take a broader view. Certainly, these issues require to be flagged, for any further work in this new and developing area will need to look at the region in a comparative framework. The historical linkages across several of these countries ensure that comparative studies of culture, religion, or nation-state formation will have much to offer, and will also be significant from the perspective of understanding ethnic conflict or containing terrorism. Again, as these countries globalize their economies and open their societies to more diverse influences, or seek to build more common ground between one another, their treatment of their own minorities will come under greater international monitoring. Though such comparative work is still relatively scarce, there is greater interest than before (Banerjee 1999; Manchanda 2010; Pfaff–Czarnecka et al. 1999).

THEMES OF THE VOLUME

Unlike in some of the other countries in its neighbourhood, in India's political and public discourses, the word 'minorities' has come to stand for religious groups other than the Hindus. Sometimes, this category includes Jains, Buddhists, and Sikhs; while at other times, it only includes Christians, Parsis, Jews, and Muslims. As we have seen, this politics of inclusion and exclusion is part of a longer tale, but, principally, the logic of 'majority–minority' has been inherited from India's Independence struggle and Partition history. This was ratified by constitutional provisions in favour of 'minorities'. The logic of social history is so compelling that though, as Michel Seymour in his chapter in this volume also seeks to remind us, the Constitution refers to both 'religious and linguistic' minorities, popular understanding generally restricts the term to religious minorities. In this series, the theme of ethnicity (covered in a separate volume) is likely to consider conflicts played out by groups claiming separate cultural and linguistic identities. As such, this particular volume on minority studies concentrates on loosely defined religious identities.

Multiple and Overlapping Identities

At the same time, the volume works within the current trends of research on ethnicity and identities in general, and queries, rather than takes for granted, the religious identification of groups. Contemporary anthropological and sociological theory treats cultures and identities as historical constructs. Thus, all identities are fluid and negotiable, rather than bring rigid and bounded. There is space for contestation and conflict. The volume tries to understand how particular circumstances bring to the fore religious identity, and how and under other conditions this identity may dissolve or break up to reveal other affirmations of caste, class, gender, or regional association.

Neither minority nor majority identities are easy to construct in homogenous terms. As several of the chapters in the volume show, in practice, the construction of a minority as a religious group has been difficult to achieve given the existence and competition of several, and sometimes contradictory, allegiances and identities. The study of minorities in India has proceeded beyond the understanding of communities as undifferentiated entities. What is considered of greater significance is the analysis of the construction of religious and minority identity and the implications and tensions that surround such constructions.

The Production of Minorities by Law and State

As the previous sections have shown, nation-state formations, modern legal systems, and the construction of national identities in turn produce minorities. Minorities are always defined by and in relation to nation states within whose boundaries they exist. The law categorizes who is or can be a minority and what claims such groups may make on the state. Even the democratic state, however, is able to accommodate only certain demands. If minorities make nationalist or sub-nationalist claims, as with Sikh nationalists or Tamil Tigers, this may lead them to be defined by the threatened state as 'militants' or even 'terrorists', waging war against the nation. Thus, the idea of the minority always comes bearing the shadow of legal, statist formulations. Moreover, as seen in the discussion of multiculturalism, in the course of such engagements, both state and minority groups end up employing politicized and essentialized understandings of culture or group identity, which have little sympathy for the actual fluidity of identities on the ground.

Matters become even more interesting when more than one legal category can be applied to a group, say, as a minority as well as an ST. When such categories become the basis for the struggle or demand for rights, the politics of identity becomes even more complex and may even turn embittered or violent. Difficulties arise when 'legally' two identities are incompatible, say, Christian minority and SC. In some cases, groups may choose to hide their Christian identity for public and legal purposes in order to be able to adopt the SC label. Kumar and Robinson (2010) record such an instance for the Malas and Madigas of coastal Andhra Pradesh.

What happens when the state itself constitutionally bequeaths us with the categories 'majority' and 'minority' and judicial decisions regularly enable the cementing of those differences by disallowing the recognition of sects within or defections from the majority religion? These troubling questions, and the implications of the use of religion as a basis for discrimination by the state, and the counter-calls for affirmative action on behalf of communities are issues discussed in the volume. The volume explores the dynamics of these and related processes and the ways in which the lives and fortunes of whole groups are implicated in and affected by what appear to be dry, textbook categorizations.

Resistance to Official Categories

While accepting that modern law creates and conditions minority identity, the volume also looks at how groups manipulate the ground-level situation to project a certain identity at a particular point of time. In other words, groups can play with the idea of being a 'minority' and this strategy may be employed for politico-economic considerations or for those of prestige. This is possible since the law seeks to categorize, but also, inevitably, leaves room for doubt. Thus, at a certain point of time, the Ramakrishna Mission or the Jain community can seek to describe themselves as, and to struggle for the status of, legal 'minorities' (see Sipra Mukherjee, Chapter 9 in this volume; Sethi 2009). On the other hand, there may be a group such as the Parsis which—though officially included in the category of the minorities—resists this identification in its worldview and self-understanding.

These battles as well as others query the 'category' of minority or turn it around for a group's own purposes in distinct ways. It is not the view of this volume, however, that authoritative categories overshadow social worlds. While the volume provides a perspective on the workings of the modern, legalistic state in the interstices of society, it also offers a crucial counterview of the dynamics of denial, manipulation, or just plain neglect of official categories that might emerge, sometimes from quite unexpected quarters.

Muslims and the Category of the Minority

The Muslims are certainly the most visible minority in India as well as in many parts of the world today. Some aspects of Muslim society—the hijab, the position of women, Muslim Personal Law, and so on—have even been seen as perhaps intrinsically incompatible with modernity and democracy. Whether it is the dispute over headscarves in Singapore or the rise of orthodoxy in Islamic communities in Malaysia or Indonesia, the Muslims find themselves at the forefront of any discussion of state-minority relations in Southeast Asia. In South Asia, certainly, history has placed Hindus and Muslims on different sides of contested borders, while leaving substantial 'minority' populations of each religious group on the opposite side. The condition of the Muslim minority in India is not directly related to what happens to Hindus in Pakistan or Bangladesh, but the reverse is not always true. Again, the battles against terrorism both in India and across the globe have identified Muslims as the frightening and untrustworthy 'Other'. Muslims, therefore, almost inevitably emerge in discussions of interstate relations.

Further, Muslims in India bear the stigma of Partition, and are constantly called upon to prove their loyalty to the nation. In Hindutva discourses, they are the principal 'outsiders' and 'enemies' of the nation. They are also India's largest minority and so, have often been wooed by political parties in areas where they can make an electoral difference. In recent times, the UPA government has made overtures particularly towards Muslims and has identified this community for specific attention due to its backwardness. All these interconnected reasons have made *Muslims* and *minorities* almost synonymous in political discourses.

This volume certainly displaces the idea that minority studies should be mainly about Muslim studies. Thus, there is an attempt to use illustrations, ethnographic field material, and data of different groups— including much smaller ones such as the Parsis (who, paradoxically, refuse the state-imposed minority label)—in order to bring out comparisons and raise issues of general concern. Further, the chapters take up these general issues, but debate them with regard to particular contexts and specific sites. As far as possible, the volume bases its themes in the specificities of historically grounded as well as ethnographically researched locations. The field material enables us to see that the category of the minority, even when applied to the Muslims, is far from fixed. Though religious leaders or the state may collude in producing the 'minority Muslim', the group designated as a minority is divided by sectarian and other differences.

Minorities and Demography

The demographic question is central to minority politics. Of course, demographic criteria alone do not necessarily define minorities. As we have discussed, ideas about marginalization, disadvantage, and even discrimination are relevant. In fact, the self-perception of threat allows us to speak of the 'minority complex' of the majority community. At the same time, the numbers cannot be avoided. In India, minorities claimed privileges from the state at the time of Constitution-making on the grounds that due to their size in the population, they were permanent minorities. The majority was assumed to be the Hindus. Further, if minorities were to participate en bloc in the electoral process, their size was certainly of some importance (Mahajan 1999: 65).

For the bio-politics of Hindu nationalism, too, the issue of demography becomes central (Foucault 1997). The threat that through defying family planning or coercively converting thousands of Dalits and tribals, the minorities might one day equal or exceed the Hindu population is a potent one in their discourse. From the perspective of this volume, it is this discourse and its implications for the relationship of the issue of demography with the politics of religious conversion that is of considerable interest. From the point of view of Hindutva ideology, conversion is a provocation as it signifies a loss in the game of numbers. It also threatens a national identity based on Hinduism. As this volume emphasizes, not only do these ideas work with a very fixed notion of religious identities, they also conflate religion with the cultural identity of the nation. Thus, Christians are rebuked for becoming 'denationalized' through conversion, with little attention paid to the many ways they are steeped thoroughly in the 'Indianness' of local cultures.

Collective Rights, Individual Wrongs: Women and the Freedom of Expression

One of the crucial difficulties that liberal theory has to deal with, even if it accepts the granting of collective rights, is the fact that minorities are often not constituted democratically internally (Carens 2000; Kymlicka 1992). Communities often resist the organization of their own internal structures in terms of liberal principles. They enforce collective community norms, and these are often detrimental to the rights of individual members of the community. In particular, traditional or religious communities often discriminate against women by imposing norms of marriage that leave women no freedom of choice, and by denying women education, employment, or other opportunities available to men. The liberal agreement on this issue (though see Kukathas 1998 for a different view) is that the right of a minority against the mainstream can be accepted, but not the right of that culture to discriminate against its own members.

In contemporary India, one of the most controversial cases that brought to the light of public discussion the discrimination implicated in permitting different communities to have their own personal laws is the *Shah Bano* case. This case became the focus of a major political storm in the 1980s. Shah Bano, a 62-year-old woman, was divorced by her husband in 1978. She had applied for maintenance under Section 125 of the Indian Penal Code (Criminal Procedure Code [CrPC]) which allows destitute, deserted, or abandoned wives (or ex-wives who have not remarried) to claim maintenance from their husbands. This was granted to her by both a high court and later, a Supreme Court judgement.

The early 1980s had also seen the beginnings of the Ayodhya movement, which claimed that the Babri Masjid in that city was built on the site of Ram's birth and where once a temple of Ram had stood. The Hindu Right had begun to consolidate itself around the movement to 'free' the Ram temple. Whether this movement played some role in increasing the threat to their identity, as perceived by the Muslims, or not, certainly the reaction to the *Shah Bano* verdict was tumultuous. Conservative Muslim leaders garnered support for the protest, and there were rallies, meetings, and strikes. The Rajiv Gandhi government capitulated and hurriedly framed and enacted the Muslim Women (Protection of Rights on Divorce) Act 1986. This exceedingly controversial Act effectively removed divorced Muslim women from the purview of secular law, that is, Section 125 (CrPC) and put the onus of maintenance on their relatives.

We may disagree that multiculturalism as a theory applies to India and prefer to see its policies, certainly its provisions for minorities— including the right to have their own personal laws—through the model of 'axiological pluralism' (Michel Seymour, Chapter 1 in this volume). However, the state still has to contend with the implications of allowing cultural autonomy to communities. Certainly, as has been pointed out earlier, India's minority rights policies have weakened the capacity of the state to protect the rights of women as equal citizens of a secular democracy. Though Hindu Personal Law has been amended from time to time by the state and though Christians have come together to make more gender-just the provisions of Christian Personal Law, the case of the Muslims remains problematic. In the end, one has to consider whether within a democracy, laws protecting community rights may be permitted to overwhelm the rights of individuals within those communities. Scholars argue that personal laws must either incorporate 'opting out' opportunities for individuals or agree to reform to accord with basic individual liberties (Kukathas 1998; Michel Seymour, Chapter 1 in this volume). The state cannot become 'an ally of social conservatism' or permit its ability 'to legislate for equal rights' (Mahajan 1999: 64, 60) to be compromised.

A further difficulty is seen when we look at the question of freedom of expression. One of the critical problems with the practice of secularism in India, with its bowing towards community rights, has been that it often amounts to the collective intolerance of the different communities and groups (Sen 1996). In the name of protecting 'religious sentiments', the state has given communities the right to express intolerance. It has created the social and political conditions for the spread of narrowness. This has simultaneously undermined the democratic underpinnings of the state, by restricting the rights of individuals and groups to peaceful dissent and to freedom of speech and expression of opinion. Any statement or action that is likely to cause wrath to any community is instantly seen as liable for a ban. The banning of Salman Rushdie's *The Satanic Verses* is an example. It is not, of course, true that the state exercises the right to ban only in favour of the minority communities. Ambedkar's *Riddles of Hinduism* was banned, and such bans have touched many issues, including a recent play reinterpreting the figure of Mahatma Gandhi.

If the practice of religions is accepted and encouraged and the rights of religious communities are protected, what is the understanding of the space of secularism that marks such a polity? What happens to the principle of the democratic right of individuals and groups to express freely views that may not be shared by others? How does the Indian understanding of secularism and the rights of minorities differ from other countries? Such questions have already been raised in this Introduction in the discussion on multiculturalism. They are taken up again later in the book, particularly in a general theoretical and comparative piece by Michel Seymour, with which the volume opens.

Stereotyping and 'Securitization'

The issue of the stigmatizing of minorities has been raised earlier. Young identifies five elements of the oppression of social groups. One of these is what she terms cultural imperialism, which essentially is: a group's experience of 'how the dominant meanings of a society render [its own] particular perspective... invisible at the same time as they stereotype one's group and mark it out as the Other' (Young 1990: 58–9). The worldview and experience of the dominant group get projected as the norm; its values and goals—even its history and culture—are the most widely disseminated in society. Hence, the perspectives of other groups are understood in terms of deficiency or negation; these groups are viewed as lacking or falling short of dominant ideals and ethos. Such groups find themselves positioned outside the pale of dominant meanings and structures of experience, inferior and stereotyped images of themselves prevail, and no effort is made to include them in the dominant vision of the world.

Stereotyping of minority religious communities along these lines is common in India. We have mentioned with respect to Christians, that they are sometimes considered 'foreign' or 'denationalized'. This kind of stereotyping and stigma is particularly clear in the case of Muslims. Hindu communal ideologies work with considerable success to demonize the Muslims. However, there are also the more insidious workings of a culture and its socialization and educational processes that take the superiority of Hindus and the 'stranger' status of Muslims for granted. The mainstream Indian media has been known to engage in such processes of 'othering', and Hindi cinema coming out of Bollywood is no different. Using this last as an example, the volume queries the cultural ingredients put together to construct the Muslim. For instance, have these always been identified with Islam or Muslims, or is the exclusive identification a product of developments in more recent times (Saeed, Chapter 11 in this volume)?

Stereotyping and demonization are essential components of the process of producing the minority as a danger—one that the nation needs to contain or to secure itself against. The threat of the Muslims, in particular, is raised at the time of communal conflict. Indeed, the threat is constructed prior to the violence and then employed to legitimize collective and state-condoned attacks targeted against the Muslims as, for instance, in Gujarat in 2002. This issue has been discussed in the volume and, further, connected to the idea of security as a productive discourse, one which not only secures but fabricates the dangers to security (Anand, Chapter 12 in this volume). India's cross-border relations with its neighbours—particularly now with the threat of terrorism—are important to understand the popular construction of Muslims as a fifth column, a danger to state and society. Throughout the South Asian region, Wæver's idea of 'securitization' (1995), wherein the rules of the democratic political system are suspended when the position of minorities is labelled an issue of national security, becomes relevant (also recall Agamben 1998).

THE CHAPTERS

The study of minorities requires an interdisciplinary effort. The contributors to this book include anthropologists, sociologists, political theorists, and scholars of history and religious studies. The first three chapters look at the category of the 'minority' in terms of an all-India perspective, raising general concerns and flagging issues of wide-ranging importance. Michel Seymour, in Chapter 1, locates India's legal provisions for its minorities in terms of a wider comparative framework. In this chapter, Seymour tries to locate theoretically what model of democracy explains India's particular and peculiar notion of secularism, as well as its capacity for the recognition of the collective rights of minority groups and their variant religious practices. He does not employ the term 'multicultural-ism' for India's formula, but calls the country 'a multinational federa-tion practising a particular form of cultural pluralism'. The chapter is important for laying out the issue of 'minorities' from a state perspective and reminding us that in the Constitution at least, these included both linguistic and religious groups. It also brings to the centre the complex issue of 'collective' versus 'individual' rights in a democracy.

The chapter recalls the problematic character of India's policies towards its minorities. As we can see, the Indian state is inhibited from evolving legislation that truly extends equal rights to all—men and women. Further, often, electoral compulsions or the character of the democracy—that legitimizes the group voice—leads to curbs on the freedom of women or of expression of individuals. In the *Shah Bano* case, Muslim women were removed from the cover of a secular law that applies to all women. As a precedent, it demonstrated the weakness of the state in performing the balancing act between equality and cultural diversity.

In Chapter 2, Rina Verma Williams links up with the themes raised by the first chapter by taking a closer look at the crucial issue of personal laws. Further, if in the first chapter statist definitions are not queried but rather made sense of, in this one, Williams finds that the category of the Muslim minority is not a fixed or bounded one but needs to be made and remade continuously. She engages with the question of how religious minority identities have been constructed in the context of modern Indian politics, particularly with regard to the 1980s battles over the definition, understanding, and application of Muslim Personal Law. Pointing to deep divides, including gender divides on the issue, she argues that the construction of an identity as a minority identity is a continuing process. It can emerge from the state and thus entail certain state policies, or it may come from other social groups or even the group thus designated itself. There are both 'top-down' and 'bottom-up' ways through which distinctions are produced and maintained.

In Chapter 3, Laura Dudley Jenkins brings out the complexity of another of modern India's legally and constitutionally created minorities—the SCs. Members of the SCs, as she reminds us, must belong to certain religions—Hinduism, Sikhism, or Buddhism—to be legally recognized as having SC status. As she points out, the cross-cutting nature of caste and religious identities complicates the very definition of who is a minority in India.

Even though religion has usually been employed to denote minorities in India, the definition of who constitutes a religious minority is contested. Jenkins employs the term macro-majority to refer to a politics of representation that sometimes projects arguably 'minority' religious communities under the rubric of Hinduism, thus rendering this majority even larger, and underplaying the distinct identities of groups such as the Sikhs, Buddhists, or Jains. Further, she employs the concept of micro-minority to speak of the fragmentation of the SC identity into subcategories based on religion or through the use of the 'creamy layer' concept. Her argument is that both the fragmentation and the amalgamation—the micro-minority and the macro-majority processes—put the minorities in a vulnerable position.

The relation between state categories, elucidated in Chapter 1, and the complexities on the ground forms the theme of the next four chapters. All these chapters connect, in different ways, with questions that arise out of the complex engagement of authoritative categorizations with the lives and experiences of communities located differently in regional cultures and hierarchical structures. Sometimes, conflicts may arise because of the competition between groups to be recognized by the state as this or that category (with its attendant privileges). Dry, legal labels take on a turbulent life when communities are willing to fight each other, sometimes with desperate commitment to an identity that, in other circumstances or spheres of activity, they may willingly relinquish.

Farhana Ibrahim, in Chapter 4, examines the idea of 'minority' among Kachchhi Muslims and among the adivasis seen as 'betwixt and between' Hindu and Muslim. Acknowledging that in Gujarat, 'minorityness' indicates not just religion but specifically the Muslim, she traces how the idea of being a minority might contain certain privileges or value for the group so designated, whereby it can legitimately demand entitlements from the state. She also examines how the Muslims of Kachchh, or even the Garasia Jatts she focuses on, are not a singular body. Sometimes, caste is more the unifier than religion, but even within the Jatt caste identity, there may be different *maslaq* (sectarian) affiliations, Sunnis or Ahl-e-Hadis, for instance. Her chapter locates the regional character of identities, while Williams's brings out the gender conflicts.

Aspects of this regional and caste complexity are also brought out in the chapter by Joseph M.T. (Chapter 5) on the Buddhists of Maharashtra. His contribution to the volume locates in the specific context of the Buddhists of Aurangabad some of the broader kinds of arguments laid out by Jenkins. He speaks of their Buddhism as Ambedkarite Buddhism and follows the dynamics of their conversion and their caste identity as Mahars. Buddhists are a minority, while Ambedkarite Mahar Buddhists are a major constituent of this group. Joseph pursues the ways in which minority identity is constructed through everyday life and practice—the *habitus* as it were of the minority. Associationalism and the domain of the '*sarvajanik*' or public are together engaged with when the Ambedkarites want to stress their particular identity as Buddhists or as ex-Untouchables. Finally, using the notion of 'political society', Joseph pursues the different ways in which the Buddhists locate themselves in civil and public spheres, tracing how a state constitutes a 'population' out of citizens, entitling such populations to enlist as beneficiaries of its practices of welfare. On the other hand, the spaces inhabited by 'populations' can also become sites for the mobility or empowerment of these designated groups.

Joseph Marianus Kujur, in Chapter 6, pursues the problem of the overlap of identities with respect to the case of Oraon Christians. He talks about the Sarna and Christian Oraons and how they have perceived and articulated their Oraon identity in recent times. Both the Sarnas and the Christians are 'STs' with constitutional entitlements. Nevertheless, the 'tribal' identity of the Christians is challenged by some sections of the Sarnas in collaboration with anti-Christian forces. While the main basis of the challenge is economic and political, Kujur argues that there is also a sense of the 'betrayal' by the Christians of their Sarna ancestry or 'parenthood'. The tribal Christians have also responded to the challenge to their 'tribal' identity by asserting their pro-tribal stance in everyday life. According to Kujur, if in the past the Christian dimension was more prominent, today, among the Christians, it is their Oraon or tribal identity that has taken predominance.

Chad M. Bauman and Richard F. Young in Chapter 7 explore the notion of minority identity through the politics of demography that rages through controversies over conversion. Arguing that conversion has been 'normal' through Indian history, they question any understanding of rigid tightly bound identities in the Indian context. Focusing on the violence in Kandhamal in Orissa, they show its complex location in the politics of caste and tribe, language, and the new Christian sectarian identities. Cross-cutting these alliances and divisions are the produced identities of 'Hindu' and 'Christian', which are invoked in the process of violence against presumed or real Christian conversion practices. As they show, therefore, violence against Christians is often justified as a response to the presumed subversive conversion activities of missionaries. Such a justification requires that the parties involved in perpetrating the violence define themselves primarily along religious lines so that each act of conversion to Christianity can be understood as a defeat in the numbers game between religious communities and can, therefore, be framed as a provocation.

The next three chapters bring out yet other aspects of the state–community relationship. Here, resistance to the state is highlighted and it emerges in three distinct forms: ignoring or refusing state-imposed labels; resistance by battling the state legally in court; and armed struggle against the state. The Parsis, as Murzban Jal points out in Chapter 8, are a community that have always disliked being referred to, or viewing themselves, as a minority. If they accept the designation at all, it is in terms of its sense of small and culturally distinct, not in terms of its denotation as a group that accepts the state's patronage. One of the possible explanations that he offers is that the 'high' Persian culture they claim they are heirs to does not permit them to see themselves as relegated to a subaltern position. Their view has been that they would not like to claim any special concessions as a minority community but would prefer to completely identify themselves as Indian and make themselves indispensable to the country. Parsis embody three traditions—Persian, Indian, and Western—and, in fact, they have embraced modernity willingly. However, this modern community which refuses to locate itself as a minority faces a crisis of its reproductive economy due to the rigid practice of community endogamy.

As Jal notes, the Parsis transcend the status in the political economy of being a minority subservient to the state; this is because their capital accumulation serves their interests far better than the state. However, as he argues, the Parsis are a very small minority and, like other minorities, face the dangers of the exclusive nationalism framed by Hindutva ideologues. Their withdrawal from this reality is due to their obsession with their distinct Persian ethnicity. Nonetheless, by doing this they appear to forget, according to the author, that a minority as such needs minority rights—which they will have to share with all minorities (including the greatly stigmatized Muslims). For this, an affirmation—within their worldview—of the system of rights will be necessary.

In 1981, the Ramakrishna Mission approached the Calcutta High Court with a plea framed against the state, claiming that it was non-Hindu and should have the status of a minority organization. In Sipra Mukherjee's chapter (Chapter 9), she traces carefully the tortured arguments and debates surrounding the Ramakrishna Mission's plea that it was a non-Hindu organization, through the 1980s and early 1990s. She questions the terms 'minority' and 'majority', arguing that when an organization with a large following among the 'majority' seeks to be identified as a 'minority', the label 'minority' comes to contain more than merely an enumerative dimension. It is not merely a bland descriptive term, but is a political one, affirming strength and indicating weakness. Numerical and sociological understandings of what constitutes a minority may not overlap. In analysing the ways in which the term can or is employed in the juridico-legal and socio-political contexts of modern India, her chapter discusses how the labels 'minority' and 'majority' can become fiercely contested ones.

How and when does a minority identity form the basis of a larger, separatist, nationalist identity? Natasha Behl examines this issue in Chapter 10 by focusing on the narrative construction of identity, exploring how actors make sense of their lives. She uses this to analyse the construction of Sikh minority identity tracing it through its various forms, even until it emerges as a nationalist identity. She captures the significance of a nationalist narrative within the Sikh community without assuming that this narrative is either uniform or monolithic. In doing so, she shows how and why Sikhs can, at a certain point of time, locate their socio-political identity in nationalist terms. A segment of the Sikh community narrates its minority identity through a public–nationalist Sikh tale, which emphasizes sacrifice, martyrdom, injury, and injustice, and leads to the emphasis on Khalsa Raj. There are specific material interests as well as enactments of privilege and dislocation that shape the nationalist construction of identity.

The important issue of the stigma of identity, particularly with regard to Muslims, is raised in the last two chapters. Separately, and together, the chapters locate how nationalism, international politics, and popular culture are co-implicated in the creation of the increasingly demonized category of the 'minority Muslim'. Yousuf Saeed in Chapter 11 looks at how popular cinema produced in Mumbai constructs a particular Muslim ethos and Islamic cultural characteristics. Tracing the progress from inclusion to exclusion, he tries to explore through some common examples from Bollywood cinema how particular cultural traits which are at present exclusively associated with Muslims were once freely accepted as normal and practiced by a majority of people. In other words, Muslim traits were part of a more embracing popular culture and were not exclusively 'Muslim'.

However, as he shows, a fifty-year transformation of Muslimness in Bollywood cinema leads to the point where the next and ultimate step becomes, quite naturally, international militancy or terrorism based on religious identity, a preferred subject in recent times. In this cinema, the Muslim has turned deceitful against his homeland, and may be shown as a Pakistani spy working against India as in *Sarfarosh* (1999) or in similar roles in other films.

The final chapter, Chapter 12, by Dibyesh Anand brings together several of the themes that have been discussed at different places earlier in the book: the ideology of Hindutva and the work of cross-border politics; and ideas of demography in the construction of the stigmatized 'Other'. The gendered character of such constructions emerges as he shows how a particular form of majority masculinity is sought to be fashioned through acts of violence. This is a masculinity that announces itself the protector of the security of the Hindus, in fact, of the imagined Hindu nation itself.

In the chapter, he uses the idea of 'security' to understand how violence masks itself as counter-violence, in the name of protection. This happens with respect to Indian minorities, particularly Muslims, wherein Hindutva ideology normalizes violence against minorities in the name of communal, national, and even international security. As he shows, recalling Wæver (1995, 2000), security is constitutive of danger, rather than merely a response to it, and it is accompanied by the dehumanization and stereotyping of the Other. The Other is labelled as the danger and is now fit object for control, policing, even extermination. The international war on terror reinforces the association of Islam and terrorism. In the Hindutva worldview, it becomes easy to conflate the Indian Muslims, terrorists, and Pakistanis.

As Anand's exploration of Hindutva ideology shows, the 'Muslim terrorist' is viewed as a grave threat to the national security of India today;

in the long run, the demographic rise of the Muslims in India produces the spectre of the defeat of Hindus in the numbers game and the annihilation of the Hindu nation, or the possible constitution of another Pakistan. The chapter is a fitting conclusion to the volume, as it also brings us back to the requirement of the consideration of our subject from a cross-country perspective. Certainly, the theme of 'securitization' links the chapter to the section on South and Southeast Asia, bringing into sharp focus the need to analyse the issues related to minorities in India in a wider, comparative framework.

FOR THE FUTURE

I agree with Bhargava (1999) that the minority–majority framework cannot easily be discarded, whether in policy analysis or academic discourse. This volume attempts to bring together some of the kind of work being done on minorities today. It sets out the main themes that occupy us at this point. However, there is considerable scope for widening the ambit of such studies.

On the one hand, the legal and policy framework will continue to be significant from the perspective of the development of the field. In this regard, I have already indicated that the slow trend towards comparative studies needs to be encouraged. Analysts of secularism, multiculturalism, and the role of the state in relation to religion in India have largely tended to compare the experience of this country directly with that of the 'West'. The ways in which other complex, traditional cultures in South and Southeast Asia have mediated the political realities of multi-religious societies in the modern period have largely been ignored. As suggested earlier, the comparative experiences and struggles with secularism of India with other plural, developing countries would be valuable for both theory and policymaking. In fact, one looks forward to more comparative analyses of the trajectories of development—social, economic, and political—in relation to increasing ethno-religious and regional discontent in the countries in South Asia.

On the other hand, the volume restricts itself to the known minorities, one could even say the officially recognized ones. Of course, at all times, it queries these categories and shows them to be historically contingent. It demonstrates as well the need for the study of minorities *in* themselves, in terms of their own understandings of themselves, and in relation to the multiple sites and complex ways in which they seek to perform their identity. Further, the study of minority religions should move towards an understanding of diversity itself, framing itself in ways that can grasp the increasing multiplicity of religious and cultural cults and movements. There are splits, divisions, and a whole host of new faith groups that form part of the terrain of minority (indeed, even majority) religions. The study of these—largely transnational—religious movements that are attracting a significant number of devotees should become part of our analyses. Through such historically located, ethnographically rich, interdisciplinary cross-cultural comparative analyses, we can reframe the dominant models of religion and culture that have thus far been the accepted knowledge.

The text of this chapter, up to this point, constitutes the 'Introduction' to the first edition of this volume published in 2012. Since then, and especially following the victory of the BJP at the national elections in 2014, several shifts have taken place on the ground including the lynching and targeted violence against Muslims and Dalits in the name of cow vigilantism, the blacking out of the media and arrest of some journalists in different parts of the country, and other forms of curtailment of basic freedoms with particularly damaging implications for minorities. It is too soon perhaps, to unravel the full ramifications of these developments; however, it is clear that 'minority studies' in the future will need to contend theoretically with the resurgence of majoritarian populist politics in our part of the world as well as in comparison with similar upsurges in other countries across the globe.

NOTES

1.   However, the new Centres for the Study of Social Exclusion and Inclusive Policy set up in many universities across the country in the recent times have inaugurated a new era. Though the central focus for the centres remains the SCs and the STs, they have also begun to show interest in the study of religious minorities.

2.   One should specify that these debates were, to a great extent, North American. On the other side of the Atlantic, as explored briefly later, the experience of multiculturalism has been more chequered.

3.   On the other hand, such discussions of the relationship between multiculturalism and citizenship could become overly concerned with the unity and viability of the democratic nation state and the potential or perceived threats posed to citizenship by minority rights (Kymlicka and Norman 2000: 40). In this work, in fact, the concern is with examining how theories of multiculturalism and minority rights affect the virtues and practices of citizenship and vice

versa. This could allow multiculturalism to be branded as an ideology for the management of minorities within the framework of the nation state (Kymlicka and Norman 2000; see also Deb 2002: 34).

REFERENCES

Agamben, Giorgio. 1998, *Homo Sacer: Sovereign Power and Bare Life*, trans. Daniel Heller–Roazen, Stanford: Stanford University Press.

Ahmad, Imtiaz (ed.). 1973, *Caste and Social Stratification among the Muslims*, New Delhi: Manohar.

—————. 1978, *Religion and Ritual among the Muslims in India*, New Delhi: Manohar.

Alam, Anwar. 2004, 'Muslim Minority, Multiculturalism and Liberal State: A Comparison of India and Europe', available at http://scholar.google.com/scholar?q=anwar+alam+multiculturalism&hl=en&btnG=Search&as_sdt=1%2C32&aS_sdtp=on (accessed 21 March 2011).

Ansari, Iqbal. 1999, 'Minorities and the Politics of Constitution Making in India', in D.L. Sheth and G. Mahajan (eds), *Minority Identities and the Nation-state*, New Delhi: Oxford University Press, pp. 113–38.

Bajpai, Rochana. 2000, 'Constituent Assembly Debates and Minority Rights', *Economic and Political Weekly*, 35(21 and 22): 1837–45.

Banerjee, Sumanta (ed.). 1999, *Shrinking Space: Minority Rights in South Asia*, Kathmandu and New Delhi: SAFHR and Manohar.

Bell, Gary. 2001, 'Minority Rights and Regionalism in Indonesia: Will Constitutional Recognition Lead to Disintegration and Discrimination', *Singapore Journal of International and Comparative Law*, 5(2): 784–806.

Bhargava, Rajeev (ed.). 1998, 'What Is Secularism For?' in *Secularism and Its Critics*, New Delhi: Oxford University Press, pp. 486–550.

—————. 1999, 'Should We Abandon the Majority–Minority Framework?' in D.L. Sheth and G. Mahajan (eds), *Minority Identities and the Nation-state*, New Delhi: Oxford University Press, pp. 169–205.

—————. 2002, 'The Multicultural Framework', in K. Deb (ed.), *Mapping Multiculturalism*, New Delhi: Rawat, pp. 77–105.

Carens, J.H. 2000, *Culture, Citizenship and Community: A Contextual Exploration of Justice as Even-handedness*, Oxford: Oxford University Press.

Conrad, Dieter. 1995, 'The Personal Law Question and Hindu Nationalism', in V. Dalmia and H. von Stietencron (eds), *Representing Hinduism: The Construction of a Religious Tradition and National Identity*, New Delhi: Sage Publications, pp. 306–37.

Deb, Kushal. 2002, 'Introduction', in K. Deb (ed.), *Mapping Multiculturalism*, New Delhi: Rawat, pp. 13–67.

Foucault, Michel. 1997, 'The Birth of Bio-politics', in P. Rabinow (ed.), *Michel Foucault: Ethics, Subjectivity and Truth*, New York: The New Press, pp. 73–9.

Hedman, Eva-Lotta. 2001, 'Contesting State and Civil Society: Southeast Asian Trajectories', *Modern Asian Studies*, 35(4): 921–51.

Hussain, Ishtiaq. 2010, 'Religious Minorities in Pakistan: Mapping Sind and Baluchistan', in R. Manchanda (ed.), *States in Conflict with their Minorities: Challenges to Minority Rights in South Asia*, New Delhi: Sage Publications, pp. 173–203.

Jaffrelot, Christophe. 2004, 'Composite Culture Is Not Multiculturalism: A Study of the Indian Constituent Assembly Debates', in Ashutosh Varshney (ed.), *India and the Politics of Developing Countries*. London: Sage Publications, pp. 126–49.

Jha, Shefali. 2003, 'Rights versus Representation: Defending Minority Interests in the Constituent Assembly', *Economic and Political Weekly*, 38(16): 1579–83.

Joppke, Christian. 2004, 'The Retreat of Multiculturalism in the Liberal State: Theory and Policy', *The British Journal of Sociology*, 55(2): 237–57.

Kukathas, Chandran. 1998, 'Liberalism and Multiculturalism: The Politics of Indifference', *Political Theory*, 26(5): 686–99.

Kumar, Ashok M. and Rowena Robinson. 2010, 'Legally Hindu: Dalit Lutheran Christians of Coastal Andhra Pradesh', in R. Robinson and M.J. Kujur (eds), *Margins of Faith: Dalit and Tribal Christianity in India*, New Delhi: Sage Publications, pp. 149–67.

Kymlicka, Will. 1992, 'The Rights of Minority Cultures: Reply to Kukathas', *Political Theory*, 20(1): 140–6.

———. 2001, 'Western Political Theory and Ethnic Relations in East Europe', in W. Kymlicka and M. Opalski (eds), *Can Liberal Pluralism Be Exported? Western Political Theory and Ethnic Relations in Eastern Europe*, New York: Oxford University Press, pp. 13–106.

Kymlicka, Will and Wayne Norman. 2000, 'Citizenship in Culturally Diverse Societies: Issues, Context, Concepts', in W. Kymlicka and W. Norman (eds), *Citizenship in Diverse Societies*, Oxford: Oxford University Press, pp. 1–41.

Lawoti, Mahendra. 2010, 'Inclusion and Accountability in a "New" Democratic Nepal', in R. Manchanda (ed.), *States in Conflict with their Minorities: Challenges to Minority Rights in South Asia*, New Delhi: Sage Publications, pp. 279–306.

Mahajan, Gurpreet. 1999, 'Contextualizing Minority Rights', in D.L. Sheth and G. Mahajan (eds), *Minority Identities and the Nation-state*, New Delhi: Oxford University Press, pp. 59–72.

———. 2010, 'Religion, Community and Development', in G. Mahajan and S. Jodhka (eds), *Religion, Community and Development: Changing Contours of Politics and Policy in India*, New Delhi: Routledge, pp. 1–35.

Mahajan, Gurpreet and D.L. Sheth. 1999, 'Introduction', in D.L. Sheth and G. Mahajan (eds), *Minority Identities and the Nation-state*, New Delhi: Oxford University Press, pp. 1–17.

Manchanda, Rita. 2010, 'Introduction', in R. Manchanda (ed.), *States in Conflict with their Minorities: Challenges to Minority Rights in South Asia*, New Delhi: Sage Publications, pp. 1–30.

Mayaram, Shail. 1997, *Resisting Regimes: Myth, Memory and the Shaping of a Muslim Identity*, New Delhi: Oxford University Press.

——. 1999, 'Recognizing Whom?: Multiculturalism, Muslim Minority Identity and the Mers', in R. Bhargava, A.K. Bagchi and N. Sudershan (eds), *Multiculturalism, Liberalism and Democracy*, New Delhi: Oxford University Press, pp. 381–99.

——. 2004, 'Hindu and Islamic Transnational Religious Movements', *Economic and Political Weekly*, 39(1): 80–8.

Mohamad, Maznah. 2006, 'Malaysia's Identity Politics', *The Times of India*, 29 September, p. 18.

Mohsin, Amena. 1999, 'National Security and the Minorities: The Bangladesh Case', in D.L. Sheth and G. Mahajan (eds), *Minority Identities and the Nation-state*, New Delhi: Oxford University Press, pp. 312–32.

Pfaff–Czarnecka, Joanna and Darini Rajasingham–Senanayake. 1999, 'Introduction', in J. Pfaff–Czarnecka, D. Rajasingham–Senanayake, A. Nandy and E.T. Gomez (eds), *Ethnic Futures: The State and Identity Politics in Asia*, New Delhi: Sage Publications, pp. 9–40.

Pfaff–Czarnecka, Joanna, Darini Rajasingham–Senanayake, Ashis Nandy and Edmund Terence Gomez (eds). 1999, *Ethnic Futures: The State and Identity Politics in Asia*, New Delhi: Sage Publications.

Sen, Amartya. 1996, 'Secularism and its Discontents', in K. Basu and S. Subrahmanyam (eds), *Unravelling the Nation: Sectarian Conflict and India's Secular Identity*, New Delhi: Penguin Books, pp. 11–43.

Sethi, Manisha. 2009, 'Hindus by Law? The Case of Jain Minority Claims', *Contemporary Perspectives: History and Sociology of South Asia*, 3(1): 155–62.

Sheth, D.L. 1999, 'The Nation-state and Minority Rights', in D.L. Sheth and G. Mahajan (eds), *Minority Identities and the Nation-state*, New Delhi: Oxford University Press, pp. 18–37.

Smith, D. 1963, *India as a Secular State*, London: Oxford University Press.

Taylor, Charles. 1994, 'The Politics of Recognition', in A. Gutmann (ed.), *Multiculturalism: Examining the Politics of Recognition*, Princeton, NJ: Princeton University Press, pp. 25–74.

Uyangoda, Jayadeva. 2010, 'Sri Lanka: Recent Shifts in the Minority Rights Debate', in R. Manchanda (ed.), *States in Conflict with their Minorities: Challenges to Minority Rights in South Asia*, New Delhi: Sage Publications, pp. 224–59.

Vijapur, Abdulrahim. 1999, 'Minorities and Human Rights: A Comparative Perspective of International and Domestic Law', in D.L. Sheth and G. Mahajan (eds), *Minority Identities and the Nation-state*, New Delhi: Oxford University Press, pp. 242–72.

Wæver, Ole. 1995, 'Securitization and Desecuritization', in R. Lipschutz (ed.), *On Security*, New York: Columbia University Press, pp. 46–86.

——————. 2000, 'The EU as a Security Actor: Reflections from a Pessimistic Constructivist on Post-sovereign Security Orders', in M. Kelstrup and M.C. Williams (eds), *International Relations Theory and the Politics of European Integration*, London: Routledge, pp. 250–95.

Wilkinson, Doris. 2000, 'Rethinking the Concept of "Minority": A Task for Social Scientists and Practitioners', *Journal of Sociology and Social Welfare*, 27(1): 115–32.

Young, Iris M. 1989, 'Polity and Group Difference: A Critique of the Ideal of Universal Citizenship', *Ethics*, 99(2): 250–74.

——————. 1990, *Justice and the Politics of Difference*, Princeton, NJ: Princeton University Press.

Zia, Shahla. 2010, 'Discrimination in Pakistan against Religious Minorities: Constitutional Aspects', in R. Manchanda (ed.), *States in Conflict with Their Minorities: Challenges to Minority Rights in South Asia*, New Delhi: Sage Publications, pp. 143–72.

1

India and the Concept of a Multinational Federation

Michel Seymour

POLITICAL LIBERALISM AS A THEORETICAL FRAMEWORK

India is a population of more than 1 billion inhabitants. It is a single nation, but at the same time, it is multiethnic in the deepest possible sense of the word, with twenty-two recognized languages, hundreds of dialects, and many ethnic communities (as I shall explain, ethnic peoples or 'tribes', cultural peoples, and socio-political peoples). It contains six religious groups (Hinduism, Christianity, Islam, Sikhism, Buddhism, and Jainism) although it is a secular state.[1] It does not seem to be possible for such a complex society to be functional in a minimal sense. And yet, it is ancient, and it is a 50-year-old democracy.

Which theoretical framework could account for India's model of democracy? What model could serve as a basis for understanding the mentality of a population involved in such a complex socio-political reality? India offers perhaps the clearest illustration of a 'social union of social unions', in John Rawls's sense (Rawls 1971: 527, 1993: 320). It is a liberal democracy and a society where toleration as respect has become a social necessity. But at the same time, it is not the usual kind liberal democracy. It is a society that must consistently find a way to adopt politics of recognition and promote liberal principles. Moreover, it is a society where rights and liberties are written in the Constitution, and also one in which the way of life of its citizens does not seem to be inspired by an individualistic conception of society and morality. It is a society that must try to reconcile a secular conception of statehood with communitarian ways of life. How could that be?

These are hard and vexing questions that cannot swiftly be answered within the confines of this chapter. Nevertheless, I shall now describe the theoretical framework that seems to be adapted to India and that could serve as an ideal norm for that kind of society. Of course, it is very important to note that there are huge problems standing in the way between what India has become and the kind of society it could be if it were to be an ideal society governed by principles of justice that every-one accepts and that everyone knows. Religious feuds, violent forms of nationalism, extreme poverty, and remnants of a caste system constitute terrible challenges affecting the Indian society. They can only be over-come after decades of further struggles. India is not yet a multinational federation in a *de jure* sense. It is rather a linguistically federal nation state (Bhargava 2010a: 51).

This young democracy does not correspond to the classical version of liberalism and can be understood only if we resort to political liberalism, that is, the view according to which liberalism must avoid any commit-ment to comprehensive theses in metaphysics (Rawls 1993: xxvii). John Rawls's 'political liberalism' can explain how it is possible for the Indian state to be liberal, democratic, and secular, while at the same time, be able in principle to recognize the collective rights of minority ethnic groups (tribes, cultural peoples, and socio-political peoples) and various religious practices.

John Rawls is usually seen as the epitome of liberal individualism. However, this wrong perception can be explained by the fact that we usually take his *Theory of Justice* (1971) as a basis for our interpretation, not noticing the changes that occurred with the publication of *Political Liberalism* (1993). It is also an interpretation that ignores his 1999 work on the law of peoples in which he ascribes collective rights to peoples, and one that fails to notice that he also welcomes principles concerning self-determination, secession, and federations for stateless peoples in the more complex version of the theory, in addition to the eight principles that he describes for the simplified version of the theory. Finally, it is also a perception that quite mistakenly maps the simplified model of justice for a closed society without immigration, national minorities, and stateless peoples to complex societies in which these groups are almost invariably present.

Political liberalism considers persons and peoples only as they appear in the political sphere, that is, with an institutional identity. It treats persons and peoples as two distinct moral agents and, thus, as two distinct and equal sources of moral worth. Finally, toleration is the basic political principle involved in political liberalism, not autonomy as in classical liberalism. Thus, political liberalism is no longer tied to moral individualism. It has disenfranchised itself in some sense from any comprehensive views about persons, society, the common good, or the good life. It is able to accommodate persons and peoples having very different conceptions about themselves. As we shall see, this approach seems to be well-suited for a diversified society, such as India.

THE POLITICAL CONCEPTION OF PERSONS AND PEOPLES

Individuals have an institutional identity and are conceived as citizens no matter how they represent themselves from a metaphysical point of view. They can represent themselves in various ways: with a single identity or with multiple identities; with an individualistic or a communitarian identity; as having a narrative or dialogic conception of the self; as having dualistic or a materialistic identity; as religious or secular; and so on. Still, they are all citizens belonging to a particular nation. Nations also have a certain institutional identity quite apart from the fact that we consider them as aggregates of individuals or as complex social wholes, as associations of individuals cooperating in a social contract or as communities held together by sharing the same conception of the good life or of the common good.

Political liberalism is a view that suggests we should not raise metaphysical issues concerning peoples. We must simply define them in accordance with their institutional identity in the political arena as single 'societal cultures' or as aggregates of societal cultures, to use Will Kymlicka's terminology, that is, as groups having a certain institutional identity (1995: 76–9). In spite of the enormous difficulties surrounding the definition of a people, we take the existence of peoples for granted. We do not hesitate to treat France, Germany, Italy, and Japan as constituting peoples, and we do not hesitate to talk about indigenous peoples. We also do not hesitate to treat the Scottish, Welsh, Catalonian, and Quebec populations as peoples. Finally, we do not and should not hesitate to consider India as a people. I believe that this is because we make use of an institutional conception of peoples.

Political liberalism does not imply a commitment to the view according to which persons or peoples are 'prior to their ends'. We can be neutral in the debate between individualists, who believe that persons are individuated independently from any moral or religious beliefs and communitarians who reject that view. But this also means that political liberalism can be implemented in a society where most individuals see themselves as defined by their ends, and this is also true of society as a whole. This is where I believe political liberalism can become quite useful in understanding a society like India. The different populations that compose this country have very different views about themselves, as persons and as peoples. But the pluralism involved in this society goes deeper than it does in most Western societies. It is a pluralism involving both individualistic and communitarian conceptions about persons and about peoples. If this pluralism is understood as durable and irreducible, how is it possible to adopt liberal principles? It is only possible if the variant of liberalism that we choose to adopt is one in which a person may understand herself as having a communitarian identity, that is, as constituted by religious beliefs, moral values, and views about the good life or views about the common good, and yet be truly liberal in the political sense.

Our institutional identity must be understood as distinct from our metaphysical identity, and this entails, among other things, that we must distinguish between institutional and moral identities. Our moral identity may change, while our institutional identity remains the same whether or not we can be considered under those circumstances as having also the same personal identity (Rawls 1993: 31). The same idea can be defended at the level of society as a whole. The institutional identity of society may also remain the same when it goes through important moral changes. So, there is also, at the level of society, a distinction to be made between its institutional identity and its moral identity. Individualists will claim that it is the same society that has undergone such a change, while communitarians will say that it has become another society.

The political liberal will be neutral in this debate and she will claim that it is only the same institutionally. The separation between the institutional identity of society and its moral identity allows us to see that the political conception of peoples, which is essential for an application of the ideas of political liberalism, can obtain even in a communitarian society, that is, in a society where a large consensus over the good life or the common good has been expressed in all its institutions. It means that it is possible to implement liberal ideals in all sorts of societies:

individualist and communitarian. Liberalism under this new approach is political, not metaphysical. But this means that it can be implemented in societies with very different metaphysical views, including communitarian views.

This way of separating the political and the metaphysical does not imply a specific kind of separation between what belongs to the public sphere and what belongs to the private sphere. The radical separation between a public political sphere and a metaphysical private sphere only occurs in an individualistically oriented society. In a communitarian society, the very same political ideals are enforced through institutions that function in accordance with communitarian beliefs, values, and ends. So, the institutions of society always reflect a certain comprehensive view, whether it is inspired by individualistic or communitarian ideas. If they are organized around a strict demarcation between the public (political) and the private (metaphysical), they conform to the individualistic conception of persons and peoples as prior to their ends. If they are organized around a particular view of the good life or the common good, they are under the influence of a communitarian conception of persons and peoples. But in both cases, these institutions can be disenfranchised from these comprehensive views if the population is living in a truly democratic society. A true democratic society is one in which the population can imagine itself as available for a potential radical transformation. A true democracy is one that can have an understanding of its institutions as potentially incorporated into very different concrete ethical communities. So, this means that it can be embodied into a communitarian society as well as an individualistic society. The concept of a communitarian democracy is not an oxymoron.

Public institutions are always concretely involved in a dominant comprehensive view, but they can be detached from any particular comprehensive view. Shall we then say that, in a sense, our institutions are somehow prior to their ends? Not really, because it is possible to see the democratic process as a continuous search of the true moral nature of society as a whole, in perfect accordance with the distinction between institutional identity and moral identity. So, the distinction between the moral and institutional concepts of identity does not mean that we must conceive of society as prior to its ends. The institutional identity of peoples can and must be detached from particular views about the good life or the common good, but at any given moment of time, it is also concretely realized in a particular ethical life. Thus, it is possible for a true liberal democracy to be embodied into a communitarian society.

In such a society, citizens are rationally autonomous, but not in the substantive individualistic sense of being prior to their ends. A rationally autonomous agent is one that can reflect upon her practices, perform strong evaluations over these practices, that is, she is able to sort out among her first-order moral judgements which are the ones she considers to be most important, and she is also able to engage into thought experiments concerning what she could be. These are the only requirements involved in order to perform our duties as citizens in a democracy. Now, this exercise in rational autonomy is perfectly possible in a society engaged in an ongoing process of self-discovery leading to a definition of oneself in terms of beliefs, values, and ends. Therefore, it is possible to be all at once rationally autonomous and communitarian. This is why one should never rule out the possibility that a given society could become a communitarian democracy. It would be a democracy concretely embodied in a society where specific views about the good life or about common good are institutionally implemented.

Just as persons have an institutional identity of citizens, peoples can also be described as having a certain institutional identity. As societies, they are perhaps always concretely understood either as associations of individuals in accordance with individualism or as political communities understood in the communitarian sense. But since a democratic society can change and can be interpreted within different comprehensive frameworks, its institutional identity can also be described as not necessarily tied to any metaphysical view. We can, thus, introduce a political conception of peoples that parallels the one that we introduced for persons (Rawls 1999). Will Kymlicka's distinction between the structure of culture and the character of culture may be of a certain use here. It reproduces at the collective level the distinction between the institutional identity and the moral identity that we could want to make at the individual level (Kymlicka 1989: 166–70). Very roughly, the structure of culture involves particularistic features, such as languages, institutions in which these languages are being used, and the historical presence of these institutions. The character involves other kinds of particularistic features, such as beliefs, values, traditions, customs, and so on.

TWO SOURCES OF VALID MORAL CLAIMS

Political liberalism also entails that individuals are not the only sources of moral worth, for peoples too understood in the political sense have an autonomous moral worth. If individuals have rights as citizens, peoples have rights in virtue of having an institutional identity. We should be favourable to an axiological pluralism in virtue of which the equal moral importance of individuals and peoples would be asserted. This leads Rawls to the admission of two distinct original positions, one for persons and one for peoples (Rawls 1999: 33–4). Ultimately, it also implies that we are seeking a balance between individual and collective rights. We reject both ethical individualism and ethical collectivism. Individual rights must not override all collective rights and collective rights must not override all individual rights. So, we must make room for full-blooded collective rights, and not only for group-differentiated rights.[2] Collective rights are not claimed on behalf of individuals, but on behalf of peoples, and their relevance is not to be explained by the value individuals ascribe to their own cultural affiliations. Peoples are valuable because they contribute to cultural diversity and because there is a growing consensus concerning the value of cultural diversity.

What is striking about India is that we do not witness the same reluctance towards group rights that one finds in Western societies. India is seeking to become a society in which both kinds of rights, individual and collective, are involved in some kind of 'cohabitation'. Therefore, it is well-suited for the kind of political liberalism that one finds in the work of Rawls. India offers the perfect case of a complex society in which the principles governing the relation between persons are to cohabit with the principles governing the relations among peoples.

TOLERATION, NOT AUTONOMY

I have argued that the kind of liberalism I favour for India is political liberalism, and that this is founded upon the value of toleration. If we were able to show that political liberalism does indeed apply to societies, such as India, we would then be in a position to argue that political liberalism is truly a universal doctrine and not one that is necessarily tied to Western societies. Many Indian intellectuals will react very strongly against the suggestion of 'importing' liberal ideals in their own society. They will see this as suggesting some kind of intellectual colonialism.

But, on the contrary, it could be argued that political liberalism takes its origins in societies that are deeply confronted with religious and cultural differences. My suggestion is that as a democratic society, India must now be clearly described as liberal, but not in the usual way, not according to the traditional individualistic model. It is much closer to the version of liberalism that I have described as political liberalism, since it is no longer based on ethical individualism. First, it is now to a large extent moving towards a communitarian conception of itself. But even more importantly, it is perhaps a microcosm of the international society. As a social union of social unions, it is composed of many different communitarian societies. But nevertheless, it could remain politically liberal if it were able also to practice toleration towards ethnic groups and religious minorities.

DEFINING PEOPLES

One of the major paradoxes of the Indian society that I have already underlined is the presence, within a single country, of twenty-two recognized languages. How could India be a nation under those circumstances? Using once again Kymlicka's terminology, we can describe nations as 'societal cultures', that is, as structures of cultures offering a context of choice. But the structure in these societal cultures usually involves a common language, a common set of institutions in which the common language is mostly spoken, and a common history which is nothing more than the history of the common institutions (Kymlicka 1995: 76–9). These structural features belong to all sorts of nations, whether their populations also conceive themselves as aggregates of persons or as complex social wholes, and as associations of individuals or as political communities. Therefore, according to this picture, nations should be monolingual societies. So, as a multilingual society, how could India be a single nation? Let us look at this matter more closely.

How could a nation be multilingual if it is to be defined with the help of the concept of societal culture and if a societal culture is monolingual? My answer to this is that if we adopt the political conception of peoples; peoples can be conceived either as single societal cultures or aggregates of societal cultures. As societal cultures, they are institutionally organized groups with a certain structure of culture. In the most simple case, a structure of culture involves only one common public language, one common public set of institutions (in which the common public language is mostly spoken), and one common public history of these common public institutions, but there are more complex cases. In the more complex case, a societal culture may itself contain many different component societal cultures. It is, for instance, the case in Canada, Great Britain, or Spain, and it is also the case with India. Multisocietal nations can unify their many diverse component cultures around a sovereign state, a common public history, and various specific values, such as multilinguism, multiculturalism, and federalism. And, they also find ties that bind their members together in the common understanding that society as a whole is an aggregate of component societal cultures.

Whether societal cultures are simple or aggregatively constituted, language appears to occupy a central position for ethnic identity. Even if it is not always a distinctive trait, it does always contribute in shaping the group's distinctive identity. It can serve this purpose by filtering cultural influences, and, thus, shaping original institutions offering a distinctive context of choice. It can also, of course, serve the purpose of differentiation with other cultures by itself being distinct. But in either case, language is a fundamental ethnic trait. This is because it is a collective property that applies initially to groups, and only derivatively to individuals. Nevertheless, it is possible to be part of a multilingual nation, because it is possible for a multiethnic group to share a common public institutional identity with all other groups.

In my previous work (Seymour 2010), I have shown that the difficulty of trying to define a people is, to a large extent, explained by the fact that there is no such thing as *the* definition of the people. There are many different ways for a people to be concretely realized in the institutions of a given polity and, for this reason, there are at least seven different types of peoples. First, there is the *ethnic people*. It is based on the idea of sharing a common ancestry. Second, there is the *cultural people* based on the idea according to which a multiethnic group shares a societal culture on a territory that is entirely contained within the confines of a sovereign state without itself being a sovereign state, and without having governmental institutions. It is to be differentiated from an ethnic nation because it is understood as multiethnic. Third, the *civic people* is a single societal culture organized into a sovereign state. Fourth, the *socio-political people* is a politically organized societal culture without a sovereign state, but with governmental institutions (province, federated state, quasi-federated state). Fifth, the *diasporic people* is a societal culture that is disseminated on many different territories and it forms minorities on each of these territories. The sixth concept is that of a *multiterritorial people*. It is a societal culture that occupies a continuous territory, but this territory does not correspond to the official boundaries of actual states. Finally, the *multisocietal people* is a sovereign state composed of many component societal cultures.

So, there are ethnic, cultural, civic, socio-political, diasporic, multiterritorial, and multisocietal types of peoples. Some peoples are sovereign, while others are not. Some have governmental institutions, but others do not. Some are confined within the territory of a sovereign state, but others are not. Some of them may contain immigrant minorities, while others do not. Some contain continuous diasporas (extensions of neighbouring nations), others do not. Some contain minority nations and are themselves multinational, others are mononational. Some exist on a continuous territory, while others are dispersed on many different discontinuous territories and are minorities on each of these territories. There are many different types of peoples and this is why the attempt to provide a single definition does not pass the test of reality. We should start looking at the empirical complexity of nationality instead of imposing a simplistic picture. The only common denominator between all sorts of peoples is the fact that they are characterized as societal cultures or as aggregates of societal cultures, and, thus, as institutionally organized cultural groups. So, the political conception of people adopted by political liberalism is an account that is able to accommodate many different sorts of peoples. When we realize this, we see that there is nothing wrong in the suggestion that the Indian population as a whole is a people. It may be described as a multisocietal people involving many component societal cultures.

India is a federation of twenty-eight states, some of which are dominated by specific languages. Hindustani speakers (including 400 million speakers of Hindi, 45 million speaking Urdu, and 25 million speaking Panjabi) are dominant in eight of those states. English is also a very important language. But in addition to these linguistic communities, more than twenty out of the hundreds of ethnic communities have their language registered in an annex contained at the end of the Indian Constitution, and this could, in principle, facilitate the attribution of a distinct state or territory for these communities. For instance, separate federal states of Nagaland (1963), Tripura (1972), and Mizoram (1986), or the autonomous region of Bodo within Assam (1993), were created after Independence. The politics of recognition instituted by the central state helped to contain, or settled, ethnic tensions that we found in these regions (Marshall and Gurr 2003: 59). In addition to the dominant linguistic communities mentioned earlier and to the twenty or so ethnic groups that are mentioned in the Constitution, there are also twenty ethnic communities whose population is oscillating between 100,000 and 7 million. Then, there are fifty ethnic communities with populations between 10,000 and 100,000. Finally, another group of fifty communities contain less than 10,000 members (Breton 2008: 30). It is, thus, not surprising to learn that India's motto is 'Unity in Diversity'. The

Constitution asserts that all groups of citizens with a distinct language, scripture, or culture residing on the Indian territory or on a part of its territory have the right to retain them. This provision is clearly referring to a collective right owned by ethnic communities within India. Furthermore, the smallest communities are listed as 'aboriginal tribes' and are subject to special legal protection.

India is, thus, a true de facto multination state, a multisocietal people containing many different ethnic communities: ethnic peoples or tribes, cultural peoples, and socio-political peoples. How could it survive in the long run as a single nation? This could only be if, among other things, it were able to put in practice a true kind of politics of recognition towards its national minorities. The federated states that it contains involve distinct dominant languages. By doing so, India is, as a matter of fact, giving precedence to these linguistic groups in their respective states. This is the beginning of a politics of recognition. By contrast, in the United States (US), all fifty states are dominated by the same language. The US exemplifies the clearest case of territorial federalism. As far as Canada is concerned, only one province is dominated by French, while all the others are dominated by English, and Nunavut is the only territory dominated by an indigenous language, Inuktituk. In order to become a true de jure multinational federation and not merely a territorial federation like the US, it is of course not sufficient for Canada to secure some kind of self-government to the Quebec or Inuit nations. The problem is that there is an imbalance between them and the most important national group in Canada. For this reason, the Canadian federation requires the adoption of further principles, such as a particular status for the province of Quebec and the Nunavut territory, asymmetrical federalism, and the right to opt out of federal programmes that are infringing provincial or territorial jurisdictions. Unfortunately, for most Canadians, the principle of equal status of the ten provinces is now accepted, but this amounts to imposed territorial federalism, and the domination of nine provinces on the province of Quebec.

In India, the domination is less evident. Hindustani dominates only 48 per cent of the population, and the situation is, for that reason, a little more balanced in terms of ethnic diversity. Of course, there have been numerous conflicts, such as those occurring in India's northeastern states. We have witnessed encroachments by central authorities into traditional cultures. Insurgent groups, such as the Naxalites, have been actively engaged in violent action in the area close to the border with Bangladesh (Marshall and Gurr 2003: 53). India has fairly stable democratic political institutions, but it also has poor human security, multiple ethnic challenges, limited resources, and a bad neighbourhood with Pakistan, especially on the issue of Kashmir (Marshall and Gurr 2003: 4).

Nevertheless, India seems to be not too far away from being able to practise politics of recognition up to a certain point. According to Marshall and Gurr (2003: 23–5), negotiated settlements were made with the Nagas (1963) and Tripura (1972). In 2003, state authorities and tribal Bodos agreed to the creation of a local autonomous council in northeast India. A final settlement with the Mizos for group autonomy has also been largely or fully implemented. This agreement provides more regional autonomy through the creation of a local council. These facts could partly explain why a diversified society like India could in the long run be able to survive as a single nation. The linguistically distinct states composing India exemplify how democracy must be practised if it is to be successful in a multiethnic state. It must incorporate politics of recognition for its component societal cultures.

Once again, let me emphasize that I am not claiming that India is doing perfectly well. After all, there are 300 million Dalits (ex-Untouchables) and even if some of them are emancipated, most of them are treated as less than human. We reach with them the limits of the politics of recognition, when it is understood as a politics of difference. Positive action policies have enabled some of the Dalits to have access to high-ranking positions, but there is simply no way to 'recognize' in the sense of 'esteem' all the other ones who belong to this group. The only acceptable 'recognition' in this case requires that we remove them from their actual situation, so that they could recover some kind of dignity (Bhargava 2010b).

Political liberalism is a conception of political philosophy that is able to account for the rights that peoples can have within a sovereign state, and that explains how it is possible to create a federation of peoples. This is why Rawls writes that the law of peoples must contain principles that condition the formation of federations of peoples (Rawls 1999: 38). It is possible for peoples to join in a federation of peoples only if the component peoples have collective rights and are recognized as peoples. For Rawls, peoples have collective rights and obligations. They, and not the state, are the owners of these rights and obligations. If peoples are equally recognized in this way, it is then possible to create a federation of peoples. This is precisely what happened in India. Nehru was initially able to implement in a somewhat rudimentary form a multinational federation. It is only by engaging oneself in a true de jure multinational federation that one can imagine a common national identity within India as a whole.

GRANTING RIGHTS TO RELIGIOUS MINORITIES

India is also a secular state characterized by six major religions, even if Hinduism is clearly the dominant one (83 per cent). There is nevertheless an important Muslim minority representing 12 per cent of the population. How could we justify the protection of various religions within a secular state? Can we accept that, in addition to peoples, religious groups could also be the bearers of rights? This creates a problem for political liberalism. If the state is to be truly secular and liberal in the classical sense, it must remain neutral towards various religious practices. So, it cannot promote a particular view of the good life and a particular view of the common good.

Is the situation any different within the general framework of political liberalism? I believe it is so. If the neutrality of the state remains a crucial issue, there are perhaps various ways to seek for neutrality. Given that it is committed to being neutral concerning the debate between individualists and communitarians, it must allow at the collective level, for the public expression of communitarian identities and not only of individualistic identities. Furthermore, on the basis of public reason alone, it could be reasonable to carve the public institutions of the state in such a way that it would reflect the dominant religion. The state could even perhaps promote a particular religion for the dominant group, but it must also, at the same time, promote the rights of minority religious groups if it is to respect the principle of liberal neutrality. Let us now see how this could be done.

First, non-ethnic religious groups must be protected fairly by a regime of individual rights. There are many multiethnic religious groups all around the world. As a matter of fact, most religious groups are either multiethnic, multicultural, or belong to different countries. This is true, for instance, in the case of Muslims, Christians, and Jews. Should these multiethnic groups have rights? If they are organized into juridical associations, they do have the rights that all formal associations may enjoy. As juridical bodies, they are the subjects of rights like all corporations, trade unions, and other formally recognized organizations.

But do they have more substantial rights? In a way yes, but these are hardly different from individual rights. The reason is that religious associations are organized around some specific individual features, such as religious belief. Therefore, the rights that are invoked by religious groups are certainly closely related to the rights of their members, even when they specifically refer to the practices of the group, or to its values, its rituals, its ceremonies, or its customs. In other words, the rights of religious 'groups' are aggregative and are identical to the sum of religious individual rights within the group. The reason is that religious belief is a property of individuals. It relates to personal identity and only derivatively to groups. So, freedom of conscience, religious freedom, freedom of expression, and freedom of association should take care of the more substantial rights that any multiethnic religious associations may have.

Apart from the rights that formal religious associations may have and the more substantial individual rights that members have within these associations, there are special rights that could be granted to minority religious groups when the wider society does not respect completely the principle of neutrality. If the Constitution, institutions, schools, ceremonies, holidays, or rituals in this society reflect a residual bias in favour of a particular religious group, then some special group rights must be granted to minority religious groups. The only way to implement the principle of neutrality in a society where the institutions have a residual bias in favour of one particular dominant religion is to provide explicit protection for minority religious groups. The members of these groups must have a right to opt out from the practices imposed by the majority group, or even have a right to adopt different practices, such as holidays, festivities, ceremonies, rituals, and so on.

Special rights, however, are not a clear case of collective right, since they appear, once again, to be rights that individuals have in virtue of their individual features. The subject of the right is the individual person and the so-called rights of the association are nothing more than a set of individual rights enjoyed by all its members. Furthermore, these are rights that are conditional on the presence of residual biases in the institutions. Now, if the biased norms are removed, the groups are no longer entitled to these rights.

What is more complex is to determine whether there are collective rights that an ethnic religious group may claim on its behalf. Here, we have to decide whether ethnic communities in general should enjoy collective rights. In the previous sections, we saw that political liberalism was compatible with granting collective rights to peoples. But at this point, we must examine one further issue. We have to see if within the framework of political liberalism, peoples can enjoy collective rights when they define themselves as having a particular cultural character, such as a religious belief. The problem is particularly delicate and complex. It is raised by the presence of communitarian ethnic communities that describe themselves as sharing the same religious beliefs. In particular, we have to decide whether we should also grant collective rights to such ethnic communities even when they form minorities on the territory of a liberal society.

Rajeev Bhargava has done some important work on different ways of implementing secularism at the level of the state.[3] He considers secular states and stretches that idea in the direction of a society that could be entitled to accept the institutionalization of religious beliefs. Along similar lines, we could wonder if we cannot also start by considering a society that is clearly not liberal in the sense of liberal individualism since it is a communitarian society. The question would then be whether it would meet the requirements of liberal secular states. The issue is whether a religious country may or may not still be secular enough in its political regime to be reasonable from the perspective of political liberalism.

In order to answer this first question, let us imagine, for example, a society in which the religious practices of a particular community, C, are accepted in the institutions of the country and perhaps even in its formal Constitution. In this society, governments conform to a calendar where holidays are determined relatively to a specific agenda of religious events taking place in C. The political parties are as a matter of fact all defending ideas that are influenced by the religious beliefs of C. The state subsidizes the religious practices of C and citizens choose their representatives partly by considering their religious claims. The education system is oriented by the religious beliefs of C, and so does the immigration policies, since they favour immigrants sharing the religious beliefs of C. Such a society is prima facie a non-liberal society, at least in the individualistic sense. It is not neutral towards a variety of views concerning the good life, and no strong separation exists between politics and religion, or the state and the church.

However, let us also suppose that citizens who wish to do so may opt out of such a political arrangement. They can send their children to secular schools, and are not forced or compelled to behave socially in accordance with the beliefs of C. Let us suppose that the state also provides subsidies for secular schools, and, more generally, to support minority religious groups that do not share the beliefs of C, and, therefore, grants collective rights to ethnic minorities having distinct religious practices. These minorities are entitled to develop their own religious institutions and the state must assist them in ensuring the viability of these institutions. Let us suppose also that citizens are entitled to express their views against the beliefs held by C and, in particular, they are entitled to defend not only different religious beliefs but also a strong separation between the church and the state. They are entitled, in addition, to form associations democratically fighting for such a clear separation between the two and can even create secular political parties whose main agenda is precisely to propose a secular state. There are democratic rules allowing for elections and on these occasions, new political parties could take power and modify the institutions of the country if they were elected. These democratic principles are also incorporated in the Constitution of the country.

What shall we say of such a society? It is best described as a communitarian democratic society rejecting the principles of liberal individualism. This approach is very different from a Western version of political liberalism, but is it not applying a different version of the same doctrine? I am inclined to answer affirmatively to this question. In those communities where the vast majority of citizens practise a specific religion, an argument based on public reason alone may force us to consider the model of a communitarian democracy. Nowadays, Turkey could perhaps illustrate such a society, even if it is not behaving correctly with the Kurds and not assuming its responsibility concerning the Armenian genocide.

Shall we say that India also corresponds to that kind of society? Here, one could say that institutionally there is residual bias in favour of the majority religious group. On the other hand, are explicit protections for minority religious groups provided? Here one should admit that there is still a wide gap between what India has become and what it could be. First, there are difficult relationships between Hindus and Sikhs. An insurgency of the Sikhs was contained in 1993, but the demand for a separate Sikh homeland is still there. There is also a growing right-wing nationalist Hindu party, the Bharatiya Janata Party (BJP), that tends to oppress religious minorities. There have also been huge tensions with the Kashmiri Muslims, especially in 2001 and 2002, that contributed to increase the tensions between India and Pakistan. Furthermore, communal violence occurred in the state of Gujarat between Muslims and Hindus. Following the killing of fifty-eight Hindus by a Muslim mob, one thousand persons, mostly Muslims, were killed in communal riots across Gujarat. The BJP is anything but tolerant and we are very far away from a situation where this party would comply with political liberal principles.

India *may* as a people democratically decide to develop religious institutions within the central state and in its various social institutions. It seems possible to imagine an Indian society controlled by a moderate form of Hindu nationalism. It is hard to imagine how the BJP could do that, but the Congress Party could be able to achieve this kind of normative ideal. The point is, however, that stateless peoples also have collective rights concerning the development, control, and creation of their religious institutions and the central state has the obligation to assist them in doing so if it is itself promoting a particular religion.

A democratic state may develop religious institutions, but it is not as a moral community that it is entitled to do so. It is rather as a societal culture having a specific structure. Kymlicka's distinction between structure and character is once again important in this context. The particular religious character of India is perhaps not an essential property of its people understood as a structure of culture. It may seem essential to India as a moral community, but being a democracy requires being able to see how as a moral community, it could change into a completely different one. So, if it is truly democratic, it must be able to distinguish its structure of culture from any particular character. This does not necessarily mean that it must renounce having a particular public character as a moral community. Its public institutions may be communitarian, but as a democratic society, it is able to imagine itself as potentially able to become quite different.

Of course, its dominant public languages, its common public institutions, and its common public history may also be the subject of very important changes, and they also are not essential to national identity. But the structural features of the group are not the same as those that relate to the character of the group. It is important to underline the fact that the character of the group could change even if the structure remained the same. So, as a people with a complex cultural structure, India could be entitled to develop its own institutions, including religious ones. It could be entitled to do so as long as it is a democracy committed to freedom of expression, freedom of conscience, and freedom of association. It must also be committed to allow for secular political parties that favour another way of understanding the separation between private and public spheres. In other words, it must be able to imagine itself as having a very different religious character. And it must also be committed to the principle of protection of minorities. Specifically, it must be able to support the different religious practices of its ethnic minorities.

COLLECTIVE RIGHTS FOR ETHNIC RELIGIOUS MINORITIES

Should we allow for collective rights enjoyed by minority religious ethnic groups, within a liberal state? We must consider the rights of groups that are all at once religious and ethnic minorities. This is so for the millions of Muslims in India who over the years, have taken on the 'minority' label and become more ethnicized through popular association with specific attributes, like Muslim Personal Law and the languages Urdu/ Arabic. We must examine how far 'personal laws' can shy away from the regime of basic rights and liberties of the state. As we just saw, it must be protected by the Indian state up to a certain point, granted that there are many aspects of Sharia law that are totally incompatible with the equality of men and women and that must therefore be rejected. But why should this be authorized within a liberal secular state? I believe that if we are willing to grant collective religious rights to the majority, it is indispensable to do the same for ethnic religious minorities. One cannot easily transcend the 'majority-minority syndrome', to use Bhargava's phrase (2005).

Like all peoples, minority ethnic religious groups have a structure of culture: a common public language, common public institutions in which that language is being spoken, and a common public history of these institutions. So, we are not promoting a particular moral character by defending their collective rights. We are defending their structure of culture and allowing them to develop their own religious institutions if they wish to do so. However, the state must defend the structure of culture of minorities, because the state is always biased in favour of the cultural structure of the majority. But how far can it go in the direction of practising politics of recognition for the religious institutions of its minorities? Here, let me just suggest that it is extremely important to constrain the collective rights of minorities if they go against basic freedom and liberties. One must not accept practices that affect the freedoms and liberties of citizens, including women and homosexuals. But in order to do so, it is not necessary to deny these ethnic minorities all their collective rights.

I would argue that only ethnic groups should be the bearer of collective rights. Religious associations cannot be the bearer of collective rights without violating the principle of neutrality that should characterize any liberal state. The members of these associations do have individual rights, but the religious associations cannot be supported as such because it would undermine the neutrality of the state. The reason is that religious belief is a property of individuals. It relates to personal identity and only derivatively to groups, while language (a distinctive ethnic trait) is a collective property and it applies initially to groups, and only derivatively to individuals. Non-ethnic religious groups would thus be protected fairly by a regime of individual rights. Ethnic minorities, whether religious or not, should enjoy collective rights.

In Quebec, we are now also confronted with the issue of the compatibility between some practices of religious immigrant Muslims and historical Jewish Hassidic minorities, and the laws of the state. A commission composed of the philosopher, Charles Taylor, and a well-known Quebec intellectual, Gérard Bouchard, has produced a report on the issue of 'reasonable accommodation' for religious groups (Bouchard and Taylor 2008). This report has been received with scepticism. One of the main criticisms was that we must establish mutual recognition if we want to stabilize the relationship between minority religious groups and the people as a whole, and we must criticize the conceptions of multiculturalism or interculturalism that are not compatible with respect to the collective rights of the people as a whole. If we are to recognize its collective rights, we must grant the encompassing people the right to adopt its own Constitution, and this Constitution might involve principles such as the equality between men and women, and the rejection of all sorts of discrimination based on sex, language, ethnicity, religious belief, and sexual orientation. Now, all this can be done while recognizing the rights of ethnic minority groups, even when they wish to develop their own religious institutions. There are reasonable limitations to 'reasonable accommodation' towards ethnic minorities, and there are also reasonable limitations that must be imposed on the collective rights of the people as a whole. There are limitations on the kind of nationalism that can be authorized. The BJP has failed to practice this kind of nationalism. As a matter of fact, if Martha C. Nussbaum (2007, 2009) is right, this conclusion may be generalized to all Indian political parties.

But how should the state react to the demand made by a particular group concerning its own identity? As a structure of culture, it may be entitled in principle to collective rights, but how shall we receive its demands concerning its own moral identity? The work of Avigail Eisenberg (2007) tells us a lot about how to assess religious identity claims made by ethnic minorities. According to Eisenberg, there are at least four identity-focused questions that can be formulated concerning a particular religious practice before we decide to grant the ethnic minority the right to develop this practice. If the state is to provide assistance, it has to be shown that the practice plays an important role in the identity of the group. What role is played by the disputed religious practice for its moral identity as a minority group? How flexible is the practice? What is the desirability of the practice for members of the group? What is the impact of the practice on individual identity and its impact on other groups? These questions are very helpful in guiding the debates if we are to assess cultural and religious identities in a transparent and fair manner. Among other things, these questions create favourable conditions for an understanding of minorities that would avoid stigmatization or reification of minority groups.

Would such an approach legitimize granting political recognition to a minority group if it turned out that a particular view about the good life were understood as part of the moral identity of the group and as constitutive of individual identities? It seems prima facie possible to arrive at such a conclusion. The problem, however, arises when the practice is interpreted as both restricting autonomy to some degree and protecting the community to some degree. Membership rules are notoriously both protective of communities and restrictive of individuals within these communities. So, how could such practices be legitimate? The only way to allow for such restrictions would be if the members of the community freely accept to impose upon themselves such restrictions. We must underline Kymlicka's insistence on the individual's capacity to revise her attachments and to his criticisms of Rawls's position according to which 'some religious commitments are neither revisable nor autonomously affirmed' (Kymlicka 1995: 158–63).

But if we are to accept Kymlicka's criticism, does that mean that we are legitimizing the classical version of liberalism based on the value of autonomy? Kymlicka does want to reinstate the fundamental principle of autonomy that according to him is at the bottom of the classical version of liberalism, and this view once again presupposes a conception of the person as prior to her ends. So, are we back to square one? Shall we have to abandon the new political version of liberalism in favour of the classical version? The crucial point is not whether a practice is more an internal restriction or more an external protection. The more important question concerns rational autonomy. Can political liberalism be reconciled with the idea of rational autonomy? I believe that there is a minimal concept of rational autonomy that can be accepted by communitarians as well as by individualists, and this concept is crucial for political liberalism.

If the members of the group are reflective (returning on their own practice), engaged in strong evaluation (thus evaluating their own first-order moral judgements), and able to perform thought experiment (imagining a possible world in which one could be different than what he or she is), they are rationally autonomous. If the population as a whole is able to engage into reflective strong evaluation and thought experiments, the members could be described as sufficiently rationally autonomous, just like in any old democracy. If a whole society of individuals were to practise this sort of rational autonomy, it could easily become democratic. And yet, the whole process could be interpretable as a process of self-discovery, and what would be discovered might be a particular religious belief that could be understood as constitutive of the individual and social selves. In a sense, such religious commitments would not be 'autonomously' affirmed, if we suppose that 'autonomy' here is to mean that persons or peoples are 'prior to their ends'. They would not be autonomously affirmed in this more comprehensive sense because they would be constitutive of the person or people. Any change that would happen in the moral identity of the person or of the people would be seen as turning the person or people into another person or another people. If the whole democratic process is a process of self-discovery, it cannot be assumed that the individual and social selves are somehow distinct from what is to be discovered.

These are the conditions under which political liberalism is able to grant collective rights to ethnic religious minorities. But no practice could be compatible with a true democracy in a society in which some of the members (women or homosexuals) cannot enjoy also basic human rights such as freedom of expression, conscience, and association. The reason is that without these rights, persons are unable to be rationally autonomous in the above sense. This suggests that India as a people should, under some circumstances, allow for a separate regime of personal laws for the ethnic Muslim community. These laws can be accepted only if they stem from an exercise in rational autonomy developed by all members within the minority. Personal laws can be accepted only if there are opting out opportunities for all these members. And they will be acceptable only if they do not violate the basic individual liberties.

That is, a balance must be sought between individual rights and the community's collective rights.

* * *

India is a multinational federation practising a particular form of cultural pluralism: axiological pluralism in which it is seeking to strike a balance between the individual rights of persons and the collective rights of peoples. I have argued that political liberalism does allow this kind of axiological pluralism to take place. India is more or less meeting the standard of a multinational federation in which ethnic minorities are, up to a certain point, constitutionally and institutionally recognized.

I have also considered different kinds of religious minority groups and argued that only ethnic groups could be the bearer of collective rights. This is because religious belief is a property of individuals and relates to personal identity and only derivatively to groups, but language is a collective property and it applies initially to groups, and only derivatively to individuals. Non-ethnic religious groups would thus be fairly protected by a regime of individual rights. Juridical entities could also, as juridical bodies, be subject to specific juridical rights. But only ethnic minorities, whether religious or not, should enjoy collective rights. Now, since the state can never be completely neutral and always tends to defend a particular structure (and may even choose democratically to develop religious institutions), it must, in order to recover a certain form of neutrality, defend the particular structures of cultures of ethnic minorities. It can do so without violating the liberal principle of neutrality, because it is not under those circumstances defending a particular character (a particular set of beliefs, values, customs, or traditions).

Finally, political liberalism prescribes that there should be reasonable limitations to 'reasonable accommodation' towards minorities that stem from the individual rights of citizens. Among these limitations, we must mention the obligation not to encroach the basic freedom and liberties enjoyed by citizens. These important restrictions to the rights of minorities are acceptable as long as the state is also willing to grant collective rights to ethnic religious minorities. The state can only be truly liberal if it secures the protection of the freedom and liberties to all its citizens, but it must also protect the collective rights of all its minorities. If it fails in this last regard, its nationalism will fail relative to the principle of neutrality, and thus fail to be liberal in the political sense of the word.

NOTES

1. See the National Portal of India, available at http://india.gov.in/ (accessed 9 May 2011).

2. Here, I depart from Kymlicka's approach, for, in his 1995 work, he clearly rejects collective rights and only allows for what he calls 'group differentiated rights'. In his view, protecting cultural affiliations is a way to pay respect to the individual's demand that their cultural affiliation be preserved. In this sense, group-differentiated rights are in most cases individual rights in disguise.

3. See Bhargava (2006a, 2006b) for an original 'Indian' perspective on secularism.

REFERENCES

Bhargava, Rajeev. 2005, 'The Majority–Minority Syndrome', in M. Seymour (ed.), *The Fate of the Nation-State*, Montreal–Kingston: McGill Queens University Press, pp. 327–56.

──────. 2006a, 'Political Secularism', in B. Honig, J. Dryzek, and A. Phillips (eds), *A Handbook of Political Theory*, Oxford: Oxford University Press, pp. 636–55.

──────. 2006b, 'Indian Secularism: A Transcultural Ideal?' in V.R. Mehta and T. Pantham (eds), *Political Thought in Modern India*, London: Sage Publications, pp. 285–306.

──────. 2010a, 'The Crisis of Border States in India', in J. Bertrand and A. Laliberté (eds), *Multination States in Asia: Accommodation or Resistance*, Cambridge: Cambridge University Press, pp. 51–80.

──────. 2010b, 'Hegel, Taylor and the Phenomenology of Broken Spirits', in M. Seymour (ed.), *The Plural States of Recognition*, London: Palgrave Macmillan, pp. 37–60.

Bouchard, Gérard and Charles Taylor. 2008, 'Building the Future: A Time for Reconciliation', Consultation Commission on Accommodation Practices Related to Cultural Differences, Bibliothèque et archives nationales du Québec, Government of Quebec, Quebec.

Breton, Roland. 2008, *Atlas des minorités dans le monde*, Paris: Éditions Autrement.

Eisenberg, Avigail. 2007, 'Identity, Multiculturalism, and Religious Arbitration: The Debate over Shari'a Law in Canada', in B. Arneil, M. Deveaux, R. Dhamoon, and A. Eisenberg (eds), *Sexual Justice/Cultural Justice*, London: Routledge, pp. 211–30.

Kymlicka, Will. 1989, *Liberalism, Community and Culture*, Oxford: Clarendon Press.

──────. 1995, *Multicultural Citizenship*, Oxford: Oxford University Press.

Marshall, Monty G. and Ted Robert Gurr. 2003, 'Peace and Conflict 2003. A Global Survey of Armed Conflicts, Self-Determination Movements, and Democracy', Center for International Development and Conflict Management, University of Maryland, College Park, Maryland.

Nussbaum, Martha C. 2007, *The Clash Within. Democracy, Religious Violence and the Future of India*, Cambridge, MA: Harvard University Press.

————. 2009, 'Land of My Dreams. Islamic Liberalism under Fire in India', *Boston Review*, 34(March–April): 10–14.

Rawls, John. 1971, *Theory of Justice*, Cambridge, MA: Harvard University Press.

————. 1993, *Political Liberalism*, New York: Columbia University Press.

————. 1999, *The Law of Peoples*, Cambridge, MA: Harvard University Press.

Seymour, Michel (ed.). 2010, 'Political Liberalism and the Recognition of Peoples', in *The Plural States of Recognition*, Houndmills, Basingstoke: Palgrave Macmillan, pp. 1–19.

2

Making Minority Identities
Gender, State, and Muslim Personal Law

Rina Verma Williams

How have religious minority identities been constructed in the context of modern Indian politics? What is the role of state and gender in these processes? This chapter seeks to demonstrate how Muslim identity was constructed as religious minority identity during the 1980s controversy over Muslim Personal Law. Like any form of modern identity, constructing minority identities, and constructing identities *as* minority identities, is an ongoing, continuous process. Identity is constructed and reconstructed over time, in iterative and cumulative—if contingent, rather than linear or predetermined—processes.

With respect to minority identity, we can posit at least two sides in the process. On one side, official designation or recognition of a 'minority' group or community can come from the state. Such a designation may, in different times and places, entail policies such as reservations to help or aid minorities. On the other side, recognition and acceptance of a group or community may or may not come from other groups in society, and within the designated group itself. That is, do other groups see the designated group as a minority? Do they see themselves as a minority? These two sides may or may not be connected to each other in different contexts. The treatment or recognition of a group as a minority on the part of the state interacts dialectically with the creation and recreation of that label in society more broadly. The official designation of any group as a 'minority' does not necessarily ensure the reception, and acceptance, of that group as a minority—either within the group or by those outside the group. Thus, minorities and minority identities must be constantly re/constructed and re/constituted, made and remade, over time. This study focuses on the 'top-down' construction of minorities and minority identities through the actions and policies of the state, rather than their 'bottom-up' negotiation or construction at the level of society (Roy 2007). It does so while recognizing the critical importance of both sides in the process, as well as the artificiality of the distinctions themselves (state–society, top–bottom) in what is ultimately a mutually constitutive process.

By the nineteenth century, British colonial rule had introduced into the discourse of Indian politics the conception of Hindus and Muslims as separate, bounded, and internally undifferentiated (if not necessarily homogeneous) 'communities'. The use of modern state instruments of enumeration such as the census worked to inscribe Muslims as a 'minority' community, together with the necessary counterpart, Hindus, as a/the 'majority' community (Bose and Jalal 2004). This conception of religious majority and minority communities represented a radical and substantive departure from the regional and localized nature of Hindu–Muslim relations in the subcontinent prior to the advent of British rule. One need neither accept nor reject a thesis of historical 'peaceful coexistence' in order to note that whatever they were, Hindu–Muslim relations in pre-British India were not patterned as majority–minority relations, and certainly not on an encompassing, all-India basis. This construction of Muslims as minority (and Hindus as majority) would shape the future of the subcontinent in myriad ways.

One critical way in which religious majority and minority communities and identities have been re/constructed over time in India is through the politics of the personal laws. In the case of Muslim Personal Law, Zoya Hasan has argued convincingly that since the 1980s, 'all efforts at identity preservation are concentrated on Muslim personal law, which has become the refuge of Muslim leaders and politicians' (1998: 86). Elsewhere, I have argued that in postcolonial India, the modern state became the institution *through which* personal laws had to be negotiated, and gender became the site *on which* they were negotiated (Williams 2010). In this chapter, I focus on these two key aspects of the construction of Muslim identity as minority identity in the 1980s. The first was the role of the state, which has become the central arbiter of changes or challenges to the personal laws of all communities. Madhavi Sunder asked the following question: Who gets to define what practices, norms, traditions, customs, or laws define any given culture? All too often, she argued, masculine or androcentric representations of culture are privileged—so that it is the interpretations of male religious, social, and political community 'leaders' that are taken to designate and delineate what practices and traditions constitute the essence and the authenticity of a religious–cultural community (Sunder 2005). I would further ask the question: If androcentric representations of culture or identity are authoritative, are privileged, then who or what is doing the privileging? How do certain representations come to be accepted and authorized over others? Here, we must look to the role of the state. While the state is certainly not the sole authority, or the sole answer to the question, it is clear that any complete answer must engage the actions of the state. This chapter will delineate the role played by the state in the 1980s, both in constructing Muslim identity as a religious minority identity and in cementing a particular conception of the Muslim community as inherently conservative, resistant to reform, and oppressive of women's rights.

The second critical aspect was the gendered ways in which these discourses were constructed. In order to construct Muslim identity as that of a religious minority, the government had essentially to deny the agency and the voice of minorities within a minority—both women and reformist Muslims (men and women alike). In so doing, the Indian state in the 1980s not only buttressed the identity of Muslims *as* a minority community but also imbued content to the substance of that identity. Since the publication of Fredrik Barth's (1969) path-breaking work on identity formation, scholars have worked with the idea that the boundaries drawn around communities of identity, and their relative permeability, proximity, and interaction with other communities or groups, are the driving force behind identity formation. In this chapter, I argue that the boundaries *as well as* the content of Muslim minority identity were shaped (though not determined) in terms that were fundamentally gendered.

The constitution of Muslims as a minority was not accomplished at a single stroke in any one period, but proceeded in contingent and cumulative fashion, reinscribed and reiterated in different periods of time. It is well-known that the then Governor General, Warren Hastings, first instituted the system that became the personal laws with his 1772 dictum that in matters of 'inheritance, marriage, cast [*sic*] and other religious usages, or institutions, the laws of the Koran with respect to the Mussalmans, and those of the Shasters with respect to the Hindoos, shall be invariably adhered to' (Griffiths 1986: 6). These family laws included laws on marriage, divorce, maintenance, inheritance, succession, adoption, and guardianship.[1] At this time, in the late eighteenth century, we see evidence of the colonial conception of Hindus and Muslims as two communities, defined first and foremost by their religious laws and customs. But there was not yet necessarily a view of Muslims as minority and Hindus as majority. Decennial censuses beginning in the late nineteenth century created categories, including 'depressed classes' and 'Indian Muslims', which would, as we know, shape the contours of Indian social and political discourses up to the present day. The conception of Muslims (and even 'depressed classes') as minorities was cemented by 1909, when the Morley–Minto Reforms awarded reserved seats and separate electorates to these groups as a form of minority protection.

In the late 1930s, the British colonial state codified but did not reform Muslim Personal Law. The postcolonial state in India, under successive regimes, continued to treat, and thus to reconstitute, Indian Muslims as a minority religious community. Under Prime Minister Jawaharlal Nehru's leadership, the Congress Party government passed through Parliament the reform and codification (on paper at least) of Hindu Personal Law, but refused to do the same for other personal laws, especially Muslim Personal Law, on the ground that these communities, *as minority communities*, must be handled in a different way. That is, they should not be forced to accept changes they did not initiate any demand for, and that they were not ready to accept. In the same vein, Indira Gandhi acknowledged demands for non-interference in minority personal laws when the Criminal Procedure Code (CrPC) was being revised and updated in the early 1970s. The controversy over reforming the Muslim Personal Law of maintenance in the 1980s represented an important inflection point in the ongoing process of constructing Muslim identity as minority identity in Indian politics. To trace the critical roles of gendered discourses and state policies/actions in these processes, this chapter will first briefly sketch the basic background to the 1980s controversy over the *Shah Bano* Supreme Court judgement and the Muslim Women (Protection of Rights on Divorce) Bill (or MWB). Then, I will examine the gendered ways the discourses of both sides to the controversy were constructed, followed by the actions of the state in negotiating conflicting responses among Muslim leaders and defining Muslim identity.

CONTEXT OF A CONTROVERSY: *SHAH BANO* AND THE
MUSLIM WOMEN BILL

Over the course of two decades, a considerable literature surrounding the events of the 1980s has been produced. A good portion of this literature was produced in the first decade after the controversy, much of it focused inter alia on: the status of Islamic law in India; the mandates of Islamic law more broadly; and women and women's rights in Islam and in India (Akhtar 1994; Engineer 1987, 1995; Hasan 1989; Mahmood 1983; Pathak and Sunder Rajan 1989). With the passage of time, a second decade of literature has expanded its scope to focus on several further aspects of the controversy and its causes and consequences. Some analysed the broader political determinants and impacts of the case (Hasan 1998; Williams 2006), while another strand of research has examined the case and the legislation as part of a system of multiculturalism in India based on the personal laws (Menon 2000; Mullally 2004). Yet others have traced the implementation of the Muslim Women (Protection of Rights on Divorce) Act (MWA) of 1986, examining how the courts have interpreted it, and the extent to and ways in which Muslim women have utilized it in the years since it was passed. Some analyses concluded that the legislation has remained—for a range of reasons—underutilized and has done little to expand and enhance Muslim women's legal and social rights to maintenance (Basu 2008; Vatuk 2001, 2008). On the other hand, these have been countered by evaluations that found courts have had notable success in balancing the needs of cultural accommodation with greater rights for Muslim women, and that the MWA has potentially increased avenues of access for Muslim women to claim maintenance rights (Mitra and Fischer 2002; Subramanian 2008).

What has been absent in this otherwise well-studied case is an explicit analysis of the role of the state in constructing Muslim identity as minority identity, which this chapter will undertake. I will also argue that progressive supporters' arguments for reforming Muslim Personal Law ended up subordinating gender to religion quite as much as did those of conservative opponents. Accordingly, the background given here does not purport to be a complete accounting of the events of 1985–6, but will highlight only those aspects most relevant to the argument at hand.

I have noted earlier that the discourse of majority and minority in Indian politics was constituted by British conceptions of the religious communities they believed they had 'found' in India. After independence, the conception of Indian Muslims as a 'minority community' had to be re/constructed and re/created in order to be perpetuated and survive over time. The *Shah Bano* controversy represented both continuity and disjuncture in these processes, and can be understood in terms of both. The controversy was certainly unique in scope and nature. It was unprecedented in the level of interference of non-Muslim groups (in this case, Hindu nationalist groups), and in representing the first instances of documented communal violence attributed directly to the personal laws (Williams 1998). Furthermore, the MWA was the 'only direct legislative interference with Muslim law in independent India' (Mitra and Fischer 2002: 112). These aspects certainly represented important breaks with previous politics around Muslim Personal Law.

At the same time, there are significant ways in which the controversy of the 1980s can also be understood in the frame of continuity, within the framework of prior politics of identity and personal law. The events of the 1980s worked to cement processes begun in the colonial era, by which religious community identity began to be linked to personal law, especially in the Muslim community. The British declined to legislate changes or reforms to Muslim Personal Law. They passed the Muslim Personal Law (Shariat) Application Act (1937) and the Muslim Dissolution of Marriages Act (1939), which served to codify—but not reform—Muslim Personal Law, aiming to standardize its application in the subcontinent and establish its primacy over regional or local custom. In the mid-1940s, even as they prepared to initiate the process of reforming and codifying Hindu Personal Law, the British colonial government made no similar move on Muslim Personal Law. After independence, the Indian government under Nehru's Congress Party continued the basic thrust of these policies, passing the Hindu Code Bills in the 1950s to reform and codify Hindu Personal Law, while making an explicit decision not to pursue any action on Muslim (or other minorities') personal laws. Nehru's language in explaining this decision was particularly revealing: 'we do not dare touch the Moslems because they are in a minority and we do not wish the Hindu majority to do it' (Mende 1956: 57).

The construction of Muslims as minority and Hindus as majority could hardly have been clearer. The resulting implication was that minority communities needed protection, ironically, both *from* and *by* the majority community, in its presumed control of, and manifestation in, the postcolonial state. That is, the (majority) community that a Muslim (minority) community needed protection from, was the very community upon which Muslims had ostensibly to rely to provide that very protection. And further, that majority community constituted, and explicitly saw itself as controlling, the state that was supposed to provide that protection.

The controversy of the 1980s had its proximate roots in events that took place a little over a decade earlier. In 1973, India's CrPC was revised and updated. One provision allowed destitute and abandoned or deserted wives and parents to claim maintenance from their husbands or children, respectively (Section 488, Section 125 of the revised CrPC). The purpose of this section was to prevent vagrancy. According to the dominant interpretation of Islamic law in India, however, a Muslim man was only required to support a divorced ex-wife for the first three months after the divorce (a period called *iddat*). Since the CrPC only required men to support destitute wives (not destitute *ex-wives*), some Muslim men would divorce a destitute and abandoned or deserted wife to avoid having to pay her maintenance. To avert this practice, the government amended the definition of a 'wife' in Section 125 to include any woman who had been divorced and not remarried.

Many Muslim leaders opposed this change, arguing that it simply did not make logical sense to define an ex-wife as a wife. More importantly, they held the revised law interfered with Muslim Personal Law.[2] Reiterating the Congress Party's commitment not to interfere in the personal laws of minority communities, Prime Minister Indira Gandhi amended a different section of the CrPC (Section 127) to allow an order for maintenance to be cancelled if a judge was satisfied that the divorcee had received 'the whole of the sum which, under any customary or personal law applicable to the parties, was payable on such divorce'.[3] This compromise did not entirely please Muslim leaders who had sought a direct exemption for Muslims from Section 125; but in the absence of any further accommodation forthcoming, it had to stand.

The Supreme Court decided two prior cases on this issue, in 1979 and 1980.[4] In both cases, a lower court granted maintenance to a divorced Muslim woman beyond what she had received under Muslim Personal Law, on the grounds that the amount had to be adequate to support her, and the Supreme Court upheld these decisions. The 1979 and 1980 judgements did create discontent, but full-scale controversy did not break out until 1985. A state high court granted a deserted (and later divorced) Muslim woman, Shah Bano Begum, monthly maintenance under Section 125. Her ex-husband, Mohammad Ahmad Khan, appealed this decision in the Supreme Court, arguing that the grant of maintenance violated Section 127 because he had already paid what he owed her under Muslim Personal Law. The Supreme Court disagreed and upheld the maintenance award.[5]

Muslim community and political leaders responded swiftly to the *Shah Bano* judgement. In May 1985, the Muslim Personal Law Board (MPLB; an association of Muslim religious scholars and political leaders) issued a resolution calling on Muslims 'to celebrate the last Friday of [the Muslim holy month of] Ramazan as "Shariat Protection Day" and organise protest meetings all over the country'.[6] The MPLB was 'encouraged by the enthusiastic response' and decided to escalate the protest. Meetings, rallies, and strikes were organized all over the country; by the end of 1985, attendance at these protests reportedly numbered in the thousands (Engineer 1987: 12).

Between May and July 1985, the Ministry of Home Affairs and the Ministry of Law examined the judgement and concluded that it could not be interpreted as interference in Muslim Personal Law. A Ministry of Home Affairs note dated 24 July 1985 concluded that the 'provisions of section 125 and 127 are a sort of social legislation meant to prevent vagrancy. It does not seem necessary to amend provisions ... to nullify the interpretation given by the supreme court [*sic*] in the judgement' (in Engineer 1987: 12). However, popular pressure on the government increased, and the scale and frequency of protest continued to grow. By December 1985, Prime Minister Rajiv Gandhi decided to introduce an official bill that would effectively nullify the *Shah Bano* judgement by preventing similar judgements in the future. The government drafted the MWB, which stated that in matters of maintenance for divorced Muslim women, the law of decision, when both parties were Muslim, would be Muslim Personal Law.

Opponents and even some supporters described the MWB as hastily drafted and flawed even with respect to classical Muslim law (Engineer 1987: 14–15). The administration introduced the MWB into Parliament with difficulty, and the MWB itself was considered—and ultimately passed—in a marathon session on 5 May 1986. Prime Minister Gandhi had issued a whip instructing all members of the ruling Congress Party to vote for the Bill, so there was no real question it would pass, which it did by an overwhelming majority: 372 votes for, to only fifty-four against. The whip left open the question of how much 'real' support the Bill actually had. After the vote, reports came out that several Congress Party members had not complied with the whip, and were absent from the House during the debates and voting. These numbers were estimated between forty and fifty-one Congress Party members (Mody 1987: 950).

GENDERED DIVISIONS: PROGRESSIVE AND CONSERVATIVE MUSLIM OPINION

In their responses to the *Shah Bano* decision and the subsequent legislation, Muslim community leaders split broadly into two camps. Conservative leaders opposed the judgement because they felt it interfered with Muslim Personal Law; as such, they supported the MWB as a way to nullify the judgement. Progressive leaders felt the Supreme Court judgement was in accordance with the basic principles of Islam, and thus did not constitute interference in Muslim Personal Law. Therefore, they opposed the MWB.

The role of women in Islam was central to how the progressive and conservative positions were defined. For both sides, the roles and rights of women were enmeshed within the framework of Islam. This did not mean that women's rights, or gender justice, or equality for Indian Muslim women were necessarily the primary concerns of any major party to the controversy. Rather, it is to suggest that both sides' arguments were discursively defined in gendered terms.

In framing their opposition to the Supreme Court judgement, conservatives defined their position almost exclusively in terms of protecting their rights as a religious minority community. These included, they argued, the right to retain their religious personal law free from state interference. Conservative Muslim leaders held that the judgement constituted such interference because it conflicted with the Muslim Personal Law of maintenance. 'This judgement is ... a flagrant [violation] of Muslim Personal Law.'[7] A prominent Muslim Member of Parliament (MP) admitted that the judgement itself 'was a very limited issue', but argued that it had caused such an overwhelming controversy because 'Muslim Indians saw it as the beginning of state interference with [Muslim personal law]' (Shahabuddin 1986a: 34). Conservative Muslim leaders held that such 'interference on the part of Supreme Court has created panic among the Muslims and they are apprehensive that these judgments by various courts would tamper with their Personal Law'.[8]

Because conservatives viewed the judgement as interference, they advocated the MWB as a means to reverse the judgement and ensure that the Supreme Court would not deliver such judgements in the future. 'If the Government takes action and removes the confusion, the courts in future, will hesitate to interfere with the personal law of any community as they would come to know that Parliament does not favour it.'[9] Muslim conservatives did not see their position as infringing on Muslim women's rights. They held that Islamic law provided for destitute, divorced women after iddat. According to Muslim Personal Law, the obligation to support such a woman fell first on her children, then on her father, her brothers and sisters, and so forth. If there were no family member who could support her, it fell to the Muslim community at large to do so. But in no case should she request or receive support from her ex-husband, since any relation between them, according to Islamic law, had been severed by the divorce.

Constitutional scholar Granville Austin has argued that economic and political interests, and not solely ideological interests, underlay conservative opposition to the *Shah Bano* judgement. The judgement, if it stood, threatened not just the sacred texts of Islam, but also the economic interests of Muslim men who might otherwise be faced with maintenance payments to ex-wives. Additionally, the political interests of the conservative Muslim leadership were threatened as well: '[I]f personal law were codified, the "ulama" and the Muslim Personal Law Board would lose much—perhaps all—of their authority to interpret the law'. For these groups, Muslim Personal Law 'is not only sacred but it is also their job security and the source of their power, religious and political', within and beyond the Muslim community (Austin 2001: 21–2).

Not all Muslim leaders shared the conservative approach. Many progressive leaders supported the *Shah Bano* judgement because they felt it returned to the true foundations of Islam. Although they did not agree with everything the judgement said, they did support its substantive conclusion: that Muslim men should provide adequate maintenance for destitute, divorced women even beyond the period of iddat. They cited Verses 241 and 242 of the Quran, which read: 'For divorced women maintenance should be provided on a reasonable scale. This is a duty on the righteous.'[10] Progressives wondered how the responsibility could be any clearer. 'What more could the Quran say than that there shall be a provision for a woman?'[11] They held that there was no firm Quranic basis to restrict maintenance to the period of iddat, an interpretation of Islamic law that they held violated true Islamic tenets. The prominent Justice Baharul Islam concluded that restricting maintenance to the period of iddat was 'not warranted by the Holy Qur'an. Such an interpretation would amount to … sacrilege' (Akhtar 1994: 292). Progressives insisted that many Muslims supported the *Shah Bano* judgement and opposed the MWB. 'I say … with force that the whole Muslim community is not represented by those people who advocate this Bill.'[12] They also argued that in matters of social justice, a progressive and educated minority must often pave the way before mass opinion follows.

The issue of women's rights in Islam was central to the progressive position. Progressive leaders argued that in its time, Islam was at the forefront in establishing equal rights for women. 'I think there is no doubt about the sanctity of the position of woman, her status, and her rights, under the Islamic Law.'[13] They held that women had actually greatly benefited from the advent of Islam, which had lifted them out of a status of degradation to a position of equality and respect. 'The women were weak and exploited and used to leading a life of inferiority. It was the crusade of Islam to secure equal rights for all.'[14] For this very reason, progressives argued, granting maintenance to divorced Muslim women who had no other means of subsistence was very much in accord with the true spirit and principles of Islam. 'A very good judgement was given by the Supreme Court … the spirit of the judgement is right according to "Koran".'[15] The MWB, on the other hand, violated the fundamental principles of Islam and trampled on the basic rights of Muslim women. Progressives argued that the legislation was 'inhuman and anti-Islamic … it will push the Muslim women back to the pre-Islamic era when women were considered as animals, chattel and part of the property.'[16]

How did Muslim women figure in the controversy? Many Muslim women supported the conservative position, but by no means all Muslim women did: 'the spirited support by some women for the divorced Muslim woman's right to maintenance [was] a noteworthy contrast to the muted and passive opposition to it by others' (Hasan 1998: 85). Muslim women had gotten involved and voiced their views as the debate over the judgement and the MWB mobilized women's organizations into action. As documented by Zoya Hasan, Muslim women participated in significant numbers in anti-MWB protests around the country, often in defiance of opposition from their families and others in the community. One activist described the campaign against the MWB as 'nothing short of a breakthrough in Muslim women's participation' (Hasan 1998: 84). Yet, there was a general sense among Muslim progressives and women's organizations that they had not been able to influence government policy, and that their voices were largely dismissed by those leaders and political institutions that were in a position to matter. Progressive Muslim leaders certainly felt that conservative rather than progressive Muslim leaders held sway over the majority of Muslim opinion in India. '"Progressive" Muslims have felt alienated from their community because their call for Islamic reform has been dismissed either as irrelevant or as opposed to mass opinion' (Pathak and Sunder Rajan 1989: 567).

There was evidence of different shades of opinion within the Muslim community as well, both during and since the 1980s. Hasan has held that the campaign against the Supreme Court judgement did not initially garner support when it was framed as an issue of maintenance, but only gained support later, when it was recast in terms of Muslim identity (Hasan 1989: 46). One survey conducted in the midst of the controversy found that only half of Muslim men and 22 per cent of Muslim women were even aware of the *Shah Bano* judgement (Rao 1985). Later, a 1995 survey of 200 Muslim women found that 88 per cent felt polygamy should be abolished. The women also supported reforms of other specific issues, such as custody (62 per cent favoured reforms) and maintenance (58 per cent favoured reforms). When asked the general question whether Muslim Personal Law should be reformed, however, only 24 per cent said yes, and only 14 per cent felt it should be replaced with a Uniform Civil Code (UCC) (Bano 1995). Finally, another national survey conducted in 1995 found that 68 per cent of Muslims in six cities across India opposed a UCC, but were fairly evenly split on the question of whether polygamy should be practised today: 44 per cent felt it should not, while 45 per cent felt it should (either unrestricted or under certain restricted conditions).[17] So, although most Muslims in India seemed to oppose a UCC, many supported some specific reforms of Muslim Personal Law, as long as the reforms were carried out within the framework of Islam. This, of course, was exactly what progressives in the 1980s advocated.

Ultimately, women's rights, for progressives and conservatives alike, were ensconced within the framework of Islam. Progressive Muslims agreed with conservatives that any changes in Muslim Personal Law must come from within the framework of Islam itself; the two sides merely differed on what Islam mandated on the topic. The implication of both the progressive and conservative arguments was that whatever difficulties Muslim women might face, they would be handled within the framework of Islam. Nivedita Menon has argued that in this way, Muslim community leaders (progressive and conservative alike, I would add) removed the issue of gender equality from the purview of the Indian state in much the same way that the Hindu community removed it from the purview of the British colonial state in the early 1900s (Chatterjee 1996: Chapter 5; Menon 2000).

Zoya Hasan has argued that there was a fundamental shift in the government's justification for the MWB. Initially, it was defended as an enhancement in Muslim women's rights. When this didn't fly, however, by May 1986, the government turned to a strategy of defending the legislation as deference to the wishes of the Muslim community (Hasan 1998: 77). As a result, the government framed and passed a bill that has had dubious benefits for Muslim women. Subsequent studies have been inconclusive at best as to the actual effects of the MWA. On one hand, some scholars have claimed that the legislation strengthened rather than damaged Muslim women's rights to claim maintenance, by providing that Muslim men must make reasonable provisions for divorced ex-wives beyond iddat. In addition, suits brought under the MWA now go directly to the criminal courts instead of getting tied up in the civil courts, making the attainment of a judgement—at least in theory—faster and cheaper, therefore, more accessible (Mitra and Fischer 2002: 120, 122; Subramanian 2008). Yet other studies have found that Muslim women still only rarely bring cases to court under the Act (Basu 2008; Vatuk 2001). Legal scholars and women's rights groups emphasized that the MWA denied Muslim women rights under the CrPC that were available to all other Indian women.

> The Bill violates the basic constitutional principle of equality before the law by denying to women of one community a protection offered under Criminal Law whose jurisdiction covers all citizens of India … the maintenance provision under the Criminal Code is meant to prevent vagrancy and destitution of all Indian women.[18]

As for Shah Bano herself, it is widely known that she recanted the maintenance award she had won after local religious leaders 'explained' to her that to accept the award would be un-Islamic (Pathak and Sunder Rajan 1989: 572).

For these reasons, women's rights advocates found little of redemption in the outcome of the controversy. The *Shah Bano* judgement and the controversy over the MWB introduced new complexities in feminist discourse about the personal laws. From this point on, the discourse could no longer be couched in terms of gender justice versus personal laws. It was precisely at this historical juncture that the conflict between individual and collective rights emerged most starkly. The involvement (or interference) of Hindu nationalist leaders and organizations in the debates over Muslim Personal Law in this period were the culmination of a long campaign—begun as early as 1956—to advocate the elimination of the personal laws altogether and the establishment of unified, territorial family laws (a UCC) on the argument that to be a unified nation, India needs uniform laws. Women's rights activists and organizations criticize the personal laws on the basis of their unequal treatment of women. Yet, the appropriation of this issue by, and the rise to national political prominence of, Hindu nationalism since the late 1990s has led feminist leaders to rethink the erasures and silencing embedded in the concept of uniformity. Women's rights organizations now avoid the term 'uniform', talking instead of a 'common', 'gender-just', or 'egalitarian' civil code (Menon 2000: 90). Further, the MWA 'damaged the state's legitimacy, for in the process of protecting minority rights it was countenancing the violation of the principle of gender equality' (Hasan 1998: 82). The qualified success of the Act in enhancing the position of Muslim women, I propose, was at least partially a consequence of the qualified extent to which the issue was defined as a matter of women's rights in the first instance. In the face of contested views within the Muslim community, then, which view would prevail? I will argue in the next section that the state 'resolved' the controversy in a way that contributed to a construction of Indian Muslims as 'essentially' conservative and opposed to legal reform for women's rights.

THE ROLE OF THE STATE: DEFINING MUSLIM IDENTITY

In the general elections of December 1984, the country rallied around the Congress Party under Rajiv Gandhi, the elder son of the former Prime Minister, Indira Gandhi, who had been assassinated in October of that year. In a wave of sympathy voting, the Congress Party won an unprecedented 48.1 per cent of the popular vote and 415 out of 542 seats in the Lok Sabha, and Rajiv Gandhi assumed the office of prime minister. Despite the apparent electoral dominance of the Congress Party, however, regional and opposition parties were perpetually poised to threaten Congress predominance, while the internal unity of the Congress Party itself seemed inherently unstable. This was the political context in which the Supreme Court delivered its judgement in 1985. As noted earlier, there was ample legal precedent for the judgement, and Gandhi's government initially supported it, at least through August 1985. At that time, a Muslim Minister of State in the government, Arif Mohammed Khan, approached the prime minister and said he wanted to make a speech in the Parliament supporting the Supreme Court judgement. Gandhi agreed, and Khan delivered his speech with the prime minister's support (Shourie 1986). Khan's speech in the Parliament represented a perfect statement of the progressive position, relying solely on Islamic sources to argue that the Supreme Court judgement was in accord with the fundamental tenets of Islam.

By the end of the year, however, Gandhi seemed to have reversed position. The government decided to sponsor an official bill to establish that questions of maintenance for Muslim divorcees would be decided by Muslim Personal Law—thus effectively (if not directly) overturning the Supreme Court's decision. The prime minister consulted with selected Muslim religious and political leaders on the contents and drafting of the bill. These included the Chairman and Secretary of the MPLB, Maulana Abdul Hasan Nadvi (known as Ali Mian); male Muslim MPs, G.M. Banatwalla, Syed Shahabuddin, and Ebrahim Suleiman Sait; and female Muslim MPs, Najma Heptullah and Begum Abida Ahmed. All those he consulted were known to oppose the Supreme Court judgement (Akhtar 1994: 358). As Zoya Hasan put it, the government's 'interpretation echoed the position of the All India Muslim Personal Law Board ... uncritically' (1998: 75). According to the then Minister of Law, A.K. Sen, no other alternatives to the MWB were ever considered or discussed by the government (Williams 2006: 138).

It is now generally believed that political considerations brought about the prime minister's volte-face. In December 1985, the Congress Party lost by-elections in two eastern states, Bihar and Assam. In the Bihar election, the Congress candidate was decisively defeated by a Muslim candidate of the Janata Party, Syed Shahabuddin. It was widely assumed that Shahabuddin won the Bihar election 'solely because of his marathon campaign against the Shah Bano judgment' (Akhtar 1994: 286), although Shahabuddin himself has denied that the judgement was an issue in the election (Shahabuddin 1986b; also see, Engineer 1987: 14). It has been argued that the prime minister took the results of these elections to mean that Muslim voters had become alienated from the Congress Party because of the government's support of the Supreme Court judgement. 'The Congress Party's response was unmistakably influenced by the political crisis that the party faced in the mid-1980s. A new strategy of conciliation and compromise was devised to try and stem the steady erosion of support for Congress. Compromise on Muslim personal law was part of the effort to win back Muslim voters' (Hasan 1998: 74).

To explain the reversal, the government explained they had come
to believe that popular Muslim opinion opposed the Supreme Court
judgement: '[O]ur information was that the average Muslim, man or
woman, was against the retention of [Section 125] of the [CrPC] on the
statue book applicable to Muslims... they said... it shouldn't be applicable to Muslims, because according to them it is against the Shariat'
(Williams 2006: 138). Faced with multiple public opinions and conflicting evidence, the government effectively chose conservative opinion
as representing 'true' or at least majority Muslim opinion on the issue.

> [O]ur understanding is that the features of the [MWB] reflect the opinion
> of the vast majority of the Muslims about their own law. It is quite true
> that about hundred or five hundred intellectuals or quite a large number
> of people outside that particular lot feel in a different way. ... But *we have
> to find the consensus of the community* and we... do not think we have
> found it wrongly.[19]

Rajiv Gandhi referred explicitly to the issue of Muslims as a minority,
arguing that secularism meant the protection of minority rights, which
in turn meant protecting the personal laws.

> The Supreme Court passed a judgement in the 'Shah Bano case' which
> caused ... uncertainties in the minds of certain minorities. Whether the
> uncertainties were founded on something concrete or not is not for us
> to judge. But the fact is that certain minorities were afraid that certain
> guarantees given to them at the time of Independence were being diluted.
> (Jain 1992: 63)

Two key conclusions that centre the role of the state emerge from
this analysis. The first is that the central role of the state itself in the
controversy was never at issue, unquestioned by any party to the debate:
progressive or conservative Muslims, Hindu nationalists, secularists, or
government leaders themselves. Progressive and conservative Muslims
alike operated on the premise that the state would negotiate whatever
the final outcome of the controversy would be. Accordingly, their appeals
were to shape and influence what actions the state would take.

Progressives seemed less concerned overall with which *branches* of
government should be engaged in such affairs than conservatives were.
They were more concerned with the substance of the final outcome, and
the extent to which it conformed to the central and defining tenets of
Islam (as they interpreted them), than with which branch of government rendered the decision. For their part, conservatives argued that
matters of personal law should be dealt with and negotiated by the

Parliament, in particular, rather than by the Supreme Court. As one MP argued, 'the courts should not interpret the Muslim [Personal] Law. If there is any such case, it should be brought to the notice of this Sovereign House'.[20] The crux of the conservative objection seemed to be the unrepresentative nature of the composition of the Supreme Court. It was noted explicitly at several points that these were, in particular, *Hindu* justices that had presumed to interpret Muslim law and the Holy Quran. On the other hand, it was suggested that Muslim leaders would be present and have some say in any such matters that came before the Parliament. It seems safe to presume that this conservative preference for Parliamentary as opposed to Supreme Court action on Muslim Personal Law was pragmatically as well as ideologically driven. But despite these differences, neither side disputed the position of the state as arbiter of the controversy.

The second and perhaps most critical factor was the role of the government in solidifying a conception of the Muslim community in India as inherently conservative and anti-reform by accepting the conservative position on the issue. The government's policies served to institutionalize a conservative interpretation of Islamic law while simultaneously marginalizing a more progressive one. The progressive interpretation would have granted greater rights of maintenance to Indian Muslim women within the framework of Islam itself—thus bringing their legal rights on par with those of Indian women of other religions. In important ways, the actions of the state under Prime Minister Rajiv Gandhi served not only to (re)define Muslims as a minority community, but to delineate a content and substance to that identity. In particular, the actions of Gandhi's government worked to define the Indian Muslim community as conservative, anti-reform, and opposed to expanded rights for Muslim women. They did this by silencing progressive or pro-reform voices within the Muslim community, and siding with conservative, anti-reform sectors. In doing so, they lent legitimacy and authority to these sectors as being somehow more 'truly' representative of a 'majority' of Muslim opinion than more progressive sectors. This is not to suggest that the 1980s was the first time state policy or action had this effect; in fact, I would argue the opposite: that the state's actions in this period worked to build on and cement the actions of prior governments, colonial and postcolonial alike.

By sanctioning the conservative view as representing the 'consensus' or 'majority' view of the (minority) Muslim community, the government effectively silenced dissident Muslim voices that were not represented by this view. Some political thinkers have begun to argue for giving precisely these dissident voices—often identified as minorities within a minority—a greater say in defining religious and cultural identity (Phillips 2007; Song 2007). In these accounts, however, it is ironically the state that is asked to protect the dissident voices of vulnerable minorities within minorities. In this case, the state was critical in sanctioning one set of views as representing the view of all or even most Indian Muslims. And far from protecting and enabling dissident, vulnerable voices within the Muslim community, the state sanctioned and authorized the voices of conservative Muslim leaders and an androcentric interpretation of the Muslim Personal Law of maintenance. As a result, the particular set of positions that were sanctioned—the *content* of the minority identity that was constructed—was that of a conservative, anti-reform Islam, resistant to gender equity or women's rights. The particular contours of this identity have had profound impacts on Hindu–Muslim relations and on the lives of Indian Muslims, reverberating through, even reshaping the discourses of Indian politics.

* * *

This analysis has centred the role of the state and discourses of gender in the making of minorities and minority identities. Since the era of British colonial rule, the Indian state has made and remade Muslims as minority and Hindus as majority. The 1980s was a critical period in Indian politics and the evolution of Hindu–Muslim relations (Menon and Nigam 2007). The eruption of the controversy over Muslim Personal Law was marked by the involvement or interference in the controversy by organizations of the Sangh Parivar and the incidence of communal violence and rioting over the issue sporadically around the country for several weeks.

The actions of Rajiv's government proved to be a critical inflection point in the definition of Muslim minority identity in India in ways that played into the hands of Hindu nationalism, and especially their political party, the Bharatiya Janata Party (BJP). Nehru's passage of the Hindu Code Bills in the 1950s, together with Rajiv Gandhi's sanctioning of the conservative position as representative of 'true' Muslim opinion in the 1980s, combined to perpetuate a narrative which constructed Hindu Personal Law (and thereby, the Hindu community as a whole) as progressive, reformed, and gender-just—contrasted with a Muslim Personal Law (and thus a Muslim community) which was constructed as inherently conservative, resistant to reform, and oppressive of women's rights, and *thus* anti-national. The Hindu Right, led by the BJP, portrayed 'the Congress government's action...as an appeasement of minority opinion' (Mitra and Fischer 2002: 112). They also managed to portray conservative Muslim opposition to reform as a refusal to integrate into the Indian mainstream, as 'antinational and a threat to national security' (Hasan 1998: 79). The ability of the Sangh Parivar to propagate their portrayal of Muslims as not only anti-reform but also further stretching this to mean anti-national, has turned critically on the actions of successive Congress governments that have contributed to the creation and recreation of this construction of Muslim minority identity.

The events of the 1980s and the actions of the Congress-led government in this period gave the BJP a foothold on which to build the discourse of a Hinduized Indian nation, which, *by definition*, has been constructed in opposition to Muslim minority identity in India, defined (with the sanction of the state) predominantly by conservative voices. The BJP built momentum on its involvement in the *Shah Bano* controversy, and this strength carried it to growing vote and seat shares and finally, to power at the centre in 1998–9. While one would certainly not draw a direct line from the controversy to the BJP's rise to national power, it is now widely accepted that the foundations for the latter were laid in the former period.

The effects of the controversy have been equally profound with respect to discourses of gender and the rights of women. Despite the centring of gender in/as discourse, the outcomes of the controversy have yielded nebulous results for women in terms of legal rights and social status. Hindu nationalist forces in the 1980s (and since) have sought to portray themselves as the saviours of Muslim women, protecting them from Muslim men, Muslim Personal Law, and indeed Islam itself. The Hindu nationalist appropriation of the issue of a UCC has led Indian feminist leaders and organizations to re-evaluate and re-examine the erasures and silencing inhering in the concept of 'uniformity' and to seek other means of attaining some measure of gender justice in the application and functioning of the personal laws (Menon 2000: 84–91). Perhaps the space for optimism lies here: as the creation of Hindu and Muslim identities, far from being *faits accomplis*, can and by definition must continue to be made and remade, the possibility is not closed that these identities could be constructed outside the clutches of the state and the discourses of minority and majority.

NOTES

1. Succession was added later in 1781. See Rudolph and Rudolph (1965).
2. Shamim Ahmed Shamim, *Lok Sabha Debates* (hereafter *LSD*) (3 September 1973), 95; C.H. Mohammed Koya, *LSD* (30 August 1973), 317; Ebrahim Suleiman Sait, *LSD* (30 August 1973), 236–6, 316, 318.
3. CrPC Section 127 (3)(b); cited in *LSD* (11 December 1973), 316.
4. *Bai Tahira v. Ali Hussain*, AIR 1979 Supreme Court 362; *Fazlunbi v. K. Khader Vali*, AIR 1980 Supreme Court 1730.
5. *Mohd. Ahmed Khan v. Shah Bano Begum*, AIR 1985 Supreme Court 945.
6. Printed in *Muslim India* (June 1985), 259.
7. Suleiman Sait, *LSD* (9 August 1985), 365.
8. Zainul Bansher, *LSD* (9 August 1985), 348.
9. Ibid.
10. Arif Mohammad Khan, *LSD* (23 August 1985), 440.
11. Ibid, p. 441.
12. Saifuddin Chowdhary, *LSD* (25 February 1986), 323–4.
13. Arif Mohammad Khan, *LSD* (23 August 1985), 434.
14. Ibid, p. 445.
15. Saifuddin Chowdhary, *LSD* (20 December 1985), 445.
16. Arif Mohammad Khan, *LSD* (5 May 1986), 451.
17. Survey conducted by Professor Ashutosh Varshney. See Varshney (2002).
18. Report from website of the Centre for Women's Development Studies. Available at http://www.womenexcel.com/law/womenlaw2.htm (accessed 25 August 2004).
19. A.K. Sen, *LSD* (25 February 1986), 353; emphasis added.
20. Zainul Bansher, *LSD* (9 August 1985), 348.

REFERENCES

Akhtar, Saleem. 1994, *Shah Bano Judgement in Islamic Perspective: A Socio-Legal Study*, New Delhi: Kitab Bhavan.
Austin, Granville. 2001, 'Religion, Personal Law and Identity in India', in G.J. Larson (ed.), *Religion and Personal Law in Secular India: A Call to Judgment*, Bloomington: University of Indiana Press, pp. 15–23.
Bano, Sabeeha. 1995, 'Muslim Women's Voices', *Economic and Political Weekly*, 30(47): 2981–2.
Barth, Fredrik. 1969, *Ethnic Groups and Boundaries: The Social Organization of Culture Difference*, London: Allen & Unwin.
Basu, Srimati. 2008, 'Muslim Women and Un-Uniform Family Law in India', *International Feminist Journal of Politics*, 10(4): 495–517.

Bose, Sugata and Ayesha Jalal. 2004, *Modern South Asia: History, Culture, Political Economy*, 2nd edition, New York: Routledge.

Chatterjee, Partha. 1996, *The Nation and Its Fragments*, New Jersey: Princeton University Press.

Engineer, Asghar Ali (ed.). 1987, *The Shah Bano Controversy*, Bombay: Orient Longman.

——————. 1995, *Problems of Muslim Women in India*, Bombay: Orient Longman.

Griffiths, John. 1986, 'What Is Legal Pluralism?' *Journal of Legal Pluralism*, 1(1): 1–55.

Hasan, Zoya. 1989, 'Minority Identity, Muslim Women Bill Campaign and the Political Process', *Economic and Political Weekly*, 24(1): 44–53.

——————. 1998, 'Gender Politics, Legal Reform, and the Muslim Community in India', in P. Jeffery and A. Basu (eds), *Appropriating Gender: Women's Activism and Politicized Religion in South Asia*, New York: Routledge, pp. 71–88.

Jain, C.K. (ed.). 1992, *Rajiv Gandhi and Parliament*, New Delhi: CBS Publishers and Distributors.

Mahmood, Tahir. 1983, *Muslim Personal Law: Role of the State in the Subcontinent*, 2nd edition, Nagpur: All India Reporter.

Mende, Tibor. 1956, *Conversations with Mr. Nehru*, London: Secker & Warburg.

Menon, Nivedita. 2000, 'State, Community and the Debate on the Uniform Civil Code in India', in M. Mamdani (ed.), *Beyond Rights Talk and Culture Talk*, New York: St. Martin's Press, pp. 75–96.

Menon, Nivedita and Aditya Nigam. 2007, *Power and Contestation: India since 1989*, New York: Palgrave MacMillan.

Mitra, Subrata and Alexander Fischer. 2002, 'Sacred Laws and the Secular State: An Analytical Narrative of the Controversy over Personal Laws in India', *India Review*, 1(3): 99–130.

Mody, Nawaz B., 1987, 'The Press in India: The Shah Bano Judgment and Its Aftermath', *Asian Survey*, 27(8): 935–53.

Mullally, Siobhan. 2004, 'Feminism and Multicultural Dilemmas in India: Revisiting the *Shah Bano* Case', *Oxford Journal of Legal Studies*, 24(4): 671–92.

Pathak, Zakia and Rajeshwari Sunder Rajan. 1989, 'Shahbano', *Signs*, 14(3): 558–82.

Phillips, Anne. 2007, *Multiculturalism without Culture*, Princeton: Princeton University Press.

Rao, P.K. 1985, 'Shah Bano's Case and Uniform Civil Code—A Survey of Public Opinion among Muslim Community at Tirupati', *Journal of the Indian Law Institute*, 27(4): 572–7.

Roy, Srirupa. 2007, *Beyond Belief: India and the Politics of Postcolonial National-ism*, Durham: Duke University Press.

Rudolph, Lloyd and Susanne Rudolph. 1965, 'Barristers and Brahmans in India: Legal Cultures and Social Change', *Comparative Studies in Society and History*, 8(1): 24–49.

Shahabuddin, Syed. 1986a, 'The Turmoil in the Muslim Mind', *Onlooker*, 16–31 March, pp. 32–7.

————. 1986b, 'Victory', *Muslim India*, January.

Shourie, Arun. 1986, 'The Arif Mohammad Affair', *The Times of India*, 3 March, p. 1.

Song, Sarah. 2007, *Justice, Gender, and the Politics of Multiculturalism*, New York: Cambridge University Press.

Subramanian, Narendra. 2008, 'Legal Change and Gender Inequality: Changes in Muslim Family Law in India', *Law & Social Inquiry*, 33(3): 631–72.

Sunder, Madhavi. 2005, 'Piercing the Veil', in W.S. Hesford and W. Kozol (eds), *Just Advocacy? Women's Human Rights, Transnational Feminisms, and the Poli-tics of Representation*, New Jersey: Rutgers University Press, pp. 266–90.

Varshney, Ashutosh. 2002, *Ethnic Conflict and Civic Life: Hindus and Muslims in India*, New Haven: Yale University Press.

Vatuk, Sylvia. 2001, '"Where Will She Go? What Will She Do?" Paternalism toward Women in the Administration of Muslim Personal Law in Contem-porary India', in G.J. Larson (ed.), *Religion and Personal Law in Secular India: A Call to Judgment*, Bloomington: University of Indiana Press, pp. 226–38.

————. 2008, 'Islamic Feminism in India: Indian Muslim Women Activists and the Reform of Muslim Personal Law', *Modern Asian Studies*, 42(2–3): 498–518.

Williams, Rina Verma. 1998, 'Reconceptualizing the Nation-State: Religion, Personal Laws and Ethnic Conflict in India, 1920–1986', Unpublished doctoral thesis, Harvard University, Cambridge, MA.

————. 2006, *Postcolonial Politics and Personal Laws: Colonial Legal Legacies and the Indian State*, New Delhi: Oxford University Press.

————. 2010, 'Hindu Law as Personal Law: State and Identity in the Hindu Code Bills Debates, 1952–1956', in T. Lubin, D. Davis Jr, and J. Krishnan (eds), *Introduction to Law and Hinduism*, Cambridge: Cambridge University Press.

3

Scheduled Castes, Christians, and Muslims
The Politics of Macro-majorities and Micro-minorities

Laura Dudley Jenkins[†]

The Scheduled Castes (SCs), a government list of the communities formerly known as the Untouchables, are one of the most complex minorities in India. Focusing on the intersection of caste and religious identities, this chapter examines the history of this official category, used for various anti-discrimination and reservation (affirmative action) policies, with attention to the political and legal developments and social movements that have complicated its definition.

Unlike the Scheduled Tribes (STs), the focus of Chapter 6 by Joseph Marianus Kujur, members of SCs must belong to certain religions (currently, Hinduism, Sikhism, or Buddhism) to be legally recognized as having SC status. In official reports, both Indian government commissions and international organizations are paying increasing attention to low-caste communities within minority religions. Nevertheless, initiatives to change reservation laws to explicitly include SC Muslims and Christians confound long-standing assumptions about caste and religion and have not succeeded.

Contemporary reports and court decisions illustrate alternative ways to recognize caste, religion, or both. Legally defining minorities is

[†] I would like to gratefully acknowledge the grants from the Charles Phelps Taft Research Centre and the Fulbright New Century Scholars Programme that made this research possible.

complicated when different types of minority identity such as caste and religion intersect or when the lines between religions are contested. Two outcomes are problematic for minorities: macro-majorities or micro-minorities. In the first case, the government 'supersizes' majorities by including minorities within them through law, policies, or politics. In the second, governments fragment minorities through law, policies, or politics that subdivide or emphasize differences within minorities.

'Intersectionality' is a useful social science concept, and even useful for policy design; yet, the political implications of intersectionality in a democracy of many, layered minority communities needs further research. Intersectionality refers to the multiple and overlapping identities that make up any society, indeed any person (Lien *et al.* 2008). Clearly, social scientists need to pay attention to the unique plight of a person who is not only low caste, but also a religious minority, poor, rural, and a woman, for example. They must also recognize that someone who is a 'minority' in one sense may be a 'majority' in another. Designers of public policies should also heed these multiple and interacting axes of identity and related advantages and disadvantages. At the same time, attention to intersectionality must be carefully balanced to protect minority rights. If a government creates administrative or legal identity categories that increasingly subdivide populations into micro minorities, valuable minority political identities may be shattered. If governments amalgamate minorities into macro majorities, they can ignore their minority rights.

THE ORIGINS OF THE 'SC' CATEGORY

Although the Constitution of India abolished untouchability and discrimination on the basis of caste (Article 15), caste discrimination persists and caste categories are legally recognized in order to implement a form of affirmative action known as reservations. The continuing use of the official 'SC' lists is an outcome of these policies, which includes quotas for candidates from the SCs in government jobs, university admissions, and legislative elections. The SCs is a government category that includes the lowest, or untouchable, castes. Many politically engaged members of these groups today prefer the label of 'Dalit', which means the oppressed or ground down.

The SC category emerged in the late colonial era, as a way to promote the rights of these groups in an era of constitutional reform and incipient independence. A previous label for these castes, the 'depressed classes', preceded the term SCs, which is still in use today. The British colonial government officially recognized the untouchable castes by listing them in 1936 as the SCs in order to implement the 1935 Government of India Act, an act that gave special electoral representation to various minority groups. The 1936 Government of India (Scheduled Castes) Order made clear that 'no Indian Christian … should be deemed a member of a Scheduled Caste'. Since Christians had special representation too, this was not immediately controversial.

This SC category emerged as a salient policy category at a time when the best strategy to uplift these lower castes was a subject of heated debate. This debate led to a stand-off between nationalist leader Mohandas Gandhi and Dr B.R. Ambedkar, activist for the depressed classes, who would become India's first Law Minister (Tejani 2007). Their disagreement stemmed from their divergent ideas about the relationship between caste and Hinduism and, thus, their different assessments about the possibilities for reform. Gandhi's strategy was to uplift India's lowest castes, which he dubbed 'Harijans', through the social and religious reform of Hinduism. Worried that distinct group rights for Harijans would be divisive during the anti-colonial nationalist movement, Gandhi fasted to protest Dr Ambedkar's demands for reserved seats and separate electorates for the 'depressed classes'.

Dr Ambedkar forcefully criticized Gandhi's reformist approach and Hinduism itself, insisting on group rights for the depressed classes. Ultimately, to end Gandhi's fast, Dr Ambedkar settled for reserved seats for the depressed classes, ensuring a percentage of seats for which only depressed class candidates could run. He gave up on separate electorates, which would have meant only voters from the depressed classes could vote for those seats, likely resulting in more forceful or radical advocates for the depressed classes gaining office. Nevertheless, with the implementation of these reserved seats, the 'SCs' became a part of India's lexicon and a political force to be reckoned with. Dr Ambedkar was so sure that reform of Hinduism was not the route to equity that at the end of his life, in 1956, he converted to Buddhism with about a half million other members of the SCs. To this day, Dr Ambedkar's devotees reject Gandhi's term 'Harijan', meaning children of (a Hindu) god, as a patronizing attempt to keep them in the Hindu fold, and they have popularized the alternative term 'Dalit', meaning the oppressed or crushed.

The tensions between Gandhi and Ambedkar and the conversion of Dalits away from Hinduism foreshadowed a recurring debate over the identification of SCs: Are there Sikh, Buddhist, Muslim, or Christian SCs? Given the escalating tendency to allocate rights on the basis of religious or caste groupings in the late colonial era, shifts between these categories took on political significance. The intersection of religion and caste would raise contentious issues for years to come.

RELIGIOUS DIMENSIONS OF THE SCs

The SC list was re-enacted after Indian independence through the Scheduled Caste Order of 1950, prepared for the purpose of continuing reservations and other protections for these castes. The SCs have reservations in government jobs, higher education, and legislative seats. As independent India's first Law Minister, Dr Ambedkar was the principle architect of India's 1950 Constitution, which prohibits discrimination on the grounds of religion, race, caste, sex, or place of birth (Article 15). Notably, a 1951 amendment made clear that nothing in Article 15 should prevent the government from 'making any special provision for the advancement of any social and educationally backward classes of citizens or for the Scheduled Castes or Scheduled Tribes' (Article 15, Clause 4). This clause refers to other affirmative action beneficiaries, the STs and the Socially and Educationally Backward Classes (also known as Other Backward Classes or OBCs). Of these three categories—SCs, STs, and OBCs—it is only the SCs who have a religious dimension to their official classification.

A Presidential Order in 1950 restricted SC reservations to Hindu SCs but was later amended to include Sikh SCs in 1956, and Buddhist SCs in 1990. Some Christians and Muslims have argued that they too face caste discrimination in India. Although Muslim and Christian religious doctrines do not recognize caste, some Muslim and Christian groups face caste discrimination and disadvantages akin to Hindu SCs.

Caste-like stratification persists in Muslim societies in India based on status distinctions between communities descended (or believed to be descended) from immigrants versus communities of local converts or descendents of local converts. Muslim hierarchies in India also derive from occupational distinctions, as in other casteist societies (Ahmad 1978; Ali 2002; Mann 1992). Although reservations for Muslims as a whole ended at independence, many Muslim communities are on the lists of OBCs, which received government job reservations at the national level in the 1990s and, in a 2006 act upheld by the Supreme Court in 2008, reservations in higher education. Some activists, however, argue that

OBC status does not reflect the extreme disadvantage of some Muslim communities. In addition to trying to get more Muslim communities onto OBC lists, the All India Muslim OBC Organization has demanded that certain Muslim communities be added to the SC lists (Jenkins 2001). The All India United Muslim Morcha's focus is to 'bring Dalit Muslims in SC category', and this organization even protested against a quota for all Muslims in Andhra Pradesh because such a quota would not target the most disadvantaged Muslims (*The Economic Times* 24 August 2004; see also Sikand 2001; *The Times of India* 19 July 2004).

Separate seats, communion cups, burial grounds, and even churches attest to the continuity of caste discrimination among some Indian Christians (Forrester 1980; Japhet 1988; Koshy 1988; Webster 1992). In their relations to the broader community, many Dalits who converted or are descended from converts continue to face caste-based social and economic discrimination related to housing, education, employment, and practices of untouchability (Kananaikil 1990). Like Muslims, Christians lost their reserved seats at independence, so their exclusion from the SC category (enforced via the 1950 Presidential Order) took on new salience. Over the years, the SC category became central to other kinds of protections, including the Scheduled Castes and Scheduled Tribes (Prevention of Atrocities) Act of 1989 and the 73rd Constitutional Amendment (1992), reserving seats on local councils for SCs, STs, and women. This expanding use of the SC category further inspired some Christians to demand a more inclusive definition of the SCs (Louis 2007). Organizations involved in this demand include the All-India Christian Council and the National Coordination Committee for SC Christians (Jenkins 2001).

Because Islam and Christianity stress equity, arguments drawing attention to caste within these communities are controversial among many Christians and Muslims. Moreover, the idea of recognizing Christian and Muslim SCs faces opposition from Hindu nationalists as well as many within communities currently classified as SCs. Current beneficiaries would have to compete with a larger pool of eligible SCs for employment, educational, or legislative opportunities reserved for members of an SC.

One example of the tensions over demands for reservations for Dalit Christians was the heated reactions to a proposal to reserve seats for Christians and Dalit Christians at Delhi University's elite St. Stephen's College in 2007. Minority-run institutions, such as the Christian St. Stephen's College, have more autonomy from government-mandated affirmative action. Yet, activists pushing for Christian SC reservations have noted the irony of simultaneously demanding SC status and maintaining the exclusivity of certain Christian colleges, which can be as dominated by privileged and upper-caste students as any elite institution in the country. St. Stephen's is one of the most elite colleges in India and known for its prominent alumni. When its Principal, Valson Thampu, created 2007–8 admissions guidelines to admit 40 per cent Christians, and within that 10 per cent Dalit Christians, criticism from alumni and the English-language media was swift and furious. (The guidelines also included 15 per cent admissions for STs and SCs—as currently defined—and 5 per cent for sports-related admissions).

Historian Ramachandra Guha (an 'old Stephenian') complained about the decline in standards: 'A few vested interests are ruining the college. It's the intellectual and cultural excellence that marks an institution. By narrowly interpreting the law, which states that minority institutes may go up to 50% reservation, the bishop and his men have turned the college into a laughing stock' (quoted in Banerjee 2008). Referring to the qualifying examination marks needed for admission to St. Stephen's, *The Times of India* reported that 'the cut-off had been brought down by 20% for Christian Dalit candidates in the Chemistry honours course, as applicants were few' (Banerjee 2008).

Thampu argued for his policy on legal, theological, and political grounds.[1] He opposed claiming minority rights (the constitutional right to run a minority educational institution) without accepting responsibilities and obligations to Christians and lower castes. He emphasized that an important aspect of Christian theology is 'social justice'. Finally, he noted that the prior 'monopoly of knowledge' allowed Brahmins to exercise a stranglehold on the economy, polity, and society in India. His purpose, he said, was 'to discover and celebrate merit in all segments of society'.[2] This high profile, non-governmental initiative to provide affirmative action to Dalit Christians highlighted political tensions over reservations and the religious dimensions of caste, and put additional pressure on the government to decide whether to recognize Christian or Muslim SCs.

GOVERNMENT ATTENTION TO CASTE WITHIN MINORITY RELIGIONS

Despite the commonly assumed link between caste and Hindu identity, social scientists and activists have noted the persistence of caste within minority religious communities in India, including Christians and Muslims. Although the government definition of SCs has not, as of now, expanded beyond Hindus, Sikhs, and Buddhists, several government reports discuss caste within other religious minority communities.

Currently, people who change religious identities through conversion may simultaneously transgress the official boundaries of the SC category. Government employees appointed to positions reserved for SCs are supposed to tell their employers if they convert to a religion that bars them from SC reservations, after which they could lose their jobs. According to the government memorandum still applied in such situations:

> Instances have come to notice where Scheduled Caste candidates on adopting a religion other than Hinduism and Sikhism, did not intimate the change in religion to the appointment/administrative authorities and continued claiming/enjoying concessions/benefits admissible to Scheduled Castes. This necessitated withdrawal retrospectively of the concessions enjoyed by them. It has now been decided that in order to avoid such instances, Ministries/Departments etc. of Government of India may in future stipulate in the letter of appointment issued to Scheduled Caste candidates that they should inform about the change of religion to their Appointing/Administrative authority immediately after such a change.[3]

In contrast to this blunt memorandum simply aimed at implementing the current policy, several government commissions have issued reports that include detailed discussions of caste in religious minority communities.

For example, Backward Classes commissions have tackled this issue. The OBCs category already includes some Christian and Muslim groups. This constitutionally recognized category is eligible for more limited forms of affirmative action than scheduled groups; thus, occasionally, an OBC group will demand to be reclassified as an SC or ST. The 2007 Gujjar agitation demanding ST status in lieu of OBC status is one example (*The New York Times* 30 May 2007).

The OBCs include Hindu low castes that are not Untouchables, as well as low-status castes or communities from non-Hindu religions. Backward Classes commissions chaired by K. Kalelkar (1955) and B.P. Mandal (1980) developed social and economic criteria for the Backward Classes, and the central government set up the National Commission for Backward Classes as a permanent body in 1993. The Mandal Commission Report eventually became the basis for national-level affirmative action in government employment in the 1990s, policies that have been expanded into higher education. In this report, the commission frankly discussed OBCs among non-Hindu communities.

> There is no doubt that social and educational backwardness among non-Hindu communities is more or less of the same order as among Hindu communities. Though caste system is peculiar to Hindu society, in actual practice, it also pervades the non-Hindu communities in India in varying degrees. There are two main reasons for this phenomenon: first, caste system is a great conditioner of the mind and leaves an indelible mark on a person's social consciousness and cultural mores. Consequently, even after conversion, the ex-Hindus carried with them their deeply ingrained ideas of social hierarchy and stratification. This resulted in the Hindu converts inadvertently acting as Trojan horses of caste system among highly equalitarian religions such as Islam, Christianity, and Sikhism. Second, non-Hindu minorities living in predominantly Hindu India could not escape from its dominant social and cultural influences. Thus, both from within and without, caste amongst non-Hindu communities received continuous sustenance and stimulus. (Mandal 1980: 60)

The Mandal report goes on to discuss caste among Muslims, Christians, and Sikhs, but notes that 'they proclaim absolute equality of all their co-religionists and any social differentiation based on caste is anathema to them. In view of this, caste cannot be made the basis for identifying socially and educationally backward classes among non-Hindu communities' (Mandal 1980: 60). Seemingly to avoid offending the minorities' egalitarian impulses, the commission suggested alternative criteria for capturing non-Hindu OBCs: '(*i*) all Untouchables converted to any non-Hindu religion; and (*ii*) such occupational communities which are known by the name of their traditional hereditary occupation and whose Hindu counterparts have been included in the list of Hindu OBCs' (Mandal 1980: 61). In practice, individual converts have not been categorized in this way, but formerly untouchable or occupationally defined communities within minority religions have made it into the current OBC lists.

The current National Commission for Backward Classes addresses the question of 'whether backward sections of the religious minorities are also eligible for inclusion on the lists of OBCs?' on its 'frequently asked questions' page online: 'The central lists of OBCs issued by the Government of India for different States and Union Territories do contain entries relating to sections of religious minorities. When a caste/community or group is included in the lists, it is included irrespective of the religion or denomination followed by the members of that caste/community or group.'[4] The studious inclusion of terms like section, community, or group circumvents the use of 'caste' alone in references to religious minorities. While recognizing caste-like disparities, government reports have tended to avoid references to caste, let alone SC status, when discussing religious minorities, until quite recently.

Another government commission took note of caste-like disadvantages within Muslim and Christian communities but did not endorse the expansion of the SC category to include members of these minorities. The Rajinder Sachar Commission was constituted to carry out a comprehensive assessment of the social, economic, and educational status of Muslims in India. Although not perfectly carried out, this was a landmark effort due to the Indian government's long-standing practice of releasing relative religious population data from the census but avoiding tabulations or publications of census data that might show Muslims are a disadvantaged community in India (*The Hindu* 13 September 2004). The legacy of the colonial census, with its often divisive attention to various religious and caste communities, contributed to this post-independence reluctance to examine quantitatively and comparatively the status of Muslims. The 2006 Sachar Committee Report is notable for its attention to inequalities between and even within minorities.

Findings included Muslims' 'relative deprivation' compared to other religious communities and the particular challenges facing Muslims in certain sub-communities:

> Our analysis shows that while there is considerable variation in the conditions of Muslims across states, (and among the Muslims, those who identified themselves as OBCs and others), the Community exhibits deficits and deprivation in practically all dimensions of development. In fact, by and large, Muslims rank somewhat above Scheduled Castes and Scheduled Tribes but below Hindu-OBCs, Other Minorities and Hindu-General (mostly upper castes) in almost all indicators considered. (Sachar 2006: 237)

The Committee recognized the presence of particularly disadvantaged communities within the Muslim community, many already included in the official OBCs lists. Rather than promoting the expansion of the SC category to include similarly situated Muslims, however, the committee's recommendations emphasized diversity and geography rather than caste. For example, they recommended policies to create incentives for institutions to become more diverse and policies to target predominantly Muslim districts for development.

More recently, two government reports have even more explicitly recognized caste within minority religions. The National Commission on Linguistic and Religious Minorities, chaired by Justice Ranganath Misra, had already begun their research on the 'socially and economically backward sections' among the minorities, when they were told to give recommendations on the issue of opening the SC category to Muslims and Christians. This new charge was inspired by several petitions pending before the Supreme Court. In the 2007 report, the Misra Commission clearly preferred that the government move away from caste categories altogether, but, as long as official SC lists remained, recommended that people of any religion should qualify. The commission promoted as an 'ultimate goal' the identification of the 'backward … based only on the educational and economic status of people and not on their caste or religion' (Misra 2007: vol. 1, p. 148). They advocated moving away from castes or communities as the unit of analysis: 'The new list of socially and economically backward has necessarily to be family/household based' (Misra 2007: vol. 1, p. 145).

Recognizing that such an overhaul could not happen quickly, most members of the commission advocated removing religion from the legal definition of the SCs, unequivocally stating that the government should 'completely de-link the Scheduled Caste status from religion and make the Scheduled Castes net fully religion-neutral like that of the Scheduled Tribes' (Misra 2007: vol. 1, p. 154). This recommendation inspired a 'dissent note' by Member Secretary Asha Das (Misra 2007: vol. 1, pp. 156–68) as well as considerable political controversy and debate (*Indian Express* 24 May 2007; Jahangir 2009: 12).

The Misra Commission's response to Asha Das's dissent provides a spirited critique of her tendency to make Hindus a 'macro-majority' at the expense of minorities: 'The statement made in the Dissent Note that "Sikh and Buddhist religions were primarily home-grown sects within Hindu religion rather than being independent religions" is deplorable as it offends the religious sensitivities of the Sikh and Buddhist citizens of India who have always regarded their faiths as "independent religions"' (Misra 2007: vol. 1, p. 169). The Misra Commission, however, has a tendency to splinter minorities into 'micro-minorities', as when it recommends subdividing the SCs into classes and excluding the upper-class 'creamy layer' from affirmative action benefits (Misra 2007: vol. 1, p. 153). Another example of their micro-minority tendency is in the conclusions of one of their meetings, recorded in the appendix to their report, where they suggest subdividing an expanded SC quota among Hindus (15 per cent), Muslims (8 per cent), and Christians (1 per cent) (Misra 2007: vol. 2, p. 81).

In 2007, the National Commission for Minorities commissioned a report on 'Dalits in the Christian and Muslim Communities: A Status Report on Current Social Scientific Knowledge'. Released in 2008, the report, by Satish Deshpande and Geetika Bapna of the Department of Sociology at the University of Delhi, provides a compendium of existing academic work on these communities, a summary of some court decisions on the status of caste in religious minority communities, and most important, original analysis of the latest National Sample Survey Organisation (NSSO) data on poverty/affluence, consumption, occupational categories, and education (Deshpande and Bapna 2008).

These tabulations allowed the authors to compare Dalit Christians and Dalit Muslims with their non-Dalit co-religionists. They also compared Dalit Christians and Dalit Muslims with Hindu, Sikh, and Buddhist Dalits. Many indicators suggest that Dalit Muslims are the worst off of all these groups. Dalit Buddhists have relatively high proportions of their population in higher education compared to other Dalit groups, and some Dalit Sikhs are relatively well off in economic terms compared to other Dalit groups. On the whole, however, the analysis shows that 'inter-Dalit economic differences across religion are not very significant' (Deshpande and Bapna 2008: xi). The authors concluded that current descriptive and statistical evidence makes a 'strong case for including Dalit Muslims and Dalit Christians in the Scheduled Caste category', and went on to note that principles of justice and fairness, as well as pragmatic considerations, further support this move (Despande and Bapna 2008: 83).

The Misra Commission Report and the report by Deshpande and Bapna include the most direct statements about caste or Dalits within religious minorities in government or government-sponsored reports, although even the much earlier Mandal report was quite frank about their existence. The politics have changed, though. The Mandal Commission took pains to identify 'backward' minorities while avoiding the term 'caste', to avoid offending Muslim or Christian religious sensibilities based on their egalitarian doctrines. Subsequently, the escalating public and legal demand by some Christians and Muslims for SCs status set the stage for the Misra Commission Report and the report commissioned by the National Commission for Minorities, which explicitly address and even support this demand.

INTERNATIONAL ATTENTION TO CASTE WITHIN MINORITY RELIGIONS

According to the 2001 Indian Census, Hindus constitute 80.5 per cent of the Indian population; Muslims, 13.4 per cent; Christians, 2.3 per cent; Sikhs, 1.9 per cent; Buddhists, 0.8 per cent; and Jains, 0.4 per cent. Yet, defining minorities depends on the geographic scale under consideration. Christians and Muslims are minorities within India but are part of the two largest religious communities in the world. The situation of Christians and Muslims attracts attention at the international level in part due to their large numbers worldwide.

Drawing international attention to minority issues within India has been one of the strategies used by activists to gain more national attention. Dalit leaders and organizations have increasingly voiced their concerns in human rights terms, including claims of discrimination based on race or descent (Bob 2009; Human Rights Watch 1999). International governmental and non-governmental organizations have reported not only on the plight of Dalits and of religious minorities within India but also, increasingly, on the unique issues facing Christian and Muslim Dalits. Thus, in addition to the increasingly explicit attention to caste within minority religions in Indian government reports, international human rights reports are heeding the complex nexus of caste and religion.

Earlier reports are less nuanced about caste and religion. For example, a 1999 Human Rights Watch Report calls caste 'a defining feature of Hinduism' (Human Rights Watch 1999: 24). Rather than discussing caste within long-standing Muslim or Christian communities, the report only mentions Dalit conversions to Buddhism, Christianity, and Islam and notes that such converts sometimes 'lose access to their scheduled-caste status and the few government privileges assigned to it' (Human Rights Watch 1999: 27).

A 2007 'shadow report' to the United Nations Committee on the Elimination of Racial Discrimination by international and New York-based human rights organizations goes into much more depth. This report notes the following:

> Dalits have responded to ill-treatment by upper-caste Hindus by convert-
> ing en masse to Buddhism, Christianity, and historically to Islam. The loss

of constitutional privileges upon conversion, however, serves as a serious impediment to their freedom to choose their religion. Additionally, most Dalits are ultimately unable to escape their treatment as 'untouchables' regardless of the religion they profess. (Centre for Human Rights and Global Justice and Human Rights Watch 2007: 75)

The report details the segregation and discrimination Dalit Muslims and Dalit Christians face within their religious communities. In addition, it also notes the quandary faced by people at the intersection of two types of minority identity: 'Dalit Christians and Muslims may be subject to multiple forms of discrimination on the basis of their caste and religion' (Centre for Human Rights and Global Justice and Human Rights Watch 2007: 77).

The January 2009 report on India by the United Nations Special Rapporteur on Religious Freedom states that 'the eligibility for affirmative action benefits should be restored to those members of scheduled castes and tribes who have converted to another religion' (Jahangir 2009: 2). The Rapporteur argues that the 'legal link between Scheduled Castes status and affiliation to specific religions seems problematic in terms of human rights standards' (Jahangir 2009: 11). She notes that the Committee on the Elimination of Racial Discrimination earlier raised similar concerns about Dalits, noting that converts to Islam and Christianity lose their eligibility for affirmative action.

Dalits' international appeals on the basis of religion, caste, and even racial discrimination have gained increasing attention. International human rights groups have heeded the intersectional arguments about the multiple forms of discrimination faced by some individuals due to the combination of religious minority and low-caste status. International reports have largely avoided the problems associated with combining groups into macro majorities or dividing them into micro-minorities, in large part because they are descriptive critiques of discrimination rather than templates for targeted policies necessitating categorization.

CONTINUING LEGAL LIMITS ON THE RELIGION OF THE SCs

Despite civil society demands for revision of the SC category and increasing recognition of caste within non-Hindu communities in some Indian and international reports, the SC category continues to exclude several religious minorities. The courts, to date, remain reluctant to expand the religious boundaries of the SCs. Sikh and Buddhist SCs have gained recognition due to legal changes to specifically include them. Muslims and Christians could be included either through similar legislative action or through a Supreme Court decision declaring their exclusion unconstitutional.

Although 'the political route may seem to be the more direct one' and has worked before for other minorities (Despande and Bapna 2008: 82), expanding the pool of eligible SCs could make a legislator politically unpopular among some Hindus from the top to the bottom of the social spectrum. Change initiated by the courts would be difficult as well. The inclusion of Sikh and Buddhist SCs built on a legal history in which these religions had been subsumed into a broadly defined 'Hinduism'. Marc Galanter argues that the courts' linkage of caste with Hinduism (or, at most, Sikhism or Buddhism) 'reflects the continued force of a view of caste groups which sees them as units in an overarching sacral order of Hinduism.... From this view of caste derived the long-standing reluctance of the courts to give legal effect to caste standing among non-Hindu communities' (Galanter 1991: 318). Islam and Christianity are exceedingly unlikely to ever be considered 'Hinduism', hindering legal recognition of caste within these religions.

The broad definition of Hinduism as a macro-majority has implications for minority rights beyond the exclusion of Dalit Christians and Muslims from SC protections. If one cannot be recognized as a religious minority due to being defined as part of a majority, minority rights cannot come into play. This situation has come up in a case in which the Jain community, legally recognized as a minority in several Indian states, was denied a separate, minority identity at the national level. (Being grouped into Hindus has not benefited Jains by allowing them access to SC benefits, although this has never been a major demand.) The denial of minority status to Jains involved several arguments, including arguments on the basis of federalism, economics, and religion; notably, the latter argument involved subsuming Jainism into Hinduism. This decision illustrates how being a 'minority' can be much more than a question of relative numbers.[5]

A Jain organization petitioned the High Court in Bombay to direct the central government to 'notify Jains as a minority under Section 2(c) of the National Commission of Minorities Act, 1992'.[6] This would give them the benefit of the attention and concern of this commission, charged with ensuring minority progress and development as well as protection of their religious, cultural, and educational rights. In *Bal Patil v. Union of India* (2005), the Supreme Court [drawing on the *TMA Pai* case 2002 (8) SCC 481] held that minority status is not determined by relative numbers nationally but rather at the state level; the Court looked to numbers within a state as well as the group's social status and conditions within that state. In addition to tossing the ball to the state level, the Court imposed some economic criteria on religious minority status and related protections and policies: 'If it is found that a majority of the members of the community belong to the affluent class of industrialists, businessmen, professionals and propertied class, it may not be necessary to notify them under the Act and extend any special treatment or protection to them as a minority.'[7] Thus, even if a community is religiously distinct, if the majority within that minority is doing well socio-economically, the Court felt that official minority status would be superfluous.

In addition, in this case, the Court questioned the distinctiveness of the Jain religion. The Court undermined the Jain community's minority status by subsuming Jainism under Hinduism, essentially making them part of the majority:

> Hinduism can be called a general religion and common faith of India whereas Jainism is a special religion formed on the basis of quintessence of Hindu religion. Jainism places greater emphasis on non-violence (Ahimsa) and compassion (Karuna). Their only difference from Hindus is that Jains do not believe in any creator like God but only worship the perfect human being whom they call Tirathankar.[8]

Disagreement over the existence of god seems to be a rather fundamental distinction between religions; yet, the Court found this insignificant.

The judges in their decision noted the legal precedent of supersizing Hinduism for purposes of personal law:

> The so-called minority communities like Sikhs and Jains were not treated as national minorities at the time of framing the Constitution. Sikhs and Jains, in fact, have throughout been treated as part of the wider Hindu community which has different sects, sub-sects, faiths and modes of worship and religious philosophies. In various codified customary laws like Hindu Marriage Act, Hindu Succession Act, Hindu Adoption and Maintenance Act and other laws of pre and post-Constitution period, definition of Hindu included all sects, sub-sects of Hindu religions including Sikhs and Jains. The word Hindu conveys image of diverse groups of communities living in India.[9]

The expansive definition of Hindu, used in this decision, has in other instances also encompassed Buddhists, as in the Indian Constitution's article on freedom of religion.[10] In another interesting manoeuvre, the *Bal Patil* decision both expanded Hinduism into a bigger majority and simultaneously shattered it into multiple minorities, ultimately breaking down the distinction between minority and majority by including the argument, 'All are minorities amongst Hindus'.

The deciding judges' ambivalence about the entire project of recognizing minorities became clear when the *Bal Patil* decision concluded with a call for the Minority Commission, which is charged with the protection of minorities, to 'gradually eliminate minority and majority classes. If, only on the basis of a different religious thought or less numerical strength or lack of health, wealth, education, power or social rights, a claim of a section of Indian society to the status of minority is conceded, there would be no end to such claims.'[11] In short, the decision called on the commission to do away with the categories it was designed to protect. If a group cannot gain minority status, the rights for which they may be eligible, however admirable and far-reaching, are moot. Legally constructing a Hindu macro-majority both disadvantages the minorities who are lumped in, such as Jains who want minority status, and those who are left out, such as Dalit Christians and Muslims who want SC status.

The courts have considered the intersection of religion and caste membership in cases involving SC reservations and other forms of assistance. In *Soosai v. Union of India and others* (1985),[12] an SC convert to Christianity claimed that denying him assistance for SCs was unconstitutional discrimination on the basis of religion. The Supreme Court held that it is not enough to demonstrate that caste membership continues; converts must demonstrate that severe social, economic, and educational deprivations continue in the new religious community. The Court noted that some Sikh communities had been recognized as SCs, attributing this to the government's consideration of evidence of their social, economic, and cultural deprivation, and pointing to a lack of detailed studies of caste and Christian society at the time of the decision. Notably, the study sponsored by the National Commission on Minorities, discussed earlier, both overviewed existing studies and provided new analysis of data from the National Sample Survey; the authors explicitly noted in their conclusions that 'In the two decades since the last major judicial pronouncement on this question in the *Soosai* case, a lot more evidence has become available' (Deshpande and Bapna 2008: 81).

Superintendant of Post Offices v. R. Valasina Babu, decided in 2006, vividly illustrates the impact of exposing the Christian identity of a supposedly SC employee.[13] A postal assistant in a job reserved for SCs was fired in 1992. When he was hired in 1980, over a decade before, '[i]n support of his claim that he belonged to Mala community, he had produced a certificate'.[14] Caste certificates issued by local authorities are routinely used to verify identities in Indian affirmative action. But in this case, an unnamed informant threw the postal assistant's identity into question: 'On an information received that the respondent in fact belonged to Christian community, a disciplinary proceeding against him was initiated.... The collector...also initiated a proceeding for cancellation of the Caste Certificate.'[15] The district collector cancelled his caste certificate. The assistant was 'dismissed from service with immediate effect which shall ordinarily be a dis-qualification for future employment under the Government'.[16] In this case, the Supreme Court applied the current categorization of SCs, with little comment on the religious dimensions of this exclusion, simply stating 'the candidate must be one who belongs to that category. If the selectee does not fulfill said basic criteria, his appointment cannot be allowed to continue.'[17]

Was the postal assistant a convert to Christianity from the Mala community? Did he convert in the twelve years between his appointment and dismissal? Were his parents or ancestors Malas? These issues are not raised in the decision, in which it was implied, but not stated, that the certificate was fraudulent by reference to another case involving a 'false certificate'.[18] Adjudicating identity fraud involving an identity as malleable or convertible as religion is a dicey legal area (Jenkins 2003). Whether he was a convert or not, the fate of the postal assistant shows that belonging to certain minority religions has tangible costs for Dalits. Losing political, economic, and educational affirmative action benefits, as well as special protections from human rights abuses under the Scheduled Castes and Scheduled Tribes (Prevention of Atrocities) Act, 1989, could dissuade someone contemplating a change of faith. In addition to the threat of losing legal protections and benefits associated with SC status, another legal disincentive to convert is the recent proliferation of state laws against 'forcible' conversions. The focus of such laws seems to be low caste or tribal communities. The law's designers seem to assume such groups (and women) are particularly vulnerable or susceptible to conversion by 'force' or 'allurement', an assumption made explicit in the higher penalties for converting women or low castes included in the laws of some states (Jenkins 2008).

Unlike SCs, members of STs may be in any religion, yet, a 2004 Supreme Court decision suggests that there may be increasing scrutiny of tribal members in minority religions in order to determine whether their tribe still accepts them as members, whether they are still disadvantaged, and whether they are still following tribal 'traditions'.[19] Such legal scrutiny may be related to the increasing social and political critiques of ST Christians, discussed in the chapter by Joseph Marianus Kujur on various efforts to de-schedule Christian tribes. The case revolved around a girl whose father was in an ST and had converted to Catholicism to marry the girl's mother, whose family had 'converted to Christianity two centuries back'. A man faced criminal charges for taking the 8-year-old girl to a classroom 'with an intent to dishonour and outrage her modesty'. He protested against additional charges under the Scheduled Castes and Scheduled Tribes (Prevention of Atrocities) Act, 1989, on the grounds that the girl's parents were Christians. 'The High Court was of the view that since the victim's parents have embraced Christianity, therefore, the victim ceased to be a member of the Scheduled Tribe.'[20]

While not agreeing that in every case conversion means exit from a tribe, the Supreme Court held that this question must be considered on a case-by-case basis. 'In such a situation, it has to be established that a person who has embraced another religion is still suffering from social disability and also following customs and traditions of the community, which he earlier belonged to.'[21] The notion of static tribal identity based on traditions and customs could result in an identity test even non-convert members might fail (Jenkins 2003: 30–1). Although there is no Presidential Order specifying religions for STs, this decision raises the possibility of a religious litmus test for STs, akin to that for SCs. This legal slicing and dicing of the SCs, and even in this case the STs, along religious lines is another example of the destructive politics of creating micro minorities.

The Supreme Court has repeatedly postponed deciding whether Christians or Muslims of SC origins should benefit from reservations. Three Dalit Christian cases[22] and one Dalit Muslim case[23] have been combined in order to be considered together. This case is partly responsible for the recent flurry of government reports, discussed earlier, but the Supreme Court has not yet come to a decision (Paul 2008).

* * *

The cross-cutting nature of caste and religious identities complicates the very definition of who is a minority in India. In India, 'minority' often connotes 'religious minority', especially Muslims and Christians. Leaving aside the point that there are many other types of minorities (based on ethnicity, language, caste, tribe, and more, as illustrated in this volume), even the definition of who constitutes a religious minority is contested. Legal and political definitions of who is a Hindu sometimes subsume arguably minority religious communities under the majority religion, Hinduism, making this majority even bigger and underplaying the distinct identity of groups such as Sikhs, Buddhists, or Jains.

The politics of defining the SCs has contributed to this debate over delineating minorities. The battles for SC benefits for SC Sikhs and SC Buddhists were successful, whereas the struggle for SC Christians and Muslims is ongoing, further reinforcing the dichotomy between macro Hinduism, in its broadest definition, and certain minority religions. Acknowledging caste within Sikh and Buddhist communities, as in Hindu communities, was an easier policy development due to legal and political precedents subsuming Sikhism and Buddhism (and Jainism) within Hinduism. Combining minorities into macro-majorities is one political move. Another dynamic that comes into play in the debate over religion and the SCs is dividing minorities into micro-groups. Although recent government reports concluded that the SC category should be open to lower castes regardless of religion, some advocate retaining distinctions between existing SC communities and any additional (Christian or Muslim) SCs that might achieve recognition. Concern about additional competitors for the same number of opportunities is justified; yet, administratively subdividing a potentially larger, uni-fied SC community could foment political divisions within a category that shares many interests, in particular, a shared dream of annihilating caste-based discrimination. Pan-religious Dalit, SC, or Bahujan orga-nizations exist in political and civil society, illustrating the potential political power of unity among the oppressed. At the same time, some members of the SCs have protested against the expansion of their cat-egory to include other religious communities, insisting that both caste and religion be considered.

Fragmenting of official identities can have two negative impacts on minorities. First, affirmative action categories could be defined in such a narrow way that there are not enough qualified applicants to fill posi-tions. For example, demands to skim the 'creamy layer' off of the SCs would reflect intersectionality by combining caste and class indicators to remove the well-off individuals from the SC applicant pool. Yet, due to educational disparities in India, many higher-level positions reserved for SCs already go unfilled, and applying the creamy layer exclusion to the SCs would increase this problem. Second, subdividing categories reinforces a sense of 'us versus them' between and within communities with some shared interests, and thus complicates political unity and action. Fracturing the official SC minority into religious subcategories, by, for example, creating a separate SC Christian or SC Muslim quota, could have this effect by reinforcing religious difference rather than socio-economic similarity. Splintering minorities into micro-minorities or amalgamating them into macro-majorities puts minorities in a precarious position. The boundaries one crosses or constructs within or between communities need careful consideration, particularly when designating 'minorities' in a democracy.

NOTES

1.   Author's interview with Valson Thampu, 3 January 2008.
2.   Ibid.
3.   D.O.P.T., O.M.NO.13/3/71-ESTT. (SCT), dated 10 September 1971, printed in Mukherjee (2006: 315–6).
4.   See http://ncbc.nic.in/html/faq5.html (accessed 26 March 2009).
5.   This section contains revised passages from Jenkins (2009), republished with permission of the editor-in-chief.
6.   *Bal Patil v. Union of India*, 2005, Case no. Appeal (civil) 4730 of 1999, available at http://164.100.9.38/judis/bitstream/123456789/9398/1/27098.pdf#search=4730 1999 (accessed 7 November 2011).
7.   *Bal Patil v. Union of India.*
8.   Ibid.
9.   Ibid.
10. Indian Constitution, Article 25(2)(b), Explanation II: '[T]he reference to Hindus shall be construed as including a reference to persons professing the Sikh, Jaina or Buddhist religion.'
11. *Bal Patil v. Union of India.*
12. *Soosai v. Union of India and others*, 1985, (supp) SCC590.
13. *Superintendent of Post Offices v. R. Valasina Babu*, 2006, Case no.: Appeal (civil) 5868 of 2006, Date of Judgement: 14/12/ 2006, available at http://164.100.9.38/judis/bitstream/123456789/6646/1/29844.pdf#search=5868 2006 (accessed 7 November 2011).
14. Ibid., p. 1.
15. Ibid.
16. Ibid.; quoting the order of dismissal.
17. Ibid., p. 2.
18. Ibid., p. 3.
19. *State of Kerala v. Chandramohanan*, 2004, SOL Case No. 091.
20. *Superintendent of Post Offices v. R. Valasina Babu.*

21.   Ibid.
22.   Writ Petition (Civil) no. 180 of 2004; no. 625 of 2005; and no. 94
of 2005.
23.   Writ Petition (Civil) no. 47 of 2006.

REFERENCES

Ahmad, Imtiaz. 1978, *Caste and Social Stratification among Muslims in India*,
    New Delhi: Manohar.
Ali, Syed. 2002, 'Collective and Elective Ethnicity: Caste among Urban Muslims
    in India', *Sociological Forum*, 17(4): 593–620.
Banerjee, Rumu. 2008, 'St. Stephens Alumni Flay New Cut-off Order', *The
    Times of India*, 19 June, available at http://articles.timesofindia.indiatimes.
    com/2008-06-19/delhi/27755906_1_christian-quota-cut-off-marks-
    supreme-council (accessed 7 November 2011).
Bob, Clifford (ed.). 2009, 'Dalit Rights are Human Rights: Untouchables,
    NGOs and the Indian State', in *The International Struggle for New Human
    Rights*, Philadelphia: University of Pennsylvania Press, pp. 30–51.
Centre for Human Rights and Global Justice and Human Rights Watch. 2007,
    'Hidden Apartheid: Caste Discrimination against India's Untouchables',
    Shadow Report to the UN Committee on the Elimination of Racial Dis-
    crimination, New York.
Deshpande, Satish and Geetika Bapna. 2008, 'Dalits in the Muslim and
    Christian Communities: A Status Report on Current Social Scientific
    Knowledge', Report prepared for the National Commission for Minorities,
    Government of India, New Delhi.
The Economic Times. 24 August 2004, 'Muslim Group Protests Quota, Blasts
    Congress', available at http://articles.economictimes.indiatimes.com/2004-
    08-24/news/27373002_1_dalit-muslims-sc-reservation-m-ejaz-ali (accessed
    7 November 2011).
Forrester, D. 1980, *Caste and Christianity: Attitudes and Policies of Anglo-Saxon
    Protestant Missionaries in India*, London and Dublin: Curzon Press.
Galanter, Marc. 1991, *Competing Equalities*, New Delhi: Oxford University
    Press.
The Hindu. 13 September 2004, 'Census Follies', Editorial, available at http://
    www.hindu.com/2004/09/13/stories/2004091302871000.htm (accessed 7
    November 2011).
Human Rights Watch. 1999, *Broken People: Caste Violence against India's
    Untouchables*, New York: Human Rights Watch.
Indian Express. 24 May 2007, 'BJP for Rejecting Ranganath Mishra Report on
    Dalit Converts', available at http://indiarightsonline.com/Sabrang/dalit2.
    nsf/a1fec1a6cddc3244e5257713005cd825/14927a37402a7417652572e70
    0325a3c?OpenDocument (accessed 8 November 2011).

Jahangir, Asma. 2009, 'Promotion and Protection of All Human Rights, Civil, Political, Economic, Social and Cultural Rights, Including the Right to Development: Report of the Special Rapporteur on Freedom of Religion or Belief, Addendum: Mission to India', 26 January, Human Rights Council, United Nations, New York.

Japhet, S. 1988, 'Caste Oppression in the Catholic Church', in M.E. Prabhakar (ed.), *Toward a Dalit Theology*, Delhi: ISPCK, pp. 176–80.

Jenkins, Laura Dudley. 2001, 'Becoming Backward: Preferential Policies and Religious Minorities in India', *Commonwealth and Comparative Politics*, 39(1): 32–50.

————. 2003, *Identity and Identification in India: Defining the Disadvantaged*, London: RoutledgeCurzon.

————. 2008, 'Legal Limits on Religious Conversion in India', *Law and Contemporary Problems*, 71(2): 109–27.

————. 2009, 'Diversity and the Constitution in India: What Is Religious Freedom?' *Drake Law Review*, 57(4): 913–47.

Kananaikil, J. 1990, 'Discrimination against Dalit Converts: With Specific Reference to Dalit Converts to Christianity', *Religion and Society*, 37(4): 60–4.

Koshy, N. 1988, *Caste in the Kerala Churches*, Bangalore: The Christian Institute for the Study of Religion and Society.

Lien, Pei-te, Carol Hardy–Fanta, Dianne Pinderhughes, and Christine Sierra. 2008, 'Expanding Categorization at the Intersection of Race and Gender: Women of Color as a political Category for African American, Latina, Asian American and American Indian Women', Paper presented at the Annual Meeting of the American Political Science Association, Boston, 28 August.

Louis, Prakash. 2007, 'Caste-based Discrimination and Atrocities on Dalit Christians and the Need for Reservations', *Working Paper Series*, 2(4), New Delhi: Indian Institute of Dalit Studies.

Mandal, B.P. 1980, *Report of the Backward Classes Commission*, Delhi: Akalank Publications.

Mann, E.A. 1992, *Boundaries and Identities: Muslims, Work and Status in Aligarh*, New Delhi: Sage Publications.

Misra, Ranganath. 2007, 'Report of the National Commission for Religious and Linguistic Minorities, Vols 1 and 2', available at http://minorityaffairs.gov. in/newsite/ncrlm/volume-1.pdf and http://minorityaffairs.gov.in/newsite/ ncrlm/volume-2.pdf (accessed 4 May 2011).

Mukherjee, Sandeep. 2006, *Guide to Reservation Policy (Work Book on Reservation in Government Services)*, New Delhi: Variety Book Publishers Distributors.

The New York Times. 30 May 2007, '14 Die in Clashes between Police and Protesters in Western India', p. A4.

Paul, Sam. 2008, 'After Four Years, India's Supreme Court Continues to Delay Decision on Dalit Case', All-India Christian Council (AICC) Press Release,

26 April, available at http://indianchristians.in/news/content/view/2065/42/ (accessed 23 January 2009).

Sachar, Rajinder. 2006, 'Social, Economic and Educational Status of the Muslim Community in India: A Report', available at http://minorityaffairs.gov.in/ newsite/sachar/sachar_comm.pdf (accessed 9 May 2011).

Sikand, Yoginder. 2001, 'A New Indian Muslim Agenda: The Dalit Muslims and the All-India Backward Muslim Morcha', *Journal of Muslim Minority Affairs*, 21(2): 287–96.

Tejani, Shabnum. 2007, 'Reflections on the Category of Secularism in India: Gandhi, Ambedkar and the Ethics of Communal Representation, c. 1931', in A. Dingwaney Needham and R. Sunder Rajan (eds), *The Crisis of Secularism in India*, Durham and London: Duke University Press, 45–65.

The Times of India. 19 July 2004, 'Muslim Body Opposes Job Quota for Muslims', available at http://articles.timesofindia.indiatimes.com/2004-07-18/india/27167624_1_dalit-muslims-job-quota-muslim-body (accessed 7 November 2011).

Webster, J. 1992, *A History of the Dalit Christians in India*, San Francisco: Mellon Research University Press.

4

Representing the 'Minority'

Farhana Ibrahim

The question of the 'minority' is, by definition, a political one; with the minority and its corollary, the 'majority', often an implicitly assumed one (against which the 'minority' emerges as a distinct category), one is in the realm of enumeration. In India, the category of the 'minority' tends to be represented as a religious one. Thus, 'minority communities' are the Christian, Muslim, Parsi, or Sikh, all emerging in their 'minority-ness' when compared to the ubiquitous mass of the Hindu majority. Linguistic or caste identities tend to not belong under the rubric of the proper 'minority'. In the case of Gujarat, the dominant paradigm for minorityness is not just religion per se; in recent years, it has come to uniquely denote the Muslim. Across large sections of urban and rural Gujarat, the 'minority community' is typically a euphemism for the Muslim alone. This is, of course, a result of its particular history of inter-religious strife. The interplay of majority–minority thus plays out here in terms of Hindu–Muslim.

Enumeration and categorization of the above sort is useful, for in a democratic context, it helps define the kinds of claims that can be made upon the state on behalf of the community. To this extent, there is always a tension between the need to homogenize within the category, thus obfuscating the incipient heterogeneity that it represents at the level of reality. This chapter will attempt to shed light on this tension using ethnographic material from Kachchh district in Gujarat. It will critically interrogate the formulation of the 'minority', to ask how it constructs itself, not just in relation to the all-pervasive majority but also vis-à-vis itself. The chapter will explore this with two sets of examples from Kachchh. Within the assumed unity of the category 'Muslim', there are numerous splits and divisions so that the identity of the community taken as a whole becomes precariously balanced between dissenting groups. Sectarian differences between Muslims are sealed as their children study in different (and often, mutually hostile) madrasas; they have their own religious leaders and advisors; and sect affiliation becomes an important criterion in determining choice of marriage partner. My second example is drawn from among the adivasi community in Kachchh, often seen as betwixt-and-between Hindu and Muslim. They are now, ironically, being assimilated as 'new Hindus' into the majority as far as public political discourse goes, yet, they are ambivalent about entirely giving up their status as a 'minority', a position that leads to other kinds of entitlements and benefits. The chapter concludes by arguing that the minority is a product of the majority context it inhabits, and that this cannot always be measured in terms of a clear-cut opposition that runs along religious or caste lines. Minorityness is more often a shifting signifier depending on the overall context of claims and entitlements on the one hand, and boundary maintenance between groups on the other.

MULTICULTURALISM, PLURALISM, AND THE DISCOURSE OF THE MINORITY

In India, discussions on the minority question often revolve around the need or continued relevance of secularism in the Indian context. Multiculturalism per se is not a very new phenomenon in terms of a mode of social organization. So-called traditional societies or even large-scale empires of the past may be said to have been more or less pluralist in their organization, if by that term we mean the coexistence of a number of social and cultural groups, each of which had the freedom to manage its own traditions. If one were to consider the societal composition under empires such as the Ottoman, Spanish, or Mughal, one would find that these societies tended to be a mosaic of ethnic and religious groups, and could perhaps be considered to be multicultural or plural, long before these terms became current in academic and social discourse. The difference between then and now lies in the fundamental nature of liberal democracy, which tends to animate the question of the minority and majority more fully. As Benedict Anderson (1983) argued in his path-breaking work on nationalism, the two great unifiers in the pre-nation state era were the 'religious community' and the 'dynastic realm'. Difference was tolerated as a prelude to assimilation into the majority, either through the unificatory use of sacred languages or personal loyalty to a monarch. This philosophy was displaced, by the time the first nation states were formed, by the rhetoric of maintaining one's own distinct traditions without sacrificing full membership in the national collective. But even this philosophy was the outcome of a later liberal political tradition. In the Western context, pluralism and multi-culturalism emerge against the backdrop of a very specific historical trajectory. The modern form of the nation state emerged as a product of the Enlightenment tradition and came of age in the specific historical experiences of England, France, and Germany. In these countries, nationalist ideologies were concerned with the idea of a shared cultural essence that bound a nation together. Carleton Hayes, an early ideologue of Western nationalism, wrote, '… nationality rests upon cultural foundations … a nationality is any group of persons who speak a common language, who cherish common historical traditions, and who constitute, or think they constitute, a distinct cultural society' (1926: 21).

It was a concern with primordial attributes such as the blood and spirit of the collective—the *volk*—that characterized the writings of German nationalists such as Fichte, Herder, and others. Built on the notions of such shared common substance, these nations have had to, in more recent times, deal with the challenge of large-scale immigration in the post-war years. How these nations have dealt with their immigrants has an important bearing on the question of how we can talk about pluralism in those societies today. What kinds of multicultural foundations are possible in these contexts where the criteria for citizenship and belonging have emerged out of very specific kind of nationalist histories? The situation is quite different in the nations of the New World, whose foundations were built on waves of immigration from Europe and, subsequently, other parts of the world. The problem of multiculturalism and religious plurality in the Western world has translated into the problem of what to do with minority religious and cultural populations. There has been an increased movement into countries such as the United States (US), Canada, and the United Kingdom (UK) due to a high volume of transnational migration, a colonial inheritance (in the case of Britain), as well as indigenous minorities (in the case of the US and Canada).

In an illuminating essay on the multicultural challenge in Britain, anthropologist Talal Asad takes the example of British Muslim protest against Salman Rushdie's controversial novel, *The Satanic Verses*, in 1989 and highlights the response of the British state. He argues that multiculturalism in the context of modern British life (that is, post-World War II, post-immigration) implies a tolerance for difference as long as there is some underlying consensus on an inherent 'Britishness', not unlike the earlier model of assimilation discussed by Anderson. In his analysis of a document released at the time of the protest, *On Being British*, Asad writes that it '... urges "cultural minority communities" to aspire to a norm. The document is an implicit description of the white cultural majority community, which supposedly sets the norm, and so of what that cultural essence is' (1993: 243–4). He also asks a question of crucial relevance for Western nations: When immigrants bring their own cultural practices with them, are they incorporated into British life, thereby extending its public scope, or are they only 'conditionally tolerated' (1993: 245) in deference to the averred policy of multiculturalism? He also asks, with respect to this document, who really counts as an immigrant? Typically, it is the non-whites who are considered to be cultural minorities rather than white Anglo-Saxons who have also immigrated in large numbers to countries such as the US.

Gurpreet Mahajan (2002) has made a case for distinguishing between pluralism and multiculturalism as analytical categories. Cultural pluralism, she argues, is not a product of modernity, but has existed in every polity where different religious or cultural groups have existed side by side, for example, the ancient empires of Persia, Egypt, and Rome, or the medieval Ottoman or Mughal empires, which were all ethnically and culturally diverse. Yet, she avers that even when different religious groups are recognized and given a legal status of their own, we cannot assume that these states are multicultural in the strict sense of the term, something that involves a conscious commitment to a different kind of value. Mahajan writes (2002: 11) that

> ... the existence of plurality at the societal level does not imply that multiculturalism as a value prevailed in these societies. The simultaneous presence of many cultures and communities within the same social space points to a plural social fabric, but it does not betoken the presence of multiculturalism. The latter entails something more than the mere presence of different communities or the attitude of tolerance in society. Multiculturalism is concerned with the issue of equality: it asks whether the different communities, living peacefully together, co-exist as equals in the public arena.

Ultimately, it is this focus on equality that is the hallmark of multiculturalism and what makes it different from pluralism in Mahajan's writing. Under pluralism, many different communities may thrive, but often, only as long as they accept the hegemony of the dominant community. In other words, they can practice their own cultural or religious norms as long as they do not overtly challenge the dominance of the majority group. Autonomy, in this sense, exists for communities only vis-à-vis their own members, that is, they have an internal autonomy, but not so much vis-à-vis the dominant group. She also makes an observation that is significant in the context of the Indian subcontinent: 'A plural social fabric or stories of collective participation in festivals and processions are, therefore, no indication of the absence of hierarchy and inequality. In fact, it often exists when the authority of the dominant community and the symbols of its power are readily accepted by others' (Mahajan 2002: 13). She adds:

> We need to go beyond the fact of co-presence and interaction and raise the issue of group equality by examining whether the different communities occupying the same social space—and at times even living amicably together—and participating in each other's cultures, have the same status in the public domain. This is essential because inequality in the public domain can, and often does, co-exist with degrees of legal and social pluralism. (Mahajan 2002: 13–14)

According to this framework, in plural—but not necessarily multicultural—societies, the dominance of a majority community is often expressed in political and symbolic terms, often with regards to the use of public space and the use of certain symbolic artefacts to the exclusion of others. Mahajan's observations become an important point of transition to discuss the issue of the minority in the Indian context, which is rather different from the Western case because of its unique historical precedents. In India, the minority is not constituted as a result of immigration as in the case of the West. Minority communities in India, whether linguistic or religious, have been an integral part of Indian society for millennia. It is with the transition to a democratic context, however, that the question of the minority assumes significance.

THE MINORITY AND THE STATE

I have been arguing that the representation of the minority *qua* minority is an important aspect of democratic politics. The minority, in a plural—but perhaps not necessarily multicultural—society such as India, in its representation as a minority, assumes an important role vis-à-vis the state. As a perceived homogenous entity, it earns for itself a bargaining potential vis-à-vis a state that otherwise may not necessarily be seen as always acting in its interests. To this extent, there is a pragmatism involved in projecting a singular group identity even though this singularity is compromised in fact. As far as the Muslim community in India is concerned, studies have pointed out how it was during the nineteenth and early twentieth centuries that the ideas of the Muslim as a representational category came up. According to Lelyveld (1981), during the nineteenth century, Muslims were transformed from only a religious community to colonial 'public'. Language played a key role in this consciousness, as Urdu came to be democratized and flowed beyond courtly and literate circles to become the language of Muslim oratory and speech. In a fledgling democratic context, by the third decade of the twentieth century, Urdu came to be seen as a quintessentially Muslim language, and its speakers came to acquire an identity uniquely associated with it. Farzana Shaikh (1989, 1991) locates this transformation in Muslim consciousness in the language of representation. The idea of representation is tied implicitly to the idea of community. She argues that if the colonial administration only saw in India a conglomeration of so many 'communities' (as opposed to 'individuals'), then all claims must be presented as speaking 'on behalf of' a community seen as a unified bloc.

How then does minority identity get constructed and 'fixed' in the public imagination? It is important to note that the process by which the 'minority' is constructed as such is the result of historical context, circumstance, and judicial process, as argued, for instance, by Shaikh, and also reiterated by Sipra Mukherjee in this volume. The process of straitjacketing multiple local identities (for example, the Tamil Muslim has a different local cultural reality from the Kashmiri or Gujarati Muslim) into a singular entity ('the Muslim') erases the multiple sites through which Muslim identity is performed in India, and reduces it to a few, stereotypical assumptions, for example, talaq, polygamy, high birth rate, and so on. Zoya Hasan (1994) suggests that religious leadership plays a key role in codifying and homogenizing, and ultimately misrepresents the community of Islam as one that is deliberately represented as singular. This singular entity is then used by the state as a criterion for policy that, once again, does injustice to the actual lived conditions of Muslims within India. While, ironically, a singular identity may help in forging a cross-regional unity and help to strengthen the kinds of demands made by the community on the state, it does scant justice to the heterogeneity contained within the category. In the rest of the chapter, I will illustrate this with the help of examples from Kachchh that will demonstrate that the 'minority' is a far from well-defined category. Although it may aspire to definitional clarity for electoral and other political purposes, the ground reality is one of a messy conglomerate of often-competing identities.

BEING 'MUSLIM' IN KACHCHH

When I first started fieldwork in Kachchh district, Gujarat, in July 2002, the anti-Muslim pogroms that had broken out earlier that year were still fresh in public memory. I was conditioned by what I had read following the violence, and also by my own ideas of the history of inter-communal strife in Gujarat, to expect a rigid Hindu–Muslim divide. This, in fact, did exist, and rumours and stereotypes concerning each group were common. In India, the religious minority is typically not exoticized (for example, Gladney 1994) as it is subconsciously feared in its Otherness (for example, Hansen 1999). Popular representations of Muslims and Christians, for example, in Hindi cinema, typically have followed a set pattern of caricatures for each group. It is now well known that in many parts of Gujarat, especially the urban areas, habitation and social interaction are rigidly defined by one's religious affiliation. It is increasingly rare for Muslim and Hindu children to attend the same schools, or for families to live in the same neighbourhoods. These trends were already set in place some decades ago, but the latest rounds of inter-religious violence have sealed the social segregation between the 'majority community' and the 'minority community', as Hindus (89.09 per cent, according to the 2001 Census) and Muslims (9.06 per cent) are euphemistically called in Gujarat. No public acknowledgement is made of the fact that there are other 'minorities' in Gujarat, such as small numbers of Jains (1.03 per cent), Christians (0.56 per cent), Sikhs (0.89 per cent), Buddhists (0.35 per cent), and Others, including Parsis and others (0.56 per cent). Jains are, interestingly, increasingly appropriated within the Hindu category, as far as popular public discourse is concerned.

The 'minority' in Gujarat, as indeed elsewhere in the country, is simply the 'Muslim'. This is not entirely unprecedented, for we can trace this kind of identification back to the colonial period, when India's Muslims came to be identified as *the* minority, as argued earlier. What

I was not conditioned to expect, however, were the deep divides that existed *within* the Muslims of Kachchh; divisions that cut across the presumed singularity of the Muslim community to reveal distinct identities based on sect affiliation. These distinctions manifested themselves in the way in which members of different Islamic *maslaq*s, loosely translated as 'way', 'creed', or 'sect', such as the Ahl-e-Hadis, Tablighi Jamaat, or the Ahl-e-Sunnat wal Jamaat interpreted the faith, and also their social interactions in and out of places of worship, even going so far as to circumscribe intermarriage across sect boundaries. The differences were much like a caste-style system of social ordering. While calls for presenting a unified identity as fellow Muslims are common, especially in the face of perceived discrimination by a Hindu nationalist state, the issue really must focus on how the Muslim community constructs itself internally, prior to any discussion that takes it for granted as a naturalized entity in contradistinction to other communities, for instance, the Hindus.

INTERNAL DYNAMICS

Muslims in Kachchh constitute a greater percentage of the population than the overall figures for Gujarat state. In Kachchh, they are 20.7 per cent of the population, according to 2001 Census figures. They tend to be preponderantly Sunnis, with a smaller percentage of Shias, primarily Ismailis (Aga Khanis) and Daudi Bohras. Among the Sunni majority, however, Muslims are divided in their loyalty to various maslaqs, chief of which are the Ahl-e-Hadis, the Tablighi Jamaat, and the Ahl-e-Sunnat wal Jamaat. The Ahl-e-Hadis and the Tablighi Jamaat are termed as such, while the largest mass, the Ahl-e-Sunnat wal Jamaat, is simply called Sunni in popular discourse, and this is what I shall take the term to mean in this chapter. In fact, the way in which sect affiliation plays out in Kachchh, to be told that one is a Sunni typically indicates that the person does not belong to the Ahl-e-Hadis or the Tablighi Jamaat and, in fact, has nothing to do with being contrasted with the Shias. The Shias are small in number and tend to keep to themselves, having their own social and ritual calendar, and more often than not, they tend to not be enumerated as Muslims at all as far as the bulk of the Muslims in Kachchh go.

The primary difference between members of the various maslaqs has to do with the centrality of the prophet as the bearer of Allah's message, and the role accorded to various saints or *pir*s in the 'properly'

Islamic lexicon. While Sunnis tend to admit various lineages of pirs into the realm of the religious (for they are all seen as means to achieve the always-present, but generally inaccessible god, Allah), the Ahl-e-Hadis are stringently opposed to them (seen, in this interpretation, as distractions from the one and only true god and, therefore, ill-suited to receive ministrations from the devotee, whose mind should be trained only on Allah), while the Tablighi Jamaat is less vociferous in their condemnation of pirs but does not openly encourage them either.

There is, in fact, a tremendous anxiety around sect affiliation among Muslims in Kachchh. This follows from the general belief that Sunni Islam is the basic, 'original', and local form of Islam in Kachchh, with the others (Ahl-e-Hadis and Tablighi Jamaat) being later intrusions and somehow responsible for corrupting the local Muslims, introducing a more hardline element in the practice of Islam by encouraging a more 'purist' approach to the religion (see, for instance, van der Veer 1992). This latter charge is most specifically levelled at the Ahl-e-Hadis, for they label as 'un-Islamic' many practices that are, in fact, part of a shared universe of belief with the local Hindu population (see, for example, Fruzzetti 1980). This tension between Sunni and Ahl-e-Hadis Muslims in Kachchh may be said to revolve around the contest between an aspiration to a certain Islamic universalism (on the part of the Ahl-e-Hadis), to belong more properly to the universal Islamic brotherhood, regardless of other cross-cutting identifying tags of race, language, or region, and a commitment to particularism on the part of the Sunnis, who see themselves squarely situated in their local regional contexts, without compromising their Islamic identity in any way.

One of the examples through which this may be illustrated is the use of language. Kachchhi Muslims speak Kachchhi, a dialect closely approximating Sindhi in syntax, grammar, and vocabulary. They also speak Gujarati if they are formally educated in either state-run or private schools, but Kachchhi is what they would refer to as their 'mother tongue'. Those who live in border villages, in the Great Rann of Kachchh, just adjoining the Pakistani province of Sindh, actually speak Sindhi. The call to prayer in mosques and the weekly *khutba* or sermon given at all mosques on Fridays, has typically been in either Kachchhi or Sindhi depending on the linguistic abilities of the local congregation. With the so-called 'conversion' of more and more Muslims in Kachchh to the Ahl-e-Hadis or Tablighi Jamaat, the language of instruction in Islamic matters, and public announcements such as the call to prayer, has changed from Kachchhi or Sindhi (the local *lingua franca*) to Arabic or

Urdu, the first being the universal language of Islam, as the Quran is written in it and is supposedly the language in which the prophet received it orally, while the second is seen as the language of Muslims in India, less universal than Arabic, but yet, it carries notions of a pan-Indian Muslim identity. Most Kachchhi Muslims are as unfamiliar with Arabic as they are with Urdu, but in the quest for a universal Islamic identity, these languages are being introduced by the advocates of Islamic universalism. Typically, Sunni mosques and madrasas continue to use Kachchhi and Sindhi today, while the more purist Ahl-e-Hadis have negotiated the switch to Arabic or Urdu. Staunch Sunnis I met during the course of my fieldwork often insisted on finding a local maulana or teacher for their village madrasa, as they wanted children to be initiated into the Sunni way, by someone familiar with their local language, customs, and traditions.

These divisions between Muslims recall fault lines between 'local' and 'foreign' Muslims that is not in itself new, for it replays the same distinctions used during the time of the Mughals in India, and subsequently, the more ubiquitous distinction between Ashraf and Ajlaf Muslims. What is interesting in this kind of discourse in Kachchh is that there is a parallel between it and the Hindutva-driven discourse of indigenous and exogenous influences in India, Islam and Christianity constituting exogenous, and therefore alien, effects. When the Ahl-e-Hadis are described in Kachchh as being from the 'outside', this space is varyingly described as external to Kachchh (Uttar Pradesh, Bihar, Rajasthan) or external to India (Pakistan, Saudi Arabia).

The tensions between Sunnis and Ahl-e-Hadis Muslims in Kachchh can be violent, without erupting into physical violence. Members of each sect are wary of eating together, for they disagree on the concept of *niaz*, consecrating food in honour of saints before consuming it; the Sunnis follow a densely populated calendar of saints' death anniversaries or *'urs*. These are important social occasions in villages as well as cities, for they bring together members of different castes and religions. Most of the 'urs festivities that I attended in Kachchh were frequented not just by Sunni Muslims, who were always the chief sponsors, but also by various Hindus who came to pay their respects to the saint in question, very often walking miles as a symbol of their devotion. Within Muslim communities, however, the 'urs is a complicated affair for it brings to light the various tensions between each group on their interpretation of correct Islamic practice. Rather than view the 'urs or the dargah as a site for inter-religious harmony between minority and majority, it is more fruitful to regard it as the site where multiple interpretations of Islam are expressed and performed (van der Veer 1992). Muslims of the Ahl-e-Hadis persuasion would tend to avoid being seen at an 'urs event, but if they happened to be around, they would be adamant about not eating. I have described one such occasion at length elsewhere (Ibrahim 2009; Ibrahim and Simpson 2008).

This kind of tension of an everyday sort between Muslims in Kachchh leads to a certain wariness between groups. In order to distinguish themselves from the Sunnis, Ahl-e-Hadis mosques will take care to issue the call for prayers with a few minutes' difference; each group has their own religious leader and mentor in Kachchh, called *Mufti*, to whom they look up to for matters both spiritual and everyday. Their respective sermons are given in different languages, and each of the larger, more recognized madrasas in Kachchh belongs to one or another of these sects with competing syllabi. When marriages are arranged, the sect affiliation of each household is given careful consideration. Strictly, Sunni households would avoid marriage into an Ahl-e-Hadis family and vice versa. Of course, sect affiliation reveals some individual preference so that members of the same nuclear family could, in theory, tend to follow different trajectories, but more often than not, the patriarch of the house tended to set the tone for what the others could or could not do.

THE JATT JAMAAT: IN SEARCH OF A COMMON IDENTITY

The above-mentioned themes will perhaps be illustrated with the help of a case study that brings to light some of the dilemmas Muslims in Kachchh tend to face in constructing a unique identity for themselves, as also the pitfalls in harbouring any assumption that they do, in fact, constitute such a singular, en bloc kind of identity. The Jatts are a semi-nomadic group of pastoralists who live on both sides of the Kachchh–Sindh border. They are divided into three distinct endogamous subunits called: the Daneta, Fakirani, and Garasia Jatts. The Garasia Jatts occupy the most widely dispersed area in Kachchh, as they are scattered across scores of villages and towns. The other two groups live in more concentrated and geographically circumscribed settlements in the district. I have described aspects of their history and social organization elsewhere (Ibrahim 2009). Here, I shall briefly describe the attempts made by the Garasia Jatts to organize their community into a single corporate body, the Jamaat, to establish itself as a political entity, not in terms of electoral politics, but to mark itself out as a recognizable Muslim minority, in order to more effectively market itself vis-à-vis the state. The period of this fieldwork coincided, as I have already mentioned, with the aftermath of one of the more vicious anti-Muslim organized pogroms in recent memory. Although Kachchh remained relatively calm compared with the rest of Gujarat, the Muslims of Kachchh found themselves shaken out of the calm that had hitherto marked their interpersonal relations with other religious groups. Despite lurking animosities, Kachchh had not witnessed the kind of large-scale communal outburst that marked the events of 2002–3. In addition, the previous year had seen Kachchh marked by a devastating earthquake that destroyed large parts of the district and countless lives were lost. As state, private, and non-governmental agencies began to address themselves to the task of relief and reconstruction, it appeared that communal propaganda also played itself out on the physical and social landscape as some communities were perceived to have received greater benefits than others. Further, as villages were reconstructed, 'unwanted' minorities such as Muslims or adivasis tended to be written out of the new construction plans, creating new villages that were socially engineered and made to order, as it were.

Against the backdrop of this darkening communal situation in Kachchh, Muslims seemed to be more and more aware of what they could gain as a 'minority right' if only they were more organized. This led to feverish attempts to rejuvenate the existing Jamaat organization, a small and exclusive community of elders, into a large-scale body known as the Jatt Jamaat that would bring under its auspices matters relating to the Garasia Jatt community in Kachchh. Underlying this impulse was the recognition that many Muslims in Kachchh remained backward, undereducated, and generally ill-equipped to understand the finer nuances of the majority–minority situation in the country.

Establishing such a Jamaat was by no means an easy task, precisely because, as I have articulated earlier, the Garasia Jatts, like Muslims in Kachchh in general, are not a singular body by any means. They may all have shared the same community or caste identity as Jatts, but within that, they were spread out across maslaq affiliations. Maslaq affiliation in itself should not have posed a problem, but as I have already mentioned, the sect that one belongs to, largely determines one's attitude towards and management of one's everyday affairs in both strictly religious as well as non-religious affairs. Matters such as education, attitudes towards the market, banking, and so on are also affected by maslaq differences. Jatt women wear a distinctive style of embroidered clothing and many of them are engaged in reproducing this traditional embroidery for the market, as they work through a dense network of non-governmental organizations (NGOs) who help in designing and marketing their wares. The decision on whether one should or should not sell this skill is also highly debated (see, for example, Ibrahim 2008), with Sunnis more opposed to marketing traditional embroidery for it is associated with a female saint revered by them and selling what is regarded as sacred is frowned upon. On the contrary, the Ahl-e-Hadis, in a bid to be seen as 'modern' and 'rational' Islamic subjects, see the marketing of a traditional skill as a way of transcending backwardness and superstition, and adopting an altogether more pragmatic approach to one's daily life. This attitude is part of the same lexicon of belief that shuns attending 'urs ceremonies and the propitiation of any object or person other than Allah, all signs of what is regarded by them as backwardness and illiteracy. Being self-aware, rational, and educated in 'correct' pan-Islamic discourse is the backbone of the Ahl-e-Hadis philosophy of the Self.

These differences ended up pitting villages against each other; villages with Garasia Jatt populations came to be regarded as either preponderantly Sunni or not, as they were rallied around key charismatic leaders who were either Sunni or Ahl-e-Hadis. Each faction drew moral support for their claims and counterclaims from their respective Muftis in Kachchh. In such an environment, it was increasingly difficult for the young leaders of this movement to create a unified Jamaat to drum up a consensus. Land was acquired and an office was inaugurated in Bhuj, the district capital, a landmark that was physically central to the district, but also important for its centrality to the powers that be, the district government, and also by implication, a more direct channel to the state government than a remote village would have been. Even as these events were unfolding, the older guard, present custodians of the existing version of the Jatt Jamaat, was uncomfortable with what they viewed as the usurpation of their power. The vanguards of the new movement were young men who regardless of their maslaq affiliations, were agreed upon the fact that the Jamaat needed to be modernized such that it was regarded as a more professional body, freed from the control of a few individuals, and one that was more representative of true Jatt opinion and an association that was altogether more democratic. If there could not be a body that would represent the voice of the Muslims of Kachchh as one, then at least there could be something that tried to adequately represent the Jatt community.

What finally appeared to clinch the debates was the question of modern, secular education. It was recognized that one of the reasons why Muslims in general, and Jatt Muslims in particular, faced discrimination in government jobs and a glass ceiling where they were successfully employed, was perhaps not solely a measure of discrimination, but perhaps also an indication that they did not perform as well in general educational terms. This was sought to be redressed by creating scholarships through donations so that deserving children could attend good quality schools in the district. It was also hoped that as the Jamaat developed and gained more recognition, it would help advertise the need of students deserving of scholarships or financial aid so that other interested funders or sponsors could step in should they so desire. It was oft-repeated during these planning sessions that I was invited to sit in on, that one of the reasons why local Hindu communities such as the Lohanas, for instance, or the Vanias had done so well for themselves was the fact that they were greatly organized and had a spirit of serving their own community through charity works, with the wealthier members of the community pitching in to help the more needy ones. It must be remembered that Kachchh has a very vast diasporic population, a trend that goes back some centuries and is not a recent phenomenon. Most communities have a substantial diasporic population in the Persian Gulf, East Africa, and the UK, and the foreign exchange remittances sent back to home villages to develop schools, community halls, temples, and public works goes a long way in stepping in for the lack of state-sponsored development initiatives in this mostly arid semi-desert region.

To return to some of the themes I articulated at the outset, sometimes emphasizing one's minority status is beneficial for it allows a certain legibility by the state and those other actors who may be in a position to step in and provide certain entitlements to the community. The above example shows that despite other bitter differences, the Jatts were finally convinced of the benefits to unite under a single banner, if only as a pragmatic step to try and further the socio-economic and political interests of the community as a whole. How far this initiative will be a success, or what its unintended consequences are vis-à-vis the internal dynamics of the community, is something that only time will tell. My second example also deals with a similar sense of pragmatism that dictates when a group would like to acquire the label of a 'minority' and when it would rather distance itself from it.

THE VADHA KOLIS: PRIVILEGED MINORITY OR ASSIMILATING TO MAJORITY STATUS?

It is complicated to make any sweeping assertions about the Kolis in India, for they occupy a range of caste and tribal identities. Most generically, they are associated with the Marathi-speaking fisherfolk known as Koli, who inhabit the coastal areas of Maharashtra. In addition, Gujarat and the Deccan also boast substantial numbers of populations called Koli, but they appear to be distinct groups. References to the Kolis are scattered in academic work, and to my knowledge, there is no systematic recent examination into this community and what seem to be its various offshoots. An ethnological article devoted to the Kolis, published in 1939, states that in the main Kolis reside in the Bombay Presidency and about 77 per cent of them reside in Gujarat (Master 1939).[1]

North Gujarat contained an even greater concentration of Kolis, with the 1891 Census enumerating the Kolis of Gujarat and Kathiawar at 23.02 per cent of the total Hindu population (Master 1939). Quoting from the relevant volumes of the *Bombay Gazetteer*, Master writes that the Kolis were officially classified as a tribe rather than a caste. There is confusion among scholars and administrators both, for there seems to be a steady process whereby these Koli were absorbed into other groups such as the Rajputs, Kanbis, and Marathas through hypergamous marriages. Presumably, each then went on to associate with the merged group, or developed sub-characteristics of their own, which makes it difficult to talk of the Kolis as a single unified group. Within Kachchh today, those who call themselves Koli appear to be those of the Kanbi–Koli or Koli–Patel variant and live much like the Hindu caste population. The 2001 Census classifies Kolis as Scheduled Tribes (ST) or adivasis, being the largest ST in Kachchh, accounting for 6.04 per cent of the total population of the district. In 2003, there was a move to revoke their ST status, it being pointed out that their socio-economic indicators revealed that it was no longer justified to classify them as 'backward' (Maheshwari 2003).

The Vadha Koli is another subgroup of the Koli in Kachchh whose characteristics are quite different from other Hindu castes. Unlike those called simply Koli, who more closely approximate Hindu caste organization, having taken to agrarian pursuits following the Kanbis or other landed ventures following the Rajputs, the Vadha Koli are described in Kachchh as people 'with no religion' or those 'who are neither Hindu nor Muslim'. Stanley Napier Raikes, British administrator in the region during the nineteenth century, wrote that the Kolis are 'tribes'

but of 'indeterminate religion' (Raikes 1977 [1856]). When describing
the Bhils and the Kolis, he admits that they are not acknowledged by
either the Muslims or the Hindus, but that they consider themselves to
be Hindus.

My fieldwork among the Vadha Kolis in the villages of northern
Kachchh, in the great expanse of the Rann of Kachchh, revealed that
they lived in close proximity with their Muslim pastoralist neighbours,
many of whom were Daneta Jatts, but also other Muslim pastoralists
such as the Mutuwa, the Halepotra, and the Raysepotra. Small groups of
Harijans, as the Dalits are called in Kachchh, also lived in these villages.
As is typical of mixed villages, each community tended to cluster in one
section of the village. These villages being in the middle of the Rann were
not structured around roads and organized landmarks but tended to be
small clusters of mud huts or *boonga*s scattered across a small area in the
Rann, a couple of kilometres inland from the main highway. Here, they
looked indistinguishable from their Muslim neighbours, often dressed
in the same kind of baggy trousers or shalwar and loose, hip-length tunic
for women and shalwars with long shirts or kurtas for men. In Kachchh,
clothing is very closely associated with caste or community, each group
laying ownership to particular styles of embroidery and style of clothing.
There is visually little to distinguish the Vadha Kolis from their Muslim
neighbours and their lifestyle also shares similarities. They do not shun
eating beef, like Hindus would, and they also bury their dead and have
a simple marriage ceremony that more closely resembles the Muslim
nikaah than a Hindu ceremony.

Slowly, however, winds of change have been sweeping through the
area. After the earthquake, many Vadha Kolis were singled out for
attention by various charitable outreach programmes run by prominent
Hindu religious groups, some of which were also close to the ruling
party in the state government. They were now at the receiving end of
post-earthquake aid not as members of a minority ST community
entitled to special benefits, but as 'new Hindus'. New developments
included the building of new houses, temples, and a new pedagogical
approach that encouraged the use of recognizably Hindu names and
forms of greeting. Yet, it is not uncommon for the Vadha Kolis to have
both a Hindu and a Muslim name, which they selectively use according
to context.

Deep in the heart of the Rann of Kachchh, barely 10 kilometres or
so south of the no-man's-land that separates India's western border from
Pakistan, is a sleepy village by the name of Dumado. This village has

small numbers of Mutuwas, who are Muslim—once upon a time, pastoralists—today leading a more or less settled life with the few animals
that manage to survive the seemingly perpetual state of drought in this
land, and working as contract labour in construction, or embroidery. In
addition, there are households of the Harijans and the Vadha Kolis. In
late 2002, soon after the resounding electoral victory of the right-wing
Bharatiya Janata Party (BJP) in Gujarat, I visited this village. By now,
there was a small offshoot of the village, newly built a few kilometres
away and renamed Madhav Nagar. The renaming of villages had become
a common sight in post-earthquake Kachchh, as smaller, sub-villages
were created out of the original parent village, such as in this example.

The Vadha Kolis of Dumado village had been selected by the Vishva
Hindu Parishad (VHP) for resettlement in the newly named Madhav
Nagar. New *pucca* or permanent houses were built for them, replacing
their old mud huts that had, ironically, not suffered any earthquake-
related damage, this area being far off from the epicentre of the earthquake,
and the use of traditional building materials such as mud precluding
much damage anyway. These houses were arranged in a circular fashion,
around a central temple that was decreed to be a Ram temple, although
construction was still ongoing. Each house was named out of a typically
Hindu lexicon: Ram *kutir*, Lakshman *kutir*, and so on. These names
lay claim to a textbook rendition of Hinduism, for they follow the
main characters of the Ramayana. We were greeted by salutations of
'*Jai Sri Ram*' which sat incongruously with their clothing that, I have
already mentioned, was the same as their Muslim neighbours and
markedly different from any Hindus in the region. When I asked their
names, equal numbers of Hindu and Muslim names were thrown up
even though when asked what caste they belonged to, they said they were
the *nava* Hindu or new Hindus. Despite the certainty with which their
newly built environment proclaimed their Hinduism, they themselves
seemed to be much more ambiguous about their identity. Later, it
transpired that even though Madhav Nagar had been formally handed
over by the VHP to the Vadha Kolis of Dumado, and although they had
publicly accepted this new village, in fact, many of them retained their
old huts in Dumado, and spent time there with their old friends and
neighbours, the Mutuwas and Harijans.

* * *

What this example tells us then is that a public proclamation of
a certain identity, in this case, a Hindu one, is not incommensurate

with a different kind of self-identification in other contexts. In an ethnographic study of Celtic identity as expressed through the Breton language movement in Brittany, northwest France, Maryon McDonald demonstrates that ethnic categories are not set sharply in stone, but rather that ethnic identity responds to its cultural, political, and social contexts. She argues that such categories acquire relevance only in the situation in which they are used and concludes that 'the identity of a people is a product of the contemporary structural context in which it exists' (McDonald 1986: 333). In the case of the Vadha Kolis, there is a tension between the incorporation of the group into the larger Hindu universe, whereby they would enter into the ranks of the majority, and remaining a privileged minority by means of which they can legitimately make exceptional demands on the state. Perhaps the former is seen as bringing with it a new set of entitlements, a sense of pride at being a member of the all-pervasive and powerful majority. Certainly during this period, the political ascendancy of the Hindu Right in Gujarat meant that Hindus were perceived as being especially privileged. Yet, this same period saw large-scale Koli protest at being de-scheduled; the removal of ST status for the larger Koli community (of which the Vadha constitute a small, much more socially and economically disenfranchised group) was met with disapproval by Koli leaders in Kachchh. The president of the Kachchh branch of the Gujarat Rajya Koli Seva Samaj, the organized body of Kolis in Gujarat, is reported to have stated, 'the government has snatched away our constitutional rights and we will fight tooth and nail to restore them' (Maheshwari 2003).

Thus, even when membership into the seductive ranks of the 'majority' are available, there is a sense in which within a democratic set-up, the status of a privileged minority is coveted too, and this is not given up without a fight. As mentioned before, this enables a positive identification by the state, and perhaps their ability to paradoxically gain status through their minorityness, and to retain some sense of autonomy with regard to their affairs, as Sipra Mukherjee argues in this volume for the case of the Ramakrishna Mission curiously seeking minority status for itself. Similar aspirations were at play with the desire to create a unified body for the Garasia Jatts with the difference, of course, that Muslims do not in any way constitute a privileged minority in the way that Scheduled Castes (SCs) or STs do. However, there was a recognition in this case that organizing under a banner of unity, no matter how fractured this unity may actually be at a number of levels, would be beneficial in order to be 'read' by the state. The irony is that such legibility could work both ways, to favour or to discriminate against. In the democratic framework, however, representation is tied up with notions of community entitlement and eventually, perhaps building up a more wholly representative political system.

NOTE

1. While the state of Gujarat as we know it today only came into existence officially in 1960, there were already, for many decades before this, various fairly well-documented ideas of what constituted Gujarat. These were based on linguistic and historical factors, and tended to exclude Kachchh and Saurashtra which became integrated into the unified state of Gujarat in 1960.

REFERENCES

Anderson, Benedict. 1983, *Imagined Communities: Reflections on the Origins and Spread of Nationalism*, New York: Verso.

Asad, Talal. 1993, 'Multiculturalism and British Identity in the Wake of the Rushdie Affair', in *Genealogies of Religion: Discipline and Reasons of Power in Christianity and Islam*, Baltimore: The Johns Hopkins University Press, 239–68.

Fruzzetti, L.M. 1980, 'Ritual Status of Muslim Women in Rural India', in J.I. Smith (ed.), *Women in Contemporary Muslim Societies*, Lewisburg: Bucknell University Press, pp. 186–208.

Gladney, D.C. 1994, 'Representing Nationality in China: Refiguring Majority/Minority Identities', *Journal of Asian Studies*, 53(1): 92–123.

Hansen, T.B. 1999, *The Saffron Wave: Democracy and Hindu Nationalism in Modern India*, Princeton, NJ: Princeton University Press.

Hasan, Zoya (ed.). 1994, 'Minority Identity, State Policy and Political Process', in *Forging Identities: Gender Communities and the State*, New Delhi: Kali for Women, pp. 59–73.

Hayes, C.J.H. 1926, *Essays on Nationalism*, New York: The Macmillan Company.

Ibrahim, Farhana. 2008, 'Islamic "Reform", the Nation-state and the Liberal Subject: The Cultural Politics of Identity in Kachchh, Gujarat', *Contributions to Indian Sociology*, 42(2): 191–217.

————. 2009, *Settlers, Saints and Sovereigns: An Ethnography of State Formation in Western India*, New Delhi and London: Routledge.

Ibrahim, Farhana and E.L. Simpson. 2008, 'Words, Tabloids and the Compulsions of the Ahl-e-Hadis', in M. Banerjee (ed.), *Muslim Portraits: Everyday Lives in India*, New Delhi: Yoda Press, pp. 156–67.

Lelyveld, D. 1981, 'Urdu as a Public Language', in P. Gaeffke and S. Oleksiw (eds), *Systems of Communication and Interaction*, Philadelphia: University of Pennsylvania Press, pp. 98–113.

Mahajan, Gurpreet. 2002, *The Multicultural Path: Issues of Diversity and Discrimination in Democracy*, New Delhi and Thousand Oaks, CA: Sage Publications.

Maheshwari, D.V. 2003, 'Kolis Want Scheduled Tribe Status Restored', *Indian Express*. Available at http://cities.expressindia.com/fullstory.php?newsid= 70229 (accessed 11 November 2011).

Master, Alfred. 1939, 'Koli or Dharalo etc.', *Bulletin of the School of Oriental and African Studies*, 9(4): 1009–13.

McDonald, Maryon. 1986, 'Celtic Ethnic Kinship and the Problem of being English', *Current Anthropology*, 27(4): 333–47.

Raikes, Stanley Napier. 1977 [1856], *Memoir on the Thurr and Parkur*, Karachi: Indus Publications.

Shaikh, Farzana. 1989, *Community and Consensus in Islam: Muslim Representation in Colonial India, 1860–1947*, Cambridge: Cambridge University Press.

————. 1991, 'The Language of Representation: Towards a Muslim Political Order in Nineteenth-Century India', in P. Corfield (ed.), *Language, History and Class*, Oxford: Oxford University Press, pp. 204–26.

van der Veer, P. 1992, 'Playing or Praying: A Sufi Saint's Day in Surat', *Journal of Asian Studies*, 51(3): 545–64.

5

Buddhists
The Political Dynamics of Conversion and Caste

Joseph M. T.

The concept of 'minority' assumes greater significance in the context of democracy. When nations are imagined into being, certain identities and collectivities claim a dominant role. Such dominance results in differentiation between different collectivities giving rise to gradations of 'large–small', 'superior–inferior', and 'superordinate–subordinate'. The basis on which these relations are defined could be race, religion, language, ethnicity, or any other such attribute. Consequently, in different contexts, the term minority can mean different groups of people.

If we understand 'nation' as a concept based on common ethnic and cultural affinities, and shared perceptions of these affinities coupled with political consciousness, minorities can be conceptualized as collectivities who have not achieved a heightened sense of such national consciousness but are nevertheless,

> ... united through race, religion, language or culture of which their members are conscious and which forms the basis of a common identity and distinguishes them from others on that basis. Such collectivities or groups are generally called minorities when they are less numerous than the other groups or when they occupy a subordinate economic, political or special position in the state. (Massey 2002: 15)

In the context of contemporary India, the different meanings that accrue to the category of 'minority' have a clear connection to the colonial intervention. The policy of preferential treatment set in place by the British was deeply influenced by the colonial understanding of Indian society which considered Indians more as societies of communities, not individuals. The groups which were accorded representation were identified as 'communities'. As other chapters in this volume point out, 'majorities and minorities ... were pigeonholed and categorized into communal electorates whose interests the British had to separate and protect from one another' (Hasan 2009: 20).

This understanding was questioned by the 'nationalists' who argued for equal rights within the shared bond of nationhood. As India became independent, the delineation of the minorities and the enunciation of their rights were done in terms of cultural rights. The discourse of disadvantage and social justice was reserved for categories of Scheduled Castes (SCs), Scheduled Tribes (STs), and later, Other Backward Classes (OBCs). The very meaning of who belongs to the SCs was given a majoritarian twist in the sense that Christians and Muslims were excluded from its purview. In the initial Presidential Ordinance of 1950, only those Dalits who belonged to the Hindu religion could claim to be SCs. This boundary was broadened in 1956 to include Sikhs, and in 1990 to include Buddhists. Thus, the conceptualization of 'minorities' in India is entrenched in a complex interplay between religion and caste.

In this volume, Jenkins looks at the process of conceptualizing minority identity in India. She shows that in the case of the SCs of India, such conceptualization takes place at the intersection of caste and religious identities. Using the criterion of religious identity, Christian and Muslim Dalits are denied the status of SCs, bringing about a fragmentation of the SCs as a minority category. This chapter takes a similar line of argument and places the Buddhists of Maharashtra as a minority community in contemporary India. The intersection of religion and caste is demonstrated in the project of conversion to Buddhism spearheaded by Dr Bhimrao Ramji Ambedkar (1891–1956), known by the honorific Babasaheb among Buddhists. The project of conversion to Buddhism was premised on a dual focus. The conversion event sought to construct a new religious identity; a modern Buddhism, as a template of a religion for engagement in civil society open to all citizens of India. It also sought to create an identity religion for the Dalits of India, particularly the erstwhile Mahars who responded in large numbers to the call of conversion by Babasaheb.

'Ambedkarite Buddhism' is the term I use for those who espouse Buddhism as followers of Babasaheb. It provides a religious ethic most suited for a democratic polity. In a sense, Babasaheb interprets Buddhism as a religion most amenable for engagement in civil society. At the same time, the logic of caste that characterizes social relations in many visible and invisible forms in India leaves its mark on the project of Buddhism among the Ambedkarites. One can observe the way Ambedkarite Buddhism has come to be seen through the prism of caste both by the adherents and outsiders. For instance, in many parts of Maharashtra, the term 'Nav-Bauddha' (neo-Buddhist) is synonymous with the older caste name 'Mahar'.

An attempt is made to trace certain similarities between the movements of the lower castes which took place in different parts of India in the late colonial period and the movement of conversion to Buddhism spearheaded by Babasaheb. The most striking similarity is the intersection of religion and caste. Appeal to universality on the one hand, and particular identities of caste or sub-caste on the other, constitute the double focus upon which many of these movements revolve. This dual, yet apparently contradictory, focus is discernible in almost all allied movements of the Buddhists of Maharashtra. This can be seen in the Republican Party of India, the movement of Dalit literature, the Dalit Panther Movement, as well as in the way Buddhists perceive their identity and affirm it in the civil society. What follows is an analysis of this dual focus.

MOVEMENTS OF THE LOWER CASTES

Engagement with modernity gave rise to many movements of the lower castes. The movement of the Untouchables in the Punjab under the leadership of Mangoo Ram; the Satnami movement among the Chamars of Chhattisgarh; the Sri Narayana Dharma Paripalana (SNDP) movement spearheaded by Sri Narayana Guru in Kerala; the Dravida Kazhagam movement in Tamil Nadu; the reform activities of Mahatma Jotiba Phule, the founder of the Satya Sodhak Samaj; and a host of similar movements raged through the length and breadth of India. An overriding similarity that one can notice among them is the way they have attempted to engage with issues of religion and caste in the context of modernity. From the outright rejection of Brahmanism as an import of the Aryan invasion and the idea that the Dravidians were the original people of the soil, which was at the heart of the ideology of the Dravida Kazhagam movement, to the more accommodationist stance of the SNDP, which configured the traditional practices making them accessible to the excluded masses, and the revivalist stance of Arya Samaj, these movements threw up an array of possibilities in their engagement with both tradition and modernity.

Many of the movements of the lower castes stood apart from engagements with modernity by the nationalist elite under the aegis of the Indian National Congress, the Socialist Party, or the right-wing Rashtriya Swayamsevak Sangh. The movements initiated and sustained by the nationalist elite had an encompassing objective of challenging the colonial rule. To that extent, they were focussed on forging a common front against the British by appealing to certain overarching characteristics through which they defined 'Indianness', and did not sufficiently address the deep-seated fissures within the Indian national milieu, especially those produced by the caste system and the condition of the Untouchables.

In contrast to the above, the movements of the lower castes addressed the interests of particular communities, sometimes even at the expense of the so-called nationalist cause. It is also intriguing to notice how the interests of the lower castes were put forward in the garb of religion. Faced with the challenge of European modernity, the movements of reform in India engaged with religion and produced an array of possibilities. One of such possibilities was the development of south Indian Buddhism. It was a modern reading of Buddhism with its relevance for certain sections of the populace. The south Indian Buddhism initiated by Pundit Iyothee Thass (1845–1914) and others in Madras (now Chennai) in the first decade of the twentieth century is a glaring example of how the untouchables of the Hindu society saw in Buddhism the resources that could be used for their emancipation. Lakshmi Narasu, a leader of this movement, authored *The Essence of Buddhism*, wherein he lays down the tenets of modern Buddhism. He sees it as, primarily, a lay religion based on the tenet of equality (see Tartakov 2004: 154).

In his study of south Indian Buddhism, Aloysius points out a feature of modern religiosity, namely, focus on the ethical–instrumental dimensions at the expense of the transcendental–experiential. Just as the studies on 'sects' in Europe and the United States (US) characterize them as anti-sacerdotal, egalitarian, and participatory in comparison to the 'churches', the modern Buddhism, as it took shape in Madras and the surrounding areas in the beginning of the twentieth century, was a modern interpretation of Buddhism. The proponents of this religion were the Untouchables who were, in the urban centres, employed in different capacities and for whom 'marginal empowerment' became a possibility

(Aloysius 1998: 44). Aloysius characterized south Indian Buddhism of that period as an example of the 'religion of the oppressed'.[1]

MODERNITY AND CASTE CONSCIOUSNESS

While the movements dominated by the upper castes circumvented the question of caste or dealt with it 'by other means', most of the movements of the lower castes talked about caste in its own terms. The stance of the upper castes is rooted in the idiom of 'nationalism' that they created in the face of colonial rule wherein the 'spiritual' or the 'cultural' is posited as the realm protected from control by the colonial power.[2] It engages with pan-Indian identities. Pandian (2002: 8) argues that if we pluralize the national culture or community, one would be struck by the domination that the valorized dominant nationalism exercises over the subaltern groups because upper-caste modernity renders every talk of caste in the material and public sphere as illegitimate and 'anti-national'.

The trajectory of lower-caste engagement with modernity has been markedly different. Their relationship with the modern is rather tenuous. 'In their response, the modern is both mobilized and critiqued, for the promises of modernity and what it delivers in practice are often in contradiction' (Pandian 2002: 18). Pandian names the lower-caste relation to the modern as 'antagonistic indebtedness' (Pandian 2002: 19). The modern is at once accepted and rejected; accepted for its promises but rejected for the way those promises are not delivered.

UNIVERSAL PRINCIPLES VERSUS PARTICULAR IDENTITY

Babasaheb's intervention in Indian society bears the mark of 'being one step outside modernity'. His commitment to modernity goes hand in hand with his enunciation of the rights of the Untouchables on equal terms with other citizens of India. The 'contradictory engagement with modernity' that Pandian talks about is seen in Babasaheb as he appealed to the universal principles of fraternity, liberty, and equality. He differentiated religions of the world into two: *religion of principles* and *religion of rules*, and identified the former with repositories of universal moral principles.

At the same time, he projected Buddhism as the religion best suited to the social location of the Untouchables. On the one hand is the appeal to the universal moral principles engendered by normative modernity, and on the other, the call to select Buddhism as a sort of 'identity religion'. He has interpreted tradition in the idioms of modernity and given birth to a modern interpretation of Buddhism. In many ways, his interpretation of Buddhism, as explained in his work, *The Buddha and His Dhamma*, is an engagement of Buddhism with modernity. In this, he has been in tune with parallel developments, especially with regard to Protestant Buddhism in Sri Lanka (see Gombrich and Obeyesekere 1988). For instance, despite notable differences, his reading of Buddhism is very much in tune with the ideas of Anagarika Dhammapala and Lakshmi Narasu.

The movement of Babasaheb was the site of a tension, between the inalienable principles of European modernity and scientific rationalism embodied in a language of rights, universal citizenship, fraternity, liberty, and equality on the one hand, and the existential concern of giving voice to the Untouchables, a significant segment of Indian population excluded from the emerging Indian 'public'—between the idiom of universal rights and the issue of particular identities.

He saw the contradiction in front of him. On the one hand was the power of modern ideas and principles, and on the other, a section of Indian population was kept away from having access to such ideas. This evolved as a dual focus of his movement and is visible in the way he has conceptualized Buddhism. Here, the argument is made that the tension between the elements of this dual focus is also present in the post-Ambedkar movement of the Dalits and in Buddhism of Maharashtra. Thus, we have two trends in the movement of Babasaheb: one that appeals to the principles most scholars enunciate as belonging to the domain of 'civil society'; and a second emphasis that borders on what has been called 'identity politics', the sort of engagements that perhaps belong to the domain of what Partha Chatterjee (2006 [2004]) categorizes as the sphere of 'political society'.

NEGOTIATING 'UNIVERSALITY' AND 'IDENTITY'

The irreconcilable tension perceived by Chatterjee (2006 [2004]) between the demands of universal citizenship on the one hand, and the protection of particular rights on the other, is played out with great force in the personality of Babasaheb. He was completely modernist. He believed in science, history, the power of reason, and in the modern state as the site for actualization of the human reason. He belongs to the whole of India as one of its tallest leaders. Post-independent India honours him as the principal architect of the Constitution. He advocated the virtues of an interventionist, modernizing state, and vouched for the modern values of equal citizenship and secularism. His interventions in Indian society and polity were anchored in a commitment to the inalienable rights of individuals, and all the campaigns that he launched were based on the notion of universal citizenship.

However, he had a firm conviction that the slogan of universality (modernity) is often a mask to cover the perpetuation of real inequalities. Therefore, there is a side of his personality that fought for the rights of the Untouchables as equal citizens of India. In the face of the homogenizing discourse of modernity and civil society that made the heterogeneous domain of the inequality of caste invisible, Babasaheb asserted the rights of Untouchables. He discerned that as per the ethos of caste system, they would be denied the right of representation and the right to hold office, the salient features of modern citizenship. Hence, he fought for the separate political representation of the Dalits and for preferential reservation or affirmative action in their favour in education and government employment. He was scathing in his attack on colonialism for denying citizenship rights to Indians and for keeping them as subjects. He was equally weary of Gandhi's idea of homogenous citizenship based on the composite identity accorded by Hinduism.

INTERPRETING BUDDHISM

This tension between homogenizing modernity and the particular identity that has an altogether different logic is evident in his interpretation of Buddhism. On the one hand, Babasaheb conceptualizes Buddhism as a social ethic and places it firmly in the language of modernity; in democracy and in the ethos of scientific inquiry and disputation. It is anchored in a social ethic which speaks the language of rights and universal principles.[3] At the same time, while he traced the origin of untouchability in Indian society, he traced it to the persistence on the part of a section of population to hold on to Buddhism, thereby giving it the aura of an identity religion for the Dalits.[4] Thus, Babasaheb's interventions in India, in both domains of politics and religion, are implicated in the '… unresolved conflict between universal affiliations and particular identities…' (Chatterjee 2006 [2004]: 24). This trend can also be observed in many of the post-conversion developments among Ambedkarite Buddhists. Here, three movements aligned with Buddhists of Maharashtra are taken up for analysis. All three portray the tension between the idioms of modernity and identity.

THE REPUBLICAN PARTY OF INDIA

The Republican Party of India (RPI), designed by Babasaheb to replace the Scheduled Caste Federation (SCF), was meant to be a broad-based party articulating the aspirations of all those segments of Indian society subjected to social discrimination and economic deprivation. That Babasaheb intended the party to be based on the idiom of modernity and civil society is evident from the announcement he made on 13 October 1956, at a press conference at the venue of the impending conversion event. He referred to the political party he planned as Republican Party and said that it '…would be open to all who accepted its three guiding principles—liberty, equality and fraternity' (Keer 2002 [1954]: 298). He had in mind the example of the Republican Party in the US, and it also evoked the Buddhist age as the age of ancient republics. The party was inaugurated on 3 October 1957. The RPI '…took pains to establish itself as a non-communal party which was dedicated to the cause of social and economic equality. It defined its clientele very broadly and avoided specific references to untouchability except in so far as it related to the larger problem of inequality afflicting Indian society' (Gokhale 1993: 217).

However, that broad focus gave way to a more particular conception of the composite identity of all the oppressed communities of India when the first manifesto of the party was prepared. Authored by famous Dalit intellectual, Shankarrao Kharat, it delineated a class-based approach and broadly divided Indian population into two classes, the oppressing and the oppressed classes, and stressed the similarities accruing among the oppressed of India. That was again given another particular identity in the form of Buddhism. '…Buddhism was to have a pivotal role in the reworking of the consciousness of the oppressed classes of Indian society…. Buddhism was to be the ideological dimension of the social revolution, which was to be directed by the RPI' (Gokhale 1993: 219). Significantly, Gokhale argues that the first split that took place in RPI in 1958 had much to do with the way a section of the RPI felt that the interests of the Untouchables and the problems faced by them called for a separate concern rather than collating it with the other oppressed classes. By 1970, the RPI had split into four factions. The electoral system itself placed constraints on parties like the RPI because the Dalit population of Maharashtra is not concentrated in large numbers in any area. It means that they needed the support of caste-Hindu votes to get elected, which necessitated the whole issue of alliances.

The RPI did not seriously engage in sustained rural mobilization and gradually, its clientele became the urban, educated 'middle-class' Dalits, and the issues which concerned them were the constitutional privileges in the areas of education and employment. Here, the focus of the party was again narrowed down to another particularity—that of getting the policy of compensatory discrimination or reservations (*savalati* in Marathi) to the Buddhists. This reduced the agenda of the different factions of RPI to the politics of reservations, which had utmost relevance to the Buddhists, not even to the other ex-Untouchable castes of the Matang and the Charmakar. 'Agitating for the extension of these facilities seemed to be the political task for which the RPI was best suited and indeed, it was most effective as a lobby in relation to the ruling party rather than as an autonomous political party in its own right' (Gokhale 1993: 251).

However, as a medium through which the Buddhists of Maharashtra and also in some pockets, the other Dalit castes of Maharashtra learnt the means of electoral politics, RPI has played a very significant role. In the post-independence era, it has been the major medium through which the Buddhists were socialized into politics and learned the ways of political participation in a democratic polity. It paved way for the development of political elite within the Buddhist community. The RPI enhanced the consciousness and political mobilization of the Dalits, particularly the Buddhists, and aided their integration into the Indian political system (Gokhale 1993: 255). The rhetoric of the representation of more general interests and identities is not given up by the different factions of the RPI. For example, the faction of RPI led by Prakash Ambedkar, the grandson of Babasaheb, has take the name, Bharatiya Republican Party—*Bahujan Mahasangh*—signalling an appeal to the bahujan, aiming at people belonging to the ex-Untouchable and other backward castes. Thus, one can notice in RPI an appeal to universal categories of citizenship in its rhetoric and a progressive development towards particular identities in its practice.

DALIT LITERATURE

Dalit literature[5] grew as a distinct genre of Marathi literature comprising of works of poetry, plays, short stories, life stories, folk songs, and novels, and got wide acceptance for its specificity. It is a literary–cultural movement, promoting the growth of a composite Dalit identity. The Dalit litterateurs perceived a close connection between literature and the society at large. Their initial revolt against mainstream Marathi litera-ture represented a rejection of the social order wherefrom such literature originated. 'They considered it their duty to expose the actual condi-tions of Indian society, to shatter the complacent illusion of middle-class Hindus, and to reveal the empty façade which scarcely concealed the unrealised dreams and broken promises of Indian Independence...' (Gokhale 1993: 311).

The predominant theme of Dalit literature is the break with the past and the transformed socio-cultural situation of the Dalits. They engage with the horrors of the past and the promise of the present. Social justice and the transformation of society resound as important themes in some of the Dalit writings. Dalit literature took upon itself to show the ugly face of varna ideology. A major portion of Dalit literature thus '...was devoted to scathing denunciations of Hinduism, derision directed at Hindu gods and goddesses, contempt for its irrationality and supersti-tions, and hatred for its principle of caste. The language used was often deliberately provocative, blasphemous, and even obscene, designed to flaunt their rebellion and shock the orthodox...' (Gokhale 1993: 312).

At the same time, Dalit literature contains strands that portray senti-ments of 'comportment'.[6] Dalit writing revolutionized Marathi litera-ture with down-to-earth phrases and language which mirrored the stark reality of lower-caste existence in the villages and cities of Maharashtra. The city, especially Bombay (now Mumbai), is represented in Dalit literature as both a locale of possibilities and a site of squalor and struggle. The poems and short stories penned by Dalit writers gave vivid details about Dalit life-worlds, ranging from the deprived sections of urban Dalit populace of the slums to the world of the Dalits working in offices of Bombay.

Dalit literature found a niche for itself in the wider domain of Marathi literature.

As early as 1970, it was accorded a place in the Marathi Sahitya Sammelan (Marathi Literary Conference), with a panel discussion on the subject. Dalit works are regularly reviewed in Marathi newspapers as well as in English language publications. With the Ford Foundation awards that Daya Pawar and Laxman Mane received, international recognition was also conferred on Dalit literature. Thus the movement has been able to acquire a stature as a serious literary–cultural form at the same time that its creators are accorded recognition as arbiters of literary–cultural values which is an unprecedented event in Indian cultural history. (Gokhale 1993: 328)

Since 1950, there have been various Dalit literary organizations. The literary journal called *Asmitaadarsh*, has remained a prominent forum for the publication of Dalit literary works. Of late, numerous publishing houses are springing up among the Buddhists of Maharashtra.

At one level, Dalit literature is steeped in notions attributable to European modernity. There is an emphasis on scientific outlook, rationality, and a concern with pedagogy of the masses. It is equally about the Dalit life-world and its attended complexities and plural ways of engagement.[7] Here, too, one can notice the tension between the idiom of the universal and that of the particular. For example, one of the points of debate among the Dalit writers was on the focus of their writing. While one group argued that they needed to address to the larger domain of the Dalits, another group wanted a specific Buddhist literature.[8] A majority of Dalit writers are Buddhists,[9] and the Buddhist themes like sentiments of devotion towards Babasaheb and the Buddha abound in some of their writings.[10]

Among works specifically belonging to a Buddhist idiom, there are popular songs that 'deify' both the Buddha and Babasaheb. These are found mostly in the pamphlets distributed at the sites of importance to the Buddhists. In her study of the songs of the Buddhists from Vidharbha region of Maharashtra, I.Y. Junghare writes of the various images of Babasaheb that are portrayed. She talks about two processes that are evident in those songs: a process of 'ascension' by which Babasaheb is raised to a level akin to that of the divine; and the process of 'descent' which positions Babasaheb like an 'avatar' (Junghare 1988: 94). She has also demonstrated that folk poetry such as the *palna* (lullabies) and the *ovi*[11] also engage with the theme of the heroism of the Buddha and Babasaheb.

DALIT PANTHER MOVEMENT

Dalit Panther movement grew on the disintegration and growing irrelevance of the RPI. It took its inspiration from a radical section of the Dalit writers.[12] It began as an extra-parliamentary group, which opposed the electoral politics of RPI and claimed to revive the class model of mobilization. In their ideology, they appealed to a broad understanding of who a 'Dalit' is.[13] 'The Dalit Panthers declared their intention of forming an alliance of all the poor, downtrodden and oppressed communities without regard to caste, and of mobilizing the rural poor to effect a radical shift of power in Indian politics' (Gokhale 1993: 264). Discussing the events that led to the formation of the Panthers, Gokhale talks about the way the young, educated, urban Dalits, located primarily in Bombay, got together to discuss the problems besetting the community. 'Arjun Dangle, a founder of the Dalit Panthers, describes a regular *salon* which was held by Baburao Bagul, the noted dalit writer and left-wing activist, at a tea shop in Dadar, Bombay' (Gokhale 1993: 267). Atrocities against the Dalits became a pressing issue and Raja Dhale, considered a founder leader of the Dalit Panthers, wrote an article in the Marathi monthly, *Sadhana*, describing the twenty-fifth independence day of India as a black day. 'On August 15, 1973, the name "Dalit Panthers" first came to public notice, as the new organization sponsored a morcha of about 200–250 people from Victoria Terminus to Azad Maidan in Bombay in honour of what was termed Black Independence Day' (Gokhale 1993: 268).[14] The Dalit Panthers followed a dual strategy of attacking the government for the growing atrocities on Dalits and opposed the RPI for its ineffective policies. The Dalit Panthers also came in conflict with the Shiv Sena as the leading followers of both the outfits in the early 1970s were the unemployed youth from the chawls of Bombay, specially Parel and Worli.

The Dalit Panthers split by the end of 1974 owing to the differences between Raja Dhale and Namdeo Dhasal, the founding leaders. One of the major differences was based on who was a Dalit. While Dhale laid emphasis on the Buddhist identity of the Dalits, Dhasal was inclined more towards communist ideas. Again, like the RPI and the Dalit literature movement, the question here is between a more universal conception and a particular identity.

> For Dhale and his group, Ambedkar was more than an extraordinary political leader; he was a prophet, and in that sense, of supra-human stature. His writings and speeches were considered quasi-divine, demanding unhesitating and unquestioning loyalty in their implementation ... for the Dhale group.... Ambedkar himself was the defining element in the identity of the dalit community, and an organising symbol which gave coherence to the history of the Untouchables through the Buddhist conversion. (Gokhale 1993: 279)

The Dhasal group viewed Babasaheb as a pre-eminent leader but steered clear of supra-human and quasi-divine qualities attributed to him by the Dhale group. They disagreed on the attitude towards communists and the implications held out by the Buddhist conversion. Dhale saw untouchability primarily as origination from the Hindu ideas of purity and pollution, varna and jati, and considered the Buddhist ideology as the most defining element of the legacy of Babasaheb. On the other hand, Dhasal saw untouchability primarily as a socio-economic problem, hence a class issue. He opposed injecting religion into the organization of Dalits and considered the accent on Buddhist religion an impediment to Dalit unity. Both legitimized their diverging emphases on the legacy of Babasaheb. Later, the Dalit Panthers split into several factions. The faction led by Dhasal split in 1975, into two groups, one led by Dhasal and his supporters and the other by Divekar and Dige. The faction led by Dhale split in 1976, into two groups, one led by supporters of Dhale and the other led by Mahatekar and Sangare.[15] Though Dhale initiated a mass movement later in 1977, the influence of the Dalit Panther movement waned over the years. However, the ideology that fired the movement is still a part of the Dalit consciousness of the Buddhists of Maharashtra.

The RPI, Dalit literature, and the Dalit Panthers movement represent the way Dalits of Maharashtra, especially the Buddhists, seek to engage in civil society armed with principles of modernity and universal citizenship. However, the rhetoric of universality is seen pitted against the assertion of particular identities.

BUDDHISTS OF AURANGABAD[16]

Buddhism of Maharashtra has gained acceptance as a religious system that has galvanized its adherents to actively engage in the civic sphere based on the ideals of democracy and the language of rights. In the lives of many of them, Buddhism is a set of values and norms that enables them to engage in the civil society as educated citizens, demanding equal rights. The higher levels of associationalism enable them to engage in political society and fight for their rights. This sense of release from the earlier imposed restrictions is epitomized in the popular saying, '*Jai Bhim Bolo, Kidhar Bhi Chalo*' (Say 'Jai Bhim' and go anywhere). Buddhists of Ambedkar Nagar referred to this saying not only to inform me of the provisions they have of travelling free of cost in the trains of the Indian Railways as they made their pilgrimage to Nagpur or Mumbai on days that were important to them,[17] it was also an expression of the difference Buddhism has brought to them—an awareness of their dignity—and the way it enables them to engage in civil society claiming for themselves equal treatment enshrined in the Constitution of the Republic of India.

In this section, I deal with the modalities of rhetoric and patterns of practice which characterize Buddhism of Maharashtra as a religion for engagement in civil society, particularly with reference to the Buddhists of Aurangabad. The dual focus of Buddhism given by Babasaheb, namely, the appeal to modern principles and values and its location in the identity of ex-Untouchables can clearly be discerned among them. First, I deal with features connected to modern ideas and principles, especially engagement with civil society, and then I go on to delineate ideas and practices of the Buddhists of Aurangabad that specifically deal with their particular identity and its articulation. I also briefly engage with the way Ambedkar Nagar as a locality can be thought of as a domain of 'political society'.

The Domain of the '*Sarvajanik*' (Public)

Buddhists of Ambedkar Nagar designate civil society as *sarvajanik* (public). It stands for the domain of custom and usage.[18] My respondents talked at length about the force of habit, custom, and usage, and its significance. They take part in all the activities which they claim as sarvajanik. They celebrate festivals and feasts in the public domain claiming that they have become sarvajanik and are no more in the exclusive domain of any tradition (religion). They conceptualize the sarvajanik in contradistinction to what is overtly designated as *dharmik* (as belonging to a particular religious tradition). In the domain of the dharmik, tradition defined by its custodians creates the norm and becomes the standard for practice. On the contrary, the domain of the sarvajanik is the sphere proper to custom and usage, outside the purview of tradition and its dispensers. There is a way in which the Buddhists of Ambedkar Nagar seek to enlarge the contours of the domain of custom and usage (the sarvajanik) at the expense of what is sought to be defined as belonging to tradition (dharmik). A case in point is their participation in practices and celebrations identified with the Hindu tradition. They rationalize such 'infringement' on tradition by taking recourse to the category of the sarvajanik.

A prominent example that Buddhists of Ambedkar Nagar cited often in this respect is that of Diwali. The difference in the way Hindus celebrate it and the way Buddhists do it is that for the former, there is a clear 'religious' meaning attached to it, while for the latter, it is just a social celebration. The children have holidays and there is a festive atmosphere all over. While talking about such festivals, Buddhists make it a point to say that they celebrate these not in a real sense (or sense of tradition), making it clear that their celebration of such festivals is a claim they make to what has been appropriated as part of the domain of the sarvajanik.

At the same time, they make it a point to assert their attachment to the growing Buddhist tradition and how there is a qualitative difference when they engage in practices proper to the Buddhist tradition and practices which are proper to another religious tradition but are appropriated by the Buddhists for the sphere of the sarvajanik. For example, Buddhists of Ambedkar Nagar would often point out that the kind of activity and enthusiasm that one can notice when the Buddhist feasts are celebrated are lacking when they celebrate feasts like Diwali. Thus, they make a distinction between a 'religious' (the domain of tradition) and a 'social' (the domain of the sarvajanik) way of celebrating a particular festival. This notion of what is in the public domain (sarvajanik) not strictly belonging to one religion (tradition) is also invoked when the Buddhists join in the practice of certain devotional practices of people around them.

During my fieldwork, I noticed that Ganesh Chaturthi was celebrated with full gusto in Ambedkar Nagar. Two Ganesh pandals were erected, one near a few Matang families and the other at the bylane near my room, just in front of the house of a Charmakar.[19] The Buddhists joined in the fun and frolic and took active part in the celebrations and the contests that were part of the programme all the ten days. The *arti*, strictly a religious act, was done by the Charmakars; no Buddhist joined in doing the arti. However, a Buddhist youth of the area made a near-perfect image, *Bhadra Maruti* (the reigning deity at the shrine of Khultabad, at the outskirts of Aurangabad), in clay and placed it near the statue of Ganesh at the pandal. He told me that Bhadra Maruti is a popular deity of the area and people would be happy to see that particular image there. The implication was that Bhadra Maruti has also become sarvajanik to a great extent. In that sense, the image of Bhadra Maruti made by a Buddhist shared space with the bigger statue of Ganesh, bought from the market. In a way, the former stood for the space of the sarvajanik and the latter for 'tradition'. On the day of immersion of the Ganesh idols, many Buddhists joined the Hindus for the procession. In fact, the whole party who played drums during the procession of the statue from Ambedkar Nagar were all Buddhists.

Some bhikkhus of Aurangabad, the self-professed custodians of Buddhist tradition, instruct the lay Buddhists to stay clear of practices that are clearly in the domain of another tradition—Hinduism. While some Buddhists are adhering to their advice, most of the Buddhists of Ambedkar Nagar view the domain of the sarvajanik large enough to include some of the practices proscribed by the bhikkhus as belonging to the Hindu tradition. Understandably, the rationale behind such celebrations is couched in terms of usage and custom—the modalities of civic participation. As one of my respondents puts it: 'We celebrate Diwali, Holi, Nag Panchami and some other festivals. Everybody celebrates them. There is a kind of national spirit that develops by the celebration of these festivals. We celebrate some of the Hindu festivals due to this. The need of the hour is to develop a friendly atmosphere between the adherents of different religions.'[20]

Associationalism

The triadic slogan, 'educate, organize, and agitate', that powered the movement of Babasaheb, has within it an accent for organization. Along with the purely religious acts like chanting the *vandana*, keeping *uposath* (Buddhist fast), and feeding the monks, the Buddhists also include acts like involvement in public life, taking part in the social concerns of the community, and social work as acts of religion of a Buddhist. In tune with the focus that Babasaheb has given to Buddhism as a religion of principles, and in a way following the example that he has shown, Buddhists have a high sense of involvement in public life. Those employed in governmental jobs are leaders of the trade unions; those who are doing private jobs also become leaders to organize the workers in the area. Buddhists in other professions as doctors and engineers are not happy to just limit their activities to their profession. They involve themselves in additional work of doing something for the Buddhist community and the society at large.

Associationalism is a hallmark of the Buddhists of Maharashtra. In Ambedkar Nagar, I noticed this tendency of the Buddhists to form associations of different nature: political, social, and cultural. In the arena of politics, it also meant factionalism, defections, and formation of new groups. Every now and then, Ambedkar Nagar would be the site of a public meeting, hosted by any of the political parties or other associations of the area. While a majority of Buddhists are involved in political parties, others are members of an array of associations ranging from the Buddhist society of India to *mahila mandals*. Associations and organizations of the Buddhists abound in the city of Aurangabad. They include cooperative unions of writers,[21] associations of the youth called *mitra* mandals in local parlance,[22] small-scale financial institutions to deposit savings, to employees' welfare associations and unions in private concerns and government companies and corporations. In the course of my interviews, all the Buddhists would state that membership in these associations is open to all citizens and that they are not associations exclusively of the Buddhists. In practice though, in many of these associations, the majority of membership is from the Buddhist community. Some associations take extra effort to enlist members from other communities, particularly the other Dalit castes of the area. In my sample, the number of women who are members of associations is relatively low.

Political Society

I have described how the Buddhists of Aurangabad invoke the sarvajanik as they assert their rights of participation in civil society. In that context, the sarvajanik is the arena of such engagement of the Buddhists with wider society, asserting a language of rights. That is not the only context when the Buddhists invoke the domain of the sarvajanik. They engage with it when it is a question of asserting their particular identity as Buddhists and ex-Untouchables. In the second case, 'sarvajanik' stands for physical spaces marked as public. In a curious way, the public space becomes the locale for the Buddhists to demonstrate their identity.

In the cities and towns of Maharashtra, one can notice the way the Buddhist identity is proclaimed through the number of the statues of Babasaheb and the Buddha erected at important locations. The celebrations of the important days of the Buddhists take place in the civic sphere with high visibility. I have witnessed the way Buddhists celebrate all of their festivals. The main attraction of the celebration of Bhim Jayanti (the birthday of Babasaheb) is the procession that is taken out in the evening of 14 April from every locality to a central place in the city (Kranti Chowk). Each locality is represented by a tableau depicting some moments in the struggle of the Dalits or in the life of Babasaheb with music blaring all the way and the young people dancing in front of these tableaux. On Buddha Jayanti, the scale of the celebrations is low. People take out a procession in the evening but the main attraction of the processionists on Buddha Jayanti is the monks. On 6 December, the monks and lay Buddhists gather together at various points, in front of the statues of Babasaheb to pay him homage. The main programme of that day in the city takes place in front of a huge statue of Babasaheb erected by the municipality at an intersection of roads called Bhadkal Gate. The monks, as usual, chant the *tisarana* and *panch shil*, and then the stage is taken over by other organizations as groups of Buddhists come together to pay respects to Babasaheb. Buddhists who belong to certain outfits, unions, organizations, and groups come together and their leaders come forward to make a speech on Babasaheb and garland the statue. The Buddhists assert their identity in the civic sphere by way of different campaigns like processions, bicycle rallies, celebration of their festivals in full public view, the naming of the streets and byways, erection of statues, naming of junctions, monuments, and institutions, naming of the university, and the turning of certain pockets in the urban geography into a Buddhist or Dalit space.

* * *

Laura Dudley Jenkins (Chapter 3 in this volume) makes a plea for 'intersectionality' as a useful tool for social science research. It is a relevant concept in studying minority communities as its stands for layers of interrelated meanings. This chapter sheds light on intersectionality particularly with reference to religion and caste set in the backdrop of modernity. Buddhists of Maharashtra constitute a minority group in India in terms of their religious affiliation, namely, Buddhism as well as their location as a Dalit community in contemporary India. In comparison to the Muslim and Christian Dalits, they have been included in the category of SCs as Buddhism is seen in the official discourse as a part of a larger definition of Hinduism. However, in their understanding, Buddhism stands outside of Brahmanic Hinduism and its principles.

Intersectionality can also be detected in the way the movements of the lower castes, particularly the Buddhists of Maharashtra, have engaged with modernity. Modern principles of universalism embodied in principles of social living are ingrained in the movements of the lower castes as well as in the construction of Ambedkarite Buddhism. However, this focus is interspersed with an enunciation of particular interests and identities. Though the principles of universality form the basis of such movements, their instrumental value lies in carving out a separate and distinct identity for the participants. Using the language of modernity and universal rights, a particular identity seeks to assert itself and construct around it a project of empowerment. Buddhism of Maharashtra is a clear example of such a project of empowerment for the Dalits, especially the erstwhile Mahars.

The interplay of religion and caste ingrained in Buddhism of Maharashtra has further strengthened the inter-community divisions between the different Dalit communities of Maharashtra, mainly the Buddhists (most of whom are erstwhile Mahars), Matangs, and Charmakars. Buddhism as a religious identity has added another twist to the differences that characterize these three communities who are classified as SC communities in Maharashtra. There is a strand of thinking among different Dalit activists of the Matang and Charmakar communities that conversion to Buddhism and the growth of a Buddhist identity has, in some way, hampered the growth of a larger SC identity.

While the nationalists and high-caste intellectuals used the language of modernity to put forward a notion of the Indian nation, consciously underplaying the interests and identities of several subordinate collectivities, leaders of the lower-caste movements like Babasaheb employed the same language of modernity to carve separate identities for diverse communities within the Indian nation, transforming them into projects of empowerment. This manoeuvre is made possible by the interplay of religion and caste, both domains contributing resources for formation of minority communities in very complex ways.

NOTES

1.   Another Buddhist organization active at the time was the Koliya Buddhist Association of Ajmer in Rajasthan, mainly with members from Untouchable castes (see Zelliot 2004: 176–7).

2.   Chatterjee (2006 [2001]) calls this a domain of culture and spirituality, while Pandian calls this 'dominant nationalism' (2002: 7).

3.   Omvedt writes that Babasaheb saw '… the necessity of religion for every historical period of society, while arguing that a modern, rationalistic, equalitarian society needs and can find a religion capable of providing a *moral code* for its purposes' (Omvedt 2004: 58; emphasis added; see also Fuchs 2004: 288).

4.   Ambedkar (1990: 229–382) argues that Buddhism emerged as a challenge to Vedic religion, especially the centrality it gave to ritualism and sacrifices. In the conflict, Brahmanism emerged victorious and they usurped some of the powerful ideals of Buddhism and adopted them with sharper focus. The beef-eating 'broken men' who persisted with Buddhism were ostracized and given the end of the villages to stay on and became Untouchables, stigmatized as *antyaj* and *antyavasin*.

5.   According to Dangle, the term 'Dalit Literature' was coined at the first-ever Dalit Literary Conference in 1958 which passed a resolution defining the term. See Dangle (1994 [1992]: xi).

6.   Ganguly deals with this theme in her analysis of Marathi Dalit literature. She reads Dalit literature from the point of view of experiences taking place in the every day life-world of the Dalits, not as products of an ideological battle. 'Comportment is not quietism or a resigned acceptance of one's place in an unjust world order. It is rather an orientation towards all that is life-giving in a slippery, treacherous, aggressive, sorrowful, oppressive, unjust world. It points to truths that are larger than the pedagogical truths of either the social sciences or those of political activism' (2005: 177). She focuses on those works of Dalits which address the issue of oppression in 'non-pedagogical and non-ideological terms', not overtly conscious of 'contributing to transforming the social order' (2005: 177).

7.   Within the literary movement, Gokhale finds three different groups of Dalits. The first comprises of well-established Dalit writers with an institutional presence. They are recognized by the other Marathi litterateurs and hail mostly from middle-class background. The second is a younger, more radical and organized group, which is more oriented towards action. The third group is that of the older, less-educated folk poets, who represent continuity from the tradition of *jalasa*, whose work is more accessible to the Dalit masses (Gokhale 1993: 299).

8.   As a consequence, a plurality of themes has developed. According to an estimate made by Gokhale, the dateline probably being in the late 1980s, there are three main groupings of Dalit writers. The first group is that of Dalit Sahitya Sansad, headed by Baburao Bagul. The second, the *Asmitaadarsh* group of G. Pantawane; and the third, the Bauddh Sahitya Parishad initiated by Bahusaheb Adsul. Each of these groups holds its conferences in different parts of Maharashtra (see Gokhale 1993: 328–9).

9.   There are also prominent non-Buddhist Dalit writers. For example, Annabhau Sathe belonged to the Matang community and his poems and other writings contain strong sentiments of revolution.

10.   For example, two poems of this variety are included in the anthology of Dalit literature in English, titled *Poisoned Bread*. They are *Tathagatha*, authored by Bhagwan Sawai, and *Yashodhara*, by Hira Bansode. See Dangle (1994 [1992]: 29–30, 31–32).

11.   'Verses, a distich of a particular measure in vernacular language, and the light air sung by women while grinding, lulling infants etc.' (Poitevin 2002: 373).

12.   Murugkar relates the rise of Dalit Panther movement with the 'militant' Dalit writers, especially of 'The Little Magazine' movement of the late 1960s. Dalit militancy found its clearest expression in a little magazine edited by Namdeo Dhasal, named *Vidroh*. The Little Magazine movement was a literary movement of the Dalit youth with a tinge of anti-establishment sentiments. Murugkar sees the Dalit Panther movement as an extension of this. See Murugkar (1991: 58).

13. In fact, the term 'Dalit' got popularized with the arrival of Dalit Panthers on the scene.

14. The Dalit Panthers was established on 9 July 1972 (cf. Ganguly 2005: 180).

15. For a graphic presentation of the splits and the various factions, see Murugkar (1991: 84).

16. This section of the chapter is based mainly on the materials collected and observations made during the fieldwork undertaken as part of my doctorate. The study mainly concentrated on the city of Aurangabad, particularly the inhabitants of Ambedkar Nagar *zoppadpatti*, N7, City and Industrial Development Corporation (CIDCO) of Maharashtra, Aurangabad, Maharashtra.

17. Many Buddhists congregate at Diksha Bhumi at Nagpur on Vijayadashami (Dussehra), a day marking the conversion of Babasaheb Dr Ambedkar and his followers to Buddhism. The day is called *dhammachakkapravartan din*. On 6 December, Buddhists come to Mumbai in large numbers to commemorate the *mahaparinirvan* of Dr Ambedkar. They come together at Chaityabhumi in Dadar where a memorial to Babasaheb has been built.

18. Professor J.P.S. Uberoi sees civil society as a domain of custom and usage. I have used this insight in this explanation of the sarvajanik (cf. Uberoi 2003: 114–33).

19. Matangs and Charmakars are two Dalit castes found in Maharashtra. However, in terms of numbers and spread of the population, the erstwhile Mahar, most of who count themselves as Buddhists (Nav-Bauddha), now outnumber both Matangs and Charmakars.

20. Interview with Ratan Kashinath Satdive, on 5 November 2003.

21. An example of a cooperative concern of writers is Kaushalya Prakashan, moderated by Dr A. Gaikwad, who operates from his clinic in the Housing Urban Development Corporation (HUDCO) area of Aurangabad.

22. Almost every locality with a sizeable number of Buddhist population in Aurangabad has one or more associations of youth. The People's Power Sanghatana (PPS) is such an association of youth in Ambedkar Nagar and has its members, young men from all the Dalit castes. They undertake different activities in the locality and are prime movers of the flagship programmes of some political parties. The members meet at regular intervals and undertake different activities to create public awareness about civic issues.

REFERENCES

Aloysius, G. 1998, *Religion as an Emancipatory Identity: A Buddhist Movement among the Tamils under Colonialism*, New Delhi: New Age International Publishers.

Ambedkar, B.R. 1990 (reprint), 'Who Were the Shudras? How They Came to be the Fourth Varna in the Indo-Aryan Society?' and 'The Untouchables: Who Were They and Why They Became Untouchables?' *Dr. Babasaheb*

Ambedkar: Writings and Speeches, Vol. 7, Bombay: Department of Education, Government of Maharashtra.

Chatterjee, Partha. 2006 [2001], 'On Civil and Political Societies in Post-colonial Democracies', in S. Kaviraj and S. Khilnani (eds), *Civil Society: History and Possibilities*, New Delhi: Foundation Books.

———. 2006 [2004], *The Politics of the Governed: Reflections on Popular Politics in Most of the World*, New Delhi: Permanent Black.

Dangle, Arjun (ed.). 1994 [1992], *Poisoned Bread, Translations from Modern Marathi Dalit Literature*, Hyderabad: Orient Longman.

Fuchs, M. 2004, 'Buddhism and Dalitness: Dilemmas of Religious Emancipation', in S. Jondhale and J. Beltz (eds), *Reconstructing the World: B.R. Ambedkar and Buddhism in India*, New Delhi: Oxford University Press, pp. 283–300.

Ganguly, D. 2005, *Caste, Colonialism and Counter-Modernity: Notes on a Post Colonial Hermeneutics of Caste*, London and New York: Routledge.

Gokhale, J. 1993, *From Concessions to Confrontation: The Politics of an Untouchable Community*, Bombay: Popular Prakashan.

Gombrich, R.F. and G.. Obeyesekere. 1988, *Buddhism Transformed: Religious Change in Sri Lanka*, Princeton: Princeton University Press.

Hasan, Z. 2009, *Politics of Inclusion: Castes, Minorities, and Affirmative Action*, New Delhi: Oxford University Press.

Junhgare, Indira Y. 1988, 'Dr. Ambedkar: The Hero of the Mahars, Ex-Untouchables of India', *Asian Folklore Studies*, 47(1): 93–121.

Keer, D. 2002 [1954], *Dr. Ambedkar: Life and Mission*, Bombay: Popular Prakashan.

Massey, I.P. 2002, *Minority Rights Discourse in India*, Shimla: Indian Institute of Advanced Study.

Murugkar, L. 1991, *Dalit Panther Movement in Maharashtra: A Sociological Appraisal*, Bombay: Popular Prakashan.

Omvedt, G. 2004, *Ambedkar: Towards an Enlightened India*, New Delhi: Penguin.

Pandian, M.S.S. 2002, *One Step Outside Modernity: Caste, Identity Politics and Public Sphere*, Amsterdam and Dakar: SEPHIS and CODESRIA.

Poitevin, G. 2002, *The Voice and the Will: Subaltern Agency: Forms and Motives*, New Delhi: Manohar and Centre de Sciences Humaines.

Tartakov, G.M. 2004, 'The Navayana Creation of the Buddha Image', in S. Jondhale and J. Beltz (eds), *Reconstructing the World: B.R. Ambedkar and Buddhism in India*, New Delhi: Oxford University Press, pp. 151–85.

Uberoi, J.P.S. 2003, 'Civil Society', in V. Das (ed.), *The Oxford India Companion to Sociology and Social Anthropology*, New Delhi: Oxford University Press, pp. 114–35.

Zelliot, E. 2004, *Dr. Babasaheb Ambedkar and the Untouchable Movement*, New Delhi: Blumoon Books.

6

Christian and Tribal

The Dynamics of Scheduled Tribe Status in the Field

Joseph Marianus Kujur

The present chapter records the dynamics of identity formation of the Oraon Christian tribals as a minority who have either themselves converted to Christianity or have inherited Christianity from their ancestors, for one or more generations, in the state of Jharkhand. It discusses the contestations of the converts' identity as Scheduled Tribes (ST) as well as the assertions that they are very much an ST by virtue of being 'Oraon', which is an ethnic identity. Thus, there is an interface of the Oraon/tribal ethnic identity and the Christian religious identity. The study probes into how the above developments within tribal society have led to a new discourse on identity within tribal society as well as outside. It also examines the nature of the discourse and the implications it has for the entire tribal society and not merely for the Christian tribals.

Two case studies have been taken for analysis. The first case is the effort by the late Kartik Oraon, a powerful tribal Member of Parliament (MP), for the de-scheduling of the Oraon Christians as ST in the 1960s; and the second case is the recent 'Nemha Bible' (Holy Bible) controversy of 2008, which became a site of vigorous contestation of the church's claim of its 'tribalness' on the one hand, and its identity assertion on the other. Both the attempts of de-scheduling of the Christian tribes are different but interrelated—the first being constitutional and the second political. While the first example is at the level of an individual with its ramification for the entire tribal community, the direct target of the second example is the institutional church itself, which claims to have a tribal character by virtue of its location in the tribal belt with a tribal congregation. The two sites of negotiation between ethnic and religious identities set the tone for the present discussion.

These two case studies have been chosen for two reasons: one, to bring to light some important issues pertaining to intersectionality between the socio-cultural identity question of the tribes in general, and of the minority Christian tribals in particular; and second, to show the second case study as a continuation of the first one. There has been an increasing discussion on the issue of minority and tribal identities among the Christian tribals, traditional Sarna tribals, as well as in the Sangh Parivar.[1] This is what constitutes the main subject matter of the present study.

Religious differentiation in tribal societies, particularly conversion from traditional religion to Christianity, has been one of the most marked processes of change. This process is alleged to be primarily responsible for the rupture in the tribal community. Conversion is perceived as a threat to the cohesion and solidarity of the community in terms of the established beliefs, practices, and norms that make the community (Viswanathan 1998: xi). Kim (2003: 4) delineates three aspects of the socio-cultural dynamics of conversion that lead to social instability: first, rigidity of the community boundaries, that is, a lack of openness to and understanding of other religions and cultures resulting in communal tension; second, a process of homogenization through the counter-conversion movement by the Hindu fundamentalists; and third, conflicting perspectives of the Hindus and Christians on conversion, the Hindu approach being 'socio-political' and the Christian 'theological'. Thus, the conversion phenomenon in India has become controversial, confusing, and chaotic. Affiliation to religions other than Hinduism (Pati 2003: 1–2), especially to Christianity (Sahay 1986: 203–26), Islam (Robinson 2003: 23), and Buddhism (Tartakov 2003: 195), is always looked upon as conflicting boundaries between the communities of the converts and non-converts.

Against this backdrop, the issue of the ST status of the Christian tribals and the absence of Scheduled Caste (SC) status for the Muslim and Christian Dalits, as in Jenkins' chapter, acquires a new significance. Though a significant section of the tribal population converted to Christianity in a short span of time after the missionaries started their activities in Chotanagpur around 1845 (De Sa 1975: 72; Mahato 1971:

18–20), the majority of the Sarna people continued to adhere to the traditional/Sarna[2] religion, which itself is a minority religion although not recognized as such by the Indian Constitution. The Sarnas also reacted sharply to the phenomenon of conversion within the community (Sahay 1986: 206–7). The contestation of the 'tribal' identity of the tribal Christians is from inside the tribal community as much as it is from outside.

Two contesting positions have been articulated over the identity question of the minority tribal Christian community. One is that the tribal Christians are not to be treated as ST (Oraon 2001; *Ranchi Express* 2001: 11–12). The other position is that the tribal Christians are as much ST as are the tribals practicing their traditional faith (Kerketta 2001: 9). This division between converts and non-converts, and intersections of ethnicity and religion, continue to haunt tribal society today as in the past. It has not only given rise to mistrust and suspicion between the two communities but has also contributed to conflict, both covert and overt. That this is so is obvious from various efforts to de-schedule the tribal Christians from the ST list.

MULTIPLE IDENTITIES

Identity is a question of perception by self and by others. This perception may be coloured by the existing social, political, and economic arrangements. That one aspect of identity prevails over the other depends on the context. Oommen (2000) raises two issues, namely, the multiplicity of identity and the prominence of one aspect of identity over others. In multiple identities, often, the primary identity is confused with the total identity. An aspect of identity, which is insignificant for self, may be blown out of proportion by others. Which aspect of identity will get prominence is determined by the situation. Gupta (1997) holds that identities are formed in a particular context. It can therefore be inferred that the identity may not necessarily be the same for all time and space. Even the identity of the same community may vary depending on the circumstances. At the same time, the identity of no two communities is identical in spite of their exposure to similar circumstances. The question of the identity of one community can be talked about only in relation to the other.

The notion of identity being relational invariably takes into account the frame of reference within which a group operates in relation to the others. Each group's boundaries are significantly demarcated. However, those boundaries are not static but fluid. The identities, in Barth's view, are 'actually quite porous, allowing individuals to shift between them, either temporarily or permanently' (as cited in Parkin 2000: 49), which can also be simultaneously manipulated and negotiated 'according to circumstance' (Parkin 2000: 49). The identity of a group needs to be negotiated among different groups because of the stake each group has for its survival or prosperity.

This chapter will examine whether a change in the religious dimension of the Oraon identity can be equated with the entire Oraon identity of a Christian tribal. In order to analyse the dynamics of the tribal status of the tribal Christians in contemporary times, two case studies have been studied.

CASE 1: A CONTESTATION OF CHRISTIANS' TRIBAL IDENTITY

The case of the negation of the ST identity to Christians by certain section of the Sarna community is also a case of the negotiations for the assertion of their own identity, as is seen in the Kartik Oraon episode.

In the 1962 general elections, Kartik Oraon, who belonged to the Sarna Oraon community, David Munzni, a Lutheran Christian from the Oraon community, and another Oraon Christian person were rival candidates for the parliamentary seat from Lohardaga parliamentary (STs) constituency. Mr Oraon was the official candidate of the Congress Party. Mr Munzni was the official candidate of the Swatantra Party, and another person was the official candidate of the Jharkhand Party. The result of the election was declared on 2 March 1962, declaring Munzni to have been duly elected. Mr Oraon polled 41,804 votes, while Munzni polled 58,173 votes and the second respondent polled 31,744 votes. The appellant therefore, filed an election petition challenging the validity of the election of respondent No. 1. It was also prayed that if that was not possible, the entire election be declared as void. While Mr Oraon was the appellant in the court, Mr Munzni and the candidate from the Jharkhand Party were the first and second respondents respectively.[3]

Mr Oraon's counsel argued that the two respondents were Indian Christians and that they had nothing to do with the animistic faith and tribal way of life. They were not following the manners and customs of the tribes and had no affinity nor any common interest, defence, or aspirations with or for the tribal people and, as such, they were not entitled to contest the parliamentary seat concerned as candidates on a seat purely meant for the STs. He also argued that although the ancestors of the two respondents were originally Oraons, they subse-quently embraced Christianity and became Christians by religion.[4]

The judge, however, decided against the petitioner. Mr Oraon next appealed to the Patna High Court, where two judges upheld the decision of the Election Tribunal: 'Oraon Tribe Members embracing Christianity do not cease to be Oraons and are entitled to rights and privileges of tribals. They can contest election to Parliamentary Seat for STs.'[5] Mr Oraon finally appealed to the Supreme Court challenging the judge-ment and decree of 14 November 1963 of the Patna High Court but lost his appeal for good. At Mr Oraon's final defeat, Mr Munzni said: 'He ought to respect the decision of the Supreme Court and never come back with his assertion that Christian Converts from the STs are no more members of the STs' (Munzni 1968).

Mr Oraon had the strong support of the Jan Sangh, a political party with the Hindu nationalist ideology. He had also the support of the late Sri Jagjivan Ram, SC MP, and Sri Morarji Desai, who later on became the Prime Minister of India. The decree in this case was sure to affect each and every Christian tribal throughout the country. Hence, it was a battle not only between Mr Oraon and Munzni but between the com-munities they represented.

Even after losing the court battle, Mr Oraon did not give up. He sent out a circular entitled, 'Task Before Tribal India' (Munzni 1970), to mobilize the Sarna against the Christian tribals. He even tried to prove his point through legislation. Mr Oraon, a member of the Joint Committee of Parliament, submitted to the Lok Sabha a bill called 'The Scheduled Castes and STs Orders (Amendment) Bill 1967'. The Joint Parliamentary Committee, under the Chairmanship of Anil Kumar Chanda, had accepted the second *anusucchi* (schedule) of Scheduled Castes and Scheduled Tribes Amendment Bill 1967, according to which anybody embracing either Christianity or Islam would not get the status of ST. This would be similar to the constitutional provisions for SCs, according to which anybody abandoning either Hinduism or Sikhism would lose his/her SC status. The committee submitted its report on 17 November 1969.

The amendment bill by Mr Oraon, in Munzni's view, was clearly biased and openly anti-Christian and anti-Muslim, as it read: 'notwith-standing anything contained in paragraph 2, no person who has given up tribal faith or faiths and has embraced either Christianity or Islam shall be deemed to be a member of a Scheduled Tribe'. Munzni in his rejoin-der (Munzi 1970) pointed out how Mr Oraon's proposed amendment was clearly contrary to the Indian Constitution, Part III, Fundamental Rights, Article 15(1), which states, 'The State shall not discriminate any citizen on grounds only of religion, race, caste, sex, place of birth or any of them.' Munzni dismissed Mr Oraon's assertion that the proposed amendment compared favourably with the provisions in the Scheduled Castes Orders 1950 and 1956 which read: 'Notwithstanding anything contained in paragraph 2, no person who professes a religion different from the Hindu or Sikh religion shall be deemed to be a member of a Scheduled Caste.' The rejoinder said:

We strongly resent this equation of the tribals with the scheduled castes. These latter are presumed to belong to the Hindu society and to form a part of it in the caste system. Once they abandon their Hindu religion, it is argued, they no longer belong to the Hindu fold. But the tribal groups are different from the Hindus precisely because they are outside this caste system. As long as they keep their ethnic identity and cultural heritage, they remain tribals. (Munzni 1970)

On Sunday, 2 May 1970, at the behest of Akhil Bhartiya Adivasi Vikas Parishad a *sabha* (convention) was organized in Morahbadi ground in which a resolution was passed to demand that those adivasis who had accepted either Christianity or Islam should not be extended the status of 'ST'. In this convention, there were about 700 delegates from Madhya Pradesh, West Bengal, Orissa, Rajasthan, and other states (Dutt 2001: 8).

The tribal Christians looked upon the proposed amendment as a 'stab in the back' of those whose ballots had largely helped Mr Oraon to become an MP. The rejoinder reminded Mr Oraon of his promises to his electorate in Barway in Gumla district that he would never work against the interests of his Christian tribals if only they voted for him as a parliamentary candidate. It asked for an explanation from him. It also asked whether such a man could be trusted. It made pleas to Kartik Oraon to withdraw his discriminatory amendment. Dutt writes that the Joint Parliamentary Committee presented an amended bill in the Parliament in November 1970. There was a clear division in the Congress Party on the issue of the tribal Christians' identity. Indira Gandhi cleverly postponed the debate. The Parliament was then dissolved before time and the amended bill could not be passed to make it into an act (Dutt 2001: 8).

Despite the above amended bill not becoming an act, the issue of tribal Christians' ST status has been raised at regular intervals in different forms. Since the Supreme Court judgement, the issue has now become a political tool for various groups, to be used, as and when required, for their own advantage. That this is so was clear from the recent 'Nemha' (Holy) Bible controversy that renewed the divide between the minority and the Sarna community, which is treated next.

CASE 2: CONTESTING TRIBALNESS OF THE INSTITUTIONAL CHURCH

The 'Nemha' Bible controversy in Jharkhand in 2008 engulfed the entire region with mutual suspicion and hatred between some splinter groups in the Sarna community and the church. It was about the Kurukh (language spoken by the Oraon tribe) translation of the Bible published by the Bible Society of India, Bangalore, which allegedly carried some derogatory remarks about the Sarna religion. The controversial verses of the Bible are as follows:

> 1 Here are the laws that you are to obey as long as you live in the land that the LORD, the God of your ancestors, is giving you. Listen to them! 2 In the land that you are taking, destroy all the places where the people worship their gods on high mountains, on high hills, and under *green trees*. 3 Tear down their altars and smash their sacred stone pillars to pieces. Burn their symbols of the goddess Asherah and chop down their idols, so that they will never again be worshipped at those places. (Deuteronomy 12: 1–3; emphasis added)

The 'green trees' in verse 2, in the Kurukh language, is translated as 'Sarna mann'. The Oraons' place of worship is called 'Sarna'. It is located in the tree groves, which is usually a thick patch of the sal trees. 'Mann' refers to trees.

The controversy started in September 2008, soon after the attacks on Christians in Kandhamal district of Orissa. After the Orissa incident, some prominent Hindutva leaders reportedly visited Ranchi and allegedly blamed the Christians, especially Cardinal Telesphor P. Toppo, for the murder of Swami Laxmanananda Saraswati,[6] in Kandhamal, Orissa, prior to the attacks on Christians.

Some Sarna leaders with close links with the Sangh Parivar, raked up the issue. On 23 September 2008, this issue was raised in the Jharkhand legislative assembly by the Bharatiya Janata Party (BJP) Members of Legislative Assembly (MLAs). A number of meetings, demonstrations, and rallies, organized by the Sangh Parivar, were held at Ranchi, Khunti,

Lohardaga, and Gumla districts to protest against the church for hurting the religious sentiments of the Sarna community. The effigy of Cardinal Toppo was burnt as a sign of protest.

In order to diffuse the prevailing tension in the state, the 'All Churches Committee' was formed, which made a joint statement apologizing for the wrong translation of certain verses of the Bible. However, despite an official apology and withdrawal of the disputed Bible, the anti-Christian propaganda escalated. On 28 September 2008, some Christian social activists were approached by the church hierarchy to resolve the problem amicably. They swung into action by contacting the Sarna leaders engaged in social, religious, and political activities, to assess the situation and find ways to resolve the conflict. Initial attempts to bring the Sarna leaders of Lohardaga on board for resolving the controversy were disappointing. However, a strategy was worked out to resolve the dispute amicably taking various Sarna groups on board.

On 2 October 2008, the annual Sarna Prarthna Mahasabha (Great Prayer Meeting) was held at Lohardaga in which about 15,000–20,000 people from the states of Chhattisgarh, Orissa, West Bengal, Bihar, and Jharkhand gathered. However, the Prathna Sabha Organizing Committee realized that there were some Sangh Parivar intruders in the crowd, who could possibly create problem for the Christian leaders. Hence, the church leaders were advised not to appear at the venue.

The Prathna Sabha started with the traditional puja (worship), but soon the Hindutva brigade reportedly hijacked the show. One certain Mr Oraon exhorted the crowd to march to the Ranchi mahapanchayat (grand assembly/meeting) on 19 October 2008 with saffron flags. 'If the Christian do not restrain themselves, Jharkhand will soon become another Kandhamal and Karnataka,' he warned. Two leaders sympathetic to the tribal Christians, exhorted the audience at the end, to restrain themselves against any kind of violence and wait for their further direction. The prayer meeting was concluded on a sober note and a core committee was formed to engage in a dialogue with all the churches' committee.

The Sarna community got divided into two factions. Those who took a moderate stand were: the Prathna Sabha; Adivasi Chhatra Sangh (Tribal Students' Union); some *parha* (confederation of villages) groups; and village leaders. They were in a reconciliatory mood and wanted to settle the problem before 19 October. The other group led by some well-known tribal intellectuals was said to have been saffronized. After days of mobilization, the dialogue took place from 6–11 October

2008, which was concluded with a joint press conference at the City Palace Hotel.

The Prathna Sabha group, Adivasi Chhatra Sangh, and parha people went to the villages of Lohardaga, Ranchi, and Gumla to make people understand that some communal forces were playing divisive politics to make the tribals fight among themselves. As a result, various parhas decided not to take part in the 19 October mahapanchayat at Ranchi. It was reported that majority of the people on the stage at the mahapanchayat in Morahbadi had allegiance to the BJP. Thus, the tension created by the Nemha Bible controversy was amicably resolved, at least for the time being. The Sarna and the Christian communities jointly formed the central 'Akhil Bharatiya Adivasi Mahasabha' (All India Adivasi Grand Assembly) to safeguard and promote the interests of the adivasis. Now, the formation of the district-level groups is in progress.

DYNAMICS OF IDENTITY ARTICULATION

Legally, the position of the Oraon Christians as ST finds legitimacy in the Supreme Court judgement. The Court has ruled that tribals could belong to various religions without losing their ethnic identity. In Civil Appeal No. 570 of 1967 before the Supreme Court, a categorical judgement was passed on 6 March 1968. As per the Constitution of India, Articles 330, 342, and 366(25)—Constitution (STs) Order, 1950, Part III, Item 25—the members of the Oraon tribe embracing Christianity do not cease to be Oraons and are entitled to rights and privileges of tribals. They can contest election to parliamentary seat meant for STs. In conformity with the Constitution of India, the Oraon tribe had been specified as ST in the state of Bihar.[7] The main arguments in favour of the ST status of the tribal Christian respondents were as follows.[8]

One, the candidates' active participation in the civic life of the tribe disproved the contention that he lacked 'common interests and aspirations' of his tribe. These respondents had taken up the cause for improvement of the condition of the tribals, including Christians and non-Christians, and both kinds of Oraons considered the respondents to be one of them for their upliftment work and were members of the Adivasi Unnati Samaj (Adivasi Development Society), of which the first respondent was the president.

Two, as regards the charge of the candidate's neglect of the manners and customs of the tribes, the Court was of the opinion that 'there was evidence that although Christian tribals did omit certain observances of tribal religion, they retained such practices as exogamy based on totemistic lineage, certain harvest rites, ceremonial eating of first fruits, birth and marriage observances, and style of writing surnames'.[9]

Three, even in the case of the tribal Christians dropping certain festivals or celebrating some in a manner different from the Sarnas, the Court ruled the 'most important thing in the matter is that the non-Christian tribals treat the converted Oraons as tribals, calling them "Christian Oraons"'.[10] This showed that they were Oraons first and Christians next.

Four, the Court also observed that the 'Christian and non-Christian Oraons intermarried and their descendants were treated as full members of the tribe. Moreover, the Christian tribals were also writing as their surnames the names of their tribe and *khoont* (lineage)'.[11] Five, Christian Oraons were invited to feasts and participated in them. Hence, conversion did not extinguish membership in the tribe. Six, the Court observed that Tana Oraons[12] did not lose their Oraonness just because they did not engage in the sacrifice of fowls and animals, without which the Oraon worship is not considered to be complete.

Seven, many members of various STs, professing the Christian faith, had contested parliamentary and assembly seats which were reserved for members of STs in the first, second, and third general elections in this country, and the successful contestants among them served their full terms as members of the respective legislature without any challenge, and that, as a matter of fact, respondent No. 2 had successfully contested his particular reserved seat in the general election held in 1957 and he served as a member of the Lok Sabha for the full term till its dissolution on the eve of the general election of 1962. Eight, three documentary evidences were presented before the Election Tribunal, namely, a sale deed (Ext. B), a *parcha* (Ext. C), and a *khatian* (Ext. D), to show that his ancestors were accepted as Oraons though their religion was mentioned as Christianity.

Nine, references were made to *The Oraons of Chota Nagpur* (Roy 1915), which gives the details of Oraon population in Bihar and Orissa. First, it gives the figures of Hindu male and female Oraons of different states. Then it states that besides these, there are males and females returned as Christians, in the Santal Parganas, Hazaribagh, Ranchi, Palamau, Manbhum, Singhbhum, and Orissa state. Thus, it appears that though an Oraon is not an animist and is of Hindu faith or of Christian faith, he is taken as an Oraon in this book for finding out the population of the Oraons in Bihar and Orissa. In other words, Christian Oraons have not been omitted from the population of the Oraons in those two states.

Ten, the Court took cognizance of the definition of the 'tribe' in *Encyclopaedia Britannica*, by W.H.R. Rivers:

> a social group of simple kind, the members of which speak a common dialect, have a single government, and act together for such common purposes, as 'warfare'. Other typical characteristics include a common name, a contiguous territory, a relatively uniform culture or way of life and a tradition of common descent. Tribes are usually composed of a number of local communities, e.g. bands, villages or neighborhoods, and are often aggregated in clusters of a higher order called nations. The term is seldom applied to societies that have achieved a strictly territorial organization in large states but is usually confined to groups whose unity is based primarily upon a sense of extended kinship ties. It is no longer used for kin groups in the strict sense, such as clans. (Rivers 1961: 465)

Thus, the legal boundary of the identity of the ST was clearly demarcated, which is inclusive of the Oraons who have accepted Christianity as their religion. However, the stereotypical criteria of a tribe pose serious problems to the identity question of all tribes irrespective of whether they are Christians or not.

The definition of the tribe by Rivers highlights its social, cultural, political, economic, linguistic, geographical, and historical dimensions. However, if manners and customs, a way of life, their affinity to the common interest, and defence or aspirations with the tribal people, and so on, are to be taken as identifiers of a tribal, most of those scheduled in the ST list will fail to fulfil the criteria today. Moreover, as for the tribal religions being animistic, some tribes are contesting the notion of their being 'animists' and they assert that they are monotheists (Lakra 1998).

Again, in the case of the Bible translation controversy, what was on target apart from the status of the Christian tribals, was the credibility of the church as tribal. There was a deliberate attempt to discredit the church as tribal. The detractors knew it well that the translation was the work of the North West Gossner Evangelical Lutheran (NWGEL) Church. However, they chose to attack the Catholic cardinal, who symbolizes the tribal church in India today. It can also be accrued that this was an attack on those Christians who claim to be tribals to benefit from the constitutional provisions but are not committed to their communities. Their argument was that if the church cannot respect the Sarna, which is a place of worship for the Sarnites, it cannot claim to be a tribal church.

The political agenda of the fundamentalist forces was clear—divide and rule. A political mileage, polarizing the Christian and Sarna votes, would be to their advantage. They triggered the religious and ethnic passion of the Sarna people. Those who considered themselves as secular created a fear psychosis that the destiny of the minorities was safe only in the hands of the non-communal parties.

For the minorities themselves, the issue of the Nemha Bible was not as serious as it was made out to be. They thought it was blown out of proportion for obvious political reasons. They claimed that they were aware of the mistake in the translation and had plans to rectify it in the second edition of the Nemha Bible. Hence, the minority communities perceived the Hindutva-supported aggression of certain sections of the Sarna community as a tactic to divert the attention of the general public from the core issues of discrimination based on caste, religion, and gender. The issues which were likely to take a back seat during the Bible controversy were other crucial issues of development, such as displacement, resettlement, migration, and so on, which are a result of the wrong policies of the government perpetrated primarily by the business and industry fraternity.

In this discourse on 'tribal' identity, two distinct aspects can be discerned. One is the equation of the Oraon identity, an ethnic category, with the ST identity, a constitutional category. As per Article 366(25) of the Constitution, 'the Scheduled tribes mean such tribes or tribal communities or parts of or groups within such tribes or tribal communities as are deemed under Article 342 to be Scheduled tribes'. They are specified by the President of India by a public notification (Verma 1990: 10). The other is that Christianity is projected by some in a diametric opposition to the ethnic Oraon identity, implying thereby that anyone converted to Christianity cannot be an ST. This notion has a far-reaching consequence. It implies that anyone converting to another religion does so at the cost of his/her own earlier cultural identity. It also means that religious and cultural/ethnic expressions are 'dichotomous', which is problematic.[13] The articulation of the Oraon identity has been approached differently by the Sarna and tribal Christian communities, which is discussed next.

THE SARNA FORMULATION

The Oraon Christians are only a tiny minority in the midst of the larger Oraon society in Jharkhand. The Christians, however, have made a mark in the areas of education, employment, living standard, and so on. The viewpoint of the Sarna Oraon community as regards the identity of the Oraon Christians has not been steady. It kept shifting with the changing political situations. The Sarna attitude towards the Christian Oraons as the 'other' has kept recurring for the de-scheduling of the Christian tribes, as seen in the earlier case studies. It is argued here that the Sarna's perception of the Oraon Christian identity either as 'tribal' or 'non-tribal' creates a space for the assertion of their own identity. If some sections of the Sarna challenge the identity of the Oraon Christians as ST, it is to bolster the assertion of the Oraon Sarna about themselves as tribals. This articulation, however, is subject to change depending upon the circumstances.

The two case studies discussed earlier reveal similar manifestations of identity—assertion of the Sarna community as ST; and a negation of the same identity to the tribal Christian minority and the church in central India, which claims to have a tribal character. The former is an example of a 'negative' campaigning for self-assertion. The effort by the Sarna intellectuals against Christians is a process of positioning themselves socially and politically. The attempt of the Christian sympathizers, however, is a positive assertion of the tribal identity at two levels: first, inclusively as one Oraon community inclusive of the Sarna and Christians; and second, their identity exclusively as Sarna Oraons.

Kartik Oraon's demand was based on two grounds: first, discrimination of the Sarna people in the Christian institutions; and second, the Sarna perception of the Christians as double beneficiaries. In the protest of Mr Oraon, there was an assertion of the Oraon identity of the Sarna. Much in the same way, in the case of the protest to the Kurukh Bible, emerges the issue of the assertion of the Sarna distinctiveness—from Christian minority as well as Hindu majority—and negotiations to the changing times.

Mr Oraon's campaign for the de-scheduling of the tribal Christians was a critique of the Christian system which was discriminating the Sarnas in admissions and use of facilities in the Christian institutions. Preferences were given to the Roman Catholics in the Catholic institutions; to the Anglicans in the Anglican-sponsored institutions; and to the Lutherans in the Lutheran Church-related institutions. In developmental projects such as digging ponds, roads, wells, and walls, Christians were the first beneficiaries. The Sarnas were ignored. It was discovered that schemes were given to the Sarna who had some association with the church. Christianity was a source of strength, resourcefulness, prosperity, and progress for those who identified themselves with the Christian faith.

Mr Oraon claimed that the Christians benefited from both the church and state-run institutions. The Sarna benefited only from the state. Mr Oraon argued that the Christian adivasis, who formed only 5.53 per cent of the tribal population, 'flagrantly' took away 60–100 per cent of the state and central services and post-matriculation scholarships and subsidies meant for the STs. He argued that the tribal Christians were 'Indian Christians' who did not need any constitutional privileges, because they were sufficiently advanced.[14] In 1970, a meeting was organized for the leaders of the All India Adivasis Convention under the leadership of Mr Oraon and a document was circulated which showed how a disproportionately large number of Christian adivasis were benefiting from the provisions offered to the STs. Facts were presented to substantiate the argument that the Christian adivasis were better placed than the Sarna people in the government jobs (Dutt 2001: 8).

According to the available data, in 1970, the number of the government posts held by the Christian adivasis was much higher than that of the Sarna adivasis. At the level of the deputy collector, out of the total thirty-nine seats occupied by tribals, the adivasi Christians held as large as thirty-three (84.61 per cent) and the Sarnas held only six (15.38 per cent). The Christians occupied all the posts of the under secretary and sub-divisional officers (SDOs). Of the fifty-four seats of the sub-deputy collector, thirty-four (62.96 per cent) were held by the Christians and twenty (37.03 per cent) by the Sarna. While seven seats of the deputy superintendents of police (DSPs) were occupied by the Christians, only one of them was held by the Sarna people. All the gazetted inspectors in various departments were Christians. In medical services, five posts were held by the Christians and three by the Sarna. Similarly, eight posts of the Bihar Judicial Services were occupied by Christians, whereas the Sarna held only five posts. In 1970, there was only one Indian Administrative Service (IAS) officer from the adivasis community and he was a Christian. Thus, of the 128 administrative posts taken for the comparison between the two communities, ninety-three (72.65 per cent) were held by Christians and only thirty-five (27.34 per cent) by the Sarna (Dutt 2001: 8).

Mr Oraon's protest against Christians was justified to some extent. Many Christian Oraons claimed to be 'tribals' where it was beneficial. At other times and situations, they refused to be 'identified' as Oraons. It is precisely against this type of attitude that Mr Oraon was protesting.

THE CHRISTIAN ARTICULATION

The Oraon/tribal Christian minority community has also been articulating its Oraon/tribal identity. What is important here is how the Chotanagpur church perceives its identity—as alien/foreign or as Oraon/tribal? The case study shows the way the church tries to prove its loyalty to the larger traditional community of which it claims to be a part. The church redefines and rearticulates its identity as 'tribal'. This the church does by identifying itself with the tribal life and culture and by standing up for the causes of the tribal community. including its negotiation with the Sarna communities on various issues of socio-cultural, economic, religious, and political significance.

The church had been supporting and reinforcing all the pro-tribal rallies openly. The collaboration of the Sarna and the Christians over tribal issues, and more recently over the Nemha Bible controversy, is a confirmation of the fact that there is a growing consciousness in both the communities of the sameness of their identity.

There has been a major shift in the stand of the church from earlier times in relation to its identity articulation: a shift of focus from the Western/Roman outlook to tribal/indigenous. At the level of religion, the church has articulated its identity as 'tribal' to thwart the idea that it is a religion imported from a foreign land. The process of indigenization in the church put an end to the speculation about church going the Western way. The detractors of the church criticize the church for its alleged distortion of the tribal culture. The mistaken translation of the Bible into the Kurukh language gave the anti-Christian forces, supported by the Parivar, fodder for further challenging the tribal identity of the church.

In response to this criticism, the minority church has a three-point programme of religious articulations of its 'tribal' identity. First, 'ideological and theological openness': a universal mandate is given through the Second Vatican Council for adaptations in the church according to the local cultures, customs, and traditions. The Second Vatican Council is revolutionary from the point of view of a paradigm shift in the theology and understanding of the Roman Church towards the indigenous cultures. There is some openness now for dialogue with other cultures and religions. Second, 'liturgical indigenization': with the indigenization of liturgy, there is scope for experimentation in the regional and local ways of worshipping and celebrating the sacred rituals. Third, 'indigenization of religious functionaries': the foreign missionaries paved way for the indigenous ones. This is a big leap in the area of indigenization of the clergy in Chotanagpur. Even converts are accepted for priesthood. This change in the clergy has given a 'tribal' look to the church, which goes in favour of the church's claim that it is indeed tribal. There is in the church, an assertion of its identity by a 'cultural *gharwapsi*' (homecoming), in the sense of going back to the tribal roots.

The church is given credit for the documentation of the tribal oral tradition; for translation of the vernaculars into Hindi and English; and also, for the literary and theological writings on tribal themes. The church has shown its interest in tribal literature, which has had its remarkable impact on the tribal community. The church is also responsible for the collection of tribal songs, seasonal music, stories, myths, legends, idioms, proverbs, and so on. A respect for tribal art and a sense of tribal aesthetics makes them safeguard tribal cultural heritage which would have otherwise disappeared. Seminars and workshops on seasonal songs and dances organized by some members of the church keep the tradition alive despite all odds. Competitions, in various schools, of tribal dances and songs make the youngsters learn their culture. Some Christian institutions in the past have pressurized the state government to allow them to teach at the primary level in tribal languages. This is the way in which negotiations between religious and ethnic minorities have taken place down the decades.

The minority church in Chotanagpur has also been encouraging the integration of tribal and Christian values and spirituality. This effort, in my view, is an attempt at legitimizing conversion and the new community that has taken shape in the tribal society. Tribal values are now publicly upheld by the church in its ecclesiological and theological writings. Often, some of the basic tribal characteristics such as harmony, solidarity, and community life are presented as a Christian monopoly. Tribal symbiosis with environment is encouraged to show their interdependence with the environment.

The term 'empowerment' is relatively new in the vocabulary of the church. The notion of empowerment in the church has primarily been looked upon as the process of enhancing the living standard in terms of philanthropic activities, such as education, employment, hospitals, social work, and development work. Of late, 'empowerment' in the church vocabulary has come to be signified as 'political action', of church's participation in the protests, demonstrations, and so on for the tribal cause and assertion of identity. The church claims to stand for the adivasis and their fundamental rights. The participation of the church in the struggles of the people gives them the feeling that it is their church and that it cares for them.

It is important to note that it was the minority Christians who initiated the process of the formation of associations among the tribes in Jharkhand. The overriding objectives of the associations were to protect and promote the interests of the tribals. Such developments eventually culminated in the formation of the Jharkhand Party. After independence, the church as an institution supported the Jharkhand movement but it was cautious in its approach. It is only since the 1970s that the church has come out openly in support of the movement.

The effort of the church is simple, namely, to show the Oraon/tribal Christians as adivasis and the minority church as adivasi. Not that there is any need to prove the Oraonness of the Oraon Christians, but the event of conversion has brought about a rupture in the community. This had been taken advantage of by the Hindutva forces, which are bent on delegitimizing the minority Christian community on the basis of their religion. But the church knows for sure that its acceptability by the Sarna and others cannot come about without its 'tribalization'. And the church has been doing that so unassumingly that one does not even take notice of the negotiations going on in the day-to-day activities of the church.

TRIBAL IDENTITY IN TRANSITION

That there is a colonial hangover even after India's independence is evident in the identification and nomenclature of the term 'tribe'. Consequently, the notion of tribe does not mean more than backwardness, isolation, inferiority, impurity, simple technology, practice of animism, and so on to most citizenry in the country. Such a conceptualization of the group is fallacious (Sinha 1993: 40), inadequate (Desai 1960: 20), and problematic (Xaxa 1999b: 3589). In the postcolonial period, the identity of the Oraons went through yet another shift—from the colonial category of 'tribe' to the constitutional category of the ST. We see the crystallization process of the new name for the Oraons and other such tribes in the *Constituent Assembly Debates* (*CAD*). The identity formulation of 'tribe' in the *CAD* was argued along two different lines of thought: first, the non-liberal Hindu line of thought, which did not necessarily represent the majority Hindus' voices, but by virtue of being vocal, it overshadowed other moderate voices; and second, the 'adivasis' (indigenous) line of thought which was in a minority in the *CAD*, but represented the tribes across the country.

The protagonist of the tribals, Jaipal Singh Munda, was vehemently opposed to the term *'vanajati'* (literally 'forest castes') for the 'tribes' proposed by the non-liberal Hindus. Munda, who claimed his people to be variously known as backward tribes, primitive tribes, and criminal tribes by the 'others', rejected the term 'vanajati'. Proud to be a *'jungli'*, a derogatory term for the jungle dwellers (*CAD* 1989: vol. 1, p. 143), Munda pleaded with the House to 'get behind the mind of the Adibasi' (*CAD* 1989: vol. 9, p. 991). He requested the House not to translate the STs as 'vanajati' (forest castes) because most of the tribes did not live in 'jungles'. Munda preferred the word 'Adibasi' to vanajati to be incorporated in the Constitution because the word 'Adibasi' has grace and because the old abusive epithet of vanajati till recently meant an uncivilized barbarian (*CAD* 1989: vol. 9, p. 992). The House instead of 'vanajati' preferred the word *'janajati'* contrary to the demand of Munda (*CAD* 1989: vol. 9, p. 993). K.M. Munshi disagreed with Munda in calling all the tribes as 'Adibasis'. Munshi found 'nothing common between one tribe and another', and hence he thought it would be fatal for the country to take them as one unit (*CAD* 1989: vol. 9, pp. 997–8). The reason why the term 'Adivasis' (or Adibasi) was not accepted was explained by Dr Ambedkar, who was of the opinion that this word was a 'general term' without any 'specific legal *de jure* connotation'. The term ST, however, as a translation for 'Anusuchit Janjati', had a 'fixed meaning' because it enumerated the tribes (Verma 1990: 11).

The constituent assembly specified the tribes as the STs under which only those tribes could be included which were to be given 'special treatment or facilities envisaged under the Constitution' (Verma 1990: 10). The Constitution does not really define nor does it lay down any criteria for specifying the STs. The President of India has the prerogative of specifying, under Article 342, by a 'public notification' the STs. The Parliament, by law, can 'include or exclude' from the STs' list any tribal community or part thereof in any state or union territory (Verma 1990: 10). One crucial clause included in the Constitution is that there is 'no religious bar for specifying a person as a member of a Scheduled Tribe'. In the case of the SCs, however, 'no person professing religion other than

Hinduism or Sikhism' can be deemed as a member of the SC (Verma 1990: 10–11).

ST STATUS AND EMPOWERMENT

Munda made a strong case for the reservation policy. He argued that the tribes had been shabbily and disgracefully treated and were neglected for 6,000 years. He was apprehensive about the fundamental rights guarantees for the 'Adibasis' and their security. However, Sardar Vallabhbhai Patel was not in favour of reservation. Patel said that there should be an endeavour 'to bring the tribal people to the level of Mr. Jaipal Singh and not to keep them as tribes, so that, 10 years hence, when the fundamental Rights are reconsidered, the word "tribes" may be removed altogether, when they would have come up to our level' (*CAD* 1989: vol. 2, p. 467). Patel seemed to have missed the point made by Munda, who had only sought to ensure the safeguarding of the adivasi identity through constitutional provisions. Munda was aware of the impact of the intermixing of the original people and the outsiders. He was also aware of the hostility between the early settlers and the newcomers called *diku*s (aliens), who were claimed to be the exploiters of the simple, ignorant 'Adibasis', looting them of their lands, expropriating them of their many rights, and taking away that jungle freedom from them (*CAD* 1989: vol. 9, p. 652). Hence, the assertion for the ST status by Jaipal Singh Munda, Kartik Oraon, David Munzni, and the tribal church was precisely to safeguard the interests of the tribals, irrespective of their religious affiliations.

It can be discerned that the administrative term 'tribe', which was first used in the colonial period, has stuck to the Oraons, as it has in the case of the other tribes, though the new term 'ST' is given to them constitutionally. Xaxa observes, however limited and problematic the term 'tribe' is, it 'has now been adopted by the tribals themselves to mean the dispossessed, depressed people of a region. There is no claim to being the original inhabitant of that region, but a prior claim to the natural resources is asserted vis-à-vis the outsiders and the dominant caste' (Xaxa 1999b: 3589). Xaxa further says, 'The identity that was forced upon them from outside precisely to mark out differences from the dominant community has now been internalized by the people themselves. Not only has it become an important mark of social differentiation and identity assertion but also an important tool of articulation for empowerment' (Xaxa 1999b: 3589).

It is this given observation by Xaxa which makes the identity articulation of the minority tribal Christians and the Sarna crucial at this juncture of the tribal history in India in general, and in Jharkhand in particular. There is, at present, a process of affirmation of its 'tribal' identity by the church in the face of some forces denying the 'tribal' status to the minority Christian tribals. The dynamics of identity formation is complex but interesting to see how these three groups perceive themselves and others and articulate their own as well as others' identity.

The issue of the identity of the tribal Christians has been a bone of contention since the independence of the country. The Constitution guarantees certain privileges to the 'STs'. Many groups in the country by virtue of their 'tribeness' are 'scheduled' as 'tribes' irrespective of their religious affiliations. Hence, a contestation over the ST status of the tribal Christians is not without nuances. This contestation is clearly over both the 'tribalness' and the 'Scheduled Tribeness'. Not only that, there is also a challenge to the *Munda*ness, *Oraon*ness, and *Kharia*ness if the Christians belong to the Munda, the Oraon, and the Kharia community respectively, which is absurd.

* * *

There is a rich and complex trajectory in the identity formation of the ethnic Christian minorities from their colonial construct to a decolonized formulation as ST in independent India. The tribalness of the convert Christians has always been a site for contestations and assertions, primarily after the formulation of the Indian Constitution. In this volume, Jenkins, in the context of SCs, points out some of the contentious issues raised by the intersection of religion and caste, which have a bearing on the tribal Christians as a minority religious group. As in the case of SCs, the tribal Christians are also one of the most complex minorities in India. Like the official category of SC, the category of ST too, used for positive discrimination for minority policies, is complicated.

However, there are differences between the SC and ST Christians. While the Christians of tribal origin can belong to any religion and have their ST status intact, in the case of the SCs, they must belong only to certain religions, such as Hinduism, Sikhism, and Buddhism, in order to be legally recognized as having SC status. Thus, the complexity of the criss-crossing between the ethnicity and religion, like the caste–religious intersections, is further intensified when different parameters are used for different minority groups. For instance, while the SCs belonging to Hinduism, Sikhism, and Buddhism are judged by one yardstick, those SC groups belonging to Christianity and Islam are not extended the same constitutional provisions. Hence, ironically, the standpoint of the Constitution in this regard looks so unconstitutional. There seems to be an inner contradiction even in the Constitution of India, which is supposed to promote equality and secularism. It should be noted that there is no homogeneity either in the Muslim or Christian community.

As far as nomenclature is concerned, the British called the persons belonging to the so-called lower castes as 'depressed classes'. Gandhiji called them 'Harijans', a term to which they are vehemently opposed. Many people labelled them as 'Dalits', meaning the 'oppressed', 'ground', and 'crushed'. For that matter, in this sense, there were efforts to bring tribals too under the ambit of the term 'Dalit', which is rejected by the tribals. The tribals argue that despite their common experience of discrimination, oppression, and brokenness, they have their own distinct culture, ethos, social organization, and so on, which are very different from those of the Dalit groups.

One common element in Hinduism and Christianity is that caste discrimination does exist in both the religions and that both of them are characterized by an absence of homogeneity. The difference, however, lies in the fact that caste stratification is recognized and perpetuated by Hinduism doctrinally and in practice, whereas although the Christianity is doctrinally opposed to any such idea of hierarchy or inequality, there are indeed caste-based discriminations within the church in practice.

Boundaries of castes are not clearly demarcated from a legal point of view, much in the same way as the boundaries of the STs. However, despite there being no legal problem regarding the ST status to tribals belonging to various religions, there are harassments and hostility to the tribals professing Christianity, which is a great cause for concern in a democracy like India.

The question of who is a minority or who constitutes a minority is important. If the present definition of minority is based on religion, how is it that the SCs belonging to Christianity and Islam do not fall under the ambit of the SC? Even for the minority tribal Christians, if they are recognized as ST by the Constitution, why should they be discriminated against the majority groups? One of the ways in which the tribal Christian minority faces institutional discrimination is the fact of ST status being state specific. Hence, the tribal migrants to the Assam tea gardens and the Andaman Islands, irrespective of their religious affiliations, are not recognized as having the ST status. Hence, as Jenkins argues, boundaries need careful consideration 'particularly when designating "minorities" in a democracy'.

Ironically, both the terms caste and tribe, which once stood for discrimination, segregation, and backwardness, have today become markers of identity assertion for Dalit and tribal communities. That is why any move for de-scheduling them from the SC and STs' lists is met with aggressive protests. The merit argument against reservation for these categories is contrary to the argument of 'equal opportunity'. Social justice, collective rights, and social responsibility are crucial to the understanding of the agitation of SCs and STs if their rights are violated.

There is caste within religious community and religion within the caste groups. Similarly, there is ethnic identity within religion and religious dimension within the tribe. Hence, there is no watertight compartmentalization. In the context of religion change of tribals and Dalits to Christianity and Islam, there seems to be a double discrimination rather than a double benefit.

This chapter has discussed the way the Sarna and the Christian Oraons have perceived and articulated their Oraon identity in the interface between their ethnic and religious identities in the contemporary times. The Oraons in the past have been called by various names. 'Tribe' is one of them. In the postcolonial articulation, the name 'tribe' was further crystallized in the ST nomenclature, which is a constitutional category. The Oraons, both Sarnas and Christians, are an ST having access to all the constitutional provisions meant for the STs.

Notwithstanding the historical sameness of the adivasis, Sarna and the Christian, the 'tribal' identity of the tribal Christians was challenged by some sections of the Sarna supported by the fundamentalist forces. The cause of the challenge was economic and political but the sense of the 'betrayal' to the parental Sarna community by the Christians cannot be overlooked. The tribal Christians also responded to the challenge to their 'tribal' identity by asserting their pro-tribal stance in everyday life.

Thus, a new era of understanding and convergence has dawned between the Sarnas and the Christians. Both the groups have worked out jointly to participate in the meetings, workshops, discussions, celebrations, demonstrations, and so on to forge unity, and to show mutual solidarity for the cause of the tribals. Greater space has been created for more representations for the Sarnas in the Christian institutions. In the identity question of the 'Oraon' Christian community, the *Christian* dimension was predominant in the past; the *ethnic* Oraon identity was latent. Today, it is the *Oraon* and the *tribal* identity that has taken prominence and the *Christian* identity has become dormant.

The argument in this chapter is that the 'minority' Oraon Christians are as much ST as the Oraons adherent to the traditional faith, which also is a minority religion although unrecognized as such by the Constitution of India. There is no loss of the Oraon identity in dropping one's traditional Oraon religion either individually or collectively. The Oraon Christian community perceives itself as much ST as the Sarna Oraons by virtue of its Oraon ethnic identity. In spite of this change in their identity, the Oraons remain 'Oraons'. In this regard, Xaxa (1999a: 1519) makes a pertinent observation. He writes that despite the fact that tribes are in transition, as in the case of Oraons who speak various languages and practice different religions, engage in a variety of occupations, and so on, they continue being Oraons 'in some socially significant sense' without losing their distinctive identities.

NOTES

1. 'Family of Associations', referring to the family of organizations of Hindu nationalists, started by members of the Rashtriya Swayamsevak Sangh (RSS) or inspired by its ideas.

2. 'Sarna' is a generic term for the religions of the tribes in some parts of central India and comes from their places of worship, which is also known as 'Sarna'. Hence, the tribes adhering to the traditional faith are also called as the Sarna or Sarna people.

3. See 'Kartik Oraon v. David Munzni & Others', AIR 1964, Patna 201 V. 51, C. 54.

4. Ibid.

5. Ibid.

6. Swami Laxmanananda Saraswati (84-years-old) along with five other people was shot dead in his Jalaspeta Ashram near Tumudibandha (Kandhamal district, Orissa) on Saturday, 23 August 2008. Naxalite groups, especially prominent in this region, had taken credit for the attacks.

7. See 'Kartik Oraon v. David Munzni & Others', p. 201; see also Galanter (1984: 293).

8. See 'Kartik Oraon v. David Munzni & Others', p. 201.

9. Ibid.

10. Ibid.

11. Ibid.

12. Tana Bhagats are a Hinduized sect of the Oraon community who are purely vegetarian and who do not drink liquor.

13. Normally, we understand 'religious organization' as one of the aspects of culture. Just by changing only one aspect of culture one cannot be said to have changed his or her entire gamut of culture holistically. Hence, it is problematic, in my opinion, to equate religion and culture on the same par in an engagement on identity. Religious identity of one may be changed without entirely changing one's cultural identity.

14. Mr Oraon had earlier argued for the de-scheduling of the Christian tribals on the basis of the 'loss' of their culture in terms of belief, customs, and affinity of interests with the tribals.

REFERENCES

'Deuteronomy', *The Good News Bible*, Chapter 12, pp. 1–3.

Constituent Assembly Debates (CAD). 1989, *Official Report*, vols 1, 2, and 9, New Delhi: Lok Sabha Secretariat (2nd reprint).

De Sa, Fidelis. 1975, *Crisis in Chotanagpur*, Bangalore: A Redemptorist Publication.

Desai, A.R. 1960, 'Tribes in Transition', *Seminar*, 14: 19–24.

Dutt, Balbir. 2001, 'Kartik Uraon ka Toofan, Jo Tal Gaya' (in Hindi), *Prabhat Khabar*, 2 July, p. 8.

Galanter, Marc. 1984, *Competing Equalities*, New Delhi: Oxford University Press.

Gupta, Dipanker. 1997, *The Context of Ethnicity*, New Delhi: Oxford University Press.

Kerketta, S. 2001, 'Chaibasa "Kuchh Sawal Eise Bhi Hain"' (in Hindi), *Ranchi Express*, 28 March, p. 9.

Kim, Sebastian C.H. 2003, *In Search of Identity*, New Delhi: Oxford University Press.

Lakra, John. 1998, 'Tribal Spirituality', *Sevartham*, 23: 3–20.

Mahato, S. 1971, *Hundred Years of Christian Missions in Chotanagpur since 1845*, Ranchi: The Chotanagpur Christian Publishing House.

Munzni, David. 1968, 'David Munzni's letter (about Kartik Oraon case) from 126, South Avenue, New Delhi–11', 12 March, addressed to Dr Philip Ekka, St Xavier's College, Ranchi.

—————. 1970, 'Long Live Tribal Unity: A Rejoinder to "Task before Tribal India" by Sri Kartik Oraon, M.P", 13 February, Ranchi.

Oommen, T.K. 2000, 'Christians Are More Indigenous than Upper-caste Hindus', in an interview by Parshuram Ray, an environmental activist for *Humanscape* (online magazine with no print edition), December.

Oraon, Vandna. 2001, 'Adivasi aur Isai Men Antar' (in Hindi), *Ranchi Daily*, date not available.

Parkin, Robert. 2000, 'Proving "Indigeneity", Exploiting Modernity: Modalities of Identity Construction in Middle India', *Anthropos*, 95(1): 49–63.

Pati, Biswamoy. 2003, *Identity, Hegemony, Resistance: Towards a Social History of Covnersions in Orissa, 1800–2000*, New Delhi: Three Essays Collective.

Ranchi Express. 2001, 'Jangan-na Men Sarna (Hindu) Likhayen: Sudarshan', 20 February, pp. 11–12.

Rivers, W.H.R. 1961. *Encyclopaedia Britannica*, Vol. 22, New York: Encyclopaedia Britannica.

Robinson, Rowena. 2003, 'Modes of Conversion to Islam', in R. Robinson and S. Clarke (eds), *Religious Conversions in India: Modes, Motivations and Meanings*, New Delhi: Oxford University Press, pp. 23–8.

Roy, Sarat Chandra. 1915, *The Oraons of Chota Nagpur*, Ranchi: Man in India Office.

Sahay, K.N. 1986, 'Christianity, and Tension and Conflict among the Tribals of Chotanagpur', in *Christianity and Culture Change in India*, New Delhi: Inter-India Publications, pp. 203–26.

Sinha, Suranjan. 1993, 'Construction of Identity', *Seminar*, 412: 39–42.

Tartakov, Gary. 2003, 'B.R. Ambedkar and the Navayana Diksha', in R. Robinson and S. Clarke (eds), *Religious Conversions in India: Modes, Motivations and Meanings*, New Delhi: Oxford University Press, pp. 192–215.

Verma, R.C. 1990, *Indian Tribes through the Ages*, New Delhi: Publications Division, Ministry of Information and Broadcasting, Government of India.

Viswanathan, Gauri. 1998, *Outside the Fold*, New Delhi: Oxford University Press.

Xaxa, Virginius. 1999a, 'Transformation of Tribes in India: Terms of Discourse', *Economic and Political Weekly*, 34(24): 1519–24.

————. 1999b, 'Tribes as Indigenous People of India', *Economic and Political Weekly*, 34(51): 3589–95.

7

Minorities and the Politics of Conversion

With Special Attention to Indian Christianity

Chad M. Bauman and *Richard F. Young*

For a 'minority', a category which calls for a modicum of homogeneity, India's Christians are very diverse. Antiquity is on their side in the Syro-Malabar Orthodoxy of the South (Bayly 1989), but so is Pentecostal dynamism, nationwide, even though only one region, the Northeast Highlands, can boast of being predominantly 'Christian', demographically. Ethnographically, being 'Christian' in India resists all attempts at simplistic reductionism. Still, the *Indianness* of Indian Christianity is constantly debated and *foreignness* remains its most durable public (mis)perception. Overshadowing everything are analytically unhelpful assumptions about 'conversion' that contribute to a reification of religious identity and to a lingering taint of betrayal, religiously and politically. We first explore how this has happened, diachronically. Following that, we problematize the nexus of factors that are commonly invoked to account for conversion. As a case study, we look at the 2007 and 2008 violence against Christians in Orissa. Finally, we reflect on a characteristically Indian form of grassroots religiosity, its unbounded openness to the 'sacred', nowadays much imperiled by the *politics* of religion and the *religion* of politics. First, though, a much-needed clarification of the word 'conversion' and of why we place it within inverted commas.

English has a large lexicon of technical terms that scholars of religion use, for which cognate terms were not readily found in the languages of India until interaction with Europe made their invention necessary. 'Religion' (in a generic sense, if such a thing exists) is one such word; 'conversion' is another. Still, there was no dearth of conversion-like phenomena before Europe overran India. From antiquity, one recalls those whom we nowadays denominate 'Hindu', who took refuge in the Triple Gem (Buddha, Dharma, Sangha). While the next great wave of conversions did not occur for roughly another 1,500 years, when masses of the population recited the Islamic shahada and publically identified themselves as Muslim (Eaton 2003; Robinson 2003), we should not forget that intra-'Hindu' conversion (one *sampradaya* to another) was a common occurrence, inflamed by sectarian rivalry (Vaishnava versus Shaiva, for example, on which, see Gonda 1970; also see, Hardiman 2003).

Clearly then, conversion has to be understood as pluriform and multidirectional (to *or* from any of India's many religions and sub-religions). One does not need to wait for colonial-era, mission-initiated Christianity to find conversion for the first time. Phenomenologically, it makes little difference whether missionaries are Buddhist, Muslim, or Christian (or even modern-day Hindu evangelists, *dharmadhutas*); they are, irrespectively, intractable visionaries who envision for others identities grounded in religious understandings of the world and of the self that are distinct from those of a convert's natal community (Burridge 1991; Young 2002). Of course, perspectives will differ, sometimes with serious social consequences, on whether conversion entails loss or gain, and that, from the vantage point of the community abandoned, 'apostasy' might be a more appropriate word than 'conversion' for the kind of change that has occurred.

Conversions are rarely imposed on hapless victims 'from above' by prelates overseas whose instructions missionaries unfailingly execute on the ground. Were it so, converts would have no agency of their own, nor would they act in their own best interests (however understood or misunderstood); they would only be acted upon, manipulatively, in (ostensibly) the worst interests of alien 'outsiders'. That, in fact, is the position of Hindutva ideologues and activists who agitate for 'protective' interventionism, and we know that such assumptions are false; historiographically, research from the 'bottom-up' demonstrates that converts need to be seen in a different light, as having an agency of their own, although agency is never unconstrained or unencumbered (for example, Dube 2010; Giddens 1984; Ortner 2006).

At a minimum, analytically, conversion must involve a rupture of *affiliation*—not of *continuity* (Zehner 2005: 588), since a total cultural break would be unimaginable—and a shift of commitment from one religious community to another, though not always at once; whether conversion also entails, over time, the wholesale reconfiguration of belief-oriented identity (of an individual or a community) is more debatable. Conversion comes in all gradations, is often prompted by a quest initiated by a crisis, and is usually preceded by a phase of try-it-out partial adhesion of variable duration. 'Conversion,' as sociologist Robert Hefner (1993: 110) argues, 'is rarely the outcome of intellectual appeal alone'. Almost always, the needs of the heart trump those of the mind. Ordinarily, these are simply the fiercely urgent, primordial needs of health and well-being, material and spiritual (Bauman 2008a: 71–100). And yet, as Young (1981) learned in a study of Maratha Brahmin convert, Nehemiah Goreh, who became a noted Anglican theologian, some individuals are extraordinarily capable of stepping back from their pre-conversion beliefs and initiating cognitive adjustments before they convert, formally and publically. The convert has never lived, however, who figures everything out ahead of time, intellectually; generally, people grow into a faith over a lifetime (naturally, some never do, and converts, as the saying goes, may backslide).

Colonial-era Christian missionaries (or, for that matter, the missionaries of other religions) are never sufficient as a cause (much less, *the* cause) of conversion; at best, they are a helpful although unnecessary presence. By and large, the most interesting action, on the ground, involves converts themselves, or those who, more properly, are engaged in the process of converting (conversion, as such, is never finally over in any aoristic sense). Still, situations occurred in which movements of conversion might not have been sustained without missionary advocacy 'from above' when yesterday's counterparts of Hindutva felt that their dominance was threatened 'from below'. Well-documented cases can be adduced, involving Anglican missionaries (Church Missionary Society or CMS) agitating for justice on behalf of their Nadar converts in Tirunelveli during the 1840s (Young and Jebanesan 1995: 81–100).

Again, historiographically, a stereoscopic approach works best. Conversion as a 'bottom-up' phenomenon looks very much as if a convert's own initiative (or that of a convert community's) is the thing that matters most; from a 'top-down' perspective, their agency may appear more constrained and encumbered, until empowered by outsiders who in past eras, may have included mission-friendly British civil servants of the Raj and not only missionary 'outsiders'. Colonial legacies die hard, and one of the most resilient is surely that of the *foreignness* of Indian Christianity, seen from the 'top-down'. This is the prevalent impression, despite the *Indianness* of Indian Christianity, even that of mission-initiated Christianity, when looked at from the 'bottom-up'.

How it came about that being Christian was so widely perceived as being un-Indian is a question that we cannot adequately consider on this occasion. Chandra Mallampalli's (2009) research locates the origins of Christianity's public marginalization (or, one might say, its transformation into a 'minority') in actions of a quintessentially 'imperial' kind. A typical instance would be the 1860s ruling of the High Court of Madras Presidency in the case of *Abraham v. Abraham*. After years of wrangling, the judges upheld the inheritance rights of an Anglo-Indian widow to the estate of her deceased husband, an anglicized Telugu Catholic. Their ruling (and others like it) had the effect of delegitimizing and displacing the *dharmashastra*s as a corpus of legal texts relevant to the affairs of Indian Christians. Her brothers-in-law, also Catholics, had claimed that, as a widow, she had had no inheritance rights at all according to the *Mitakshara* (wherein a widow has a right to maintenance but not to property). 'The story that emerged,' Mallampalli observes, 'is that of the Raj de-Indianizing an Indianized Catholicism' (2009: 145).

MAKING INDIA'S CHRISTIANS THE 'OTHERS' WITHIN

The emergence of Indian Christianity as an increasingly distinct political bloc contributed to the impression, already well-established in some circles, that the unity of the Independence movement was under siege, and that 'foreign' religious loyalties were part of the problem. And then, in the 1920s and the 1930s, the mass movements of conversion to Christianity (Pickett *et al.* 1956) raised the spectre of Hindu extinction.

Related at least in part to these developments, a number of prominent Indian thinkers began to explore the grounds of Indian unity or 'Indianness'. Some, like Savarkar (1989 [1923]), posited a common cultural essence. Savarkar suggested that what held Indians together (or what *should* hold them together) was Hindutva ('Hinduness'). As he articulated it, Hindutva was not merely a religious identification, but many understood it that way, and the term certainly had the effect of suggesting that Hinduism was at least *part* of what it meant to be

Indian. Golwalkar, the influential head of the Rashtriya Svayamsevak Sangh (RSS), went a step farther in his book of 1939, *We or Our Nation Defined*, suggesting that minorities should be asked to pledge their allegiance to certain symbolic elements of Hindu identity (Jaffrelot 2007: 15, 97).

The views of Savarkar, Golwalkar, and others constituted an alternative to the more inclusive nationalism of Gandhi. But even Gandhi worried about the unity of the Independence movement. Knowing that swaraj (self-rule) would require a unified effort, he tried fiercely to hold together India's diverse communities. He was particularly determined to counteract centrifugal forces within the Hindu community. He protested with a fast unto death the proposed British Communal Award, providing for separate electorates for many of India's religious communities, including the Hindu 'depressed classes' (Coward 2003). Gandhi also began to oppose the work of Christian missionaries, who he feared were luring the Harijans away from the Hindu community (Frykenberg 2003: 7–8; also, Harper 2000: 292–345). Other groups opposed conversion more directly. During the same period, the Arya Samaj was conducting *shuddhi* (purification) ceremonies to restore converts to Christianity and Islam to the Hindu fold (Llewellyn 1993: 99–103).

During constituent assembly discussions (1946–50), leaders of more conservative Hindu groups proposed a constitutional ban on conversion. The proposal was rejected, but the concerns which lay behind it remained salient in the immediate postcolonial period, the psycho-social byproduct, perhaps, of long-term colonization (Jones 1981: 448). Many Hindus feared that Hinduism, which they conceived of as a non-missionary religion, would be overrun by the aggressive proselytizing of Christians and Muslims. Such a prospect was particularly unsettling given prevalent anxieties about the survival of the Indian nation in the face of internal and external threats and the widespread belief that Christians and Muslims, with their alleged ties to foreign states, might prove unpatriotic and disloyal in a time of true crisis (Bauman 2008b: 194–6). To those apprehensive about such things, the decision of India's constitutional framers to guarantee all Indians the freedom of 'profession, practice and propagation of religion' appeared to be a monumental folly.

These postcolonial concerns were clearly brought out in the 1956 Christian Missionary Activities Inquiry Committee Report, or the 'Niyogi Report'. The Report was commissioned by the Madhya Pradesh government in response to allegations that Christian evangelists were luring lower-caste Hindus and adivasis to Christianity in large numbers with jobs, education, medical care, and even cash bribes. Though the Report was even-handed at points, it suggested that Dalits and adivasis were becoming Christian in large numbers, that the Hindu community was declining in the region, and that the aim of Christian evangelistic work was not just religious but also political, namely, the establishment of a Christian-dominated state within India, or an independent nation for Christians (Kim 2003: 60–73).

Christians denied these claims and accused the report of bias, with some justification. For example, there was only one Christian on the committee, an individual who was, moreover, not known for being particularly pious. The questionnaire contained blatant insinuation and asked a number of leading questions. Nevertheless, the report's allegations and recommendations were influential in the formation of state laws limiting conversion in, for example, Orissa (1967), Madhya Pradesh (1968), and Arunachal Pradesh (1978). These laws generally borrow the language of the Report and prohibit conversion by 'force', 'fraud', 'inducement', or 'allurement' (Bauman 2008b: 192). Such words render the laws, at times, ineffective and meaningless, and at other times, open to manipulation by those who would act on their grievances against local Christians by having them booked on farcical charges of 'forcible conversion'.

Since the 1950s, the Report has become a touchstone of public debates on conversion in India. In particular, for BJP politicians and others, it remains accurate and relevant despite fifty intervening years, greater missionary sensitivity (generally speaking) to the potential pitfalls of certain evangelistic methods, and a seismic demographic shift in missionary personnel (from Westerners to Indians) (see Shourie 2007 [1994]). The Report's language of 'forcible conversion' or conversion by 'force', 'fraud', 'allurement', or 'inducement' has become a kind of shorthand for what critics of conversion in India believe (or proclaim) Christians to be up to, as well as a justification for acts of violence against them. What opponents of Christianity mean when they speak of 'forcible conversion' is conversion by material allurement, whether explicit or implicit. Of course, many sensitive and liberal-minded Christians themselves have struggled with and sometimes spoken out against what they perceived as illegitimate forms of conversion (Kim 2003: 88–131). We will analyse this issue next, but the audacity and cultural power of the Hindu Right is worth noting here, as it attempts, and in some ways succeeds, in rhetorically transposing what is an ethically ambiguous issue (namely, allurement) into the implied key of an ethical absolute (that is, the reprehensible and inexcusable use of physical force).

'ALLUREMENT' AND ITS ETHICAL AMBIGUITIES

Certainly, there is little ethical ambiguity in the act of offering explicit incentives (cash, jobs, legal help, and so on) to potential converts. Today, nearly all Christians and Hindus in India would be willing to condemn this kind of inducement. But the ethics get murkier when one considers more indirect kinds of allurement. Is it allurement, for example, if Christian educational facilities guarantee admittance or offer reduced tuition rates to Christians, as they still sometimes do? Is it allurement if Christian medical facilities do the same? Is it allurement if Christian doctors pray over their patients before treating them and thereby suggest that their healing power derives from Jesus, the 'Divine Physician', rather than from scientific medical practices? Is it allurement if churches educate their congregants about hygiene and this then leads to better health and fertility rates among Christians (see Bauman 2008a: 133–65)? Is it allurement if Christian agriculturalists form religiously exclusive cooperatives and thereby outperform and out-compete their non-Christian neighbours (see Aaron 2007: 16)?

Further, if conversion results from a complex mix of material and 'ideal' interests, then the issue of allurement gets even more complicated. If a Dalit Hindu woman converts to Christianity because, in her oppressed condition, she derives inspiration from Christian visions of a loving and egalitarian community, can Christians—who have never perfectly realized this vision in India or elsewhere—be accused of rhetorical allurement, of inducement by utopian propaganda? Is the vision of a world where all are treated equally itself a kind of inducement in a Hindu context where many (but not all, it should be emphasized) still believe social stratification to be the result of just and unalterable *karmic* processes (Clarke 1998, 2003)?

The rhetoric of conversion by 'force, fraud, and inducement' also assumes that there are no material reasons why a person would want to remain or become a *Hindu*. But there are, in fact, 'inducements' to Hindu affiliation as well, though they are perhaps less obvious. The power of tradition and the expectations of family loyalty are substantial and a Hindu who might wish to convert and thereby rebel against family cannot generally do so without serious social repercussions, sometimes tantamount to 'social death'. Moreover, Hindus remain the numerical and political majority, and association with hegemony naturally has its benefits. Additionally, there is the Indian 'reservation' system, which sets aside seats in educational, political, and civil service institutions for Dalits, adivasis (tribal peoples), and Other Backward Classes (OBCs). Dalits who convert to Christianity cease, in the eyes of the law, to be Dalits, and thereby lose access to reservations. Mukul Kesavan argues, with some justification, that this constitutes an inappropriate inducement for Dalits to remain Hindu (Kesavan 2001: 70–2; also, Kumar and Robinson 2010: 3; Mosse 2010).

Therefore, Indian Christians often argue that the Niyogi Report's allegations were exaggerated even in the 1950s, and are offensively out of date when applied to Indian Christianity in the present. Such Christians point out that mainstream Indian Christian groups such as the Roman Catholic Church (RCC), the Church of North India (CNI), and the Church of South India (CSI) openly reject any use of force or explicit allurement in their evangelistic efforts. They might also point out that these same groups hardly involve themselves in any proactive proselytizing activities at all, preferring instead to minister to those already Christian and convert only those non-Christians who initiate a relationship with the church. At the same time, many of these same Christians would defend their right to convert those who find Christianity attractive, without government intervention or regulation.

Additionally, a new and rapidly growing class of independent Christians, many of them with vaguely Pentecostal or conservative Evangelical roots, have returned to more aggressive forms of evangelizing, undermining the efforts of mainstream Indian Christians to present Christianity as a non-threatening, irenic, and tolerant *Indian* religion which, in principle, provides relief and development assistance to *all* citizens, regardless of religious affiliation. This 'new breed' of missionaries puts 'an emphasis on speed' and evangelism (over social service) and is 'returning to practices of proselytizing that were long ago abandoned by the mainline missionaries because they were seen as offensive' (Baldauf 2008). In certain cases, this new breed of pastors and evangelists is absolutely independent, accountable to no one but themselves. In other cases, they are at least loosely affiliated with para-church organizations, often with foreign funding and roots.

Such groups have outspoken critics, who object to the substantial amounts of money they pour into India from foreign sources; the critics insist that impoverished Indians will surely convert, or even take jobs as professional missionaries, in order to gain access to that cash

(Malhotra 2011). Even many Christians in India worry that funding from abroad creates among Christians in the developing world, an unhealthy syndrome of helplessness. A high-profile organization typical of its kind is the Gospel for Asia (GFA), which rejects this criticism, and along with it the conventional wisdom of most mainline mission organizations since midway through the twentieth century. The GFA asserts that 'It is not outside money that weakens a growing church, but outside control. Funds from the West actually liberate the evangelists and frees [*sic*] them to follow the call of God' (GFA 2009).

Of equal concern to Hindu nationalist groups in India is the fact that organizations like GFA unabashedly privilege evangelism over social service. According to GFA's website: 'One lie the devil uses to hinder Gospel work and send people to hell is, How can we preach the Gospel to a man with an empty stomach? Because of this lie, for a hundred years much missions-designated funding has been invested in social work rather than in spreading the Word' (GFA 2009).

Clearly, GFA would not provide its own wide range of social services for reasons of compassion alone, but also as a strategy to spread the Christian gospel. Critics of such practices would argue that this consti-tutes an improper use of foreign funding, since it forces underprivileged Indians, who might have no other alternative than GFA services for access to education or clean water, to submit (or feign acquiescence) to evangelistic overtures so as not to forfeit their opportunities (Malhotra 2011: 349–53). And there is a long history, from Gandhi forward, of Indian critics of Christian evangelism suggesting that the ulterior motive of conversion undermines the value of the social services provided.

WHY THE VIOLENCE AGAINST CHRISTIANS IN ORISSA?

Given the more critical and controversial practices of independent evangelists and those associated with para-church groups like GFA, it is perhaps unsurprising that they bear the brunt of everyday violence against Christians in India. In 2007, Bauman collected information on 223 incidents of violence against Christians reported by media outlets in India and abroad. Of these, twelve (or 5 per cent) targeted GFA workers, despite the fact that there are fewer GFA workers in India than workers associated with the RCC, CNI, or CSI. Only the RCC (twelve inci-dents) was targeted as regularly as GFA. Most mainline groups escaped almost unscathed. For example, the CNI and CSI were involved in only one incident each, and the historic Mar Thoma churches were targeted in a total of two incidents. With few exceptions, nearly all of the remaining 195 incidents involved independent missions, churches, or pastors. While mainstream Christian groups might interpret these data as an affirmation of their indigenization and awareness of Indian cultural sensibilities, groups like GFA might suggest that the lack of violence against mainstream Christian workers is a measure of their evangelistic apathy.

If those involved in isolated, localized acts of violence against Christians display a certain selectivity in their targeting, venting their displeasure most frequently on assertively evangelistic Christians, those involved in more generalized anti-Christian violence, such as that in the context of the sustained and widespread violence against Christians in Orissa, or later in Karnataka, do not demonstrate the same degree of precision. In fact, where generalized anti-Christian violence occurs, it is directed as much at *property* as against *people*. In such cases, the older, established denominations with a more impressive and recognizable institutional presence are targeted as much if not more than others. The mob violence is often committed by non-locals who, because of a lack of knowledge about demographics on the ground, must attack obvious targets. Further, in the midst of generalized violence, specific grievances give way to global concerns, a process particularly visible in the anti-Christian violence in Kandhamal district, Orissa, starting with four days of anti-Christian violence in December 2007 and continuing with another string of attacks in 2008, which began in August and lasted much longer. Nearly a hundred people were killed, hundreds (maybe thousands) of homes were destroyed, dozens of Christian institutions were burnt, torn down, or desecrated, and around five thousand people, mostly Christians, ended up in refugee camps. (There were reprisal attacks carried out by Christians, particularly in the first round of violence, and a significant proportion of the homes destroyed belonged to Hindus.)

The Orissa violence drew force from long-standing tensions between the Hinduized adivasi Kandhas, and the largely Christian Dalit Panas. Both groups speak Kui, but in the eyes of government, the Kandhas are a Scheduled Tribe (ST) and the Panas a Scheduled Caste (SC). The ST converts to Christianity retain their claim to reservations, but SC converts do not. For this reason, the SC Panas had been making an effort, through legal petition, to be reclassified as Kui adivasis, that is, as an ST community. Still, the Christianized Panas had become, over the years, visibly wealthier than the Kandhas. And the Kandhas, who resented the Panas for that extra wealth, and for what they felt was an historical pattern of Pana exploitation of Kandhas, saw the Pana legal petition as nothing more than a coldly calculating power play. Accordingly, a pro-Kandha social organization, the Kandha Kui Samaj Coordination Committee (KSCC), announced a *bandh* (strike) to protest, on the 24 and 25 of December, 2007, the decision of the Panas (*The Hindu* 22 September 2007). The bandh corresponded with the Christmas holiday, and coincided with anniversary celebrations organized by the party in power, the Biju Janata Dal. These celebrations siphoned off the Kandhamal police, who were needed in the capital, Bhubhaneshwar. This fact, and the large numbers of trees felled across important traffic arteries by the KSCC as part of its bandh, prevented an effective police response to the violence when it erupted on Christmas eve in the village of Brahmanigaon in Kandhamal district.

The immediate provocation was a dispute over Christmas preparations and decorations. Christians had built and decorated a pandal (a tent) near the largest church in town, and had pressured local authorities to keep the Brahmanigaon market open on the 24th (despite the KSCC bandh), in order to purchase items necessary for the holiday celebrations. Some local Hindus objected to the pandal, though in previous years they had not minded, as well as to Christians ignoring the bandh. A scuffle ensued and one Christian was shot and wounded; violence soon spread to other villages, along with news of the original altercation.

Two interrelated factors contributed to the transformation of this stereotypical village imbroglio into one that was broader and more toxically communal. The first was the involvement of Swami Laxmanananda Saraswati, a well-known and locally popular octogenarian anti-conversion activist with ties to the RSS and Vishva Hindu Parishad (VHP). Soon after the initial scuffle described above, the Swami's automobile, which was on its way to Brahmanigaon when it got stuck in traffic, was allegedly attacked by a group of Christians. The Swami claimed innocence, saying that he had been seriously wounded in the attack. Christians dispute the details of his version of the story, and contend that his bodyguards were the aggressors. Whether his arrival in Brahmanigaon on that day had anything to do with the earlier Brahmanigaon violence cannot be determined. But as news of the attack on the Swami spread, it displaced the initial scuffle in Brahmanigaon as explanation and justification for vengeful Hindu attacks on Christians.

The second issue was the early and significant involvement of other local, regional, and national Sangh Parivar leaders. These leaders exaggerated the viciousness of the attack on the Swami's entourage, even claiming at one point that the Swami himself had been killed (VHP 2008). They also linked the attack to an alleged larger (Western) Christian conspiracy to conquer India through conversion. Some Sangh Parivar groups, in fact, alleged that in the ensuing violence no Christians had been attacked, and that the Christians were burning their own homes and churches in order to provoke an outpouring of foreign Christian aid (VHP 2008). At the same time, Sangh sources that acknowledged attacks on Christians portrayed them as a 'natural' response to years of offensive missionizing efforts by local Christians (Tripathy 2008).

Sangh Parivar rhetoric, therefore, effectively linked this local conflict to larger, Hindu concerns about 'forcible conversions', the survival of Hinduism, and the integrity of the Indian nation, thereby contributing to the transformation of local tensions into a broader Hindu–Christian conflict. Tambiah (1997: 81) has called this process 'transvaluation', and sees it commonly at work in ethno-religious conflict throughout South Asia. Likewise, Paul Brass (1997: 16) has described a class of 'conversion specialists' who, in the context of communal violence, 'convert' local conflagrations, through insinuation, rumour mongering, and rhetorical exaggeration, into countrywide, inter-religious conflicts.

Clearly, Sangh leaders appear to have played this role prominently in the violence against Christians in Orissa, as they have done elsewhere. But it should also be noted that the Christians' alleged attack on the Swami made it easier for them to do so, since he himself was a potent symbol of Hindu resistance to the alleged neocolonial aims of putatively 'foreign' proselytizers. The Swami's symbolic potency fuelled the second round of violence as well. Eight months after the Christmas violence, in August 2008, as the last of the refugees returned to their homes, he was gunned down in his ashram while celebrating Krishna's birthday. Naxalites immediately claimed responsibility, but the motive for the murder seemed obviously to serve Christian interests, and so it was easy for Sangh leaders once again to 'convert' the assassination into a call to arms in defence of Hinduism. As this volume went to press, the case remained unsolved, though a number of alleged Naxalites, some of them Christian, have been arrested (for additional discussion, see Bauman 2010).

RELIGIOUS IDENTITY: FLUID OR FROZEN?

As indicated, violence against Christians in India is often justified as a response to the putatively subversive conversion activities of missionaries.

Such a justification requires that the parties involved in perpetrating the violence define themselves first and foremost along religious lines, so that each conversion to Christianity can be construed as a defeat in the inter-religious numbers game, and made into a provocation.

This dynamic confirms Amartya Sen's (2006: 2–4) contention that conflict between different communities is often premised on the 'illusion' of fixed and singular identities (see also Kaviraj 1991: 73–8; Pandey 1990). Sen goes on to argue that there is always at least a modicum of *choice* involved in how individuals and communities define and identify themselves (Sen 2006: xiii, 4). As we noted at the outset, choice is never unlimited. An ethnic or linguistic identity to which one has no real claim cannot become one's own merely by fiat. Choice comes into play, according to Sen, in the relative weight that one gives to the various elements of one's identity (Sen 2006: 5, 34). From that angle, no particular reason can be adduced for why it is that communities in conflict with each other *necessarily have to privilege* their religious elements over other elements of their identities, ones that might highlight their commonalities instead (nationality, regional identity, ethnicity, language, class, and so on).

Excepting religion, the Hindu Kandhas and Christian Panas who clashed in Orissa had quite a bit in common; potentially, they could have maximized these commonalities had they not succumbed, through internal and external pressure, to the singularization of their identities (that is, to the privileging of their religious identities). Hindu–Christian violence is also premised on the assumption that 'Hindu' and 'Christian' are reified, mutually exclusive categories. Even scholars who criticize such violence, often uncritically labour under this misapprehension, and therefore view conversion as a movement *from* one hermetically sealed religious worldview, practice, and community *to* another. Converts sometimes perceive things this same way, understanding themselves to be moving from one faith to another in a linear trajectory.

Religious identities, however, are not always so clearly delineated. Discussions of conversion become more complicated—and more interesting—when one keeps this fact in mind. There is, for example, a cross-cultural process of metabolization, which ensures that one cannot speak of a singular template for 'Christianity' and another for 'Hinduism'; rather, one must speak of multiple, localized versions of each. Moreover, scholarship on cross-cultural appropriation confirms that any religion in any context is likely to assimilate, or to have assimilated, elements of the cultures and religions which predate its arrival.

Certain indigenizations are arguably more superficial and mimetic, such as those borrowed from local religious dress, custom, or gesture. For example, like virtually everyone else, in many churches, Indian Christians usually remove their shoes before entering; other churches segregate the sexes during worship; and still others employ elaborate processional vehicles to publically display images of the divine (Waghorne 2002). Phenomenologically, such organic indigenizations as these, which result from the natural and often unconscious interaction of religious worldviews, cultural mores, and social assumptions, localize all religions in thorough, unpredictable, and uncontrollable ways (Bauman 2008a: Chapters 4 and 5). Besides the cross-cultural appropriation process, which to some degree blurs the boundaries between religious traditions, there are a variety of cases where Hindus and Christians consciously and premeditatedly transgress their assumed religious boundaries. Such transgressions are most easily seen at the level of religious *practice* (Raj and Dempsey 2002: xvii; see also Mosse 2006; Ram 1992).

There are a number of reasons why the assumed lines between Christianity and Hinduism are crossed over. For one, at ground level, these lines are not always very clear. As a Hindu, one might perform one's devotions (through prayer, for instance, or votive offerings) at a church or shrine where Christians venerate the Virgin Mary or a Catholic saint, or one might perform them at a temple enshrining a local god or goddess; shared notions of sacred power and its unbounded accessibility make it possible to cross from one to the other without a troublesome sense of 'cognitive dissonance'. That means that for many Indians (Hindu, Christian, or otherwise), religion is less about maintaining loyalty to a particular dogmatic tradition than it is about instrumental efficacy, for the sake of health, prosperity, and well-being (cf. Bauman 2008a: 135, 144; see also Bayly 1989: 414–19; Caplan 1985; Mosse 2006). Therefore, if a Hindu village woman's child is ill, and she hears that prayers given at the shrine of a local Christian saint have curative value, she might not hesitate to visit and pray at that shrine. (Fertility concerns are also a common reason for ritual boundary crossing; cf. Raj 2002: 98). Likewise, and for similar reasons, Christians may visit shrines of Hindu saints, or participate in Hindu rituals; one finds, however, more resistance to such ritual transgression from Christian clergy than from Hindu ritualists and gurus.

Similarly, converts to Christianity tend to be unwilling or unable (because of tradition, religious anxieties, or social pressure) to abandon all their former practices, and therefore maintain at least some of them (usually surreptitiously). This happens even as they participate in the life of their new religious community; it means, in effect, that the church has to be recognized for what it is, an in-between kind of space where individuals and communities try out their new identities, as it were. At the same time, there are Hindus for whom the life and teachings of Jesus are appealing, and who may quietly nurture devotion to Jesus Christ, but may not be willing or able to abandon the immemorial Hindu practices of kin and clan. In such cases, which Raj (2002: 43) termed 'multiritualism', we see a blending of religious practices and a blurring of religious distinctions.

Yet another major reason is the monolatry so distinctive of Hindu worship practices; this allows for devotion to a particular Hindu god or goddess (or to one divine family), but does not necessitate rejection or denial of other divinities, even those that are extra-Hindu. Few Hindus would ever refuse to participate in the religious celebrations and festivals of their neighbours, if invited to join; moreover, to take part in them with a certain degree of genuine religious devotion would seem natural. While fewer Christians might reciprocate, enough have been significantly influenced by inclusivistic Hindu notions of the sacred that boundary crossing is not infrequently bidirectional during festivals and ceremonies. In any case, the greater the spectacle and the more carnivalesque the atmosphere, the higher the likelihood that participants will be drawn in from a plurality of seemingly distinct religious traditions (Meibohm 2002).

Such are the phenomena of everyday religious life; they call into question the rigid, tightly bounded identities (usually Sanskritic and Brahmanic; see Pirbhai 2008) idealized by Hindutva ideologues and activists who assume that conversion is the movement of persons or people from one clearly demarcated religious community to another and who see conversion as threatening their majority position. Still, the practices of everyday religious life that we observe at the popular level where folks of all communities meld together are rarely heeded by zealots of the Sangh Parivar who construe their anger at conversion—the most controversial and controverted boundary crossing of all—as compensatory acts of retaliatory justice (cf. Sail 2003). Yet, at the same time, there are Christians in India (those especially who associate themselves with para-church organizations such as GFA) whose aggressively proselytizing activities may inadvertently lend support to the Sangh Parivar and others who hold conversion in contempt. Worse, such Christians may, in fact, unwittingly perpetuate the illusion of Christianity's foreignness, so very prevalent in Hindutva circles, while also reinforcing the mistaken notion that religious identities are invariably singular and monoform.

No aspiring civil society would want this kind of 'blowback', especially at the most ordinary and natural level at which Christianity and other religions are lived and practiced, among people of all communities who commingle throughout India's villages, towns, and cities. This is especially the case since, as we saw, conflict involving minorities is rarely (if ever) monocausal or exclusively 'religious' in the sense of being a local outbreak of primordial rivalries based on irreducible differences of belief and practice. Rather, our discussion shifts attention from alleged incompatibility in the realm of 'ideals' to the clash of material interests. Many of these (or all) are susceptible, as Paul Brass (1997) observed, to manipulation, invidiously, by outside 'specialists'. And that, we submit, is how tension is often transmuted into tragedy.

REFERENCES

Aaron, Sushil J. 2007, 'Contrarian Lives: Christians and Contemporary Protest in Jharkhand', Asia Research Centre Working Paper No. 18, London School of Economics and Political Science, London.

Baldauf, Scott. 2008, 'A New Breed of Missionary: A Drive for Conversions, Not Development, Is Stirring Violent Animosity in India', *Christian Science Monitor*, 1 April, available at http://www.csmonitor.com/2005/0401/p01s04-wosc.html (accessed 26 June 2008).

Bauman, Chad M. 2008a, *Christian Identity and Dalit Religion in Hindu India, 1868–1947*, Grand Rapids, Michigan: William B. Eerdmans Publishing Co.

——————. 2008b, 'Postcolonial Anxiety and Anti-Conversion Sentiment in the Report of the Christian Missionary Activities Enquiry Committee', *International Journal of Hindu Studies*, 12(2): 181–213.

——————. 2010, 'Identity, Conversion and Violence: Dalits, Adivasis and the 2007–08 Riots in Orissa', in R. Robinson and J.M. Kujur (eds), *Margins of Faith: Dalit and Tribal Christianity in India*, New Delhi and Thousand Oaks, CA: Sage Publications, pp. 263–90.

Bayly, Susan. 1989, *Saints, Goddesses and Kings: Muslims and Christians in South Indian Society, 1700–1900*, Cambridge: Cambridge University Press.

Brass, Paul R. 1997, *Theft of an Idol: Text and Context in the Representation of Collective Violence*, Princeton: Princeton University Press.

Burridge, Kenelm. 1991, *In the Way: A Study of Christian Missionary Endeavors*, Vancouver: University of British Columbia Press.

Caplan, Lionel. 1985, 'The Popular Culture of Evil in South India', in D. Parkin (ed.), *The Anthropology of Evil*, Oxford: Basil Blackwell, pp. 110–27.

Clarke, Sathianathan. 1998, *Dalits and Christianity: Subaltern Religion and Liberation Theology in India*, New Delhi: Oxford University Press.

—————. 2003, 'Conversion to Christianity in Tamil Nadu: Conscious and Constitutive Community Mobilization towards a Different Symbolic World Vision', in R. Robinson and S. Clarke (eds), *Religious Conversion in India: Modes, Motivations, and Meanings*, New Delhi: Oxford University Press, pp. 323–50.

Coward, Harold (ed.). 2003, 'Gandhi, Ambedkar, and Untouchability', in *Indian Critiques of Gandhi*, Albany: State University of New York Press, pp. 41–66.

Dube, Saurabh. 2010, *After Conversion: Cultural Histories of Modern India*, New Delhi: Yoda Press.

Eaton, Richard. 2003, 'Who Are the Bengal Muslims?' in R. Robinson and S. Clarke (eds), *Religious Conversion in India: Modes, Motivations, and Meanings*, New Delhi: Oxford University Press, pp. 75–97.

Frykenberg, Robert E. (ed.). 2003, 'Introduction: Dealing with Contested Definitions and Controversial Perspectives', in *Christians and Missionaries in India: Cross-Cultural Communication since 1500*, Grand Rapids, Michigan: William B. Eerdmans Publishing Co., pp. 1–32.

Giddens, Anthony. 1984, *The Constitution of Society: Outline of the Theory of Structuration*, Berkeley: University of California Press.

Golwalkar, M.S. 1939, *We or Our Nation Defined*, Nagpur: Bharata Prakashan.

Gonda, Jan. 1970, *Visnuism and Sivaism: A Comparison*, London: Athlone Press.

Gospel for Asia (GFA). 2009, 'Frequently Asked Questions', available at http://www.gfa.org/faqs (accessed 1 June 2009).

Hardiman, David. 2003, 'Assertion, Conversion, and Indian Nationalism: Govind's Movement among the Bhils', in R. Robinson and S. Clarke (eds), *Religious Conversion in India: Modes, Motivations, and Meanings*, New Delhi: Oxford University Press, pp. 255–84.

Harper, Susan Billington. 2000, *In the Shadow of the Mahatma: Bishop V.S. Azariah and the Travails of Christianity in British India*, Grand Rapids, Michigan: William B. Eerdmans Publishing Co.

Hefner, Robert W. (ed.). 1993, *Conversion to Christianity: Historical and Anthropological Perspectives on a Great Transformation*, Berkeley and Los Angeles: University of California Press.

The Hindu. 22 September 2007, 'Communal Trouble Brewing Up in Kandhamal Dist.', available at http://www.thehindu.com/2007/09/22/stories/2007092252750300.htm (accessed 26 June 2008).

Jaffrelot, Christophe (ed.). 2007, *Hindu Nationalism: A Reader*, Princeton: Princeton University Press.

Jones, Kenneth W. 1981, 'Politicized Hinduism: The Ideology and Program of the Hindu Mahasabha', in R.D. Baird (ed.), *Religion in Modern India*, New Delhi: Manohar, pp. 447–80.

Kaviraj, Sudipta. 1991, 'On State, Society, and Discourse in India', in J. Manor (ed.), *Rethinking Third World Politics*, London: Longman, pp. 72–99.

Kesavan, Mukul. 2001, *Secular Common Sense*, New Delhi: Penguin.

Kim, Sebastian C.H. 2003, *In Search of Identity: Debates on Religious Conversion in India*, New Delhi: Oxford University Press.

Kumar, Ashok and Rowena Robinson. 2010, 'Legally Hindu: Dalit Lutheran Christians of Coastal Andhra Pradesh', in R. Robinson and J.M. Kujur (eds), *Margins of Faith: Dalit and Tribal Christianity in India*, New Delhi and Thousand Oaks, CA: Sage Publications, pp. 149–68.

Llewellyn, J.E. 1993, *The Arya Samaj as a Fundamentalist Movement: A Study in Comparative Fundamentalism*, New Delhi: Manohar.

Malhotra, Rajiv and Aravindan Neelakandan. 2011, *Breaking India: Western Interventions in Dravidian and Dalit Faultlines*, New Delhi: Amaryllis.

Mallampalli, Chandra. 2009, 'Caste, Catholicism, and History "from below", 1863–1917', in R.F. Young (ed.), *India and the Indianness of Christianity: Essays on Understanding—Historical, Theological, and Bibliographical—in Honor of Robert Eric Frykenberg*, Grand Rapids, Michigan: William B. Eerdmans Publishing Co., pp. 144–57.

Meibohm, Margaret. 2002, 'Past Selves and Present Others: The Ritual Construction of Identity at a Catholic Festival in India', in S.J. Raj and C.G. Dempsey (eds), *Popular Christianity in India: Riting between the Lines*, Albany: State University of New York Press, pp. 61–83.

Mosse, David. 2006, 'Possession and Confession: Affliction and Sacred Power in Colonial and Contemporary South India', in F. Cannell (ed.), *The Anthropology of Christianity*, Durham: Duke University Press, pp. 99–133.

———. 2010, 'The Catholic Church and Dalit Christian Activism in Contemporary Tamil Nadu', in R. Robinson and J.M. Kujur (eds), *Margins of Faith: Dalit and Tribal Christianity in India*, New Delhi and Thousand Oaks, CA: Sage Publications, pp. 235–62.

Ortner, Shirley. 2006, *Anthropology and Social Theory: Culture, Power, and the Acting Subject*, Durham: Duke University Press.

Pandey, Gyanendra. 1990, *The Construction of Communalism in Colonial North India*, New Delhi: Oxford University Press.

Pickett, J.W., A.L. Warnshuis, G.H. Singh, and D.A. McGavran. 1956, *Church Growth and Group Conversion*, Lucknow: Lucknow Publishing House.

Pirbhai, M. Reza. 2008, 'Demons in Hindutva: Writing a Theology for Hindu Nationalism', *Modern Intellectual History*, 5(1): 27–53.

Raj, Selva J. 2002, 'Transgressing Boundaries, Transcending Turner: The Pilgrimage Tradition at the Shrine of St. John De Britto', in S.J. Raj and C.G. Dempsey (eds), *Popular Christianity in India: Riting between the Lines*, Albany: State University of New York Press, pp. 85–111.

Raj, Selva J. and Corinne G. Dempsey. 2002, *Popular Christianity in India: Riting between the Lines*, Albany: State University of New York Press.

Ram, Kalpana. 1992, *Mukkuvar Women: Gender, Hegemony and Capitalist Transformation in a South Indian Fishing Community*, New Delhi: Kali for Women.

Robinson, Rowena. 2003, 'Modes of Conversion to Islam', in R. Robinson and S. Clarke (eds), *Religious Conversion in India: Modes, Motivations, and Meanings*, New Delhi: Oxford University Press, pp. 291–322.

Sail, Rajendra K. 2003, *Conversion in Chhattisgarh: Facts and Myths*, Raipur: Indian Social Action Forum.

Savarkar, V.D. 1989 [1923], *Hindutva: Who Is a Hindu?* New Delhi: Bharatiya Sahitya Sadan.

Sen, Amartya. 2006, *Identity and Violence: The Illusion of Destiny*, New York: W.W. Norton.

Shourie, Arun. 2007 [1994], *Missionaries in India: Continuities, Changes, Dilemmas*, New Delhi: Rupa & Co.

Tambiah, Stanley J. 1997, *Leveling Crowds: Ethnonationalist Conflicts and Collective Violence in South Asia*, Berkeley and Los Angeles: University of California Press.

Tripathy, Rama Prasad. 2008, 'Pseudo-Seculars Deliberately Trying to Shun Facts', *Kamal Sandesh*, 1–15 February, pp. 20–2.

Vishva Hindu Parishad (VHP). 2008, 'Christian Atrocities in Kandhamal, Orissa', Press Release, 14 January.

Waghorne, Joanne Punzo. 2002, 'Chariots of the God/s: Riding the Line between Hindu and Christian', in S.J. Raj and C.G. Dempsey (eds), *Popular Christianity in India: Riting between the Lines*, Albany: State University of New York Press, pp. 11–37.

Young, Richard Fox. 1981, *Resistant Hinduism: Sanskrit Sources on Anti-Christian Apologetics in Early Nineteenth-Century India*, Vienna: Institut für Indologie der Universität Wien.

————. 2002, 'Some Hindu Perspectives on Christian Missionaries in the Indic World of the Mid Nineteenth Century', in J.M. Brown and R.F. Frykenberg (eds), *Christians, Cultural Interactions, and India's Religious Traditions*, Grand Rapids and London: William B. Eerdmans and Routledge Curzon, pp. 37–60.

Young, Richard Fox and S. Jebanesan. 1995, *The Bible Trembled: The Hindu–Christian Controversies of Nineteenth-Century Ceylon*, Vienna: Institut für Indologie der Universität Wien.

Zehner, Edwin. 2005, 'Orthodox Hybridities: Anti-Syncretism and Localization in the Evangelical Christianity of Thailand', *Anthropological Quarterly*, 78(3): 585–617.

8

Parsi Ethics and the Spirit of Indian Modernity

Murzban Jal

PRELUDE: METHODOLOGY AND PHILOSOPHY

A methodological remark is necessary to understand the sociology of minority communities, especially the Parsis, who claim to be both an ethnic and religious community. Studies with regard to this community have been scholarly as well as notorious; scholarly because considerable amount of research has gone in these studies, and notorious because these studies have been determined in the last resort by the discourses of Orientalism. It has been said, usually following Karaka's nineteenth century monumental work, that it is with the advent of the British in India that the Parsis suddenly appeared back into history (Karaka 1999). It was, as if, they were unknown since their history in Iran (that is, till at least 651 AD). Following this logic, the Parsis appear as the colonial elite, or if not *the* colonial elite, then another form of an elite that would be the grave diggers of British colonialism in India.

The notoriety of Parsi studies lies in the absence of good anthropological and historical data, and most importantly, the absence of the understanding of the Asiatic mode of production with Indian historians. Because of the absence of the understanding of the Asiatic mode and the absence of the understanding of Indian village communities, the Asiatic cities, and the nature of the precolonial state in India, not only do we lack the understanding of how a native bourgeoisie was born from non-feudal society, but we also lack the understanding of how the Parsis played the role of both this emerging national bourgeoisie as well as the organic intellectuals of early liberalism in South Asia.

Besides actually existing ethnic communities in South Asia, there is also the role of what Benedict Anderson called 'imagined communities' in the makings of modern imagination of the nation state (Anderson 1991). Because the place of locating 'minority communities' has a history that is located in the last resort in colonial history—especially after the defeat of the Indian revolution in 1857—the role of 'imagined communities' gets more prominence. Thus, one has to note that after 1857, the history of ethnic and religious minorities gets more nuanced. The legacy that the present Indian state has inherited is from the British policy of *community production*—a peculiar type of commodity production—that transforms the fetishism of commodities into the fetishism of manufacturing communities.[1]

Though *the ideology of manufacturing communities* is as ancient as the origin of class societies, 'identity' is a modern term that emerges with the rise of capitalism. 'Parsi identity' (or to be precise, *the politics of Parsi identity*, the politics of inclusion and exclusion) is likewise linked to the rise of capitalism in India and that is inexorably linked to colonialism, especially the colonial law that shaped the 'manufacture' of the Parsi community. Four points have to be noted in this context: first, the question of 'Parsi identity' emerged with the Parsi elites, when R.D. Tata married a French woman, Suzanne Brière, and had her initiated to the Parsi faith and then sought social approval, only to be legally confronted with the conservative Parsi Panchayat, led by the bourgeois baron, Sir Jamsetjee Jeejebhoy, IV Bart.[2] Second, the judges to 'try' this case were the orthodox Parsi, Justice Dinshaw Davar (who infamously sentenced Tilak for sedition), and the theosophist, arch conservative, and supporter of the Hindu caste system, Justice Frank Beaman. Helping the Parsi orthodox in this case was the Parsi solicitor and orator, J.J. Vimadalal (a member of the conservative Ilm-e-Khshnoom sect and advocate of eugenics and race theory). Third, the reference to the myth of the 'pure Persian' that practiced endogamy and the myth of the Parsis not allowing people of other faiths into the Parsi religion was rooted in the discourses of Orientalism and the emerging field of 'Iranian studies' in European and American universities. And fourth, the space that colonial modernity took with the rise of British imperialism was modernity that walked on one foot, the foot of the British Empire. It is keeping these points in mind that we turn our attention to the study of the Parsis as (and as not) a minority.

The Parsis are the smallest religious community in India of Persian descent, comprising barely 0.016 per cent of the Indian population (Writer 1994: 34). They are seen as an 'affluent' community and are known to be agents of social change in modern India, the pioneers of social reform and modern education, the founders of scientific institutions, and one of the architects of India's freedom from British colonialism. The following factors have to be kept in mind in order to understand this ethnic community. First, Parsi identity spans three historical epochs: the Iranian; the Indian (or more specifically, the Gujarati epoch); and the European epoch. What one may define as modern Parsi identity finds its *real roots* in the encounter of these 'Indianized-Persians' with British colonialism and the rise of capitalism in India.

Presently, there are competing versions of Parsi identity that emerged in the middle of the nineteenth century defined by the struggle between the English-educated liberal Parsis and the religious–orthodox Parsis, followed by the intervention of colonial law. Three versions of Parsi identity became dominant since the intervention of colonial law: the patrilineal version (a Parsi man could marry a non-Parsi and his progeny could be Parsis, but not vice versa); the more exclusive eugenic-based racial model (marriage strictly between Parsis), where the orthodox Parsis borrowed their ideology from the ideologies of European imperialism; and the subaltern one that has hitherto defied both the patrilineal as well as the racial–colonial model of classifying ethnic communities in South Asia.

Besides the construction of ethnic identity in the period of late colonialism, it is important to note that classical Persian legacy was mobilized during this same period, wherein the Parsis reinvented themselves as the harbingers of the Protestant ethic in early capitalist India.[3] In this second reinvention, the Parsis claimed to represent individual as well as social responsibility defined by the ancient Persian precepts of the dialectical philosophy of the struggle between good and evil. And lastly, we have the triumph of secular values and the impact of European liberalism and humanism, especially the 'Doctrine of the Rights of Humanity and the Citizen', on the Parsis which propelled them to become both the dominant class and also the dominant ethnic community in India. With the triumph of secularism, the class of anti-colonial organic intellectuals led by Dadabhai Naoroji emerged. One must, however, stress that the most important point is to understand how the Parsis emerged as the dominant class–ethnic community due to the absence of caste in their system, thus allowing them greater social mobility, especially in the period of rising industrial capitalism. In this context of the caste system in India and the relation of the Parsis to it, one could say that Albêrûnî's (2002: 3) statement: '… they [that is, the Indians] totally differ from us in religion, as we believe in nothing in which they believe, and *vice versa*',[4] could well have been said by a Parsi.

Despite the fact that the Parsis are a very small community, the same vicissitudes that are present in larger religious and ethnic communities are similarly present. To a large extent, heterogeneity is veiled and gender and the question of labour are almost totally ignored. Stress is put on their distinct ethnic identity (their 'Persian-ness') whilst forgetting that it was at the initiative of the Parsi elites, helped by colonial law in late nineteenth century and early twentieth century, that a certain type of this 'Persian-ness' emerged. Since the matrix of contradictions defines the history of the Parsis, we shall try to locate the contradictions between diasporic cosmopolitanism and ethnic exclusivity that make up modern Parsi identity.

That the Parsis are a not only a minority, but the smallest religious minority in India is an undeniable fact. Yet, there is a strong contrast in the narrative of the Parsis, namely, that they maintain their distinctiveness and want to be recognized as a ('minority') community only in terms of maintaining their exclusive identity. They do not want 'minority' status for getting privileges from the state (Hinnells 2005: 62–3).[5] That the modern Parsis prefer citizenship to this latter type of 'minority' status that is subservient to state patronage should be kept in mind. The history of this lies in late nineteenth and early twentieth century with the initial triumph of the Western-educated liberal Parsis over the conservatives. The deeper historical materialist logic is the transformation from village community to mercantile and industrial capitalism, the birth of the organic intellectuals in the community, and the ultimate triumph of the idea of multicultural India over sectarianism promoted by the British.

Like most communities in South Asia, the middle of the nineteenth century is the watershed in the making of modern Parsi identity. European liberal education led to the birth of the three important Parsi organic intellectuals who shaped both the makings of the modern Parsi as well as modern liberal Indian: Naoroji, Pherozeshah Mehta, and Dinshaw Wacha.[6] But this period is itself complex where different factions of the Parsis clashed, mainly on the issues of reinterpreting the Parsi faith in relation to modern scientific knowledge and the role of the Parsis in the emerging nationalist movement. The site of the struggle witnessed the struggle between the modernists and secularists on the one hand, and the Parsis gripped with the politics of Parsi identity on the other hand. What we find in the modern Parsis—the community that sees itself as a proud and distinct ethnic community, but seeks no privileges from the state—is found in early twentieth century social and political history.

It is not the case that the Parsis came to the site of cultural modernity without a bitter struggle. Already in the times of Naoroji, Mehta, and Wacha, the conservative section of the Parsis were plagued by the politics of Parsi identity and the fear that independent India would be a Brahmanical India governed by conservative Hindus who would not grant minority rights to the many ethnic and religious minorities. Unlike the political revolutionaries, and like the social reform movement in India, the conservatives chided those struggling for Indian freedom. The Home Rule agitation—Naoroji was its first president—was opposed by the conservative Parsis. What they proposed was a grand alliance of smaller communities, as a balance between the Hindus and the Muslims, a Grand League that would include backward classes and the Sikhs. But both this ideology of the *Grand League of Smaller Minorities* and the politics of separate electorates failed to grip the imagination of the Parsi masses, not to forget the almost Quixotic idea of the autonomous state of Parsistan in the state of Gujarat (Kulke 1978: 199). What came to stay was the modern idea of the Parsi, the Persian who insists on its Parsiness, is not only a national citizen but a world citizen, and yet, does not demand privileges from the state.

At the outset, I would like to state that the communitarian view of understanding ethnic communities is not what I would subscribe to. One motif of this writing of Parsi history is that the Parsis are seen as an exotic community (to be precise, the authentic 'Aryan' community) that is not 'contaminated' either by the Muslim Arabs, nor the Hindus in India. Instead, I will start with Anderson's view of 'imagined communities' based on the cultural politics of the Lacanian triad of the real, imaginary, and the symbolic. It is from this complex moment that one understands how this minority community of Iranian descent moved from the position of exile and marginality to the epicentre of power.

As an exilic community, it is almost inevitable that Benjamin's depiction of exile, messianic historicism, and human emancipation comes up, where one is compelled to forget one's 'hatred and its spirit of sacrifice for both are nourished by the image of the enslaved ancestors rather than that of liberated grandchildren' (Benjamin 1979: 262).

What is remarkable is that the Parsis (like Benjamin's proletariat) have forgotten their apocalyptic past, the collapse of the Persian Empire, and the enslavement of their ancestors. Yet, like Benjamin's (1979: 259–60) angel of history, it is inevitable that the Parsi 'face is turned towards the past' despite being blown forward by the storm of progress. Looking backwards is antithetical for the Parsis for they believe that the European idea of progress is an essential part of their ancient faith. And yet, it is ancient Iran which they continuously refer to, when talking of their community identity. To talk of present Iran would not be so much heresy or a matter of prudence. It would be a matter of radical politics, which the Parsis seem to comfortably abjure. Somehow, Iran (both ancient and modern) would not escape the Parsis.

As we will see, the greatest crisis haunting the Parsis is the crisis of the libidinal economy. If the entire world is gripped by the global economic crisis, the Parsis are faced with the libidinal problem. If bourgeois economics they seem to have mastered, bourgeois libido they seem to have forgotten. To save Parsi identity, it would be then seem that they would have to turn to Iran with the abundance of 'pure' Persians there. If colonial law had created a problem for the Parsis in the beginnings of the nineteenth century in creating a closed identity, they would be creating another one, not so much for the Parsis, but more for the right-wing Islamic state of Iran. Earlier, the Iranian mullahs had banned left-wing politics. Now, they may just have to ban the 'pure' Persians from seeking the resolution to their problem of libidinal economy. Earlier, the Islamists in Iran shouted 'The communists are coming!' Now they may have to shout 'The Parsis are coming!'

SOCIOLOGY OF THE PARSIS

Presently, the largest group of the Parsis resides in India. They also have a well-knit diaspora, with their population scattered in Pakistan, the United Kingdom (UK), the United States (US), Canada, Australia, and New Zealand. Iran (their former homeland) also has a substantial population. Historians claim that the Parsis have preserved their community and religious identity for the last 3,500 years (Boyce 1978; Boyce and Grenet 1991; Humbach 1991; Modi 2004; Zaehner 1961). Currently, in India, they number only 69,000, and there are fears that this community will wither away. This number has been contested and other figures mention 100,000 in India, a number that has remained constant for at least 200 years. Monier–Williams (1914) had mentioned 70,000 Parsis in 1870, whilst quite recently, Hinnells has claimed that the Parsis have declined in numbers at the rate of 10 per cent every ten years. Hinnells (1981: 41) counts 92,000 Parsis in 1971. Since then, in *The Zoroastrian Diaspora* (Hinnells 2005) he has detailed the drastic fall in numbers.

It is often said that the fundamental characteristic of the making of the Parsi is that (like the Brahmin and the orthodox Jew) one has to be born a Parsi (Hinnells 1981: 234). To this orthodox and closed rendering of the Parsi community is a contrasting claim that the Parsi faith has always been an open faith which has had not only the Iranians as their followers but also people of other nationalities. Following the orthodox rendering, the Parsis find themselves in the company of Hindus and Jews, in the sense that the Parsi, Jewish, and Hindu religions have not been able to achieve 'universal' (or proselytizing) status, like Buddhism, Christianity, and Islam.

The Parsis are called by this nomenclature (the 'Parsis') from the place of their original residence—the province of Pars in the central part of Iran. Many a times, the terms Persia and Iran are used interchangeably. This is incorrect; the Persians are just one of the many ethnic Iranian groups. The Parsis are literally both Persian and Iranian. To understand the sociology of the Parsis and to simplify the issues of terminology, I will identify three groups:

1. *The Parsis*: This is the starting concept in the understanding of this ethnic community. They are the group of Persians who migrated to India after the Arab conquest of Iran. It is well known that the date on their coming to India is shrouded in ambiguity. The reference is based on the early seventeenth century text, *Kisse-i-Sanjan* (The Story of Sanjan). Their mother tongue is Gujarati. Sociologists have mentioned Iran as their homeland, or as Hinnells (2005: 709) calls it, *their ultimate homeland*. India is said to be their motherland, or their 'second home' ('Kisse-i-Sanjan' 1920: 101), their place of residence that they promise to nurture and protect. After Partition, around 2,000 Parsis found themselves on the 'other side' of the colonially constructed divide. For them, Pakistan is their motherland. Hinnells (2005) shows the privileged place that the Parsis find themselves not only in India, but also in Pakistan. Just as the Parsis were prominent in the making of modern Bombay (now Mumbai), so were the Parsis prominent in undivided India in the making of Karachi. Ironically, not only was the wife of Jinnah (the founder of Pakistan) a Parsi, his descendents are also Parsis.

2. *The Iranian Zoroastrians*: The second group is the Iranians or the Iranian Zoroastrians who stayed on in Iran and faced persecution. This is one of the subaltern Parsi groups largely marginalized due to the reactionary state of Iran. Some of these people migrated in the nineteenth and twentieth centuries to India. Their mother tongue is Persian but they adapted to Gujarati on their coming to India. Whilst the first group is called 'Parsi Zoroastrians' (or simply 'Parsis'), the second group is called 'Iranian Zoroastrians'.

3. *The Zoroastrian diaspora*: This is also another subaltern group largely erased from nationalist imaginations. This is the largest term that includes 'Parsis' and 'Zoroastrian Iranians'. But this group is both larger as also more inclusive as is known to the world at large. It is the international Parsi subaltern group. It also includes the Kurds who had approached the Imperial Court of the Shah of Iran to be included as Zoroastrians (Hinnells 2005: 8–9). It can include the Yazids and the Al Haqqs as belonging to a subaltern Zoroastrian sect, though externally they seem to be Muslim (Kreyenbroke 2002). In India, there is a Zoroastrian sect called the Ilm-e-Khshnoom, rallying around Meher Master Moos, which has connections with the people of Tajikistan who claim to be Zoroastrian. Besides the Tajiks (they have named their Press Trust, *Avesta*, following the holy book of the Zoroastrians), it is also the people of Uzbekistan who claim to be of Zoroastrian descent (Hinnells 2005: 9). This group of Zoroastrians would become even larger if one includes large groups of Shiite Iranians claiming to be Zoroastrian. One also has neo-Zoroastrians, of European, North and South American origins, largely belonging to the Zarthushtri Assembly, a group following Ali Jafarey's (born a Muslim in Karachi and who in searching for his 'roots' found the ancient faith of the Parsis, converting consequently to Zoroastrianism) teachings. If the response of the Parsis is cautious to the claims of the Kurds, Tajiks, and Uzbeks, they are hostile to the neo-Zoroastrians. The North American Parsis led by Jafarey openly defy the orthodox and racial interpretation of the Parsi religion. According to this school of thought, the Parsis, in following the orthodox high priests, are being deluded in believing that the 'good religion' (as the Parsi religion is called) is only meant for a few people of Iranian descent defined by blood descent. Such claims would not merely mimic the Hindu caste system, but be in total opposition to their own philosophy which talks of human freedom and rational choice making.

Largely, the Parsis, especially of Mumbai, are orthodox. However, since the culture of modernity and cosmopolitanism governs the community, there is no sharp social division between the liberals and the orthodox, despite issues like intermarriage leading to fierce debates and now, ex-communication of rebel priests. The orthodox—led by the high priests (*dasturs*)—are wary of the liberal followers of Jafarey, since (as they claim) the politics of Iran is central to his imagination and since he wants to convert Islamic Iran into Zoroastrian Iran, he could disturb the peace that the minority Zoroastrians have with the Islamic state. The Zoroastrians in Iran are (like the Jews and the Christians) a protected as well as a persecuted people.

If Benjamin's angel of history was looking backwards despite being blown forward by the great storm of progress, the Parsis are looking everywhere: to India; the New World (America, the Middle East, Australia, and New Zealand); and also to Iran. They hear with keen interest what the arch-conservative Iranian mullah, Ayatollah Rafsanjani, once claimed, that Shiite Iranians can convert back to Zoroastrianism if they wished (Hinnells 2005). In the early 1990s, the same reverend mullah had also made a call to the international Parsi community to come back and settle down in Iran. Presently, the Parsis make regular trips to Iran and the Parsi press regularly advertises these trips to their former homeland. The political turmoil, somehow, seems to escape their imagination.

The view of the politics of multiculturalism in West Asia (and the role of the Parsis in this cultural politics) is largely not known to the outside world. What appears in the worlds of both cultural anthropology and popular imagination is the image of the Parsis as the 'colonial elite' of the British Raj. Since the Parsis reappear on the stage of history with the coming of capitalism in India, they appear dressed as the colonial elite with 'all of the virtues reconfigured and acquired during the Raj—the honesty of commercial trustworthiness, the purity associated with European-like racial superiority to the native Hindus, the philanthropy of successful business, the English style rationality and the progressiveness of Parsi religion, life-style …' (Luhrmann 1996: 120; see also Palsetia 2001).

What one calls the complexity of social factors in determining the history of an ethnic community is forgotten. One also forgets the 1857 revolt against British imperialism and the brutal crushing of this revolutionary movement. To my mind, there is no study of what the Parsis did in this period of radical revolution. Ironically, the Parsis found themselves in the rather Marxist situation in colonial India: 'England has to fulfil a double mission in India; one destructive, the other regenerating—the annihilation of old Asiatic society, and the laying of the material foundations of Western society in Asia' (Marx 1976: 82). This, to my mind, is the accurate moment—the liberal Parsis (like Marx) knew that the old Asiatic society with its myriad of castes and patriarchal oppression had to be actively destroyed and from these ruins of Asiatic despotism, modern India would have to emerge.

If Max Weber had said that one needed in Europe a 'spirit of capitalism', and this spirit would not be served by the feudal Catholic ideology that had become (to borrow Engels's phrase) 'an international centre of feudalism' (Engels 1975a: 383), but by Protestantism, so too in India, one needed this self-same spirit. The Parsis were ready to wear the hat of the bourgeoisie. However, first and foremost, the crowns of the Asiatic despots had to be knocked off. For that, they would have to knock down caste with its system of unfree labour, which, ironically, though history presented them a chance—Ambedkar took admission in a Parsi hostel as a young student in Baroda (around 1917) claiming to be a Parsi, and the reactionary–orthodox Parsis drove him away—they let it slip away from their grasp (Omvedt 2004; Sharafi 2006: 31n68).

A certain cynical reading of the space of ethnicity compels us to remember that the history of modern India would have been different if the Parsi conservatives had not confronted the young Ambedkar. What if Ambedkar had continued as a Parsi? Would then Ambedkar's critique of the caste system find solid foundations when his call for annihilating castes had found echoes in the old Persian philosophy of smashing the caste devils (*devas*)? Would, then, not this very modern type of *Parsinized Buddhism* have created a cultural revolution unimaginable in India? What if there had not been only a great alliance between the Dalits and the Parsis, but had the Dalits converted to Ambedkar's 'Parsi faith' and then, one had literally a new ethnic and political group called the *Persian Dalits*?

THE 'STRANGER' AS 'RATIONAL' CITIZEN

Since this now remains at the level of speculation, we need to turn our attention to the Parsis as they are, and not as they should have been. We begin with Georg Simmel's idea of the stranger and relate the Parsi as the quintessential stranger who becomes the 'rational' citizen. We take the later idea from Max Weber's idea of the new type of entrepreneur in *The Protestant Ethic and the Spirit of Capitalism* (1958). For Simmel, the stranger (as distinct from the wanderer) has a very specific place in modern capitalism. The stranger is 'far off, and yet very near'. He comes from distant lands, but comes to stay. He is apart from the main national–ethnic group and yet, penetrates deep into the national life-world. The stranger is objective in his assessments that is marked by the *strange phenomena* of the nearness that comes from a distance (Simmel 1950: 402–7). It is both this objectivity and rationality that marked the Parsis to become the Protestant capitalists in South Asia.

And since this *rational objectivity* was harnessed by the Parsis since the seventeenth century, the modern Parsis could construct the ideology of their group identity in modern and secular terms. And this rational objectivity had to sublate their ethnic identity into modern national citizenship—'sublate' meaning, not negation, but a transcendence which preserves as well as abolishes its ethnicity in the modern multicultural context. It is important to note that an Indian Parsi is an *Indian*, whilst a Pakistani Parsi is a *Pakistani*. One will not find the sites of the Parsi identity and the citizen clashing. But the emergence of the religious right-wing in South Asia, both in India and Pakistan, has however put this equation into question. Consider how in pre-Taliban days, the Pakistani Parsi was perceived. According to the late Pakistani President Ayub Khan, the philosophy of the Parsis is a source of infinite inspiration for all humanity and Pakistan was proud of the 'patriotic' Parsi citizens who have contributed so much to the progress and development of the nation (Hinnells 2005: 224).

Since the Parsi does not fit in the imperialist politics of damning civilizations, at least in modern imagination, the Parsi as the 'citizen' (be it the Indian or the Pakistani Parsi) is imprinted. Besides the translation of Simmel's and Weber's ideas into the Indian context, there has been no satisfactory explanation as to why this ideology of the Parsi as the stranger-cum-rational citizen prevails even in popular imagination. In addition to the idea of the stranger who becomes the 'rational' subject, another feature is that the place of the Parsis in colonial imagination was not registered as the 'hostile other', but a native like other natives involved in riots and the mayhem of Partition. Another explanation is that these 'rational strangers' have taken the role of the social democratic bourgeoisie with their welfare measures, thus letting the nationalisti-cally defined 'patriotism' have real social effects.[7] One will have to point out that the site of divisions functioning in modern capitalist societies (that of the *clash* between the private and public realms, the religious and the secular identities that Marx so eloquently pointed out in

On the Jewish Question) is very cleverly negotiated by the Parsis because of the triumph of cosmopolitanism inherent in the principles of secularism and modernity (see Marx and Engels 1975).[8] The Parsis are comfortably Parsi and Indian, Pakistani, Iranian, American, and so on. They become a community without borders.

What the Parsis have done is marginalize the conservative sections within their community and put the programme of modernity onto the forefront. Unlike the Bohra community that put the orthodox priest-hood (*Da'i'*) with an authoritarian church-like structure at the head of their economics, whereby the priesthood could control the community and manage dissent, the Parsi bourgeoisie was totally separated from the priesthood. And yet, this type of secularized modernity had made them remain in the framework of their religion and not made them turn their backs to it. This they have done by transcribing their precepts to suit modern contexts. Nietzsche's (1992: 127–8) phrase that good and evil form the central axis of all existence and is 'the actual wheel in the working of things' found roots in political economy, where 'good' was translated as economic wealth and 'evil' became underdevelopment. If one was told to fight 'evil' with 'righteousness' (in the old language of Persian theology), in the new language of political economy, one now fought the political economy of underdevelopment with the programme of economic development. Since the destruction of evil as the removal of scarcity is central to the philosophy of the Parsis, their religion has been christened: 'the philosophy of action' (Taraporewalla 1979: 31–7). And since performance as material praxis formed the crux of their ethics, they could be the ideal class for accumulating capital in the period of early capitalism. And since their worldview is unlike caste-based Hinduism with its emphasis on unnecessary rituals, the segregation of people into caste-based hierarchies (thus pre-empting the emergence of 'free labour', the necessary condition for the emergence of capitalism), not to forget their understanding of the world as maya or illusion to be renounced in order that humanity be emancipated (moksha), for the Parsis, the world is real, and above all good, to be nurtured and protected.

Whilst recent research claims that the advent of the Parsis into the world of modernity (especially the modern judicial system) was a work of the inner dynamics of the colonial Parsis (Sharafi 2006, 2007), theories of Simmel and Weber, Sombart's (1982) *The Jews and Modern Capitalism*, and Schumpeter's (1949) *The Theory of Economic Development* serve to illuminate how a non-indigenous ethnic commu-nity could serve as agents of social change. Schumpeter's (1949) views on how the new type of entrepreneur modelled himself on old principles of dynasties and empires of classical antiquity, almost attempting to create kingdoms, could serve to understand the emergence of the Parsi business houses.[9] Likewise, Sombart's (1982) thesis on the relation between piety and political economy, especially his understanding on the relation between Jewish piety and the rise of Jewish wealth, could be transcribed in the understanding of the modern Parsis. For the Parsis, being 'religious' is not abstract, nor ritualistic. 'Want to be pious?' the Parsi asks. 'Then grow corn' is the reply.[10] To have material wealth, and have it in abundance, is important as a religious imperative.[11] After all, what they call the Holy Spirit (*Spenta Mainyu*) is literally the 'Bountiful Spirit' or the 'Spirit of Plenitude', a socialist type of economic surplus, which is not exploitative capitalist surplus value, nor a surplus that is a result of fate, but which has to be made through hard collective labour.[12] The ancient battle between good and evil has now become the modern war between surplus and scarcity, where surplus guarantees piety through a full stomach.[13] If bourgeois morality is realized through production of surplus, then Parsi morality is revealed through sobriety—'all men should become sober', so a Parsi text once said, 'by drinking wine in moderation' (Menok i Khrat in Zaehner 1956: 117). To grip the modern imagination of the nation state, the rational strangers had to play the role not only of the liberal welfare state, but also the hedonist. The latter role they would play to perfection.

PARSIS AND THE IRONY OF NATIONHOOD AND CITIZENSHIP

The question of nationhood and citizenship is always a problematic question. For the Parsis it is not only problematic, since their foreign origins are never concealed, but also ironical, when studies on the Parsis today refer to the 'Zoroastrian nation' (Writer 1994). That the ideological reference point for Parsi tradition is Persia and Iran is a point that has never been questioned. Both in the popular imagination of the Indians as well as the Indian state, the Parsi is always the 'good Parsi'. That the Parsis as a community stand in direct opposition to the right-wing fascist ideology of Hindutva is also never thought out. Neither is India their *punyabhumi* (Savarkar's fascist 'holy land'), nor is it the *pitrabhumi* (the fascist 'fatherland'). Nor is the repertoire that Savarkar argued for a 'Hindu India', namely, the acceptance of the literature from the Vedas to the Gita, acceptable to the Parsi imagination. But most offensive is Savarkar's claim that the official ideology of a 'Hindu' India ought to be based on the theology of *Devayasna* (literally, 'devil worship' for the Parsis).

Despite their basic ideological schism with Brahmanical Hinduism, the Parsis became an inseparable part of India. This is because the Parsis have learnt to adapt themselves to changing conditions by continuously secularizing their religious narrative without losing their status as the dominant class and ethnic group. It is most certainly not the loss of the colonial grandeur that the Parsis lament, but the growing communalism in India since the 1990s. Probably nothing has disturbed the Parsis more than the destruction of the Babri Masjid in 1992, the consequent rise of the right-wing Bharatiya Janata Party (BJP) to power, and the Gujarat anti-Muslim genocide of 2002. The Parsis have also been very critical of the evangelic imperialist policies of the American state.

Despite a plethora of research on the Parsis, it has never been asked as to why and how an exilic people of Iranian origin could be accepted in the discourse of nationhood despite the fact that their foundational ideology—the raison d'être of their existence—is based on the radical critique of the foundational ideology of Hinduism. No serious study of secularism and assimilation can ever ignore this question, especially in the era of manufacturing communalism. Nor can the question be ignored as to how and why could two groups of people (the early Parsis and the Hindus) who had once bitterly fought now be reconciled as the meeting of two lost siblings. One must note that right from the time of their prophet, the speakers of this *Great Lie* were said to be the devas— or the gods of the early Hindus, led by Indra, the god of thunder. In this case, why did the Parsis come to the land of what they thought to be the land of the demons? And why and how did the followers of the alleged demons accept them? How could they reconcile two opposing facts: of cursing the devas every morning and accepting citizenship in the land of these 'demon worshipers'? How could they pray that Indra be banished from the country[14] and yet live in the country of Indra? The answer is, at first hand, very simple—*practice determines ideology*. The problem is ideological and is negotiated within the realm of ideologies. In this sense, the Parsi would say, following Marx: 'We are not aware of it, nevertheless we do it' (Marx 1983: 78–9).

To understand the formation of Parsi identity as the stranger who is also a rational citizen, one has to understand not the *foundational religious ideology* of the Parsis, but the *foundational sociological ideology* (that now appears as the foundational ideology per se, the foundational ideology that defines them as the rational citizen). This image is that which the Parsis draw on their arrival in India. This first image that the Parsis draw after landing in this new land is not of the old ideology of imperial Persian hegemony and destroying the Indian demons, but that of assimilation and the imperative that people with incompatible religious ideologies can live together. The Parsis are greeted by a chieftain, sometimes called 'prince' sometimes 'king'—a certain Jadi Rana ('Kisse-i-Sanjan' 1920: 103–6). They ask the Rana for refuge. The chieftain is wary of the presence of these Persians. He gives them a glass full of milk filled till the brim indicating that his land is full and it would not be possible to accommodate them. In response to this, the Parsi leader puts a pinch of sugar in the milk indicating that they would be like the sugar and not upset the balance of forces. Sugar also signifies sweetness. They would henceforth sweeten this new land that they would adopt and make it their home. An older dogma to destroy the devas was forgotten. After all, when one moves from a position of hegemony to periphery, then ideology too changes. From henceforth memory takes a different form. Besides, the Parsis are asked to give up their mother tongue and adopt the local language, Gujarati ('Kisse-i-Sanjan' 1920: 102). If language is the *House of Memories*, then if not memories, at least the language of memories would have to change. However, one claim is largely buried in this discourse of 'assimilation'—assimilation is determined by the politics of majoritism: *the Parsis have to forget their mother tongue and adopt Gujarati.*

But more than the discourse of milk and sugar signifying a new passion for survival and a new cultural exchange, it is the law of political economy, and thus the law of equal exchange—the driving force of civilizations—which helps not only the Parsis survive in India, but thrive. The exchange between milk and sugar (rather commodity 'A' and commodity 'B') was, on the one hand, a symbolic gesture of peace and goodwill. One the other hand, it was the reliving of probably the most ancient act of human history—the exchange of commodities. And, as usually told by the Marxists, this most ancient act is the secret of our modern civilization—the creation of surplus value and economic wealth. The Parsis who came to India knew this. Spenta Mainyu or the 'Holy Spirit' would not be a mere theological term for them, but as signifying bountifulness would imply the creation of material wealth that is justly distributed.[15]

The Parsi philosophy of abundance transcends not only scarcity but also surplus value (as 'unpaid labour'); thus, neither excess nor deficiency (but *Paymān* or the correct measure as distributive justice) forms the ethics of their political economy. As it was once said, the legendary Jamshid (the hero of the Parsis) once went to the devil and put his hand in his buttock to extract this correct measure (Shaked 1995b: 243). Good and evil are totally separate for the Parsis. But Jamshid, like Faust, would even flirt with the devil in order to obtain this correct measure that transcends both surplus value and scarcity. Maybe, he would also flirt with the devil to have a socialist distribution of wealth. Wealth without doubt, the Parsis have created, but next to the production of wealth is the reproduction of the human species. This, the Parsis, despite their materialism and hedonism have forgotten. The fault, it seems, lies not with hedonism, but with a fetish—the fetish of the alleged 'pure Persian'. Whether this fetish can be resolved in far away Persia, or nearby India, remains to be seen.

PARSI ORTHODOXY AND THE LIBIDINAL PROBLEM

We saw the rationality of the Parsis. But next to reason marches irrationality, just as next to the citizen marches the fundamentalist. One will have to look at this too. If the New Class talked of citizenship, the Old Class led by the high priests fused religion with the European ideas of race and blood descent. According to the latter view, 'mixed marriages are condemnable for Parsis, calamitous to the very existence of our community, and detrimental to the interests of the Parsi girl, who thoughtlessly embarks on the perilous voyage' (Davar 2005: 21). A more distinct type of exclusion (patriarchal exclusion) states that the Parsi faith talks only of the 'the religion of the husband of a married woman', where one cannot even recite the name of a non-Parsi in the Zoroastrian prayer.[16] Like all religious orthodoxy, Parsi conservatism accepts the idea of civil law, but entirely subservient to religious dictums.[17] Even more reactionary–racist views are held that prohibit organ donation (Hathiram 2007). Fortunately, the liberal Parsis immediately oppose these views, claiming them to be ideologies of 'religious apartheid' and 'ludicrous mentality' similar to that of Hitler and the Klu Klux Klan (Hinnells 2005: 644).

Ironically, it is a very non-Persian idea governing the ideologies of the religious orthodox—the ideology of the Hindu caste system and the right-wing European ideas of race and apartheid. The 1906 legal observation of the colonial judge, Beaman, marked the actual makings of 'Parsi identity', modelled on the Hindu caste system.[18] It becomes even more obvious that this 'Parsi identity' was ideologically manufactured by the Orientalists,[19] when one reads that the 'Irani Zoroastrians have never opposed conversions though, historically, seeking to convert Muslims means death' (Boyce 1979: 153).

What Naoroji said in 1861 is pertinent even today. If the Parsis have embodied the spirit of modernity, they are also stuck with race theories inspired by British colonialism. Ironically, endogamy which the right-wing Parsis propagate, is also the ancient consanguineous marriage system—ironically, the 'first stage of the family' as Marxism calls it (Engels 1975b)[20]—where brothers and sisters become naturally husbands and wives. It is however true that the fear of incest—the foundations of Western civilization—was never present with the Persians (Marx and Engels 1976: 174). In one Persian text, a Persian court philosopher, to disprove materialism and atheism, marries all his seven sisters and goes into the netherworld and narrates his voyage of heaven and hell (Vahman 1986). Western historians, with fetish for the pure unspoiled 'Aryan', claim that the Persian nobles and kings practiced endogamy, implying that the Parsis ought to continue the same mythical tradition (Boyce 1979). Parsi texts, however, suggest that the Parsi faith is open to all and that even Hindu *servants* of the Parsis can follow the 'Good Religion' if they so wish (Dhabhar 1932). But wishes are not to be followed. What the alleged followers of free thought follow is caste-based ideology,[21] where the 'tradition of all the dead generations', to borrow an excellent phrase from Marx, 'weighs like a nightmare on the brains of the living' (Marx 1975: 96).

For the entire world, the nightmare is the global economic crisis. For the Parsis, it is libidinal economy. And thus, it has to be stressed that if the world is facing the crisis of political economy, the Parsis are facing the crisis of libidinal economy. Outside Iran, there would most certainly be scarcity of 'pure' Persians. It is thus to Iran—with its abundance of 'pure Persians—that the Parsis may just have to turn to. It is in this site of irony—a minority community that refuses to recognize itself as a *real minority*, burdened also with the weight of the past—that Benjamin's angel of history is seen once again. This time the gaze is not directed towards the past but to the present, to Iran. And then the crisis of the libidinal economy of the Parsis as well as the crisis of the right-wing theological state in Iran may just compel Benjamin's angel to land in Iran with the Parsis perched on its back. One wonders if there would be anyone waiting for them with a glass of milk!

NOTES

1. This fetishism becomes clear when minorities are made to deny their rights as religious minorities, by simply denying that they are minorities. In the *Indian Express* (28 September 2005), the leader of the fascist Rashtriya Swayamsevak Sangh (RSS), K. Sudarshan, said that only Jews and Parsis are minorities. The *Organiser*, the mouthpiece of the Indian fascists, has for long been attacking the idea of minority and minority rights. To pre-empt this fascist fetish, the Parsis created a counter-fetish—that they are a distinct ethnic minority (the fetish of the 'pure' Persian) who, however, transcend their status in the political economy of religious minorities subservient to the state. In this sense, the Parsis transcend the programme of the economy of minorities and the state to become libidinal economists. They then become postmodernists before the advent of postmodernism! And this is simply because capital accumulated by them serves their interests better than the state. But the danger promoted by the right-wing forces simply does not find a place with the Parsi elite, represented mainly by the Parsi Panchayat. Whilst the 2002 anti-Muslim genocide in Gujarat was abhorred by the Parsis, in April 2011, the orthodox Parsi priesthood praised Chief Minister Narendra Modi (the chief architect of the genocide) and even wished that he may become the Prime Minister of India. There is not only narcissism with the orthodox Parsi elite but also a type of psychosis, in the sense that they seem to have totally withdrawn from reality. They seem to forget that a minority needs minority rights as such, which they will have to share with all minorities, especially Muslims. For that they have to affirm the regime of rights and stop being obsessed with so-called Persian ethnicity.

2. The two sides that comprised the makings of contemporary Parsi identity were Sir Cowasji Jehangir, Sir Dinshaw Petit, Sir Ratan Tata, and R.D. Tata (the plaintiffs) on the one side, and Sir Jamsetji Jeejebhoy, IV Bart, H.E. Albess, J.C. Jamsetjee, M.M. Cama, and B.D. Petit (the defendants) on the other. They were what Rashna Writer calls 'the cream of the "Parsi aristocracy"'. See Writer (1994: 133).

3. For the analysis of 'rational' behaviour as the cultural logic of capital accumulation and Parsi–Zoroastrian philosophy, see Robert E. Kennedy (1962). Early Parsi bourgeoisie perfected the art of *productive consumption* whereby money could be transformed into surplus value.

4. Emphasis in the original. But this difference between the caste-based Indians and the Parsis cannot be construed as the colonial difference between the native Indians and the British. T.M. Luhrmann (2002) bases her research on the latter paradigm.

5. Hinnells however notes that with the rise of right-wing communal parties in India, the contemporary Parsis feel excluded from mainstream India (Hinnells 2005: 63).

6.   With Anqutil du Perron's (1731–1805) 'discovery' of the Avesta in Surat in Gujarat in 1759 and the later discovery of philology and historical linguistics, the Parsis got a new strength—the strength of secular disciplines like philology, archaeology, and history—for the interpretation of their history. With the fusion of European studies and classical Parsi tradition, modern Parsi ideology was born in which the Parsi religion was deconstructed in its secular narrative.

7·   Despite this hegemony of the *imagination of welfare* constructed by the Parsis, if one leafs through historical documents, one sees that besides the 'good' liberal bourgeoisie, there were a certain section of Parsis who had talked of a separate homeland (either in Gujarat, or in Baluchistan, or East Africa).

8.   When I say that the idea of the Parsi is sublated into the practice of citizenship, I use the Hegelian term *Aufhebung* in order to understand the term sublation (sometimes also translated as supersession and transcendence). The logic of sublation (Aufhebung) 'lifts up' social identities to a higher level, thus preserving as well as abolishing them, simultaneously. But why does this Hegelian logic work amongst the Parsis? The answer is simple—the Parsi faith is itself dialectical. Remember that Hegel had said that the prophet of the Parsi faith was the first dialectician in world history (Hegel 1985: 153).

9.   Not much has been thought on the relation between the Parsi capitalist houses and the ancient Persian Empire. Likewise, not much has been thought or written on their old hatred for lies. According to the Parsis, the Persian 'Fall' was due to the mythical first lie spoken. Herodotus (1942: 77) says: 'the most disgraceful thing in the world … [for the Persian], is to tell a lie; the next worse, to owe a debt: because among other reasons, the debtor is obliged to tell lies.'

10.   *Pahlavi Vendidâd (Zand=Î Jvît-Dêv=Dât)*, transliteration and translation by B.T. Anklesaria, III, 31, Mumbai: K.R. Cama Oriental Institute, 2002, p. 31.

11.   Ibid., III, 3, p. 39.

12.   Ibid.

13.   Ibid., III, 34, pp. 57–8.

14.   *Pahlavi Vendidâd*: '*I*-drive-away (the dêv) Indra; *I*-drive-away (*the* dêv) Saurva; *I*-drive-away Naonhaithya-dêv from *the*-house, from *the*-street, from *the*-village, from *the*-country.' See also pp. 12–13.

15.   According to a ninth century Parsi text: 'The religion of Ohrmazd is (but) one word, the Measure; that of Ahriman is two words, excess and deficiency' (Shaked 1995a: 218).

16.   See Firoze M. Kotwal, 'Religious Implications of Mixed Marriages', available at http://tenets.parsizoroastrianism.com/mixrel33.html (accessed 16 December 2011).

17.   'While I am aware of the provisions of the Special Marriages Act, which permits persons belonging to different religions to have a legally valid marriage, I would like to stress with all emphasis at my command, that such a marriage has no sanctity in our religion' [see http://tenets.parsizoroastrianism.

com/mixrel33.html (accessed 16 December 2011)]. What is important to note is the anti-secularist position reflected by the ideology of the Parsi orthodox.

18.   Justice Beaman's Judgement, 'Suite no. 689 of 1906, Sir Dinsha Manekji Petit and others v Sir Jamshedji Jejeebhoy and Others', in *Indian Law Reports*, vol. XXIII, Bombay Series, 1908, p. 538, quoted in Boyce (1984: 153). See also Sharafi (2010).

19.   A.V. Williams Jackson (1965: 20) is an example of how an American scholar came to manufacture South Asian identities. Mary Boyce (1979) continued this Orientalist reading of the Parsis when she said that Cambyses (the Achaemenian Persian king) was 'the first person known to have practiced '*khvaētvadatha*', that is, the next-of-kin marriage. According to the Pahlavi books, this form of marriage was highly meritorious, and never more so within the close family circle—father with daughter, brother with sister, even mother with son. The term itself occurs in the Zoroastrian creed, the *Fravarne*; but, it is oddly placed there, appearing towards the end in a section otherwise concerned with noble generalities, and so may be well interpolated. The passage in question (Y 12.9) runs: 'I pledge to the Mazda-worshiping religion, which throws off attacks, which causes weapons to be laid down, which upholds *khvaētvadatha*, which is righteous' (p. 53). Likewise, Boyce notes Herodotus and Xanthas of Lydia who claim that the Magian men (that is, the ancient Parsi priests of Iran) co-habit with their mothers, daughters, and sisters (p. 54). It is good that the Parsis do not take the Orientalists literally!

20.   In an 1882 letter Marx (no longer preserved) says that: 'In primeval times the sister *was* the wife, and *that was moral*' (in Engels 1975b: 472–3).

21.   The orthodox Parsis rely on the reading of the Zoroastrians in medieval Iran by Boyce (1979: 178). The Zoroastrians in Safavid Iran were 'noticed' as not 'mix(ing) at all with other people, especially not with Mohometans'. This is most certainly due to the persecution and violence that the Zoroastrians had to face in Iran and discretion taught them to keep to themselves.

REFERENCES

Albêrûnî. 2002, *India. An Account of the Religion, Philosophy, Literature, Geography, Chronology, Astronomy, Customs, Laws and Astrology of India about A.D. 1030*, New Delhi: Rupa Publications.

Anderson, Benedict. 1991, *Imagined Communities. Reflections on the Origin and Spread of Nationalism*, London: Verso.

Benjamin, Walter. 1979, 'Theses on the Philosophy of History', in *Illuminations*, trans. Harry Zohn, Glasgow: Fontana/Collins, pp. 255–66.

Boyce, Mary. 1978, 'The Continuity of the Zoroastrian Quest', in W. Foy (ed.), *Man's Religious Quest*, London: Croom Helm, pp. 603–19.

————. 1979, *Zoroastrians: Their Religious Beliefs and Practices*, London: Routledge.

Boyce, Mary. 1984, *Textual Sources for the Study of Zoroastrianism*, Manchester: Manchester University Press.

Boyce, Mary and Franz Grenet. 1991, *History of Zoroastrianism*, Vol. Three, *Under Macedonian and Roman Rule*, Leiden: E.J. Brill.

Davar, Firoze C. 2005, 'Parsis and Racial Suicide', *Parsi Pukar*, 10(3): 21–3.

Dhabhar, B.N. (trans.). 1932, *The Persian Rivayats of Hormazyar Framroz and Others*, Bombay: Cama Oriental Institute.

Engels, Fredrick. 1975a, 'Socialism: Utopian and Scientific', in *Marx Engels: Selected Works*, Moscow: Progress Publishers, pp. 375–428.

———. 1975b, 'The Origin of Family, Private Property and the State', in *Marx Engels: Selected Works*, Moscow: Progress Publishers, pp. 449–583.

Hathiram, Marzban. 2007, 'Can Parsis Donate Organs after Death?' *Frashogard*, 17 September, available at www.frashogard.com (accessed 16 December 2011).

Hegel, G.W.F. 1985, *Introduction to the Lectures on the History of Philosophy*, trans. T.M. Knox and A.V. Miller, Oxford: Clarendon Press.

Herodotus, 1942, *The Persian Wars*, trans. George Rawlinson, New York: The Modern Library.

Hinnells, John R. 1981, *Zoroastrianism and the Parsis*, Bombay: Zoroastrian Studies.

———. 2005, *The Zoroastrian Diaspora: Religion and Migration*, Oxford: Oxford University Press.

Humbach, Helmut (in collaboration with Josef Elfenbein and Prods O. Skaervo). 1991, *The Gāthās of Zarathushtra and Other Old Avestan Texts, Part I*, Heidelberg: Carl Winter Universitätsverlag.

Karaka, Dosabhai Framji. 1999, *History of the Parsis*, New Delhi: Cosmo Publications.

Kennedy, Robert E. 1962, 'The Protestant Ethic and the Parsis', *American Journal of Sociology*, 68(1): 11–20.

'Kisse-i-Sanjan'. 1920, in S.H. Hodivala (ed.), *Studies in Parsi History*, Bombay: Sharpurji Hormasji Hodivala, pp. 92–117.

Kreyenbroke, Philip. 2002, 'Modern Sects with Ancient Roots: The Yezidis and the Ahl-e Haqq of Kurdistan', in P.J. Godrej and F.P. Mistree (eds), *A Zoroastrian Tapestry: Art, Religion, & Culture*, Ahmedabad: Mapin Publishing Pvt. Ltd, pp. 260–77.

Kulke, Eckehard. 1978, *The Parsis in India: A Minority as Agent of Social Change*, New Delhi: Vikas Publishing House.

Luhrmann, T.M. 1996, *The Good Parsi: The Fate of a Colonial Elite in a Postcolonial Society*, New Delhi: Oxford University Press.

———. 2002, 'Evil in the Sands of Time: Theology and Identity Politics among the Zoroastrian Parsis', *Journal of Asian Studies*, 61(3): 861–89.

Marx, Karl. 1975, 'The Eighteenth Brumaire of Louis Bonaparte', in *Marx Engels: Selected Works*, Moscow: Progress Publishers, pp. 96–179.

Marx, Karl. 1976, 'The Future Results of the British Rule in India', in *Marx Engels: On Colonialism*, Moscow: Progress Publishers, pp. 173–6.

—————. 1983, *Capital*, Vol. I, Moscow: Progress Publishers.

Marx, Karl and Fredrick Engels. 1975, *Collected Works*, Vol. 3, Moscow: Progress Publishers.

—————. 1976, *The German Ideology*, Moscow: Progress Publishers.

Modi, Jivanji. 2004, *A Few Events in the Early History of the Parsis and Their Dates*, Mumbai: K.R. Cama Oriental Institute.

Monier–Williams, Sir Monier. 1914, 'The Towers of Silence', in Eva March Tappan (ed.), *The World's Story: A History of the World in Story, Song and Art*, Vol. II, *India, Persia, Mesopotamia and Palestine*, Boston: Houghton Mifflin, pp. 234–44.

Nietzsche, Friedrich. 1992, *Ecce Homo*, London: Penguin.

Omvedt, Gail. 2004, *Ambedkar: Towards an Enlightened India*, New Delhi: Penguin Books.

Palsetia, Jesse S. 2001, *The Parsis of India: Preservation of Identity in Bombay City*, Leiden: Brill.

Schumpeter, Joseph. 1949, *The Theory of Economic Development*, Cambridge, MA: Harvard University Press.

Shaked, Shaul. 1995a, 'Paymān: An Iranian Idea in Contact with Greek Thought and Islam', in *From Zoroastrian Iran to Islam*, Hampshire: Ashgate Publishing Ltd, pp. 217–40.

—————. 1995b, 'First Man, First King: Notes on Semitic-Iranian Syncretism and Iranian Mythological Transformations', in *From Zoroastrian Iran to Islam*, Hampshire: Ashgate Publishing Ltd, pp. 238–56.

Sharafi, Mitra. 2006, 'Bella's Case: Parsi Identity and Law in Colonial Rangoon, Bombay and London', Unpublished PhD dissertation, Princeton University.

—————. 2007, 'Judging Conversion to Zoroastrianism: Behind the Scenes of the Parsi Pachhayat Case (1908)', in J.R. Hinnells and A. Williams (eds), *Parsis in India and the Diaspora*, London: Routledge, pp. 159–80.

—————. 2010, *Colonial Parsis and Law: A Cultural History*, Mumbai: K.R. Cama Oriental Institute.

Simmel, Georg. 1950, 'The Stranger', in K.H. Wolff (ed.), *The Sociology of Georg Simmel*, New York: The Free Press, pp. 402–7.

Sombart, Werner. 1982, *The Jews and Modern Capitalism*, London: Transaction Books.

Taraporewalla, I.J.S. 1979, 'The Religion of Action', in *The Religion of Zarathushtra*, Bombay: B.I. Taraporewalla, pp. 31–7.

Weber, Max. 1958, *The Protestant Ethic and the Spirit of Capitalism*, trans. Talcott Parsons, New York: Schiber.

Williams Jackson, A.V. 1965, *Zoroastrian Studies. The Iranian Religion and Various Monographs*, New York: AMS Press.

Writer, Rashna. 1994, *Contemporary Zoroastrianism: An Unstructured Nation*, Landham: The University of America Press.

Zaehner, R.C. 1956, *The Teachings of the Magis: A Compendium of Zoroastrian Beliefs*, London: Allen & Unwin.

——————. 1961, *The Dawn and Twilight of Zoroastrianism*, London: Weidenfeld and Nicholson.

9

The Curious Case of the Ramakrishna Mission

The Politics of Minority Identity

Sipra Mukherjee[†]

When the well-known religious group, the Ramakrishna Mission, approached the Calcutta High Court in 1981 with the plea that it was non-Hindu and claimed the status of a minority organization, there was a furore both within and outside the Mission. The disturbance increased even more when, in its judgement, the Calcutta High Court upheld the Mission's claim of being non-Hindu. The discussions surrounding the judgement spanned a diverse landscape from the nature of religion to the nature of social opportunities. The case went up to the Supreme Court and, after many years of protracted arguments and debates, it reversed the High Court judgement on 2 July 1995. The Mission's claim of being non-Hindu was rejected and its status as a Hindu organization affirmed.

It is through the Ramakrishna Mission case study that this chapter seeks to question the terms 'minority' and 'majority'. When an organization with a large following among the majority seeks to be identified

[†] I am grateful to Comparative Religions Programme, University of Washington, for its Luce Grant project on 'Religion and Human Security: Negotiating the Power of Religious Non-state Actors', 2008, which first led me to this study of the Ramakrishna Math and Mission.

as minority, the label 'minority' is revealed as possessing more than an enumerative dimension. Contemporary history has repeatedly shown that the term 'minority' is no longer an innocuous descriptive term, but a political one. The label 'minority' has, in its complex contemporary usage, come to designate a weakness and affirm a strength (Grew 2001: 1). This connotation of the term is evident in Jal's discussion on the Parsis in this volume, who reject the label as allocating a subaltern status to the group, thereby indicating characteristics more complex than an innocent quantifying of their numbers.

The Ramakrishna Mission study underscores the perceived discrepancy between numerical and sociological minority-hood. Such strategic use of the terms may encourage multicultural communities to position themselves as one singular monolithic entity as is seen in Ibrahim's study of the Muslims and the Kolis of Kachchh in this volume. A seemingly homogeneous community that is really heterogeneous and multicultural, like the Kachchh Muslims, or a largely different group like the Vadha Koli tribals, may be coaxed and cajoled into the Hindu fold. The identity of a uniform harmonized community is chosen because the numbers, under the labels of 'minority' and 'majority', strengthen the demands made by that community on the state. By analysing the ways in which the terms are used, or *can* be used, in the socio-political situation of modern India, this chapter discusses how these identities can become fiercely disputed ones.

The case of the Ramakrishna Mission is interesting because, despite its alleged political benefits, the minority identity was not acceptable both to a majority within the organization and to a large section of the Hindu community outside it. The non-Hindu tag was, in fact, aggressively resisted by the Mission's 'outside' supporters,[1] who emotionally/ spiritually felt themselves to be connected with the Mission. While this group was willing to identify themselves as a denomination within Hinduism, they were not willing to be called non-Hindus. Since the Court had to first come to an understanding of Hinduism, the majority's religion in India, before it could reach a conception of 'minority', the terms 'denomination', 'sect', and 'religion' were debated endlessly.

The fact that being identified as a Ramakrishnaite and a non-Hindu was not acceptable either to the insider or outsider devotees throws into relief the complex associations of the Hindu identity within India. These ideas, if placed beside the rapid growth of the Hindutva ideology around this time, and their perceived association between Hindu and Indian, would reveal why unusually intense attention was focussed on this case by the Hindutva group. In fact, a survey of the media reports shows that this court case was most zealously followed and discussed in those newspapers and journals which saw themselves as carrying the onus of 'protecting'/'rescuing' the Hindu religion in India.

The other question that this case study raises is the role of the judiciary in India in delineating religious identities. The first case in independent India that attempted to define Hinduism, with regard to a religious group that claimed non-Hindu status, was the *Shastri Yagnapurushdasji and Others v. Muldas Bhundardas Vaishya and Another*[2] in 1966. The judgement which decided whether the Swaminarayan Sampradaya was Hindu or not, has served as reference point for all later cases involving religious identity, and is significant because it singled out certain features of Hinduism as most important: '... tolerance, universality, a classical core and a search for fundamental unity' (Sen 2006: 15). The Ramakrishna Mission case, too, illustrates the role of the Indian courts in questions that straddle the division between the secular sphere and the religious. Both these cases amply demonstrated that, unlike most civil–political rights, religious freedom and religious identity are questions that cannot be comprehended solely through the individual–state framework (Balakrishnan 2009). These questions are often cast, as the Chief Justice of India says, in terms of the relations between the religious majority and the different minority groups rather than in the domain of individual or group rights enforceable against the state (Balakrishnan 2009).

One might add to this the domain of relations among the various groups within the majority community. While in traditional India, various sections (villages, sects, castes) enjoyed a legal autonomy, in modern India, these groups have been viewed as components of modern India, committed to secularism, democracy, and the protection of the minorities' rights. This has led to the loss of the earlier isolation and autonomy, and the legal system has emerged as 'a link or hinge between the secular public order and religion' (Galanter 1998: 268). The definitions of the terms religion, denomination, Hinduism, minority, and majority-hood are therefore continuously undergoing redefinition and transformation since the 'nature of the emerging secular order is dependent upon prevalent conceptions of religion, and the reformulation of religion is powerfully affected by secular institutions and ideas' (Galanter 1998: 268).

BACKGROUND

The Ramakrishna Mission petition for minority-hood, which came up in the Calcutta High Court in 1980, had a brief history. The Mission had earlier, in 1969, petitioned for and been granted the status of a minority organization in the state of Bihar. The petition in West Bengal was possibly seen by the Mission as a similar strategic move. But, unlike the Bihar case, the case in West Bengal drew much attention, in all likelihood because the Ramakrishna Mission is much more active, recognized, and supported within this state which is its birthplace. The final judgement passed by the Supreme Court was in two parts. While the first part of the judgement went against the Mission, rejecting its claim of minority-hood and establishing the Mission as Hindu, in its second part, the Court granted the organization special powers of administration generally inaccessible to the 'majority' of India, agreeing that it could be identified as a religious denomination of Hinduism. This effectively turned the defeat of the Mission into a victory, and has been viewed as such by its supporters. The Mission thus retained its Hindu status, while at the same time, remaining independent in the administration of its institutes.

Interestingly, it was a mundane and entirely secular matter that led to these rather profound questions regarding the nature of Hinduism and Ramakrishna Mission's ideology being raised at court. On the northern fringes of the city of Kolkata, not very far from Baranagar where the first Math had been set up by the monastic followers of Ramakrishna, is the Vivekananda Centenary College of Rahara. This college had been set up by the Ramakrishna Mission monks with financial support from the Government of West Bengal, then led by the Indian Congress Party in 1961. The administration of the college was singular in the fact that certain norms mandatory to the other colleges were not imposed upon it, though, like these colleges, the Mission college too operated on grants received from the West Bengal government.[3] This difference had been accorded approval by the Calcutta University and the state government and this approval was, from time to time, obtained from them by the college authorities.[4] The teachers who worked in the college had run into conflict with the Mission monks on an earlier occasion when, in 1975, a service rule was introduced which made the teachers employees of the Mission and empowered the authorities to transfer them to any institution under the Ramakrishna Mission Boys' Home or to terminate their services with three months' notice. The teachers of the Vivekananda

College succeeded in getting these rules withdrawn in 1978 after a pro-longed agitation. However, their principal complaint against the method of administration remained: unlike other undergraduate college teach-ers, they could not be a part of the governing body of the college and consequently, had no significant role in administrative decisions. This was seen as a violation of the West Bengal College Service Commission Act of 1978 and the West Bengal College Teachers (Security of Services) Act, 1975.

In 1980, when the Principal of the college, Swami Jitatnanda, retired, the teachers refused to acknowledge the appointment of the new Principal, Swami Shivamayananda, demanding that the authorities follow the norms laid down for government-funded colleges in matters of appointment. In accordance with these rules, the Teachers' Council of the college placed the senior-most teacher among them in the position of the teacher-in-charge, to act as the principal as long as that position remained vacant. This amounted to a taking over of the administration of the college, and the incident created a few ripples in some other edu-cational institutions run by the Ramakrishna Mission. While the West Bengal College and University Teachers' Association remained silent on the issue, the Scientific Workers' Forum, West Bengal, submitted a memorandum signed by sixty-seven teachers and researchers support-ing the teachers of the college and calling for a 'science education free from religious control' (Dutta 1986: 476). On 18 December 1980, the teachers of the Rahara College filed a petition in the High Court, with a three-point demand: the removal of the nominated principal; reconsti-tution of the governing body of the Mission college in accordance with the standard pattern of those of sponsored colleges; and implementation of the West Bengal College Teachers' Service Security Act. The Mission authorities reacted to this 'untoward incident' (as the Supreme Court termed it in its judgement)[5] by instituting a civil suit in court seeking a declaration that the action of the teachers was illegal.

The situation was further complicated at this time by three notices sent by the University of Calcutta to three other educational institutions run by the Mission. The notices, directing the colleges to reconstitute their governing bodies, and sent at this particular time when the writ petition was pending in the court, indicated that there were possibly other issues involved besides the indignation that the college teachers felt against the arbitrary administration of the college. What was also at issue here was control over the administration of the institution and 'the limits of state action with regard to institutions run by the Mission'

(Sen 2006: 19). In its judgement, the High Court dismissed the petition and quashed the notices sent by the university on the grounds that the Ramakrishna Mission was a minority organization and its institutions were therefore protected under Article 30(1) of the Constitution. The Mission argued that as the followers of Ramakrishna, a renowned mystic of Bengal and guru of the patriot saint Swami Vivekananda, the religion they followed was Ramakrishnaism and that they were a non-Hindu minority.[6]

REACTIONS TO THE DEMAND FOR MINORITY STATUS

The case may perhaps have passed without too much notice if the media had not taken it up. But after the High Court ruling of the Ramakrishna Mission being a non-Hindu organization, the case was hotly debated and discussed, radically polarizing the public on the issue.[7] The case moved to the Supreme Court of India in 1985 and, over the decade and a half during which the long-drawn-out legal battle played out, the newspapers and journals publicized the opinions of people who, formally or informally, believed they had some claim to the organization. The views of these diverse, non-state, and non-organizational players were reflected in the media as the issue of majority–minority politics was brought into the public sphere. In the discussions on this case, one is struck by the manner in which the social, political, and religious trajectories repeatedly criss-cross each other, revealing the substantially varied dimensions to the seemingly neutral descriptive term, 'minority'. The concerns and issues which framed the discussions of the case in the non-legal, public arena are as interesting and intriguing as those within which the case was argued in the Court. The Court proceedings went into detailed deliberations of the meaning and definition of the terms religion, sect, and denomination. But the out-of-court discussions often rejected completely the Hindu/non-Hindu aspect of the case, focussing instead on minority rights, majority rights, and minority privileges.

The non-Hindu plea of the Mission was viewed with irritation, impatience, or embarrassment by its many followers, but was not taken seriously by any. It was acknowledged that the Mission's move for minority-hood was solely to find a way out of the restrictions that framed the workings of non-minority institutions. In these non-legal discussions, the point at issue was always whether the Ramakrishna Mission should be allowed to administer its institution without interference from the state.[8] These discussions often revolved around the belief that the Hindus, being a numerical majority, had been divested of sociological powers and privileges that were enjoyed by the minority. The Supreme Court judgement, in fact, addresses this issue directly, by giving the Mission the right to administer its own institution. But it does so without going into the controversial majority/minority rights, and maintains its focus on the alleged concern of the case: the definitions of religion and Hinduism.

The disparity between the stated position of the monks of the Ramakrishna order and the wider public was explicitly articulated through the outright refusal of the supporters and followers of the Mission to even consider a non-Hindu status for the Ramakrishna Mission. Though most of the Mission monks preferred to remain silent about the Mission's attempted move away from the Hindu name, the few monks who did speak to the media agreed that it was more a tactical move to evade governmental interference than a decision based on ecclesiastical reasons. 'Sometimes bending down a little is good,' says Swami Satchitananda, 'at least for the time being, rather than destroying yourself if you know that you cannot fight it out. Then you are taking the victorious withdrawal for political reasons…. As an organization you must think like the King' (*Hinduism Today* 1986). These words lend support to McLean's view that it was more pragmatism than religious sentiment that lay behind the Mission's decision to go to court seeking the minority status (McLean 1991: 100).

The kind of censure evinced by the common public[9] was not heard from the monks. In fact, if it may be so phrased, the monks showed themselves more amenable to adapt to practical necessities than did the secular public. Beckerlegge writes that after the High Court ruling of the Mission as non-Hindu in 1985, 'the claim reverberated through the Ramakrishna movement, causing anger and distress among those members who were convinced that they were Hindus and that Ramakrishna and Vivekananda were authentic spokesmen of the Hindu tradition' (Beckerlegge 2000: 62). The monks, in an admirably nuanced argument, stated that while being a Ramakrishnaite and a Hindu were not contradictory, temporal circumstances may necessitate strategies that may appear unexpected and different on the surface, but which did not really indicate any changes in the ideology of the Mission.[10] It is intriguing that a decision regarding the name of a religious order which appears to have been acceptable to the monks of that order, albeit for strategic purposes, should appear so completely unacceptable to the larger majority of its lay supporters. The answer to this riddle possibly lies in the fact that, for many of the followers of Hinduism, what was at issue here was not the majority or the minority tag, but that of the Hindu and non-Hindu. As Swami Bhasyananda said in an interview to *Hinduism Today*, 'the emphasis should be given on the minority religion status and not on "abandoning Hinduism." That's where the mischief is coming.'[11]

The logic of the 'minority' identity is entirely based on the relatively modern concepts of census and enumerated communities. The idea of the Hindu, however, is as entirely based on what Sudipta Kaviraj calls 'the fuzzy community' of the pre-modern times. The concept of the fuzzy community he explains as being based on 'an idea of identity, which is predicated in turn on some conception of difference' (1992: 20). These communities, usually reaching back to very early times, variously defined, tended to be fuzzy in two ways: one, they had fuzzy boundaries, because communities of religion, caste, and endogamous groups were not territorially based; and two, unlike modern ones, these traditional communities were not enumerated. Yet, as Kaviraj points out, the history and narratives of these traditional and fuzzy communities are of crucial importance to the creation of the modern communities which make up the nation state. This is because the idea of the community as one that has always existed since ancient, immemorial times, gives to the modern community a romance that justifies and sanctifies its existence today. Kaviraj gives the example of nationalism which, despite its modern origins, 'tries to steal, to use Marx's phrase, the poetry of primordiality from [the ancient communities], to try to argue about and justify itself through a wholly illegitimate discourse of immemorial aspirations and indissoluble community' (Kaviraj 1992: 21).

The idea of the Hindu similarly, is an identity that is based on the idea of a fuzzy community and was, in the late nineteenth century, constructed in a similar manner. Like the two-headed Roman deity Janus, it looks backwards into the past as well as forward into the future (Nairn 1997). Though in the modern nation state of India, the Hindu is an enumerated and well-mapped community, yet, it derives its identity from a discourse which draws on the past. This discourse validates its existence in the present as belonging to a romantic hoary past whose horizon is beyond the reach of mortal historians. The term 'minority' is, in comparison, a term bare of the glory of this lineage. To ask the Hindu Indian to surrender his Hindu identity for a non-Hindu one, is asking her/him to surrender a glorious history that he feels a part of.

SITUATING THE HINDU DISCOURSE IN RECENT HISTORY

In the more recent history of India, this purportedly ancient (and consequently considered significant) discourse of the Hindu has been situated in the age of nationalism and in the turbulent struggle against a foreign power. The nationalistic discourse of India repeatedly drew its images and metaphors from Hindu traditions of worship, creating a discourse that fused together the contemporary with the ancient. Among the many sages of Hinduism, it is the name of Vivekananda especially which has a particular significance within the tradition of Indian nationalism. The Ramakrishna Mission that he began, despite its religious anchoring, is commonly viewed as being 'Vivekananda's greatest political contribution to the building up of "New India"' (Rao 1979: 248).

Towards the end of the nineteenth century, when Bengal was caught up in the rousing fervour of nationalism, Vivekananda transformed Ramakrishna's purely spiritual legacy into one that embraced the secular facet of patriotism. Ramakrishna's censure of Western materialism and his discourse on asceticism, devotion, and worship were translated by Vivekananda into the idiom of service to the nation. Through this discourse, it became possible to bring the domains of the religious and the secular closer to each other, making him the 'patriot prophet' (Dutta 1954).

Partha Chatterjee's (2004: 121) analysis of the Indian nationalistic discourse is essential to understanding the immense success that Vivekananda found all over India. Chatterjee explains the contemporary nationalistic discourse as one that created a distinctive Indian identity based on India's own superior spiritual heritage. This allowed Indians to retain and employ the concepts of modernity imbibed from the West without any consequent feelings of inadequacy. Through Swami Vivekananda's (1970) discourse of 'practical Vedanta', Hindu spirituality could now work towards progress and the material uplift of the people, thus creating a nationalism based on Indian spiritual heritage, but capable of working in the secular field. Vivekananda's role in inspiring patriotism in leaders like Subhas Chandra Bose, whose popularity in India cuts across religious, linguistic, and regional divides, has situated the Mission firmly within the nationalistic tradition. In a letter to Vivekananda's brother, Bhupendranath Dutta, Hemchandra Ghose, a young revolutionary from Dhaka, writes that the revolutionaries perceived Swami Vivekananda to be more a political prophet than a religious leader (*Prabuddha Bharat* 2007: 605). Romain Rolland noted that 'the Indian nationalist movement smouldered for a long time until Vivekananda's breath blew the ashes into flame and erupted violently three years after his death in 1905' (quoted in *Prabuddha Bharat* 2007: 605).

This legacy of Vivekananda has been vital in making the Mission a 'modern' religious organization, with an ideology that is attractive to the urban, educated middle classes. Vivekananda's determined yoking together of spirituality and the more Western idea of institutionalized service to society made the Ramakrishna Mission a religious organization that set social reform on as high a plane as spiritual development. In fact, the one was inextricably linked with the other. Agehananda Bharati (1970: 278) writes that modern Hinduism has rejected the old-fashioned, non-English-speaking, peregrinating, or ashram-bound sadhu who does not contribute to modern life. 'Yet, all "modernities" overtly or covertly admire and venerate the "scientific", "modern" man who wears monastic robes' (Bharati 1970: 278). Swami Vivekananda became then, and has remained since, an undisputed culture hero not only of all modern Bengali Hindus, but of all modern Hindus because they 'derive their knowledge of Hinduism from Vivekananda, directly or indirectly' (Bharati 1970: 278).

Through an able and efficient administration, the Ramakrishna Math and Mission has been tremendously successful in reaching social, medical, and spiritual aid to hundreds of thousands of Indians, establishing itself as 'a model for modernity within Hindu monasticism' (Miller 1999: 121). Consequently, the Mission has come to occupy the unique position of a Hindu religious organization whose ideals include both those of the past and the present. The 'ancient' ideals of asceticism, renunciation, and devotion perceived as being uniquely 'Indian' were brought together with the more 'modern' ideals of liberalism, social responsibility, and human rights. This has contributed greatly to the growing support which the Mission enjoys among Indians all over the world. Open acknowledgement of the Mission's role in the social and spiritual development of India by leaders like Jawaharlal Nehru have also strengthened this modern religious image. References to Vivekananda as the 'mentor' of Nehru (Edwardes 1972: 247) known more for his scepticism regarding benefits derived from religion and for his secularism, have also contributed to the idea of the Mission's positive influence on secular India. At a time when the nation was reeling under the injustices and humiliations of the colonized identity, Vivekananda's inspiration and encouragement to Jamsetji Tata during their chance meeting in 1893, both bound for Chicago on the ship to Vancouver, revealed Vivekananda's mission as one that had nation building as its ideal.[12] The Mission was therefore, from its inception, seen as a religious organization intimately connected with the growth of the nationalist movement.

The associations of the 'Bengali Hindu' identity, too, were shifting around this time. From the frail and the feminine, it underwent a transformation into the virile and masculine, reaching its culmination in the figure of Vivekananda (Chowdhury 2001). Chowdhury demonstrates the centrality of gender in the formation of the colonial discourse which used the stereotypes of the 'effeminate Bengali' and the 'manly Englishman' to dominate the Orient. She analyses how Ramesh Chander Dutt, Bankimchandra Chatterjee, and others negotiated these identities through the nationalist project and how, towards this end, the historiography of Bengal was remodelled to lay claim to 'a past that was both civilized and glorious: a past where he could renounce his dispirited, feeble self and adopt instead a valiant one' (Chowdhury 2001: 59). Bankimchandra's construction of the *'santans'* in his Ananda Math as sannyasis who renounced everything to free their enslaved motherland found articulation in reality through the persona of Vivekananda. Repeatedly feted in the newspapers as 'the warrior monk' and 'the cyclonic monk', Vivekananda's image carried explicit echoes of the Hinduism–nationalism blend which had already been accepted into the nationalist discourse. Removing the Hinduness from the identity of Ramakrishna Mission would mean disconnecting the Hindus from this glorious era of history that they have for so many years seen as their own.

This brings us to the very detailed delineation and meaning of Hinduism given by the Supreme Court in the judgement it passed in 1995. The principal argument that the Mission had used to vindicate its non-Hindu identity was its ideal of inclusiveness. They cited this specific element in their ideology, arguing that the ability of Ramakrishnaism to include the Muslim, the Christian, and followers of any of the diverse religions of the world within its fold, without conversion, was what marked it out as being a religion that was different from Hinduism. Koenraad Elst cites Swami Lokeshwarananda who said in 1983, 'Is Ramakrishna only a Hindu? Why did he then worship in the Christian and Islamic fashions? He is, in fact, an avatar of all religions, a synthesis of all faiths.'[13] It is striking therefore that the Supreme Court used exactly the same argument of inclusivism to deny the Mission a non-Hindu status. It cited 'a grander inclusivism' (Minor 1999: 165) that brought within its fold innumerable traditions, creeds, and practices of worship as the singular characteristic of the Hindu religion, and argued that the Ramakrishna Mission followed one of the many paths possible within Hinduism.

The language that the Supreme Court used to define Hinduism was borrowed largely from the writings of the Orientalist Monier–Williams and from the philosopher Sarvepalli Radhakrishnan. Since the discourse of both these scholars is far removed from the dispassionate and cogent language usually characteristic of law, the lengthy quotations included bring to the Supreme Court judgement a language which frequently veers more towards the language of poetry than that of analysis and investigation. That complicated strand of 'enumeration and exoticization', which was part of the colonial project of Orientalism (Appadurai 1993: 323), may be observed in these quotations. Citing Monier–Williams, Hinduism is described as 'a complex congeries of creeds and doctrines which in its gradual accumulation may be compared to the gathering together of the mighty volume of the Ganges, swollen by a continual influx of tributary rivers and rivulets, spreading itself over an ever increasing area of country, and finally resolving itself into an intricate delta of tortuous streams and jungly marshes....'[14]

This view of Hinduism as a union of diverse creeds is echoed by Radhakrishnan whose concept of Hinduism was characterized by tolerance and inclusivism. Ironically, Radhakrishnan had cited Vivekananda to elucidate this 'grand inclusivism'. He believed that Vivekananda had shown 'that the Hindu religion was both scientific and democratic, not the religion as we practice it, which is full of blemishes, but the religion which our great exponents intended it to be' (Radhakrishnan 1956: 192). Therefore, despite the many smaller faiths and creeds practised by the Hindus, the actual essence of the Hindu faith lay in the philosophy espoused by the Vedas. The philosophy of Radhakrishnan was in accordance with the nineteenth century reformist frame of Hindu faith. Based on the Vedanta philosophy and patronized by the modern, liberated middle class, this philosophy was famously described by Radhakrishnan (1957: 77) in his Upton lecture at Oxford, in 1926, as 'more a way of life than a form of thought'. Accordingly, a particular kind of tolerance and inclusivism was viewed as an integral characteristic of Hinduism.

ATTEMPTED DEFINITIONS OF HINDUISM AND THEIR IMPLICATIONS

The definition of Hinduism in Indian judicial discourse has centred on the characterization and now-accepted legal definition of its inclusiveness from the very first case (*Yagnapurushdasji v. Muldas*) in independent India to attempt a definition of Hinduism. Both in this case and that of the Ramakrishna Mission's, Radhakrishnan's ideas were quoted in the Supreme Court judgement. Echoing Radhakrishnan, the Court spoke of the plurality within Hinduism:

> When we think of the Hindu religion, we find it difficult, if not impossible, to define Hindu religion or even adequately describe it. Unlike other religions in the world, the Hindu religion does not claim any one prophet, it does not worship any one God; it does not subscribe to any one dogma; it does not believe in any one philosophic concept; it does not follow any one set of religious rites or performances; in fact, it does not appear to satisfy the narrow traditional features of any religion or creed.[15]

Yet, this very feature that 'had been the obstacle to constructing a model of Hinduism which would fit the concrete data is turned into one of its major characteristic—it is inclusive' (Baird 1971: 51). In this light, the various religions and cults begun by saints who were Hindus by birth are viewed as reform movements within Hinduism: '... [F]rom time to time saints and religious reformers attempted to remove from the Hindu thought and practices elements of corruption and superstition and that led to the formation of different sects. Buddha started Buddhism; Mahavir founded Jainism: Basava became the founder of Lingayat religion, Dhyaneshwar and Tukaram initiated the Varakari cult; Guru Nanak inspired Sikhism....'[16]

Such an approach to the faiths of Mahavira, Buddha, and the others effectively dilutes the challenge to Hinduism that most of these movements embodied. Hinduism is thus seen as characterized by innumerable smaller traditions of faith, which are all essentially myriad expressions of the core, higher Hinduism. The core Hinduism, a religion of the spirit, remains unaffected by the different traditions or even beliefs that the syncretic or breakaway faiths might profess. Hinduism is thus viewed as a large umbrella faith, within which diverse smaller faiths of various kinds can exist because the larger overarching faith was a 'religion of the spirit' that could accommodate the smaller faiths with their beliefs in rituals and traditions. It is consequently an inclusivism that is tacitly based on the acceptance that differences may exist between the core essential philosophy of Hinduism and the many diverse ways in which it is practised, and that such differences were inconsequential when compared to the higher philosophy that they all shared. Quoting Radhakrishnan, the Supreme Court declares that the worldview of all Hindus is similar, because 'all of them accept the view of the great world rhythm. Vast periods of creation, maintenance and dissolution follow each other in endless succession....'[17]

This interpretation of the Hindu faith implies a hierarchy between the many diverse creeds with their diverse rituals and traditions, and the purely spiritual creed espoused by the Vedanta. All the other traditions are viewed as various forms of that one absolute reality termed as Brahman, the 'monistic idealism' which, according to the Court, can be said to be the general distinguishing feature of Hindu philosophy. By accepting this view, the Court has given voice to the characteristic of Hinduism being an inclusive religion: 'In a sense the State has put its weight behind the Gita itself' (Derrett 1968: 121). Analyses of Radhakrishnan's inclusive faith have, however, been interpreted as an inclusivism of 'the hierarchic, subordinating type', 'a form of religious assertion', and the tolerance of a 'superior who tolerates the weaknesses of an inferior' (Minor 1993: 309–10).

The Mission's claim in the document submitted to the Court was that it had a religion of its own, called 'Ramakrishnaism'. It argued that 'the Ramakrishna religion was distinct and separate from the Hindu religion'. It also stated that the followers of the Ramakrishna Mission look 'upon Sri Ramkrishna as an illustration and embodiment of the Religion Eternal which constitutes the core of all religious ideals and permits his worship through his image'. Ramakrishnaism was not only non-Hindu, but was also not inconsistent with Christianity and Islam, and that, unlike in Hinduism, 'there are persons coming from Hindu fold as well as from the followers of Islam, Christianity and other religions' among the followers of Shri Ramkrishna's religion (AIR 1995, SC 2089: 12). The claims to inclusivism that both the Mission and the Court makes for Hinduism are interesting when compared to each other. The Mission claimed their inclusivism on the grounds that Ramakrishnaism, unlike 'other religions', does not 'claim absolute authority in all matters to the exclusion of all others' (AIR 1995, SC 2089: 12) The claim to inclusivism made by Radhakrishnan, on the other hand, is substantially different since it is based on the assumption that the differences within the creeds of India are 'non-essential' when placed beside the more significant similarities arising out of their acceptance of the Vedas.

It may be argued that this construction of the Hindu religion is a reflection of the composite character of the Hindus, who are not one people but many. Yet, much of this delineation of Hinduism that the Supreme Court uses in its rulings to decide what does and does not qualify as Hindu is, of course, embedded in a discourse on classical or high Hinduism that originated with the nineteenth century reformation of Hinduism. Vivekananda and Radhakrishnan were the two most notable practitioners of this inclusivist and tolerant Hinduism, basing much of their interpretation on the Advaita Vedanta. Legal history shows that, for the greater part of its existence in independent India, the Court has appropriated this discourse on classical Hinduism to emphasize the inclusive and tolerant qualities of Hinduism (Sen 2006).

In his discussion on the Court's judgement of Hinduism, Sen (2006) points to Paul Hacker's argument that the inclusivism of Hinduism is often confused with tolerance and to his claim about the displacement of tolerance by inclusivism within Hinduism.[18] Sen argues that 'the Court, by adopting the inclusivist model of Hinduism, also contributed to the construction of a homogenous Hinduism which was inimical to variations in beliefs, practices and doctrines' (Sen 2006: 7). Moreover, as Balakrishnan (2009: 20) writes, in this delineation, the Court has remained faithful to its usual trend of characterizing 'reformist or breakaway groups as coming within the larger Hindu fold'. The key issue here, consequently, remains the Court's 'essentialising' role in shaping religious identities (Balakrishnan 2009: 7), a role that the colonial courts had played in India. Grappling with the diverse religious sects and the customs of communities with 'syncretic' practices, the judicial 'construction' of identities made by the colonial courts was not always limited to 'syncretic' groups but also extended to breakaway movements.

Thus, Hinduism can include any faith, any tradition, any ritual, and any philosophy that originates on Indian soil. The famous 'way of life' speech defines Hinduism as: 'more a way of life than a form of thought. While it gives absolute liberty in the world of thought it enjoins a strict code of practice. The theist and the atheist, the sceptic and the agnostic may all be Hindus if they accept the Hindu system of culture and life' (Radhakrishnan 1957: 77). Such a definition of Hinduism is in accordance with the reformist, enlightened, yet Brahmanical frame of the neo-Hindu faith that is patronized by the modern, liberated, secular urbanized middle class. In the Swaminarayan sect's temple entry case,[19] the satsangis claimed the status of a separate religion, being the followers of Swaminarayan, and sought protection from the Bombay Harijan Temple Entry Act. Galanter (1998) cites this case to argue that the 'reformist' inclination of the Court indicated the influence of the modernized Western-educated governing elite of India. Balakrishnan (2009) too feels that the Bihar cow slaughter case[20] is one which may be seen as an attempt by the Court to progress towards the ideal of democratic citizenship.

In both these cases, the Court sought to curb retrograde practices: caste discrimination in the first case; and cow slaughter being used to incite communal violence in the second. However, despite its adherence to the constitutional ideals of democracy and religious freedom, the Court used the religious discourse in these cases to justify its stance. Both the cases consequently served to essentialize religious identities because what was held up by the Court was a distinctive version of the group's identity and not its actual heterogeneous character. In the process, the discourse articulated an inclusive pattern of self-definition that posits Hinduism as an apparently uncontested religious ideology. Challenges to the majoritarian sway over Indian society from any breakaway sect from Hinduism are diminished because the majority is constructed as including all possible challenges, differences, and variations. This also reinstates the Muslims and Christians as minority. This discourse of Hinduism therefore, though acceptable to the socially powerful Hindu middle class, uses a language that *others* those communities who fall outside it. An institution which is capable of using such an emancipatory discourse of modernity and can claim to speak with the voice of the Universal Man, the unmarked citizen, or often, in Vivekananda's words, 'the Indian', is a voice at home with the arrangement of self and community as it exists. It is not the voice of the minority that 'readies arrangements of self and community aimed at subverting and replacing' the existing order (Tharu 1996: 2019).

The strongest criticism of this inclination to create a grand narrative for all faiths born on Indian soil has come from Kanchi Ilaiah who avoids the conception of Brahmanism as religious precept or ritual order, and conceives it instead as contemporary practice and as cultural, economic, and political power in today's world. The heterogeneity of the many sects being brought under one umbrella leads to the new smaller sects being appropriated by the discourse of Hinduism. In the *Yagnapurushdasji v. Muldas* case,[21] the suit was dismissed by the Court on the grounds that 'the apprehension entertained by the appellants' was 'founded on superstition, ignorance and complete misunderstanding of the true teachings of Hindu religion and of the real significance of the tenets and philosophy taught by Swaminarayan himself'.[22] This role played by the Court in deciding which practices are correct or 'essential' religious practices and which are not in a given religious order, gives the judiciary the power to accept or dismiss groups which claim to have formed a new religion or religions sect. Moreover, with the definition of Hinduism being given near-universal applicability, it appears extremely unlikely that any faith born within the geographical precincts of the Indian subcontinent will be given a status significant enough for its challenge to have any impact on society.

This has a significant impact on the equations between the majority and the minority communities in the society. If the master narrative of the majority community is such that it cannot, by whatever means, be challenged or diminished in any way because the totalizing narrative has, even before the challenges have been made, legitimized them all, then the majority and minority become permanent and fixed numbers. Talking of how we have come to live with the notion of a permanent Hindu majority, and similarly permanent Muslim, Christian, Sikh, or untouchable minority, Gyanendra Pandey (2006: 178) cites Partha Chatterjee's explanation of the minority groups as an actually existing category of Indian citizenship—constitutionally defined, legally administered, and politically invoked. Thus, the very discourse of state which gives us our constitutional provisions, government policy, and legal practice, also gives us our notions of 'majority' and 'minorities', along with an idea of the communities which occupy the domain of nationalist politics. As Pandey (2007: 163) writes, the communities in question, those who will be party to particular political dialogues, are conjured up to a large extent by this powerful political discourse:

> It is necessary to note, however, that this privileged discourse is itself the enunciation ... of particular, powerful classes and communities—which have considerable leverage within the institutions of the state. ... Political parties, associations and movements are central to the negotiations that produce the particular distribution and hierarchical arrangement of communities that marks contemporary Indian discourse. So, of course, is the state and its legal apparatus.

The setting for the Ramakrishna Mission court case was a decade when religion and religious identity came to the forefront of the Indian socio-political context. After the Mandal agitation, which was often openly supported by the upper-caste middle class, came the rise of the Bharatiya Janata Party (BJP), the political wing of the Sangh Parivar. On 6 December 1992, the Babri Masjid was razed, and violent communal riots broke out in various parts India. The decade ended with the 2002 Gujarat riots, pushing to the foreground of Indian politics and society uncomfortable questions regarding the Indian majority and the minority. Set within this decade, the Ramakrishna Mission, prompted by either religious or secular reasons, articulated their philosophy as a religion that is tolerant and universal. They argued that though Vivekananda had gone to Chicago as an aggressive Hindu monk, he had returned a preacher of a religion basically different from Hinduism. Upon this was based Vivekananda's claim that through the Mission, 'we shall speak to all men in terms of their own orthodoxy!' (Noble 2005: 389).

The assumption that Hinduism *could* include a faith which unambiguously stated itself as being distinct from Hinduism exposes the power differentials that lie behind the objective numerical differences of the terms majority and minority.

NOTES

1.   The Ramakrishna Mission enjoys great support in India, especially in West Bengal. While many of its devotees join the prayer assemblies, or attend the lectures arranged by the Mission, they are not all formally members of the organization, or followers who have taken the '*diksha*' from the Mission monks. There are also many who are not devotees and who may not attend the religious functions of the Mission, but have faith in and support the Mission's activities. This large community constitutes its 'outside' support.

2.   . *Shastri Yagnapurushdasji and Others v. Muldas Bhundardas Vaishya and Another*, AIR 1966, SC 1119.

3.   The letter of the Director of Public Instructions (DPI) dated 29 August 1962 informed the Registrar of the Calcutta University that the Rahara college would function as a sponsored college with financial assistance from the state government and union government.

4.   See memo dated 16 January 1971, conveying the approval of the Governor of West Bengal for the common pattern of governing bodies of sponsored colleges, and specifying that this composition of the governing bodies of the sponsored colleges did not include governing bodies of sponsored colleges run

by missionary societies on the basis of agreement with respective missions. Also, see memo dated 18 April 1978, advising a change in the compositional pattern of the governing bodies of colleges, but excepting 'the colleges ... run by Missionary Societies on the basis of agreement with the respective Missions'. Both these memos were referred to in the Supreme Court judgement.

5. *Bramchari Sidheswar Shai v. State of West Bengal*, AIR 1995, SC 2089.

6. The Ramakrishna Mission's demand was to have itself declared a non-Hindu minority wherein its members could legally still be treated as Hindus in matters of marriage and inheritance (that is, according to the Hindu law), but would be recognized as non-Hindus in the religious sense. This would mean that the Ramakrishnaites would have the same status as Sikhs and Buddhists: recognition as 'legal Hindus and religious non-Hindus'.

7. Among the many sharp reactions to the event was that of Professor G.C. Asnani, who wrote to the Chief Justice of India, Justice P.N. Bhagwati, stating that the action of the Mission authorities had aggrieved 'millions of Hindus in general and many Hindu disciples of Shri Ramakrishna and Swami Vivekananda' in particular (Dutta 1986: 476).

8. 'State control over education invariably brings with it an access to funds, which gives the state as well as the party cadre scope to arm-twist the educational authorities. It also empowers the state and the party to doctor syllabi. The fracas of the Communist Party of India (Marxist) with the Ramakrishna Mission-run institutions led the latter to contemplate acquiring minority status' (Biswas 2002).

9. Devotees and supporters of the Mission used the words 'grief', 'anger', 'disappointment', and 'unexpected' when recounting this phase of their association with the Mission in interviews with this author.

10. 'We are proud that we are Hindus. We would not say that we are not Hindus.... It was just to get that advantage. If we can get those advantages as a minority, then why should we not do so?' (Swami Bhasyananda 1986).

11. Ibid.

12. Jamsetji's letter to Vivekananda, written to ask him to guide the planned Research Institute (later, the Indian Institute of Science [IISc]) speaks of his hopes to encourage the spirit of asceticism and science—two spheres usually treated as disparate. 'Tata Steel and Vivekananda', Letter from Jamsetji to Vivekananda, 23 November 1898, IISc Archives, Bangalore.

13. 'Are Hindu Reformists Hindus?' Who Is a Hindu? Voice of India, New Delhi, 2001, 'The Koenraad Elst Site', available at http://koenraadelst.voi.org/books/wiah/ch6.htm#5#5 (accessed 18 December 2011).

14. AIR 1995, SC 2089: 8.

15. Ibid.

16. Ibid., p. 11.

17. Ibid., p. 10.

18. According to Hacker, inclusivism 'consists in claiming for, and thus including in, one's own religion what really belongs to an alien sect' (Hacker cited in Sen 2006: 8).
19. *Yagnapurushasji v. Muldas*, AIR 1966, SC 1119.
20. *Mohd. Hanif Quraishi and Others v. State of Bihar*, AIR 1958 SC 731.
21. *Yagnapurushdasji v. Muldas*, AIR 1966, SC 1119.
22. AIR 1966 SC 1135.

REFERENCES

AIR 1995, SC 2089, Text of Judgment by Supreme Court of India, Bramchari Sidheswar Shai v. State of West Bengal, Judgment delivered on 2nd July 1995, available at http://judis.nic.in (accessed 18 December 2011).

Appadurai, Arjun. 1993, 'Number in the Colonial Imagination', in C.A. Breckenridge and P. van der Veer (eds), *Orientalism and the Postcolonial Predicament*, Philadelphia: University of Pennsylvania Press, pp. 314–36.

Baird, Robert D. (ed.). 1971, 'On Defining Hinduism as a Religious and Legal Category', in *Religion and Law in Independent India*, New Delhi: Manohar, pp. 41–58.

Balakrishnan, K.G. 2009. 'Individual Rights in India: A Perspective from the Supreme Court', Paper presented at the International Roundtable Conference, University of Georgia, 3–6 April.

Beckerlegge, Gwilym. 2000, *The Ramakrishna Mission: The Makings of a Modern Hindu Movement*, New Delhi: Oxford University Press.

Bharati, Agehananda. 1970, 'The Hindu Renaissance and Its Apologetic Pattern', *Journal of Asian Studies*, 29(2): 267–87.

Biswas, Susanta Kumar. 2002, 'Schooled in a New Set of Rules', *The Telegraph*, Kolkata, 31 December, available at http://www.telegraphindia.com/1021231/asp/opinion/story_1457193.asp (accessed 18 December 2011).

Chatterjee, Partha. 1998, 'Secularism and Tolerance', in R. Bhargava (ed.), *Secularism and Its Critics*, New Delhi: Oxford University Press, pp. 345–79.

———. 2004, '*The Nation and Its Fragments: Colonial and Postcolonial Histories*', in *The Partha Chatterjee Omnibus*, New Delhi: Oxford University Press.

Chowdhury, Indira. 2001, *The Frail Hero and Virile History*, New Delhi: Oxford University Press.

Derrett, J.D.M. 1968, 'Hindu: A Definition Wanted for the Purpose of Applying a Personal law', *Zeitschrift fur vergleichende Rechtswissenschaft, einschliesslich der ethnologischen Rechtsforschung*, LXX: 110–128.

Dutta, Bhupendranath. 1954, *Swami Vivekananda: The Patriot Prophet*, Calcutta: Nabobharat.

Dutta, Nilanjan. 1986, 'Religious Privilege vs Academic Freedom', *Economic and Political Weekly*, 21(12): 476.

Edwardes, Michael. 1972, *Nehru: A Political Biography*, New York: Praeger Publishers.

Galanter, Marc. 1998, 'Hinduism, Secularism, and the Indian Judiciary', in R. Bhargava (ed.), *Secularism and Its Critics*, New Delhi: Oxford University Press, pp. 268–93.

Grew, Raymond. 2001. 'Introduction', in A. Burguiere and R. Grew (eds), *The Construction of Minorities: Cases for Comparison Across Time and Around the World*, Ann Arbor: University of Michigan Press, pp. 1–14.

Hinduism Today. 1986, 'A Chat with Swami Satchitananda', October, available at http://www.hinduismtoday.com/modules/smartsection/print.php?itemid= 390 (accessed 12 December 2011).

Kaviraj, Sudipta. 1992, 'The Imaginary Institution of India', in P. Chatterjee and G. Pandey (eds), *Subaltern Studies VII: Writings on South Asian History and Society*, New Delhi: Oxford University Press, pp. 1–40.

McLean, M.D. 1991, 'Are Ramakrishnaites Hindus? Some Implications of Recent Litigation on the Question', *South Asia*, 14(2): 99–117.

Miller, David. 1999, 'Modernity in Hindu Monasticism: Swami Vivekananda and the Ramakrishna Movement', *Journal of Asian Studies*, 34(1): 111–26.

Minor, Robert Neil. 1993, 'S. Radhakrishnan and Religious Pluralism', *Studia Missonalia*, XLII: 307–27.

————. 1999, *The Religious, the Spiritual and the Secular: Auroville and Secular India*, Albany: State University of New York Press.

Nairn, Tom. 1997, *Faces of Nationalism: Janus Revisited*, London: Verso.

Noble, Margaret E. 2005, *The Master as I Saw Him: Being Pages from the Life of the Swami Vivekananda*, Calcutta: Kessinger Publishing (Printed by S.C. Ghose: Lakshmi Printing Works).

Pandey, Gyanendra, 2006, *Routine Violence: Nations, Fragments, Histories*, Stanford: Stanford University Press.

————. 2007, 'The Secular State and the Limits of Dialogue', in A.D. Needham and R.S. Rajan (eds), *The Crisis of Secularism*, Durham and London: Duke University Press, pp. 157–76.

Prabuddha Bharat. 2007, 'Politics, History and Swami Vivekananda', Editorial, 112(11): 605.

Radhakrishnan, Sarvepalli. 1956, 'Presidential Address', 21 February 1954, on the 92nd Birthday Celebrations of Swami Vivekananda, New Delhi, in S. Radhakrishnan, *Occasional Speeches and Writings*, The Publications Division Ministry of Information and Broadcasting, Government of India, Calcutta: Saraswati Press.

————. 1957, *The Hindu View of Life*, New York: Macmillan.

Sen, Ronojoy. 2006, 'Defining Religion: The Indian Supreme Court and Hinduism', Heidelberg Papers in South Asian and Comparative Politics, Working Paper No. 29, South Asia Institute, Department of Political Science, University of Heidelberg.

Rao, Vijendra Kasturi Ranga Varadaraja. 1979, *Swami Vivekananda—The Prophet of Vedantic Socialism*, Builders of India Series, New Delhi: Publications Division, Ministry of Information and Broadcasting, Government of India.

Swami Bhasyananda. 1986, 'RK Mission Seeks Protection from a Communist Government', *Hinduism Today*, March, available at http://www.hinduismtoday.com/modules/smartsection/item.php?itemid=363 (accessed 18 December 2011).

Swami Vivekananda. 1970, 'Practical Vedanta and Other Lectures', in *The Complete Works of Swami Vivekananda*, Vol. 2, Calcutta: Advaita Ashram.

Tharu, Susie. 1996, 'A Critique of Hindutva-Brahminism', Review, *Economic and Political Weekly*, 21(30, 27 July): 2019–21.

10

Sikh Minority Identity Formation
Nation and Politics in Postcolonial India

Natasha Behl

When asked about the treatment of Sikhs in India, Hardev Singh Saini, a 43-year-old backward-caste man, said: 'In the nation, when people see a Sikh, about 70 per cent of those people are actually against him. They are opposed to Sikhs because Sikhs have their own identity, their own religion, their own everything.' When asked the same question, Hardeep Kaur Bedi, a 55-year-old Khatri woman, answered:

> We don't need anyone to give us anything; we Sikhs have our own separate law. We love our religion; we have our own way of dress; we have our own identity; we have created our own social norms of how we interact and interrelate. We have created all of this on our own. Our *qaum* [nation or community] is just like this; no one needs to give us anything. We don't need anything. Our Gurus have given us so much, and they continue to watch over us, and we actually do better on our own, as the lions that we are.

The statements made by Saini and Bedi raise interesting questions about Sikh identity. How does one make sense of a Sikh minority identity that values separateness and distinctness from India? How is this minority identity constructed? What discourses are at play in this particular identity formation process? How can the continuities and variabilities of this identity formation be conceptualized? And last, who is privileged and displaced by these particular continuities and variabilities?

The literature on minority studies provides some insight on the formation of minority identities. Some scholars, for example, explore the way in which modern law (constitutional, personal, and case law) creates and conditions minority identity. Others approach identity formation by focusing on issues of minority representation. Some scholars of minority studies examine the nexus between knowledge and power to demonstrate the ways in which colonial institutions and practices create and condition minority identity formation. This project contributes to the understanding of minority identity formation by examining the narrative construction of identity. I argue that one can understand minority identity formation—how it is created, maintained, and challenged—by exploring the narratives that social actors use 'to make sense of—indeed, to act in—their lives' (Somers 1994: 618).

This chapter makes sense of Sikh minority identity formation in the postcolonial Indian context by drawing on Margaret Somers' notion of narrative identity to explain the process through which minority identities are created, maintained, and challenged. By reading interview responses through a public Sikh nationalist narrative rooted in truth, justice, and recognition, one is able to better understand the formation of a separate yet narrow Sikh nationalist identity through which respondents develop a shared way of conceptualizing the socio-political world. Narrative identity is premised on an interpretation of narrative that is not limited to representation, but defines 'narrative and narrativity as concepts of *social epistemology and social ontology*' (Somers 1994: 606). This conception of narrative posits 'that it is through narrativity that we come to know, understand, and make sense of the social world, and it is through narratives and narrativity that we constitute our social identities' (Somers 1994: 606). In short, Somers argues that 'all of us come to *be* who we *are* by being located or locating ourselves in social narratives *rarely of our own making*' (Somers 1994: 606). For the purposes of this analysis, the most relevant dimension of narrativity is public. Public narratives are 'attached to cultural and institutional formations larger than the single individual, to intersubjective networks or institutions' (Somers 1994: 606) and can range from the narratives of one's family to those of the workplace, church, government, and nation.

In this analysis, I use interview responses from ordinary Sikhs to query rather than take for granted the minority religious identification of individuals and groups. By doing so, I am able to ask how, when, and why people interpret social experience in ethnic, religious, racial, or gendered terms. The emphasis shifts not only to questions about how people get classified but also to questions about how gestures, utterances, situations, and events are interpreted and experienced. I follow the lead of multiple authors such as Rogers Brubaker, Taeku Lee, and Harjot Oberoi, who argue that scholars of identity need to take concepts like ethnicity, race, and religion as subject to, rather than prior to, empirical study. For example, Brubaker argues that ethnicity or ethnic common sense 'is a key part of what we want to explain, not what we want to explain things *with*; it belongs to our empirical data, not to our analytic toolkit' (Brubaker 2004: 9). Similarly, Lee argues: 'An expectation of a preordained identity-to-politics link can potentially distort our understanding of race and ethnicity, especially when taken as prior to, rather than subject to, empirical study' (Lee 2008: 461). Oberoi argues that historians of religion often come to questionable conclusions because they assume a one-to-one correspondence between the religious categories on the one hand, and the way people actually experience their everyday lives on the other (Oberoi 1994). In response, Oberoi calls for an examination of 'religion as a social and cultural process; not something given, but an activity embedded in everyday life, a part of human agency' (Oberoi 1994: 1–2). In accordance with Brubaker, Lee, and Oberoi, I shift my analytic attention towards the process of identity formation through an examination of narrative identities, rather than taking identities as given.

This analytic approach to identity provides two specific benefits: first, it offers resources for avoiding what Brubaker calls 'groupism',[1] while at the same time, helping to account for its tenacious hold on our social imagination; and second, it helps to elucidate and concretize a notion of identity as a way of seeing and being in the socio-political world. This approach avoids the problem of taking groups for granted because it does not treat groups as 'substantial entities but as collective cultural representations, as widely shared ways of seeing, thinking, and conceptualizing the social world' (Brubaker 1994: 23). In other words, I shift my analytic attention towards the process of group making rather than taking groups as a basic unit of analysis. Equally important is the fact that this approach also suggests that identity is a way of seeing and being in the world; it is, as Linda Alcoff argues, a way of inhabiting, interpreting, and working through—both collectively and individually—an objective social location (Alcoff 2006).

Similarly, my use of a qualitative, exploratory research design has distinct advantages when trying to understand identity formation processes. First, qualitative methods permit the definition of key concepts like martyrdom and Khalsa Raj to be determined by ordinary members of the Sikh community, not by religious and scholarly elites. Second, a qualitative approach does not assume that Sikh nationalist identities are a simple reflection of Sikh scripture or Sikh religious history; rather, it builds an understanding of Sikh nationalist identities from the ground up. In Spring 2009, I conducted forty semi-structured, in-depth interviews in Punjabi with Sikhs of all walks of life. The interviews were primarily conducted in two districts of Punjab, India—Mohali and Amritsar—with approximately the same number of men as women from each of the three major caste groups—Jats, Khatris, and Scheduled Castes (SC)/Backward Castes. Also, I conducted interviews with respondents of varying ages (from 21–71 years) and educational levels (from illiterate to highly educated). In addition to conducting in-depth interviews, I had the opportunity to gather crucial information through follow-up interviews, informal conversation, and observation of religious and social activities. This research also builds on one summer of preparatory research conducted in 2005.

SIKH NATIONALIST NARRATIVE

Interview data provide evidence to support the arguments that: (*i*) a segment of the Sikh community narrates their minority identity through a public Sikh nationalist narrative, which emphasizes the pursuit of truth, justice, and recognition, and is characterized by four narrative themes: sacrifice and martyrdom, injury and injustice, Khalsa Raj, and visible identity; and (*ii*) this particular narrative identity is tied to specific material interests, narrative methods employed to maintain and challenge these interests, and social actors who are, in turn, privileged and displaced. It is important to note that a Sikh nationalist narrative is only one way in which Sikhs understand their minority position in India. A Sikh narrative of integration, in addition to others, also helps to engender a sense of minority identification among Sikhs. Unlike a Sikh nationalist narrative, an integrationist narrative envisions a more harmonious relationship with the Indian state.[2]

Sacrifice and Martyrdom

A narrative theme of sacrifice and martyrdom connects individual Sikhs to one another, both historically and contemporarily. Respondents construct this narrative by drawing from the Guru period (1469–1708),

Khalsa Raj (1765–1849), Indian independence struggle (1920s–47), and militancy period (1980s–90s). Respondents employ this narrative to understand their lives in relation not only to the lives of other Sikhs, but also to the lives of the gurus, which allows them to understand their personal history as part of a larger set of sacred communal memories. A narrative of sacrifice and martyrdom allows respondents to interpret and weave together disparate and disconnected historical events in nationalist terms, a shared socio-political conceptualization rooted in truth, justice, and recognition.

One way in which this shared conceptualization is achieved is through the Sikh *ardas* (petition or prayer closing congregational worship). According to Gurinder Singh Mann, 'Sikhs believe that the events in the lives of the Gurus were part of the revelation, and that subsequent historical developments continue to reflect the divine design' (Mann 2001: 16). Consequently, Sikhs tend to interpret their history as a set of sacred memories, which is actualized through the ardas. The ardas, according to Mann, constitutes a record of the historical memories of the community from its founding to the present day, in which 'Sikhs express gratitude to Vahiguru [god] for guiding the community's destiny in the past, seek divine blessings in dealing with current problems, and reaffirm their vision of establishing a state in which the Sikhs shall rule' (Mann 2001: 16).

According to Sikh tradition, the concept of martyrdom in Sikhism 'was first established by the Sikh Gurus, in particular Guru Nanak (AD 1469–1539) and Guru Gobind Singh (AD 1666–1708), and sustained by two Guru-martyrs and countless brave Sikhs who suffered death fighting tyranny in the face of an overwhelming enemy' (Fenech 1997: 625). For Sikhs, sacrifice and martyrdom thus represents a fundamental institution, one perhaps present since the faith's very inception.[3] According to Fenech, the ardas is the greatest testament to the importance of martyrdom in the Sikh community:

> Those male and female Singhs who gave their heads for the faith; who were torn limb from limb; scalped, broken on the wheel, and sawn asunder; who sacrificed their lives for the protection of the sacred gurdwaras, never abandoning their faith; and who zealously guarded the sacred *kes* [hair] of the true Sikh: O valiant Khalsa, keep your attention on their merits and call on God, saying *Vahiguru*. (Fenech 1997: 625)

Fenech argues that this particular portion of the ardas, which asks Sikhs to call to mind past sacrifices, is 'firmly lodged in the minds and understanding of its citers and listeners' (Fenech 1997: 625). Interview respondents confirm Fenech's claim as they make sense of Sikh socio-political realities through a narrative emphasis on sacrifice and martyrdom—an emphasis that makes sense of the present by pointing to the sacrifices of the past.

Many respondents, such as Hardeep Kaur Bedi, discuss the Indian independence struggle as part and parcel of a larger Sikh narrative of sacrifice and martyrdom:

> Many young people, like Bhagat Singh, who were shrewd and sharp, are now identified as the martyrs of that time, the martyrs of the independence movement. But nowadays if they were among us we would call them militants. We would, right? Many people rose to the occasion, and the British attempted to put down the movement. Some like Mahatma Gandhi would agitate half-naked in front of official buildings. He would refuse to move and the British said, 'This old man is very obstinate.' And for us, these people are martyrs, and for the British they were militants. They used to call Guru Gobind Singh a militant because he fought for his nation; he sacrificed his entire family for his qaum.

Bedi connects Bhagat Singh and Mahatma Gandhi to Guru Gobind Singh, thus connecting three individuals from two different time periods with different religious, political, and ideological commitments through a narrative focus on sacrifice and martyrdom. Bhagat Singh, for example, explicitly framed his participation in the Indian independence struggle vis-à-vis his Marxist, atheist, and anarchist beliefs. Mahatma Gandhi, in contrast, understood his participation in the Indian independence struggle through his particular conception of Hinduism. Unlike Bhagat Singh and Mahatma Gandhi, Guru Gobind Singh's sacrifices are arguably best understood through his creation of the Khalsa, the Sikh brotherhood. Bedi seamlessly brings together these three men because she makes sense of these two time periods through the common narrative theme of sacrifice and martyrdom, and consequently she is able to make sense of the Indian independence struggle and the Guru period as part and parcel of a public Sikh nationalist narrative.

A narrative of sacrifice and martyrdom is not only apparent in the way in which respondents understand a Sikh socio-political reality, but is also evident in their concern for external recognition of a visible Sikh identity.[4] For example, when discussing the Indian independence movement, Fateh Singh states: 'Sikhs are the ones who gave up their lives, who martyred themselves to gain independence for this country.' He continues by stating that, in the present day, the Indian government does not sufficiently recognize the sacrifices of the Sikh community:

> This thing [Sikh sacrifice] bothers the Indian government. They don't count the sacrifices that we have made. For example, the government presents Indian history on TV or in other mediums by characterizing Sikhs as nothing. Why did they do this? See, no one has made the type of sacrifice that Sikhs have made. If they [Indian government] recognize our sacrifice, then they become nothing because they have admitted that they didn't sacrifice. As long as they keep Sikhs down, characterize Sikhs as zero, as nothing, and as long as they keep a divide-and-rule policy, then they can continue to rule.

According to Fateh Singh, Sikhs sacrificed and martyred themselves for Indian independence, but this sacrifice and martyrdom is not acknowledged in dominant accounts of Indian nationalist history. For Singh, according to a public nationalist narrative of truth, justice, and recognition, the Indian government is required to publicly recognize the sacrifices made by the Sikh community for the Indian nation.

Injury and Injustice

A public national narrative theme of injury and injustice allows respondents to connect their lived experience under Hindu/Congress rule[5] to the lived experience of Sikhs during Mughal and British Raj. Respondents emphasize the narrative of injury and injustice in order to: (*i*) create a connection between Sikhs irrespective of time and space; and (*ii*) explain their commitment to truth, justice, and recognition, which, for a segment of the respondents, is attainable only through Khalsa Raj. A narrative of injury and injustice can be read as another way in which respondents come to know, understand, and make sense of the socio-political world in nationalist terms.

Respondents, such as Beena Kaur, a 65-year-old Khatri woman, claim that Sikh history and contemporary life are best characterized through a narrative of injury and injustice:

> Behind all these things there are some very deep issues; our history is very deep. It is a very painful history. For example, if we begin to speak of our history, it becomes difficult. It is difficult to speak of the small, small children whose throats were squeezed; at one point, their necks were squeezed, and later they were covered with tires.

Beena Kaur's version of Sikh history is intelligible only through a narrative emphasis on injury and injustice. She is able to discuss the physical abuse of Sikh children during Mughal rule and the brutal mistreatment of Sikh children during Congress rule—specifically the 1984 riots in Delhi[6]—as a seamless narrative. The memory of the physical abuse of Sikh children during Mughal rule is alive for Kaur even though she was not alive to witness it. She expresses pain at the thought of 'small, small children'[7] being brutalized in different ways, in two distinct eras and contexts. Irrespective of these differences, Beena Kaur is able to speak of these atrocities as connected because both are rooted in a sense of pain and trauma experienced by Sikhs under foreign rule, be it Mughal or Hindu/Congress.

Fateh Singh, a 42-year-old SC man, and Surinder Singh, a 22-year-old Jat man, connect their demand for justice with the injury experienced by Sikhs in the 1984 anti-Sikh riots. For example, Fateh Singh focuses his attention on the state's inability to provide justice:

> There [in Delhi] innocent people were burned to death with tires. How many years has it been? It's been 24, 25, 26 years. But justice has yet to be attained. Justice hasn't been served. Why hasn't it? Our politics is beholden to the chair, to the seat of power. If politicians seek justice, then they lose their seat. They lose their seat. Then why do these individuals claim that they are the rightful representatives of the Sikhs? These people are the enemies of the Sikhs. Since 1984, these people haven't been able to prosecute the perpetrators of this crime; these people haven't been able to pursue justice. Ask who has suffered through this incident: those individuals who lost mothers, fathers, sisters; those individuals who are now orphans.

Fateh Singh is outraged by the fact that so much time has passed since the atrocities of 1984, yet the victims have not received justice. According to Fateh Singh, in the current political structure, a politician who actually pursues justice will lose his or her position of power. Fateh Singh is criticizing the very structure of the state by claiming that the state and its agents (that is, politicians) cannot pursue justice if they want to remain in power, and therefore, in his narrative formulation, Sikhs will never attain justice within the current Raj. He concludes by stating that it is the victims who continue to suffer—it is the victims who endure injury and injustice on a daily basis. Similarly, Surinder Singh raises questions regarding accountability and justice:

> Take, for example, the 1984 riots: it's been 25 years and there still hasn't been a resolution. If Tytler[8] didn't have a hand in the riots, then who did?

> Someone has to behind the riots; if it isn't Tytler, then whom should we hold responsible? Someone was behind these riots, and if it isn't you, then who is it? Someone is behind this, and we still don't know who it is.

Surinder Singh repeatedly asks, 'If Tytler didn't have a hand in the riots, then who did?' Singh claims that someone has to behind the riots, and he or she must be held accountable. Interestingly, Surinder Singh was born after the riots occurred, but this fact does not diminish the pain he experiences. The memory of the riot is alive for him even though he was not alive to witness it.

Respondents connect a discussion of injury and injustice to the need for Khalsa Raj, where truth, justice, and recognition can be attained. To make such an argument, many respondents explain that foreign rule fails to provide justice. For example, Fateh Singh states:

> The state doesn't think it's a sin to kill innocent people. The state simply says, 'A big tree has fallen; no big deal, some will die.' But was the big tree right? Was the big tree just? If you bring injury to someone's religion, then the religion will rise. Even if people like me stay sleeping, there are some out there that have been filled by the religion, and they will rise. That injury gave rise to a call for justice.

Fateh Singh integrates the language used by Prime Minister Rajiv Gandhi following Indira Gandhi's assassination into his nationalist narrative to underscore the injustice of Congress rule. According to Rao, Rajiv Gandhi 'explained away this unprecedented orgy of violence [1984 anti-Sikh riots] comparing it with a natural phenomenon: "there is a shaking of the earth, whenever a big tree falls"' (Rao 1984: 2066). Fateh Singh interprets the 'big tree' as Indira Gandhi and the 'shaking earth' as the killing of innocent Sikhs. This narrative formulation allows Fateh Singh to question if actions that took place after Indira Gandhi's assignation were just. Fateh Singh follows with a statement in which he argues that if the Sikh religion is injured, then it will rise in the name of justice. Thus, Fateh Singh explicitly connects the experience of injury to a Sikh nationalist narrative that claims to pursue truth, justice, and recognition.

Similarly, Beena Kaur argues, 'If the nation gave us justice, then we wouldn't need Khalsa or Khalsa Raj.' However, the fact that Sikhs have yet to attain justice for the atrocities committed in 1984 allows Kaur to maintain that Sikhs need Khalsa Raj. The need for Khalsa Raj is justified not only through the unjust treatment of Sikhs under Hindu/Congress rule but also through references to past atrocities inflicted by other rulers, such as Mughal and British rulers. Thus, the narrative of injury and injustice allows respondents to frame their response to a history of atrocity as a pursuit of truth, justice, and recognition that, according to some, is only attainable through Sikh rule, Khalsa Raj.

Khalsa Raj

Khalsa Raj is both a historical period[9] in Sikh history and, as discussed in the context of injury and injustice, a contemporary normative goal for a segment of Sikhs. Khalsa Raj, therefore, plays an interesting role in a public nationalist narrative because it is pointed to as both a collective historical achievement and collective normative goal. As a result, Khalsa Raj is significant for understanding how, when, and why people interpret social and political experience in nationalist terms.

A majority of respondents narrate the historical memory of Khalsa Raj with great pride and dignity. Hardeep Kaur Bedi boasts about Ranjit Singh's rule:

> Maharaja Ranjit Singh was an amazing raja; his reign was outstanding. Before the British Raj the Sikh religion really grew; this happened during Maharaja Ranjit Singh's time. He was able to bring all Hill Kings into his kingdom. He won over all of Punjab including Peshawar and Lahore, he conquered all the way to Pakistan and Afghanistan, all the way to Kabul. His rule was strong up 'til Kabul. But the Sikh nation was badly damaged by the British when Maharaja Ranjit Singh's son Dalip was kidnapped and held against his will in England. And that was the end of the Sikh nation in the world.

Bedi describes with pride the way in which Ranjit Singh was able to build a Sikh Empire that spanned from current-day Punjab through Pakistan to Afghanistan. Bedi also points out that the Sikh religion grew during Khalsa Raj. She ends her narrative by stating that initially the Sikh nation was damaged by the British, and ultimately brought to an end.

Other respondents, like Jatinder Singh, a 24-year-old SC man, take pride in the international connections that were forged during Khalsa Raj: 'During Maharaja Ranjit Singh's time we had a connection with Europe—we had established links with Europe. For example, the French people traveled here to give [military] training, and therefore our identity was known in foreign lands.'[10] Singh takes pride in the knowledge that a Sikh identity was recognized around the world. Many respondents look back to this historic period with pride and honour because this is one of the few times when the religious symbol of Khalsa Raj took concrete form, thus leading to the growth of Sikhism.

Other respondents speak of missed opportunities by narrating moments at which Khalsa Raj was potentially attainable. A few, for example, describe the period of the militancy as a missed opportunity when Khalsa Raj could have been established under the leadership of Jarnail Singh Bhindranwale.[11] But many more respondents discuss the period of Indian independence as a missed opportunity. For Jatinder Singh, the period of Indian independence marks a significant moment:

> They [Sikh political leaders] didn't become aware at that time. If they had become aware, then we [Sikhs] could have had some success—we could have had our demands met by the British. But we experienced failure during this time. Sikhs could have gained a state during this time, but they failed. Muslims were absolutely smarter. For example, Muhammad Iqbal[12] writes '*Saara jahan se achchha, Hindustan hamara*' [Better than the entire world, is our Hindustan]. But after that he is a staunch supporter of Pakistan—of independent Pakistan. How did this man's thinking change? How could he at one point say that Hindustan is the best and then so soon thereafter demand Pakistan? We have been let down by our political leaders.

This period, according to Singh, represents the moment when Sikh demands for an independent Sikh state—for Khalsa Raj—could have been met. Unlike their Muslims counterparts, Sikhs were let down by their political leaders. To reinforce this statement, Singh turns to a narrative description of Dr Muhammad Iqbal, who, according to Singh, was initially a supporter of Hindustan, but seized the opportunity to help create a new Muslim state, Pakistan. For Singh, this is where Sikh leaders failed: Sikh leaders were not able to translate this potential for the creation of Khalsa Raj into a concrete reality.

Beena Kaur argues that Sikhs made a grave mistake by collaborating with Hindus:

> Pundits are not our friends. This is Pundit Raj [Hindu rule]; they aren't our friends. The pundits said that we [Sikhs] would receive our piece; when Pakistan and Hindustan divided they told us, 'For now give us your support, and then you will be given your own territory where you will be able to rule yourself—where you will be able to spread your religion.' And later we [Sikhs] were told by the pundits, 'The time for Sikh self-rule has passed.' They [pundits] backed down.

According to Kaur, after Partition, Hindus backed down on their promise of Sikh autonomy, thus destroying the possibility for reinstating Khalsa Raj and instead subjecting Sikhs to pundit rule. The idea of a missed opportunity resonates with a specific segment of the Sikh community. According to Mann, '…with the departure of the British, the Akali Dal leadership's hope of recreating a new Khalsa Raj collapsed and the period closed on a profoundly sad note: Hindus got Hindustan, Muslims got Pakistan, but what did the Sikhs get?' (Mann 2001: 65).

Other respondents, however, like Jasveer Singh Gill, a 54-year-old Jat man, equate the creation of a Punjabi-speaking state in 1966 with Khalsa Raj:

> In 1966, the Punjabi Suba [Punjabi-speaking state] was created. Akalis [Sikh political party] participated in peaceful agitations—they went on strike, they were jailed, and they managed to create a Punjabi Suba—but the Congress people say they were wrong in doing so. But I don't say this. I think that they [Akali Party] did the absolute right thing. It is the right thing because today's Punjab, doesn't matter what the count is, it could be 40 percent, 30 percent, 25 percent Hindus, but ultimately whose state is it? Punjab is a Sikh state. This is the one demand of ours that has been met. If we still had a *maha*-Punjab [super Punjab, composed of Punjab, Haryana, and Himachal], then Punjab would never be a Sikh state. It would have been a Punjab of Punjabis, or a Punjab of those who live in Punjab, but today it is a Punjab of Sikhs; Punjab is a Sikh state.

After the language-based reorganization of Punjab, the demographics of Punjab shifted dramatically. Sikhs, who were a minority in Punjab, became a majority. Currently, Sikhs represent over 60 per cent of Punjab's population. This demographic shift, according to Gill, also signals a shift in power. A demographic shift can be equated with a shift in power relations because the Khalsa is a form of religious state formation. In short, Punjab is a Sikh-majority state, and therefore, for a segment of the Sikh population who adopt a nationalist narrative, it is also Khalsa Raj. This particular formulation of Khalsa Raj is significant because the state Punjab is majority Sikh, but not solely Sikh; Hindus, Muslims, Christians, and Jains also live in Punjab.

Visible Sikh Identity

A public Sikh nationalist narrative is also characterized by a visible Sikh identity. A visible Sikh identity is important because it delimits the contours of what it means to be Sikh. In other words, being Sikh in the socio-political world is defined in terms of one's visible identity. And therefore, who belongs in the Sikh community—who counts as Sikh—is intimately tied to a visible identity. Sikhs can be differentiated by degrees of religious observance categorized as *amritdhari* (bearer of amrit or nectar), *kesdhari* (bearer of long kes), and *sahijdhari* (bearer of slowness). After implementation of the *khande di pahul* (baptismal ceremony),[13] the Sikh community was composed of two segments. The first was the 'kesdharis or Singhs, who had undergone the ceremony of the khande di pahul and had taken up the mission of establishing the Khalsa Raj' (Mann 2004: 99). The other segment included the sahijdhari, who had not undergone the khande di pahul. In the nineteenth century, a third category, amritdhari, was created to describe those who keep unshorn hair and have undergone the baptismal ceremony, while kesdhari came to refer to those who keep hair but have not been baptized. It is amritdharis alone who have access to political power within the Sikh governing committee.

Most respondents adopt the aforementioned concepts to define and delimit who is a member of the Sikh community. According to some respondents, Sikhs are only those who have undergone the khande di pahul and live according to *rahit* (Sikh code of conduct).[14] Others, however, define Sikhs more inclusively as those who keep unshorn kes. Still other respondents define Sikhs as simply those who live according to gurbani (word of god) irrespective of outward appearance, which is the most inclusive definition. Jasveer Singh Gill defines Sikh identity by focusing on kes:

> A Sikh's heart should be full of Sikh teaching even if a Sikh doesn't conform completely to the required outward appearance. But I also don't believe that a Sikh can cut all their hair. The main characteristic of Sikh identity should remain intact; the most important Sikh character-istic is a Sikh's kes. If a Sikh keeps his kes, if he ties his turban, then he looks like a Sikh; he looks to be a Sikh. But if this same Sikh cuts his kes—even if he is wearing a *kirpan* [sword]—then he doesn't look to be a Sikh. This is the identity that I believe in.... You must have hair, you must tie a turban, and your beard can be cut, but it needs to be cut, not shaven. People like this should be considered pure Sikh and should receive full respect and dignity.

According to Gill, kes and turban are the most important characteristics of Sikh identity because this is what makes a Sikh look like a Sikh. For Gill, if an individual appears to be a Sikh, then he should be considered pure

Sikh, and in turn be granted full respect and dignity. Gill's emphasis on a Sikh's visible identity is reinforced by his explicit exclusion of sahijdhari Sikhs: 'Sahijdhari Sikhs aren't like me; sahijdharis are those who belong to the Sikh religion, but they cut their hair, so I don't consider them Sikhs.' Sahijdhari Sikhs do not look Sikh, and therefore Gill does not consider them to be part of the Sikh community.

Many respondents share Gill's concern regarding a visible Sikh identity. For example, Hardeep Kaur Bedi describes Sikhs as those who can be identified: 'Unlike Americans or Chinese, Sikhs have a visible identity. Sikh identity is, you know, of his turban, of his beard; Sikhs have a separate identity.' Bedi's narrative description includes both amritdhari and kesdhari Sikhs because both categories of Sikhs are visible through their unshorn hair, beard, and turban. As such, both Gill's and Bedi's narrative descriptions of Sikh identity can be read as fairly inclusive, excluding only sahijdharis. Both Gill and Bedi want to maintain a separate Sikh identity by emphasizing one's hair, beard, and turban as a boundary marker, but they also want to open up the religion to those who have not undergone the khande di pahul ceremony.

According to Gill, the Sikh religion needs to become more liberal by opening up its ranks to less observant Sikhs in order to avoid decline:

> I believe that the Sikh religion needs to change—it needs to become more liberal. It needs to change in a manner, for example … every time a religion has fractured, it has happened due to increased rigidity—increased conservatism. The change that needs to be brought about is that the Sikhs who cut and trim their beards, like myself, they should receive complete respect and dignity in the Sikh religion—in the Shiromani Committee, our Sikh [democratically elected] body. Sikhs like myself should receive full respect. Sikhism will grow only if this change is adopted; otherwise, Sikhism will go into decline because to keep a beard and to become a true Sikh isn't something everyone is capable of. To maintain this position one needs to work extremely hard. And when you have to work harder and harder to maintain Sikhism, then little by little people will begin to leave the religion.

According to Gill, the prescriptions associated with amritdhari status are too burdensome, and therefore people will begin to leave the Sikh fold. However, if one opens up the religion by granting kesdhari Sikhs the same rights as amritdhari Sikhs, then the Sikh religion will grow.

Gill's definition of who should count as a Sikh demonstrates the variability within a nationalist narrative; this variability is controversial because it can disrupt the current power structure in the Sikh community.

If kesdhari Sikhs are elevated to the same position as amritdhari Sikhs, then they will be granted full rights and privileges in Sikh institutions, including the Shiromani Gurdwara Prabandhak Committee (SGPC), an elected body of the Khalsa that first came into being in response to the 1920s Gurdwara Reform Movement. Since its inception, the SGPC has managed and maintained gurdwaras; prepared a standard edition of the *Guru Granth*; issued authoritative statements on Sikh history, beliefs, and code of conduct; and built a chain of schools and colleges. According to Peter van der Veer, since the 1920s, '... the control of this committee has become the most coveted prize in Sikh politics' (van der Veer 1994: 74). Another point of contention is the ongoing debate regarding the SGPC's definition of a Sikh (see, for example, Axel 2001; McLeod 1989; Takar 2005). Thus far, the SGPC has defined a Sikh in a relatively exclusionary way by only permitting amritdhari Sikhs to be full participants in the electoral process. Gill's call for the Sikh religion to become more liberal, therefore, has vast implications. If kesdhari Sikhs are given the same rights and privileges as amritdhari Sikhs, this will enable them to be part of the SGPC electoral process. Because kesdhari Sikhs actually outnumber amritdhari Sikhs, kesdhari control of the SGPC could lead to a dramatic change in the understanding of who is a Sikh, and this change could, in turn, impact distribution of resources and access to benefits.

The narrative descriptions of Sikh identity can be read as both inclusionary and exclusionary. Gill and Bedi, for example, deviate from the orthodox definitions of Sikh identity by narrating a more inclusive Sikh identity that creates room for kesdhari Sikhs, but they simultaneously exclude Sikh women by emphasizing male markers of Sikh identity, such as turban and beard. Both Gill and Bedi equate Sikh identity with male identity by consistently referring to *his* hair, *his* turban, and *his* beard. According to Brian Axel, Sikh men have become the privileged site for negotiating who is recognized as a member of the Sikh *Panth* 'by means of particular bodily techniques, religious practices, visual representations, and narratives of Sikh "identity"' (Axel 2001: 4). Even though Gill's and Bedi's narrative construction of Sikh identity is more inclusive towards kesdhari Sikhs, their narratives are simultaneously exclusive because Sikh women are written out of a Sikh nationalist narrative and a male Sikh identity is adopted as the norm. A Sikh nationalist narrative helps to elucidate and concretize the process through which a segment of the Sikh community adopts a nationalist way of being in the world, one that is intimately tied to gendered bodily practices—keeping unshorn hair and wearing a turban—that mark a distinct Sikh identity.

* * *

By analysing identity through narratives, I am able to avoid groupism while also elucidating and concretizing a notion of identity as a way of seeing and being in the socio-political world. In short, I am able to demonstrate how and why ordinary Sikhs at times inhabit, interpret, and work through, both collectively and individually, their socio-political location in nationalist terms. I am able to demonstrate that: (*i*) a segment of the Sikh community narrates their minority identity through a public Sikh nationalist narrative, which emphasizes the pursuit of truth, justice, and recognition, and is characterized by four narrative themes: sacrifice and martyrdom, injury and injustice, Khalsa Raj, and visible identity; and (*ii*) this particular narrative identity is tied to specific material interests, narrative methods employed to maintain and challenge these interests, and social actors who are, in turn, privileged and displaced.

In particular, it is from within a public Sikh nationalist narrative that one can make sense of the relations between a segment of Punjab and the rest of India, among a segment of Sikhs within Punjab, and among a segment of men and women within Sikhism. For example, Hardev Singh Saini's statement first examined at the opening of this article is best understood as part and parcel of a public Sikh nationalist narrative. Saini is giving voice to a Sikh nationalist identity, which, for him, is tied to the narrative themes of unrecognized and unacknowledged sacrifice, martyrdom, injury, and injustice. By doing so, Saini attempts to elevate and privilege a minority Sikh nationalist identity over an Indian identity. In the same way, one can make sense of Gill's definition of Sikh identity in relation to a narrative theme of visibility. While upholding this narrative theme, Gill simultaneously opens up the religion by granting kesdhari Sikhs the same rights as amritdhari Sikhs; a move that has the potential to radically shift the power balance among Sikhs. In short, Gill reinforces the narrative theme of Sikh visibility in an effort to elevate kesdhari Sikhs to the same position as amritdhari Sikhs, and provide kesdhari Sikhs access to material benefits that have been historically denied to them. Similarly, one can make sense of Bedi's narrative construction of a visible Sikh identity as part and parcel of a public Sikh nationalist narrative that emphasizes the need for recognition. However, this very need for recognition rooted in the narrative emphasis on visible identity simultaneously displaces Sikh women. Sikh women are written out of a Sikh nationalist narrative because they do not have access to the markers of a Sikh visible identity, and therefore the male Sikh identity is privileged—by both men and women—as the normative Sikh identity.

By taking individual and group identification as subject to, rather than prior to, empirical study, one can be more attentive to the process by which people, gestures, utterances, situations, and events are interpreted and experienced in nationalist terms. This approach enables one to explore the 'how' of identity formation processes. This analysis has explanatory value because the particular theoretical approach to identity combined with a qualitative research design allows for: (*i*) definitions of key concepts to be determined by ordinary members of the Sikh community, not by religious or scholarly elites; and (*ii*) an understanding of Sikh nationalist identities from the ground up, rather than assuming that Sikh nationalist identities are a one-to-one reflection of Sikh scripture or history.

NOTES

1. I draw this term from Brubaker who defines groupism as 'the tendency to take discrete, bounded groups as basic constituents of social life, chief protagonists of social conflicts, and fundamental units of social analysis' (2004: 8). For Brubaker, most scholars adopt groupism in their treatment of ethnic groups, nations, and races by assuming that they are 'entities to which interests and agency can be attributed' (2004: 8). This tendency to reify groups manifests in scholarly treatment of groups such as

> Serbs, Croats, Muslims, and Albanians in the former Yugoslavia, of Catholics and Protestants in Northern Ireland, of Jews and Palestinians in Israel and the occupied territories, of Turks and Kurds in Turkey, or of Blacks, Whites, Asians, Hispanics, and Native Americans in the United States as if they were internally homogenous, externally bounded groups, even unitary collective actors with common purposes. (Brubaker 2004: 8)

2. Bachittar Singh Walia, a 40-year-old Jat man, states, 'Sikhs are a minority; for example, they are two to three percent [of the Indian population].' Walia also adds, 'Sikhs have an identity that is recognized worldwide. But we can't say that Sikhs have a specific or special national identity.' Thus, for Walia, a minority identity does not give rise to a separate national identity among Sikhs. When asked explicitly about the treatment of Sikhs in India, Walia states that the treatment of Sikhs is 'fine'. He adds, 'There aren't any major problems, because India is an independent nation in which all religions are given an equal degree of respect. The state doesn't adopt any policies that privilege one

religion over another; all religions are treated equally and given equal respect.' For Walia, Sikhism, like other religions, is recognized and respected by the state. And more specifically, the state does not adopt policies that privilege one religion over another. And therefore, Walia's understanding of a Sikh minority identity is narrativized as harmonious with the state and its policies towards religious minorities. Even though Walia's narrative does not completely resonate with the narrative themes emphasized in a Sikh nationalist narrative—injury and injustice, sacrifice and martyrdom, Khalsa Raj, visible identity—he does recognize Operation Blue Star as one of the most important moments in Indian history since independence. For Walia, Operation Blue Star injured Sikh sentiment, and this is an injury that Sikhs are still recovering from. Walia understand himself through, and takes action from, an integrationist narrative, but this does not foreclose his capacity to recognize the importance of injury and injustice, especially in relation to Operation Blue Star.

3.   There is debate regarding the veracity of the popular belief that Sikh Gurus established martyrdom. Louis Fenech argues that the current under-standing of martyrdom that is prominent and pervasive in the Sikh community is not directly connected to the Guru period. Specifically, Fenech challenges the dominant belief among Sikhs that Guru Arjan, the fifth Guru, was the first Sikh martyr. Fenech is able to decentre this belief through a three-prong strategy: (*i*) Fenech's critical examination of primary sources 'demonstrates that many scholars of the Sikh tradition extrapolate far too much from them, filling in the numerous gaps in these sources' narrative with popular understandings forged in later years' (Fenech 1997: 627); (*ii*) Fenech determines that 'a conceptual system of posthumous recognition and anticipated reward' (Fenech 1997: 630) necessary for the accommodation of martyrdom did not exist during the time of Guru Arjan; and (*iii*) Fenech comes to the conclusion that the terms *sahid* and *sahadat* when used in Sikh literatures are used in its Islamic sense rather than what would later come to signify the Sikh martyr (Fenech 1997). Based on these three arguments, Fenech comes to the conclusion that Tat Khalsa ideologues in the nineteenth century appropriated a profound and powerful 'rhetoric of martyrdom' in an effort to produce the far less inclusive definition of the Sikh martyr (Fenech 1997: 642).

4.   Many respondents describe Sikh military service as part of Sikh sacrifice and martyrdom. Santokh Kaur, a 46-year-old Jat woman, for example, states: 'Sikhs are always ready to fight; they are always ready to give their lives, but no one respects this sacrifice. Take a look at all the borders; the borders are full of Sikh regiments.' According to Kaur, Sikhs sacrifice their lives for Indian national security; however, these sacrifices are neither acknowledged nor respected.

5.   Many respondents who adopt a Sikh nationalist narrative use the terms Congress Raj and Hindu Raj interchangeably. For these respondents, secular-ism is read as a thinly veiled pursuit of Hindu Raj. For example, Fateh Singh states, 'Look, before British rule, there was Muslim rule, after the British there

is Hindu Raj, Congress Raj. Hindu Raj and Congress Raj are one thing. Their porridge is the same; the only difference is that one speaks to your face and the other says, "We believe in and respect every religion".'

6.   According to Barbara and Tomas Metcalf, public rage in response to Indira Gandhi's assassination took its most hideous and brutal shape in Delhi, with mobs roaming the streets in pursuit of revenge. For three days, gangs of arsonists and killers in criminal collusion with the police and Congress Party politicians were allowed to rampage freely. Consequently, over 1,000 innocent Sikhs were murdered in Delhi, and thousands more rendered homeless. No one was ever brought to jail for these crimes (Metcalf and Metcalf 2002). For further details, see Metcalf and Metcalf's chapter entitled, 'Congress Raj: Democracy and Development, 1950–1989'. Others such as Amiya Rao argue that closer to 5,000 Sikhs lost their lives (for further details, see Amiya Rao 1985).

7.   Women and children play an integral role in a narrative of injury and injustice. For example, when Beena Kaur makes a distinction between Sikh and Singh, she justifies this difference by describing the mistreatment of Sikh women during Mughal rule. According to Beena Kaur, 'When there was Muslim rule the degree of violence and atrocity was very high. They would kidnap daughters and sisters. When Guru Sahib saw that these atrocities were occurring, that our daughters were being kidnapped before our eyes, he asked, "Are we so weak that we can't protect our own daughters?"' According Beena Kaur, Guru Gobind Singh initiated the *khande di pahul* ceremony to create Singhs, whose duty is to fight for justice and to protect daughters and sisters against injury and injustice.

8.   Jagdish Tytler is a Congress Party politician who recently withdrew from Lok Sabha elections. Tytler was being investigated by *Central Bureau of Investigation* (CBI) for alleged participation in the anti-Sikh riots of 1984. In April 2009, the CBI released a report clearing Tytler of any responsibility. This led to widespread protests by Sikhs in Punjab and Delhi. The Congress Party asked Jagdish Tytler to withdraw from the Lok Sabha election in order to avoid further protest. Tytler ultimately withdrew, but maintains that he is innocent.

9.   According to Mann, the goal of the Khalsa is political power and autonomy: 'As directed by Guru Gobind Singh and firmly etched on the pages of Sikh history and every Sikh heart, the goal of the Khalsa is political supremacy (*bol bala*)' (2001: 67). In 1765, the dream of Khalsa Raj took concrete form with the establishment of Sikh political power in the Punjab. This era of Khalsa Raj was marked by a new set of symbols: 'a new capital city at Mukhlispur [city of the purified], a new official seal, new coins, a new calendar, a new insignia, and a new flag (*Nishan Sahib*)' (Mann 2001: 48). In 1799, Ranjit Singh unified Sikh principalities, which ultimately led to the creation of a Sikh Empire (Mann 2001). Ranjit Singh expanded Khalsa Raj to the territories between the river Satlej and the mountain ranges of Ladakh, Karakoram, Hinukush, and Sulaiman.

10.   Jatinder Singh is referring to fact that Ranjit Singh hired European officers, several of whom served under Napoleon Bonaparte, to train the Khalsa army (Mann 2004).

11.   According to the Indian government, Jarnail Singh Bhindranwale and his followers were fundamentalists and terrorists. However, for a segment of the Sikh population, Bhindranwale is considered a *gursikh* (true Sikh), a defender of *gurbani* (word of god) and the social and economic interests of the Sikh qaum. Also, it is worth noting that Bhindranwale was referred to and continues to be referred to as *sant* (saint) by a segment of the Sikh population.

12.   Dr Muhammad Iqbal was instrumental in the creation of an independent Muslim state, Pakistan. He is also widely regarded as the author of *Saare Jahan Se Achchha*, an anthem celebrating independent Hindustan.

13.   According to Peter van der Veer, Gobind Singh's 1699 inauguration of the Khalsa brotherhood was a major development that enabled Sikhs to formulate their own nationalism. In 1699, Guru Gobind Singh declared that: (*i*) he was the last in the succession of Sikh gurus; and (*ii*) from then on, the authority and unity of the Sikhs would lie in the sacred scripture of the Sikhs, and in the judgement of the entire brotherhood. The formation of the Khalsa brotherhood 'was a major development that later enabled the Sikhs to formulate their own nationalism, distinct from that of the Hindus. From then onward, Khalsa Sikhs can be clearly distinguished from those followers of Guru Nanak who did not opt to become part of the Khalsa' (van der Veer 1994: 54).

14.   Amritdhari Sikhs are required to wear the following five items: *kachha* (shorts), kes (hair), *kangha* (comb), *kirpan* (sword), and *kara* (steel bracelet).

REFERENCES

Alcoff, Linda Martín. 2006, *Visible Identities: Race, Gender, and the Self*, Oxford: Oxford University Press.

Axel, Brian. 2001, *The Nation's Tortured Body: Violence, Representation, and the Formation of a Sikh Diaspora*, Durham: Duke University Press.

Brubaker, Rogers. 2004, *Ethnicity without Groups*, Cambridge: Harvard University Press.

Brubaker, Rogers, Mara Loveman, and Peter Stamatov. 2004, 'Ethnicity as Cognition', *Theory and Society*, 33(1): 31–64.

Fenech, Louis. 1997, 'Martyrdom and the Sikh Tradition', *The Journal of American Oriental Society*, 117(4): 623–42.

Lee, Taeku. 2008, 'Race, Immigration, and the Identity-to-Politics Link', *Annual Review of Political Science*, 11(1): 457–78.

Mann, Gurinder Singh. 2004, *Sikhism*, Upper Saddle River: Prentice Hall.

McLeod, W.H. 1989, *Who Is a Sikh? The Problem of Sikh Identity*, Oxford: Clarendon Press.

Metcalf, Barbara and Tomas Metcalf. 2002, *A Concise History of India*, New York: Cambridge University Press.

Oberoi, Harjot Singh. 1994, *The Construction of Religious Boundaries*, Chicago: University of Chicago Press.

Rao, A. 1985, 'When Delhi Burnt', *Economic and Political Weekly*, 19(49): 2066–9.

Somers, Margaret. 1994, 'The Narrative Constitution of Identity: A Relational and Network Approach', *Theory and Society*, 23(5): 605–49.

Takar, O.K. 2005, *Sikh Identity: An Exploration of Groups among Sikhs*, Burlington: Ashgate Publishing Company.

van der Veer, Peter. 1994, *Religious Nationalism*, Berkeley: University of California Press.

11

From Inclusive to Exclusive

Changing Ingredients of Muslim Identity in
Bombay Cinema

Yousuf Saeed

One of Mumbai's most prolific film directors, the late Manmohan Desai,
said in a recorded discussion: 'If the Muslims don't like a film, it flops'
(Masud 2005). It is difficult to say how true this generalized statement
is or what era or geographic location it applies to, but it does signify
the Muslim ethos or cultural characteristics that have been integral to
the success of much cinema produced in Mumbai since the inception
of its film industry around the 1930s. Many of the all-time favourite
Indian movies such as *Mughal-e-Azam, Pukar, Chaudhvin ka Chand,
Aan, Garam Hawa,* or *Umrao Jan* were largely based on Muslim ethos,
though one cannot easily define their themes as specifically belonging to
Islam (the religion) or Indian Muslims (the community) per se. Although
each of these films were great artistic creations, appealing to all section
Hindustani audiences, their producers were often also trying to cater
specifically to thousands of north India's conservative Muslim families,
where cinema and other forms of sensuous entertainment, including
romantic novels, were looked down upon, and it was certainly taboo for
an unmarried girl to go to the cinema with friends, and more specifically,
watch films with glamorous or 'immodest' content.

While their main aim was entertainment, these movies attracted more
conservative audiences by portraying Muslim women as role models of

modesty, morality, and *tehzeeb* (etiquette), though themes of courtesans and decadent aristocracy were also central to many of them. However, one should not assume that only Indian Muslims watched such films, or that they did not appreciate films without 'Muslim' content in them. In fact, the very act of writing on such a topic has the risk of essentializing an identity that has already been the subject of much stereotyping. While many Indian movies used literatures, historical themes, costumes, or architectural motifs originating in Arabia, Persia, or Turkic regions, or even in Mughal courts, or may have used Islam's devotional element, it may not be appropriate to club them all into a monolithic genre like the 'Muslim Social', a phrase some film advertisements and posters used at the time of their release, or even a generic term 'Islamicate' that some authors have used lately (Dwyer 2006). The diversity and overlapping of their themes has been far too complex to see these films only through the eyes of Islamic identity.

Many commentators have pointed out that through a deliberate portrayal of Muslims as the 'other' community, mainstream Indian media in general, and the Mumbai film industry in particular, has created a stereotypical image of Indian Muslims, often strengthening the popular perception about them as a 'minority' in India (Chadha and Kavoori 2008). Such portrayal basically associates some specific traits such as dresses, linguistic expressions, greetings, architectural motifs, and societal behaviours with Muslims and Islam in the public imagination. In fact, this vision of minority, or 'Muslimness', has also transformed more recently from the images of naïve Muslim piety into political subversion, criminal behaviour, and militancy in many films, thus creating a demonic image of the community in the popular imagination (Chakravarty 2005). What are these cultural ingredients that constitute the 'Muslim' identity in cinema or in real life? Have they historically been attributed only to Muslims and Islam? Or, has there been a shift in the identity formation through the decades? Although religion and religious identity has been an integral part of Indian cinema, is it appropriate to classify films through religion? These are some of the questions that need to be addressed while discussing the Muslim themes in Bombay cinema. Much debate has also ensued about the etymology of terms such as Muslim, Islamic, Islamicate, popular, Bombay cinema, and so on, which I try to use here in the conventional manner, often interchangeably, but with caution (Saeed 2009a).

My argument here is that many cultural ingredients in the pre-cinema or early cinema stages were not always considered exclusively Muslim or

Islamic—they had an inclusive or pan-regional appeal to a large section of people. In fact, many of these traits reflected a unique amalgamation or hybridization of Indian and Perso-Arabic cultural strains, permeating the society without distinctions of religion or creed. It is only later (mostly after the 1960s) that such cultural entities started slowly being associated with Muslims. And deliberately or otherwise, India's popular cinema, media, and education system have been responsible over the decades for the creation of this image of 'minority' via typecast images (Saeed 2009b). Through some common examples from Bombay cinema and other popular media, I will explore how particular cultural traits that are now associated exclusively with Muslims, were accepted initially as a norm in India, and practised by an eclectic set of people. For instance, until the middle of the twentieth century, wearing a *sherwani* (long robe), churidar (tight) pyjama, and a crooked cap was in vogue for men of the elite whether Hindu or Muslim. Similarly, the learning of Urdu and Persian languages and composing poetry in them was considered a mark of high society both among Hindus and Muslims. And some of these traits were reflected in early cinema too, although my observations about cinema should not be seen as an exhaustive representation of all of popular Indian media—many other contemporary media such as music records, radio, novels, calendar art, or newspapers/periodicals might have followed different patterns of representing the minority community stereotypes (Farooqi 2009).

EARLY INDIAN CINEMA AND ITS 'MUSLIM' INGREDIENTS

The evolution of Indian cinema was not simply an adaptation of a technological medium imported from Europe. There were several indigenous precursors to cinema in the form of traditional entertainment, mainly the local theatre and music performances, puppetry, street arts, narration of epics, religious dramas, and popular literary practices, all over India, and particularly in Mumbai, Kolkata, and Chennai, where the earliest movies were made. Among the most dominant of these art practices were, for instance, the folk *nautanki* and Urdu–Parsi theatre of northwestern India that incorporated, among other things, popular themes of Persian and Arab romantic sagas and tales of wonder such as *Alif–Laila*, *Shirin–Farhad*, *Laila–Majnun*, or *Alibaba*, using Urdu poetry, Indo-Persian music, and verbose dialogues (Hansen 2001). Since these were commercially the most successful forms of public entertainment besides being part of the popular textual or printed literatures available at that time, it was natural for them to have been adapted into early cinema. Hence, some of the earliest Indian movies such as *Alam Ara* (1931), *Laila–Majnun* (1931), *Gul-e-Bakavli* (1932), *Yahudi Ki Ladki* (1933), or *Ab-e-Hayat* (1933) were basically dramas with Muslim themes that were performed on stage earlier. In fact, after the arrival of sound in Indian cinema in 1931, the movie versions of these plays drove the Parsi theatre out of business. Many other themes or sub-themes of Muslim ethos were also incorporated into Indian movies throughout the twentieth century.

Some of these themes could be roughly grouped in the following pattern (with some prominent examples), although this listing is not restricted to any specific era of production:

- Muslim historical sagas: *Anarkali* (1935); *Pukar* (1939); *Shahjahan* (1946); *Mughal-e-Azam* (1960); *Razia Sultan* (1983).
- Indo-Persian/Arabic folklore: *Shirin Farhad* (1931); *Misar Ka Khazana* (1935); *Hatim Tai* (1947); *Gul-e-Bakawali* (1956).
- Magic, fantasies and horror tales from the Perso-Arab world: *Sair-e-Paristan* (1934); *Tilasmi Duniya* (1946); *Alladin Aur Jadui Chiraagh* (1952).
- *Nawabi* (aristocratic) and courtesan fiction: *Chaudhvin Ka Chand* (1960); *Mere Mehboob* (1963); *Bahu Begum* (1967); *Pakeeza* (1971).
- Muslim devotional/social dramas: *Nek Parveen* (1946); *Dayar-e-Habib* (1956); *Idd Ka Chand* (1964); *Dayar-e-Madina* (1975); *Aakhri Sajda* (1977).
- Identity crisis after 1947/Hindu–Muslim communalism: *Garam Hawa* (1973); *Salim Langde Pe Mat Ro* (1990); *Bombay* (1995); *Mammo* (1995).
- Portrayal of Indian Muslims in adverse roles (underworld, militants): *Border* (1997); *Ghulam-e-Mustafa* (1997); *Sarfarosh* (1999); *Mission Kashmir* (2000).

The given list is only indicative of broad themes, but one could find hundreds of movies under each category. Since many of them also overlap in several films, these should not be seen as fixed categories. Moreover, one may find plenty of films that do not strictly belong to these categories but, nevertheless, feature various Islamic ingredients. It would be worthwhile if one made a survey of the topics explored in such films produced in different decades since the 1930s, in order to map their emerging trends, that is, which themes were being explored in what decade more than the other times and why. More importantly, what are the cultural ingredients in some of these movies that today sound 'Islamic' due to their prevalent stereotypes, but might have not been so at the time of their production or circulation. For this, I have been compiling a tentative list of films from Mumbai that have featured Indo-Muslim ethos in various forms. Besides a large number of well-known films that one knows or has seen, a sizeable portion of my list includes films that are either inaccessible or have not been seen by many of us, but were enlisted as their titles suggested Muslim or Indo-Persian ethos. For example, while making the list, one doesn't need to see all eight versions of *Alibaba Aur 40 Chor* (a story from the *Arabian Nights*), four versions of *Razia Sultana* (a Muslim woman ruler in the thirteeth century Delhi), five versions of *Shirin Farhad* (a Persianate romance), and innumerable remakes of *Laila Majnun* (an Arab romantic saga) to figure out what themes they represent. Similarly, one could safely enlist titles like *Noor-e-Islam*, *Noor-e-Wahdat*, *Dayar-e-Madina*, or *Auliyae Islam* as popular devotional Muslim movies, even if some of them are not accessible.

But the very fact that for someone growing up in the late twentieth or the early twenty-first century, a mere reading of the names of many older movies evokes a Muslim or 'Islamicate' image says a lot about how the stereotypes of language and visual identity have been formed in our minds of late. Mukul Kesavan (1994) has shown that not only the stock of Bombay cinema is Islamicate but also a majority of Indian movie titles and dialogues use Urdu or Perso-Arabic words. A simple watching of a large number of such films breaks the stereotype that Perso-Arabic vocabulary was confined to Muslims alone. Such vocabulary actually cuts across early films of all genres and story lines, including some even dedicated to Hindu devotional themes!

By observing the continuity and change in the use and representation of cultural and linguistic diversity in twentieth century Bombay cinema, one could probably construct a history of how the real cultural identity and language of north India transformed over the century. I use the examples of a few movies, especially produced between the 1940s and the 1970s, to explore how certain cultural ingredients, which were part of the 'mainstream' at the turn of the twentieth century, slowly became marginalized, and then got associated exclusively with Muslims. Some of this change seen in the cinema could also be perceived in real life as we shall see here briefly. Since I am mostly (although not exclusively) focusing on the early cinema and its transformation, the scope of this chapter comes to a halt around the time when Bombay cinema started excessively depicting Muslims as underworld dons and 'Islamic' militants, with references to Pakistan as India's enemy. I avoid these references not because they are uncomfortable or sensitive, but because I consider these images as end products of a long-term transformation of cultural identity, which is what needs to be explored first. My effort is to break the stereotypes of the cultural ingredients as they are viewed in today's India at the beginning of the twenty-first century.

MUSLIM ETHOS AS INCLUSIVE AND PLURAL

The silent era of Indian cinema (pre-1930s) already had enough movies with Muslim themes, especially related to historical sagas or Indo-Persian fantasies, such as *Razia Begum* (1924), *Shah Jahan* (1924), *Sirajud-Daula* (1927), *Adle Jahangir* (1930), *Gul-e-Bakavali* (1924), *Bulbul-e-Paristan* (1926), and others. But many films even with non-Muslim themes were not devoid of Indo-Muslim cultural overtones. Although India's first talking film, Ardeshir Irani's *Alam Ara* (1931), was based on a fairy tale-style Parsi play, it contained several Islamic ingredients such as its hit song, '*De de khuda ke naam pe pyaare*', sung by Wazir Mohammed Khan (probably the first ever song in Indian cinema), besides two other songs that invoke god's name in them, although the story itself does not involve a Muslim theme. Of course, a large number of early talking films with specific Muslim themes do naturally use chaste Urdu, Islamicate architecture, and poetic idioms to evoke the Muslim ethos, some important examples of this being *Pukar* (1939) and *Najma* (1943).

While the story of *Najma* (directed by Mehboob Khan) revolves around the typical nawabi characters trying to cope with modernity, the film opens with the shot of a mosque's minaret with the sound of *azan* (*Allah-o-Akbar*, a call for Muslim prayer) in the backdrop, followed by a namaz (prayer) inside where the poor people and the nawab stand in the same row, stressing on the egalitarianism of Islam. There are several similar scenes in the film that set the ball rolling for the iconic Muslim stereotypes, such as the image of a praying Muslim woman with hands raised forward and an open Quran kept before her, or her offering a song–prayer on seeing the crescent of Eid festival. Similarly, the lead actor, Ashok Kumar, is featured here as a despotic Muslim nawab in relation with a *tawaif* (courtesan), a role that he was to play repeatedly in many Muslim Social or courtesan films until the 1980s. Somehow the very image of Ashok Kumar in large parts of his career became that of a sherwani-clad dandy nawab with a stick in his hand. However, with the logic of popular stereotype, one would expect the 1949 film *Mahal*, featuring Ashok Kumar and Madhubala, and directed by Kamal Amrohi (who later made the legendary *Pakeeza* and *Razia Sultan*), to be a typical courtesan/nawabi movie. But no, the *Mahal* is not a nawab's haveli (an aristocrat's mansion)—it is an eerie house called Sangam Bhawan in Allahabad, and Ashok Kumar plays a Hindu character named Shankar in the film!

One could find many more examples of the merging of identities, or situations, where an odd religious identity does not get unnecessarily contrasted in certain films. The peculiar story of *Shahjehan* (1946) depends on a girl named Ruhi, whose extraordinary beauty attracting hundreds of suitors becomes a bane for her father. Young men of the entire town are yearning to marry her, singing songs in her praise on the streets, and often fighting with each other to get to her. She finally gets invited to live securely in the royal palace by King Shahjahan and Queen Mumtaz Mahal, who promise to find her a suitable husband. But oddly, Ruhi's father is a *thakur* (upper-caste) Hindu. She finally gets married to an Iranian sculptor named Shirazi who, according to this story, designed the Taj Mahal for Shahjahan! Similarly, a film named *Sheesh Mahal* (1950), using a heavy dose of Urdu in the dialogues and song lyrics, is a story about Thakur Jaspal Singh whose emphasis in everyday life on *sharafat* (civility) and *faraghdili* (generosity)—traits that one finds in Muslim socials, although not exclusive to Muslims—ultimately drives his family bankrupt, and Sheesh Mahal, their palatial house, had to be mortgaged to pay the debts. One should note here that the traits of social morality such as sharafat, tehzeeb, and faraghdili were also dominant themes in much of fiction produced in Urdu literature in late nineteenth and early twentieth centuries, especially in the novels of Munshi Premchand where the protagonists were not necessarily Muslim.

Unlike the representation of Muslim protagonist in newer films (1960s onwards) where they are usually given a *special* role to highlight their 'Muslimness', the Indian Muslims in early cinema could do normal things without getting contrasted against a non-Muslim. For instance, *Dard* (1947) is a story of a rich and generous Muslim man who adopts a young orphan boy (besides having his own daughter of the same age) who grows up to become a medical doctor, and risks his life by going out to help the poor when an epidemic of plague breaks out. The same character also falls in love with the daughter of one of the patients he treats, unaware that the daughter of his adopted father too loves him. Although this film elegantly uses all the essential ingredients of

Muslimness—domestic items such as *paandan* (a metallic case for betel nuts), *ugaldan* (spittoon), and *surahi*s (water jugs); women's dresses such as *sharara*s, *gharara*s (elaborate skirts), and *dupatta*s (scarves); Mughal jewellery; and so on (some of the promotional black and white stills for the movie are classic portraits of Muslim aristocracy)—it treats the Muslim characters as ordinary persons without playing too excessively with their religious identity.

In contrast, when director Abdur Rashid Kardar's *Dil-e-Nadan* (1953) starts with a scene of a mother lovingly dressing her six-year-old son in a golden sherwani with floral patterns and an elegant crooked cap, also worrying if such a pretty child might attract an evil eye ('*Mere chand ko nazar na lag jaye*,' says the mother), one immediately assumes this to be a Muslim family, not realizing that the child's name is Madan and this is a Hindu household. Madan's father Mohan, a celebrated violinist (as we later see in the flashback), had difficulty pursuing a career in music as *his* father, Munshi Popat Lal, could not tolerate music learning in his *sharif* (respectable) family. While breaking his son's violin in rage once, he said, '*Ek arzi navees ke khandan mein yeh bhand mirasiyon ka kaam kisi ne nahin kiya. Kal se qalam–davat lekar tumhe mere sath kachehri ke bahar bethna hoga*' (In this respected family of application writers, no one ever indulged in such work of lowly musicians. From tomorrow, you must come with a pen and inkpot and sit with me outside the court to find work). Many movies from Mumbai, in fact, made fun of the music-teaching pandits or gurus, portraying elements of their classical music in mocking terms (Booth 2005). But while the learning and practise of music was rejected by the 'respectable families' of early twentieth century as a 'lowly' job of *mirasi*s (professional singers) and courtesans (in a Muslim/nawabi sense), this approach seems to have been reversed in real life in the recent times. Islam and Muslims are today seen as opponents of music and arts, whereas more and more Hindu families are getting their children to learn the 'traditional' Indian music by the pandits or gurus, who are no longer mocked in the films. The last film that could still show a Muslim family's daughters practising music as respectful professionals was *Barsat ki Raat* (1960).

North Indian art music and its unique Indo-Persian vocabulary have often been used to create ambiguity of identities in real as well as reel life. A 1960 film, *Kohinoor* (name of a diamond from the Mughal period), whose title itself tricks us into thinking of it as a Muslim historical, is actually about the court of an imaginary ruler named Maharaja Chandrabhan Singh of Kailashnagar. The Hindu king's palace in the film uses elaborate Islamic (as well as European!) architecture, the court language has heavy doses of Urdu and Persian words (*bashinde, zanana bagh, wafadari,* and so on), and strains of music such as that in the *Arabian Nights* can be heard in the background, somehow typifying the very image of regality with Islamic or Persianate ethos. The prince of this court (enacted by Dilip Kumar), a music maestro, gets a hyperbolic introduction by his assistant (Mukri) in a language that mockingly blends Persian and Indian words, including musical terms: '*Shahanshah-e maharajgan-e mausiqi wa badshah-e ustadan-e bandooqi, aali jaah-e jaijaiwanti, alam panah-e thumri, khudawandane jhanjhooti, wa aalishan, aaliban, wa aalitan, sangeetkar maharaj Kohinoor baba'.*

An abundance of films in the 1950s and the 1960s focusing on nawabs, tawaifs, and their indulgence in music and dance not only created a strong image of Muslim extravagance, but also addressed a general sense of loss of culture and heritage by the Muslims through the tragic events of 1857 and 1947 (Ansari 2008). But besides the Muslim historical movies whose sole purpose was to recreate the lost history and heritage, the films with nawabs and courtesans are not simple depictions of heritage. They are contemporary stories where the 'tradition' is mostly problematized as it meets 'modernity'—a crisis most of the upper-class north Indian Muslims were, in reality, grappling with in the early twentieth century (Dwyer 2003). A large number of such films are either about crumbling aristocrats or landlords who escape from their family/wife to find refuge at the *kotha* (courtesan's quarter), or about tawaifs trying to find more respectable modes of sustenance. But despite this problematic, the picturization and the music or poetry used in such films, with an essential backdrop of Lucknow/Awadh, does create an exotic image of the Muslims' obsession with courtesans, and completely ignores the fact that *kothewalian* or courtesans also existed in other communities and regions of India, for instance, by the names of *baijis* and *devadasi*s in central/western India. The Muslimness of the courtesan is certainly exoticized and overemphasized. At the beginning of *Benazir* (1964), a courtesan film produced by Bimal Roy, even the English text of the credits list is calligraphed and stylized through symbols of Arabic/Urdu vowels (*zer, zabar, pesh,* and so on) to create an 'Islamic' milieu.

Certain stereotypes never age. Urdu poets and their poetry recitations are naturally shown as the hallmark of a cultivated Muslim society in innumerable films, such as *Barsat ki Raat* (1960), *Ghazal* (1964), or *Dayar-e-Madina* (1975). But some *sha'er*s or poets also happen to be non-Muslim characters. In fact, in many nawabi/courtesan films where the Muslim male actor is trying to woo his female counterpart by composing romantic poetry, he often has a sidekick friend, usually with a Hindu name (and played by humorous actors such as Johny Walker), who too composes Urdu poetry and participates in the *mushairas* (poetry soirees) with the lead actor, or supplies secret information about the woman and so on. But Urdu poetry is certainly not confined to Muslims only. At least one film, *Pyasaa* (1957) by Guru Dutt, tells the story of a rebel Urdu poet, Vijay, who struggles hard to get his poetry recognized and published, while he has an affair with a tawaif, Gulabo. Some believe that the film was based on the story of a real Urdu poet, such as Sahir Ludhyanvi (who is one of the lyricists of the film) or Majaz Lakhnavi who died two years before the release of the film (Taneja 2009). But in reality, there is no dearth of non-Muslim Urdu poets (or connoisseurs) in India who regularly participated in mushairas.

But the reason for an overdose of Urdu and Persian vocabulary and aesthetics in early cinema is not merely because a majority of Mumbai's film writers, actors, and crew were Muslim, or came from Awadh/Lucknow region as some would believe (Dwyer 2006), but probably because such ethos was truly the mainstay of north India's popular culture of entertainment, printed literature, legal terminology, and many other facets of life. Of course, this changed over the years. Especially after 1947's partition of India, the stress on nationalism affected the spontaneous cultural plurality in real as well as reel life. Most importantly, Urdu was officially removed as a medium of education, or even a subject of study, in most schools and colleges of north India. Urdu was not simply a linguistic mode or a medium of instruction—it contained in it centuries of shared cultural heritage. Thus, in its absence, there grew an entire generation of people who were devoid of such heritage in their upbringing. The isolation or alienation of cultural ingredients started showing through the popular cultural forms such as cinema, although many filmmakers continued to use the Islamicate ingredients in syncretic ways. Interestingly, a large number of cine artists and song writers migrating to Mumbai from Punjab that became part of Pakistan after 1947, who were well trained in Urdu and its rich ethos, continued to keep some plurality and syncretism alive in cinema.

Qawwali, the mystical form of music commonly performed in India and Pakistan, has also been used as a major icon for Muslim identity in the movies, for several purposes. The most common and clichéd scenario is a qawwali's heightened performance by a dramatically dressed troupe in Sufi shrines where a distressed (Muslim) protagonist comes to pray for the resolution of his/her crisis. While the character is praying before the tomb of the saint, a ray of light miraculously falls from the dome or sky, often through the *jali* (lattice) of the shrine, and the devotee's problems instantly get resolved. Qawwalis at Sufi shrines are also used as a meaningful backdrop for the miraculous meeting of two lost friends or characters in some movies. Qawwali has been used in many non-Muslim contexts too. Weddings and family functions in Muslim families are the most common venues for qawwali. It is probably Bombay cinema that invented or ushered in the style of 'qawwali competitions', often between male and female troupes, singing non-devotional and often bawdy lyrics, that became a rage in hundreds of movies produced between 1960s and the 1990s; *Barsat ki Raat* depending largely on such a scenario. But in many situations, it becomes difficult to distinguish women's qawwali and a *mujra* (courtesan song and dance sequence).

One could find many other examples of the qawwali's use in non-Muslim situations. The film *Rustom-e-Rome* (1964) about a great warrior of Rome is neither based in India nor the Arab/Islamic world, but uses popular Islamicate ethos—the actors, in strange Greek/Egyptian costumes, have names like Sulaiman and Shabana, and speak '*Ya Allah*' and '*Salam*', since this may originally have been a Parsi-style play. Most interestingly, the Roman soldiers, once stuck in an alien terrain, perform a qawwali, '*Husn walon ki kya baat hai*' (what to say of the people with beauty), with tablas and harmonium, in the voices of the emerging *qawwal*s, Ismail Azad and Jani Babu. Somehow, for Indian film industry, the very concept of classical romance gets its suitable image only through the Perso-Arabic sagas. It should be noted that between 1922 and 1982, as many as eighteen films were produced in Mumbai based on the story of *Laila Majnun* (de Groot 2006).

Of course, qawwali has also been used in other unusual situations such as a secular entertainment in a train excursion (*The Burning Train*, 1980). But the most memorable non-Muslim use of qawwali is probably from the film *Waqt* (1965), where '*O meri zohra jabeen*' is sung in family festivity of a Hindu businessman in Peshawar/Punjab. Qawwali was also used in certain derogatory or mocking scenarios. Extreme gestures and clownish clothing used by qawwals in some movies introduced an element of frivolity and idiocy with qawwali, best exemplified by Rishi Kapoor in *Amar Akbar Anthony* (1977), when he jumps like an acrobat onto the concert stage to sing as poet Akbar Ilahabadi. The very concept of purdah (veil)—normally associated with Muslim women—has been mocked and typified in many ways in this song as well as others, where the stereotypes of Muslim community, especially about women's clothing, continually get strengthened. More recently, the qawwali has also been used as a backdrop for sequences of criminals chasing each other or even murder and mystery scenes, which, of course, have something to do with Muslimness of the characters, such as in movies *Gunaah* (2003), *Haasil* (2003), and *Gangster* (2006).

THE MUSLIM CULTURE AND CHARACTER AS 'THE OTHER'

Usually, the body language and costumes given to the qawwals in the movies are what makes them the most typical 'Muslim' characters created by Bombay cinema—a shiny achkan (robe) and velvety crooked cap, lips red due to paan (betel leaf and nut) in the mouth, a flowing handkerchief with pink border in a hand, and a wicked smile. When clapping during a qawwali, they press both hands in a twisting fashion as their chest comes forward. This is exactly how Pran performs a qawwali in the film *Adhikar* (1971) where he acts as Banne Khan Bhopali, a Muslim side character who plays small but significant role to save the story at the end. Muslims in many films post 1960s did get a lot of such funny and side character roles. There is the inimitable Soorma Bhopali from *Sholay* (1975) with an accent that is supposed to exemplify a Muslim-dominated urban neighbourhood in north India. The character of Soorma became so popular that not only did Jagdeep (the person behind it) make a new film by the same name (in 1988), but other minor films too featured their villainous or side characters with this Bhopali accent, such as in *Aakhri Sajda* (1977) or *Khwaja ki Diwani* (1981), both Muslim devotional movies.

As Muslim side characters, the benevolent Rahim Chacha (*Deewar*, 1975) or Karim Baba (*Dayavan*, 1988) are always old, bearded men living under a thatched roof in the wilderness on a rainy and scary night, saving an endangered main character, without which the story would have probably sunk. Some of them also come as turbaned pathans from Afghanistan or Pashtun area into the Hindi-belt India, often being aggressive, but finally soft-hearted and sacrificing, such as in *Kabuliwala* (1961) and *Zanjeer* (1973), and also *Khuda Gawah* (1992), although it is a more mainstream film. These Muslim characters usually save others through their good conduct, and often end up sacrificing their lives for the lead characters, but always remain sidelined from the main story. Thus, the 1970s is a period when one can see the slow disappearance of Muslims (and Muslimness) from Bombay cinema as the mainstream feature—Muslim cultural ethos being marginalized as something special, something other than the norm, although the 'bad character' roles are still not assigned to any specific ethnic or religious identity.

But this is also the time when a large number of low-budget Muslim devotional films were produced by lesser known directors/producers for a niche audience, with titles such as *Shan-e-Khuda* (1971), *Noor-e-Elahi* (1973), *Niaz Aur Namaz* (1973), *Mere Garib Nawaz* (1973), *Dayar-e-Madina* (1975), *Noor-e-Islaam* (1978), *Sultan-e-Hind* (1978), *Deen Aur Iman* (1979), and *Auliyae Islam* (1979). Many of these films featured common actors, actresses, and crew members—almost a mini-industry working within the Bombay cinema. Some common names in the credit list of the abovementioned films are Sona, Tarique, Raza Murad, Satish Kaushal, Mukri, Shakti Kapoor, Veena, Tabrez, Husn Bano, and Nazir Husain, among others, as if many of these had signed contract with the producers to do a series of Muslim devotional films (although the directors keep changing). It is also possible that some of the actors were stereotyped by their repeated appearance to look like a Muslim wife, lover, husband, nawab, maulvi (cleric), tawaif, sister-in-law, poet, or a villain, and found comfort in those roles.

One could argue that while Muslimness was pushed to the corner in mainstream cinema in the 1970s and the 1980s, the typical Muslim audience who longed to see movies they could culturally relate to, found an added comfort in the low-budget devotional movies in the same era. Even if a light-hearted attempt was occasionally made to 'integrate' the different communities or elucidate the concept of Hindu–Muslim unity through films such as *Amar Akbar Anthony* (1977), where long-lost brothers (three sons of the same mother) are brought up as Hindu, Muslim, and Christian, the devotional cloistered theme of Muslim films continued to get more typified. Thus, a few years later, the hero of *Allah Rakha* (1986) sings, '*Na Amar, na Akbar, na Anthony, mera naam hai Allah Rakha...*' (I am neither Amar, nor Akbar, nor Anthony. My name is Allah Rakha—the one rescued by God). Could that be seen as a doubting of the concept of cultural integration or inclusiveness, and falling back on the exclusive identity of a Muslim?

Finally, we come to an important question: were the Muslim Social or devotional films addressed primarily to a Muslim audience? The Mumbai film industry, especially its distribution networks, certainly believed in a section of the film market they called the 'Muslim belt' (Mazumdar 2003), which comprised of the cinema halls in a few towns (such as Hyderabad, Bhopal, Lucknow, Patna, and localities in Mumbai and Kolkata) or rural areas in north and central India, which brought the maximum revenue from the Muslim socials and devotionals. This is probably the reason why the stories and characters of many devotional films are typically set (and sometimes shot) in towns like Bhopal, Hyderabad, and Mumbai, or heavily use the local linguistic accents. Until 1947, most such stories were also set in Lahore, although a bulk of the shooting was done inside studio sets. In contrast, the metaphor of Lucknow has been used mostly for courtesan and nawabi themes, whereas Delhi and Agra often become the setting for historical films, besides imaginary historical towns in Persia/Arabia.

Many blockbuster films were/are scheduled, whenever possible, to be released on Eid, not because it's an auspicious occasion, but for the money the working-class Muslims would spend on watching movies, often the same film more than once if they liked it. But there is no reason why the same can't be said about the average 'Hindu' cine-goers, since the number of films released on Diwali are often more in number than those on Eid, irrespective of the themes or their 'intended' audience. Hence, while the religious segregation of audiences might sound like a generalization, the film producers do seem conscious of the niche religious audience they are catering to.

The Muslim side characters were nevertheless also brought to the centre stage in the 1980s, but only while keeping their odd Muslim characteristics intact. They became the grand heroes and saviours of urban slums or Muslim ghettoes, in films like *Coolie* (1983), *Allah Rakha* (1986), or *Ghulam-e-Mustafa* (1997), where the protagonist helps and fights for the poor and the weak, but could not break his link from crime and the underworld, or his religious practice. Some of the most sophisticated gang lords and smugglers of Bombay cinema are shown with a rosary in hand and a pink-and-white checkered Arab scarf on their shoulders. Such a character can be seen as the epitome of an almost half-century long transformation of Muslimness in cinema, for whom the next and ultimate step is naturally the international militancy based on religious identity, a favourite subject of present-day Bombay cinema. The romantic Urdu poet of the 1960s, who composed and sung melodious ghazals for his beloved, now turns deceitful against his homeland and becomes Gulfam, a Pakistani spy working against India, in *Sarfarosh* (1999).

Although it would be unfair to make comparisons between films that were produced over half a century apart, it seems equally unfortunate to note that the ingredients of fine poetry, language, art, and aesthetics that regaled, inspired, and entertained millions of movie watchers in the early and middle part of twentieth century in India, have slowly been swept aside and now associated only with a certain religious community, which itself is probably too insecure today to revive its creative talents that could once again bring life to plurality in Bombay cinema. The oddness of what is treated as the 'Muslim attire' and mannerism is often presented mockingly in many recent movies. Some films depicted a nawab from Lucknow wearing an archaic sherwani, chewing paan, and speaking in poetic Urdu, being heckled by others for appearing so old-fashioned. In fact, Urdu poetry and its mushaira-like recitation itself has been made a subject of ridicule in the movies as well as television and radio. The latest, for instance, is a series of mocking audio-drama clips called *Babbar Sher* on a private FM radio station (Radio City 91.1) available in Delhi, Mumbai, and other cities, where a man recites raunchy and often-nonsensical poetry in a Bihari/Bhojpuri accent, with a noisy group of men applauding in equally despicable manner, as if in a mushaira. For the new generation of listeners who are not used to traditional mushairas and ghazal recitations, such radio limericks will probably appear to be the real face of Urdu or Islamicate culture. But the same could probably be said about other forms of traditional Indian cultural practices too (such as Hindustani classical music), which today have either disappeared from the mainstream media, or shown in irreverent manner, such as a funny competition between two tabla players for an advertisement of a chewing gum!

All is not lost though. There have been a few recent efforts where a Muslim could be seen as a regular character without any peculiarity, such as in *Munnabhai MBBS* (2003), where a man named Maqsood can be a cleaner in a hospital, and Zaheer, a cancer patient, without their religious identity or appearance playing any role in the plot. Similarly, *Chak De! India* (2008) is about a Muslim hockey coach (Shahrukh Khan) who tries to break many stereotypes about Indian Muslims (Sharma 2009). In *3 Idiots* (2009), one out of the three friends is a Muslim boy (Farhan Qureshi) who does not invoke anything from his religion or cultural identity, and appears as a regular Indian boy aspiring for a successful career. One hopes to see more of such balancing acts in Bombay cinema of the future that might offset the stereotypes of a 'minority' that have been created for over half a century. More importantly, even if we have to highlight cultural traditions, such as what is popularly perceived as

'Islamicate' art, literature, music, or architecture, it could better be presented as an inclusive heritage of all rather than of only Muslims.

REFERENCES

Ansari, Usamah. 2008, '"There Are Thousands Drunk by the Passion of These Eyes": Bollywood's Tawa'if: Narrating the Nation and "The Muslim"', *South Asia: Journal of South Asian Studies*, 31(2): 290–316.

Booth, Gregory. 2005, 'Pandits in the Movies: Contesting the Identity of Hindustani Classical Music and Musicians in the Hindi Popular Cinema', *Asian Music*, 36(1): 60–86.

Chadha, Kalyani and Anadam Kavoori. 2008, 'Exoticized, Marginalized and Demonized: The Muslim as Other in Bollywood Cinema', in A. Kavoori and A. Punathambekar (eds), *Global Bollywood*, New York: New York University Press, pp. 131–45.

Chakravarty, Sumita S. 2005, 'Fragmenting the Nation: Images of Terrorism in Indian Popular Cinema', in J.D. Slocum (ed.), *Terrorism, Media, Liberation*, New Brunswick: Rutgers University Press, pp. 232–47.

de Groot, Rokus. 2006, 'The Arabic–Persian Story of Laila and Majnun and Its Reception in Indian Arts', *Journal of Indian Musicological Society*, 36–37: 120–48.

Dwyer, Rachel. 2003, 'Representing the Muslim: The "Courtesan Film" in Indian Popular Cinema', in T. Parfitt and Y. Egorova (eds), *Jews, Muslims, and Mass Media: Mediating the 'Other'*, New York: RoutledgeCurzon, pp. 78–92.

———. 2006, *Filming the Gods, Religion and Indian Cinema*, New Delhi: Routledge.

Farooqi, Athar (ed.). 2009, *Muslims and Media Images: News versus Views*, New Delhi: Oxford University Press.

Hansen, Kathryn. 2001, 'Parsi Theater, Urdu Drama, and the Communalization of Knowledge: A Bibliographic Essay', *The Annual of Urdu Studies*, 16: 43–63.

Kesavan, Mukul. 1994, 'Urdu, Awadh and the Tawaif: the Islamicate Roots of Hindi Cinema', in Z. Hasan (ed.), *Forging Identities: Gender, Communities and the State*, New Delhi: Kali for Women, pp. 244–57.

Masud, Iqbal. 2005, 'Muslim Ethos in Indian Cinema', *Screen*, New Delhi, 4 March, available at http://www.screenindia.com/old/fullstory.php? content_id=9980 (accessed 29 December 2008).

Mazumdar, Ranjani. 2003, 'The Bombay Film Poster: The Journey from the Street to the Museum', *Film International*, 1(4): 13–18.

Saeed, Yousuf. 2009a, 'Muslim Exotica of Hindi Filmdom', *The Book Review* South Asia Special, XIV(August–September): 23–4.

Saeed, Yousuf. 2009b, 'This Is What They Look Like: Stereotypes of Muslim Piety in Calendar Art and Hindi Cinema', *Tasveer Ghar*, available at http:// tasveerghar.net/cmsdesk/essay/78/ (accessed 8 November 2010).

Sharma, Sanjukta. 2009, 'The New Bollywood Muslim', *Live Mint*, 25 June, available at http://www.livemint.com/2009/06/25202438/The-new-Bolly-wood-Muslim.html (accessed 26 December 2011).

Taneja, Anand Vivek. 2009, 'Muslimness in Hindi Cinema', *Seminar*, Special issue on Circuits of Cinema, 598: 36–40.

12

The Violence of Security
Hindutva's Lethal Imaginaries*

Dibyesh Anand

This chapter, originally published in *The Roundtable: Journal of Commonwealth Affairs* in 2005, is a journey into the recent spectacle of collective communal violence in India, its (extra)ordinariness, and the gestures that seek to translate corporeality of violence into abstraction. These enabling gestures can be understood as part of a discourse of security. It is the logic of this discourse of security that enables extreme violence—in particular, against minorities—to be normalized, systematized, and institutionalized. Politics of hate, of which the Hindu Right (Hindu nationalism; also called Hindutva) in India[1] is a good example, feeds upon, as well as shapes, local societies' conceptions of security and insecurity. Hindutva's politics of hate is targeted prinicipally at the Muslim and Christian minorities and seeks to tame, if not annihilate them, at the same time as it transforms the state into its vision of a Hindu *Rashtra*. The global environment, with its own dynamic politics of representation of dangers, has a direct impact on the local societies' conceptions. An example of the so-called 'Hindu–Muslim' communal

* This is a reprint (with revision/modification) of Dibyesh Anand, 2005, 'Violence of Security: Hindutva in India', *The Roundtable: The Commonwealth Journal of International Affairs*, 94(379): 201–13, ISSN 0035-8533. Reprinted with permission of Routledge, Taylor & Francis Ltd. Available at http://www.informaworld.com.

riot in India is from Gujarat (a state in the federal set-up of India) in 2002,[2] where more than a thousand people (mostly minority Muslims) were killed in the space of a couple of months.

The chapter is divided into four sections. It starts with an outlining of the political context of communal violence in India and then moves on to conceptualize security as a productive discourse—one that produces 'dangers' to security as well as the object to be secured. The third section discusses the centrality of particular representations of threatening Muslim masculinity (the figure of 'The Muslim') in Hindutva discourse. 'The Muslim' is seen as constituting the danger against which the Hindu body politic needs to be secured. This legitimizes the use of violence against Muslims in the name of securing the Hindu Self. The last section visits Gujarat 2002 (a shorthand I use for violence, overwhelmingly against Muslims, that took place during 2002 in Gujarat) as the most (in)famous site that can be best made sense of within the (meta) discourse of security. The chapter concludes by re-emphasising that the violence of the kind witnessed in Gujarat 2002 is made possible, probable, and even inevitable by the logic of violence and abstraction that is part of the discourse of security. The main argument of this chapter is that the violence against minority Muslims is facilitated and justified in the name of achieving security for the Hindu Self at individual, community, national, as well as international levels. The arguments about centrality of violence, fear, gender, sexuality, narcissism, and paranoia in Hindu nationalist politics is expanded in my writings (especially Anand 2011) that followed the original article in *The Roundtable*.

THE HINDU RIGHT IN INDIA

Communal violence in India should be understood within the larger context of the struggle and debate over the secularism of the postcolonial Indian state (for perspectives on secularism in India, see Bhargava 1998). This has become especially significant since the 1990s, the decade that saw the end of Indian National Congress's dominance and the rise of the BJP, a Hindu nationalist party. The victory of Congress-led alliance in the national elections in 2004, and in 2009, does not signal the demise of Hindu nationalism as a political movement. It merely reminds that the electoral politics in India, at this point in time, can absorb ideologically distinct political formations.

The history of Hindu nationalism in India is as long as that of the mainstream nationalism represented mainly by the Congress (see Jaffrelot

1999; Misra 2004; Zavos 2000). The attitude of many Congress leaders and activists towards majoritarian communalism (of which Hindu
nationalism is an articulation) and even communal violence has been
ambiguous. Yet, BJP and its Hindutva ideology are different and distinct
from the dominant ideals of the Indian state as secular. Its rhetoric of
democracy, rights, and nation is based on a simplistic majoritarian principle and runs along the following lines: since Hindus are the majority,
it is 'natural' and 'democratic' that their 'rights' should be promoted
by the Indian state which hitherto has been 'pseudo-secular' because of
its appeasement of the minorities! The Hindutva movement therefore
is a 'conservative revolution', combining paternalist and xenophobic
discourses with democratic and universalist ones on rights and entitlements (Hansen 1999: 4). The Hindutva movement is targeted at transforming the Indian state and controlling the Muslim and Christian
minorities. At the same time, the primary goal is to transform the
Hindus, to 'awaken the Hindu nation' (see Chitkara 2003; Hingle 1999;
RSS 2003). There is a schizophrenic shuttling between the idea of a pre-
existing monolithic Hindu nation and a lamentation that most members
of this supposed nation do not fit in Hindutva's template of an ideal
citizen of the Hindu nation. A Hindutva website's call illustrates this
well: 'No Hindu politics is possible unless there is Hindu-Awakening.
And that Hindu-Awakening is not yet in sight' (Swordoftruth.com
n.d.). Hindutva is self-recognized as being as much about representing
the Hindu nation as it is about fabricating one. This has been the case
throughout the twentieth century (see Noorani 2002).

What was different at the start of the twenty-first century was the
respectability and influence gained by the exponents of Hindutva
through participation in the government at the federal level as well as in
various states allowing them to gain access to the resources of the state.
For instance, leaders who were seen as firebrand ideologues during the
1990s became members of the government; non-Hindutva politicians
competed over who is a more authentic Hindu; school children were
taught a history where militant Hinduism was normalized and minority religions such as Islam and Christianity (and as a corollary, Indian
Muslims and Indian Christians) were alienated; government employees
could join Hindutva organizations; and the prime minister pronounced,
in a cavalier manner, that the Muslims are a source of 'problems' everywhere in the world (as Atal Behari Vajpayee did in 2002; see Rediff.com
2002). Thus, there was a visible shift to the Right in Indian politics, and
the ascendancy of Hindutva forces was its clearest manifestation.[3] Even

during the election campaign in 2009, which the BJP lost, one witnessed frequent presentation of Narendra Modi, Gujarat's Chief Minister most closely associated with anti-Muslim violence in 2002, as an efficient pro-business political leader as if his record of having presided over anti-minority violence was excusable. Hindutva's ascendancy is clearly not a foregone conclusion, nor is it even throughout the country. But, at the very least, it is there as an important force in the Indian political landscape that seeks to create a more Hinduized India (Hinduized on terms set by Hindutva forces and not in its traditional, fuzzy, and fluid forms) and discipline the religious minorities.

Communal violence in India remains a debated subject amongst actors, including politicians, activists, and scholars (for various intellectual positions, see Basu *et al.* 1993; Brass 2003; Brass and Vanaik 2002; Das 1990; Hansen 1999; Huntington 1993; Jaffrelot 1999; Kakar 1996; Nandy 1988; Pandey 1990; S. Sarkar 2002; Varshney 2002). The Hindutva shares the neo-Orientalist belief in the primordial naturalness of Hindu–Muslim violence in India ('historic clash', as most Western media tend to report). I reject this and argue that 'riots' (spectacular incidents of inter-communal collective violence) are not a direct product of communalism (where communities are seen as bounded, historical, and given). Instead, I adopt a social constructionist position that sees 'communal' riots as being exercises in the construction of communities through the mobilization (of the 'Self'), purification (erasure of commonalities), and definition (through violence of what is the Self and what is the Other). Communalism is not merely a reflection of a pre-existing community but the will to create a bounded community (see Pandey 1990). Communalism as an ideology operates at the level of the individual as well as the collective—the identity and interests of individuals are seen as coinciding with that of the collective, the community. In this sense, it is deterministic. For instance, in the case of Hindu–Muslim communalism, every individual is reduced as only a Hindu or only a Muslim—no other identities matter. As several testimonies after riots have shown, identification with community becomes stronger since one suffers on account of being a member of that community.

Patwardhan in his film, *Father, Son and Holy War* (1994), finds that the Muslim women who were identifying their common interests with Hindu women before the 1993 riots in Mumbai felt that during violence, it is their 'Muslimness' that marked them and their being a 'woman' became irrelevant. The reduction of individuals to only one form of identity is generally more common in representations of the minorities by the majoritarian discourses. The idea being that while 'we', the majority, can experiment with identities, 'they', the minorities, are overdetermined by what marks them as minority. While the Hindus have multiple layers of identity, every aspect of a Muslim is supposed to be determined by her/his Muslimness. The determinism of communal discourses dehumanizes the Other and poses it as a danger to the security of the Self.

THE PRODUCTIVE DISCOURSE OF SECURITY

Security is a central concept in the theory and praxis of not only international relations but local, inter-local, as well as translocal relations. In positivist literature on security, it is assumed to possess an ontological and epistemological certainty where the sources of insecurity as well as the referent of security are givens. In line with the literature of critical international relations (see Campbell 1998; Krause and Williams 1997; Lipschutz 1995; Weldes *et al.* 1999), I conceptualize security as a productive discourse that produces insecurities to be operated upon as well as defines the identity of the object to be secured. This challenges the dominant conceptual grammar of security that treats insecurities as unavoidable facts while focusing attention onto the acquisition of security by given entities. It foregrounds the processes through which something or someone (the Other) is discursively produced as a source of insecurity against which the Self needs to be secured. Thus, discourses of insecurity are about 'representations of danger' (Campbell 1998; Dillon 1996). Insecurities, in this view, are social constructions rather than givens—threats do not just exist out there, but have to be created. All insecurities are culturally produced in the sense that they are produced in and out of 'the context within which people give meanings to their actions and experiences and make sense of their lives' (Tomlinson, in Weldes *et al.* 1999: 1). Insecurities and the objects that suffer from insecurities are mutually constituted.

That is, in contrast to the received view, which treats objects of security and insecurity themselves as pre-given and natural and as separate things, we treat them as mutually constituted cultural and social constructions and thus, products of processes of identity construction of Self–Other. The argument that security is about representations of danger and social construction of the Self and the Other does not imply that there are no 'real' effects. What it means is that there is nothing inherent in any act, or being, or object that makes it a source of insecurity and danger.

Security is linked closely with identity politics. How we define ourselves depends on how we represent others. This representation is thus integrally linked with how we 'secure' ourselves against the Other. Representations of the Other as a source of danger to the security of the Self in conventional understandings of security is accompanied by an abstraction, dehumanization, depersonalization, and stereotyping of the Other. The Other gets reduced to being a danger and hence, an object that is fit for surveillance, control, policing, and possibly extermination (cf. Foucault 1977, 1988). This logic of the discourse of security dictates that the security of the Self facilitate and even demand the use of policing and violence against the Other. This can be illustrated through the case of Hindutva's politics of representation that legitimizes anti-Muslim violence in the name of securing the Hindu body politic at various levels.

While the focus in the chapter is on Hindutva's stance towards the Muslim minorities, they do not leave the Christians alone. Both Muslims and Christians are portrayed as enemies of Hindu India. As a saying among Hindutva sympathizers goes, '*pehle kasai, phir isai*' (first the butcher—pejorative term for Muslims—and then the Christians). On rare occasions, Christianity is seen as equal or a greater threat. For instance, an ideologue writer, Paliwal, reminds his readers that in independent India, 'the tactics, strategies and modes of operation of the christian missionaries have been more subtle, cunning, fraudulent and indirectly of far reaching consequences than that of the Muslims' (2003: 31). The anti-Christian violence in Orissa in recent years shows that the specific politics of enemy construction by Hindu nationalists depends on the regional/local dynamics. As the chapter in this volume by Bauman and Young shows, the process of Othering of Indian Christians performs a function that is similar to that of Indian Muslims in this chapter. What may be different is the heavier investment in hate and violence against the Muslims because they are seen as the enemy number one within Hindu nationalist worldview.

'The Muslim', a stereotype of Muslim males, is posed as a danger to the body of Hindu women and through her, to the purity of Hindu nation. At the same time, it is seen as a threat to national, state, and international security. These representations of 'The Muslim' as a danger to the security of Hindu body politic facilitate the politics of hate against the Muslims in India.

REPRESENTING 'THE MUSLIM' AS A DANGER

'The Muslim' as an object of insecurity in the Hindutva discourse inhabits the levels of the personal, local, national, as well as international. 'The Muslim' is discursively constructed as a site of fear, fantasy, distrust, anger, envy, and hatred, thus generating desires of emulation, abjection, and/or extermination. My argument is that these desires are not confined to the subscribers of Hindutva but are prevalent in the wider society amongst those describing themselves as Hindu. The Hindutva movement is not an inevitable result of these prejudicial desires but scavenges upon them and, in turn, fuels and fossilizes them. The desire of emulation, abjection, and extermination is intextricably linked to certain threatening representations of 'The Muslim'. The politics of Hindutva is one where the construction of a desired masculinity (ideal Hindu male, virile yet with controlled sexuality) requires the destruction of competing masculinities and men. In the words of V.D. Savarkar, one of the 'founding fathers' of Hindutva, the aim of the Hindu nationalism is to recuperate manliness and 'Hinduize all politics and militarize hindudom' (in Pandey 1993: 263).

Hindutva's politics of representation is one replete with myths and stereotypes. Let me provide you with some snapshots.[4] Hindutva discourses construct a myth of the Hindu self as virtuous, civilized, peaceful, accommodating, enlightened, clean, and tolerant, as opposed to 'The Muslim' Other, which is morally corrupt, barbaric, violent, rigid, backward, dirty, and fanatic. The myth borrows from various stereotypes and motifs that are prevalent in India and elsewhere, including the West. The prophet's sex life, licentious Arabs buying young girls and boys, men with four wives, Muslim prostitutes, lack of democracy in the Muslim world, all these motifs are mobilized to 'confirm' the immorality and corruption of Muslims. Halal meat, circumcision, the history of the spread of Islam through sword and rape, forms of punishment in the Arab world, Islamic terrorism—these images are deployed to provide an alibi to the supposed barbaric and violent character of Islam and Muslims. This is encapsulated by Savarkar's statement: '...where religion is goaded on by rapine and rapine serves as a hand-maid to religion, the propelling force that is generated by these together is only equalled by the profundity of human misery and devastation they leave behind them in their march' (Savarkar 1999: 26). Refusal to modernize, the veil, Sharia law, low status of women, all these stereotypes characterize the Muslims as rigid and backward. Muslims supposedly have a penchant to live in small houses in ghettos and walled cities which goes with 'The Muslim' predilection for filth and dirt. As Kakar in his analysis of stereotypes about Muslims points out, '… the image of Muslim animality is composed of the perceived ferocity, rampant sexuality, and demand for instant gratification of the male, and a dirtiness which is less a matter of bodily cleanliness and more of an inner pollution as a consequence of the consumption of forbidden, tabooed foods' (Kakar 1996: 107).

Fanaticism of Muslims is a motif that needs no elaboration since it is deployed by many states and groups around the world in contemporary times. This 'fanaticism' (of which Al-Qaida is the most recent incarnation) is supposed to flow out of Islam (the prophet's personal character, Quran's rigid instructions, and spread of Islam through violence). At the same time, it is claimed to be a result of the physical and moral character of Muslims. Empirical studies (see Brass 2003; Datta 1993; Jayawardena and Alwis 1998; Kakar 1996; Ludden 1996b; Pandey 1993; Sarkar and Butalia 1995), anecdotal evidence, and personal experience show that these myths are not confined to Hindutva forces only but are increasingly becoming a part of a 'common sense' amongst other Hindus (especially upper caste) too. These images borrow heavily from the Orientalist and imperialist writings by the West (see Kabbani 1986; Lewis 1996; Said 1978). In recent times, Hindutva proponents, especially in cyberspace, scavenge voraciously from racist writings about Islam and 'Muslim mind' coming out of the West (see Note 4). The so-called international 'war on terror' has only reinforced this association of Islam with terrorism. The most common image of the Muslim amongst Hindutva today is of 'terrorist'. As the writings of proponents of Hindutva show, Muslims and terrorism are seen as inseparable. For instance, Chitkara laments that 'Common Hindu is surprised why riots take place when Muslims have already been given a separate home-land Pakistan? Terrorism shows that their appetite has not been quenched' (Chitkara 2003: 38, xi–xii). This conflation serves to criminalize large sections of Muslim males. The supposed 'terrorism' of Muslims is seen as a justification to discriminate against them and marginalize them from 'sensitive' government posts (see Khalidi 2003).

While 'The Muslim terrorist' is constructed as a grave threat to the national security of India today, in the long term, what is seen as even more dangerous to the existence of the Hindu nation is the spectre of 'overpopulating Muslims'. Every census in India since the late nineteenth century has been followed by hue and cry about the relative strength of Hindus vis-à-vis Muslims. The idea of demographic decline has been

entrenched in Hindutva since the early twentieth century. This was
encapsulated by U.N. Mukherji's analysis of Hindus as a dying race in
1909 that 'they count their gains, we calculate our losses' (in Elst 1997).
After an alarmist (and erroneous) report on the 2001 Census, the debate
resumed about how Muslims are breeding like rabbits and are going to
overtake Hindus (see Dayal 2004; Rajalakshmi 2004). There are various spectres: obliteration of the Hindu nation (in a few hundred years);
defeat of the Hindus in the numbers game (in few decades); and another
Pakistan, as in few years time, Muslims will constitute 30 per cent of
population (the way it was during 1947) bolstering their claim for partition. Acharya Dharmendra, a Hindu religious leader, proclaimed in a
public meeting in 2003: 'Muslims breed like rabbits and their population would soon overtake that of the Hindus' (Gandhi 2003). The
scientific arguments against unduly alarmist readings of demographic
figures that expose lies about the alarmism or that rationalize differential
population growth amongst religious groups (see Datta 1993) do not do
away with the common 'knowledge'/myth of overpopulating Muslims.
This becomes clear when one participates in conversations with many
Hindus in middle-class drawing rooms, university cafes, tea stalls, and
other public and private gatherings.

The 'overpopulating Muslim' is linked not only to religion but also
to the virility of Muslim men (and the over-fertility of Muslim women).
This imagined virility is used to construct an image of Muslim masculinity that is marked by an uncontrolled and uncontrollable lust, and
is hence a danger to Hindu women. The handsome Muslim who is a
master in the art of seduction, the lecherous Muslim, and the Muslim
rapist, all these images play upon each other as a danger for 'innocent'
Hindu females (see Gupta 2001). This then encourages the mobilization of Hindu women for Hindutva in the name of self-defence and
protection of the body of Hindu women and the Hindu nation.[5] But
more crucially, it exhorts Hindu men to 'protect' their innocent Hindu
mothers, sisters, and daughters. This implies defending Hindu women
from 'the Muslim' who is lecherous and a potential rapist. It also entails
protecting Hindu women from the seduction of Muslim men by policing interactions between Hindu women and Muslim men, casting any
relationship based on this interaction as an indicator of sly Muslim men
polluting, converting, and oppressing Hindu women. Any agency of
the Hindu woman in such relationships is denied. The close connection between demonizing the Muslim and policing (Hindu) woman's
sexuality is well illustrated in debates during early twentieth century

when Hindu widow remarriage was promoted as necessary to 'control' the passion of Hindu widows who would otherwise become prey to the designs of Muslim men (see Gupta 2001).

Thus, a militant aggressive masculinity is called for in the name of defence and security of the Self (women, family, community, religion, nation, state). The construction of 'the Hindu' draws its legitimacy from the representation of 'The Muslim' as a danger to the Hindu body and, in turn, legitimizes the use of 'any means' to protect and take revenge. The Hindu male is expected to protect Hindu women, and in the process, if required, is justified in castrating Muslim men and raping Muslim women. This violence is masked by the Hindutva forces as self-defence. As Bacchetta points out, '...the counterpart to the chaste Hindu male is the Muslim male polygamist or rapist, and to the chaste motherly Hindu woman is the Muslim woman as prostitute or potential wife' (Bacchetta 2004: 101).

Thus, 'The Muslim' as a gendered figure is constructed to mobilize the Hindu male and female and awaken the Hindu nation. The fact that Hindutva forces are not dominant politically in India does not reduce the danger of such vicious representations of the Muslim in fermenting collective anti-Muslim violence. As I pointed out earlier, what is more disturbing is that these representations scavenge upon, and in turn shape and fossilize, prejudicial desires that are common in the popular imaginary amongst many Hindus in India and abroad. Not enough attention has been paid to the 'highly selective and manipulative process by which myths and stereotypes about the marauding and libidinous Muslim, the innocent and motherlike Hindu woman, the tolerant Hindu man, have entered and entrenched themselves in public memory and conscious-ness' (Butalia 1995: 79). Hindu fanaticism is seen as a contradiction in terms by some Hindus who, while politically shunning the Hindu Right, buy into the myth of Hinduism as marked overwhelmingly by tolerance. Though Hindu chauvinism is widespread, it is not hegemonic as there are many Hindus who do not subscribe to it. Rejecting the charge of Hindu communalism, the apologists of Hindutva will present communal conflicts as 'an unintended by-product of Hindu national self-assertion that results from adverse reactions from minority commu-nities and from the Indian state' (Ludden 1996a: 16). In most commu-nal riots in contemporary India, Muslims are overwhelmingly victimized in terms of loss of life, dignity, and livelihood. Yet, this screaming fact is silenced by blaming the victims—the loss is sad, but 'they' (Muslims) asked for it! Why did they start the riot, why do they support Pakistan, why are they terrorists and criminals, why do they create problems and strife everywhere in the world, why cannot they be like us?—these questions rid many Hindus of their guilt consciousness and leave intact the self-image of the enlightened, tolerant Hindu. Anti-Muslim riots in Gujarat in 2002 illustrate well this 'blame the victim' ideology and the role the imagining of 'The Muslim' as a danger to the security of Hindu body plays in making sense of this kind of violence.

VISITING A SITE OF COMMUNAL VIOLENCE: GUJARAT 2002

The anti-Muslim violence in Gujarat in 2002 was masked as 'inevitable' and 'understandable' acts to secure the Hindu Self. The (meta)discourse of security offered the forces of Hindutva a tool to legitimize violence as non-violence, killers as defenders, rape as understandable lust, and death as non-death. I do not go into details of the violence and explanations of it here (see *Communalism Combat* 2002; IIJ 2003; *Labour File* 2002; *Lessons from Gujarat* 2003; Mander 2002; Varadarajan 2002. What I propose is one of the ways in which we can make sense of the complicity of a significant number of Hindus in this violence, borrowing the analysis from various reports just mentioned.

During February 2002, the VHP, one of the constituents of the Sangh Parivar (see Note 1), was carrying on with its agitation over the building of a temple in Ayodhya.[6] After some altercation, one coach of the *Sabarmati Express*, a train returning from Ayodhya and carrying many Hindu *kar sevaks* (activists), was burnt at the Godhra station in Gujarat on 26 February killing fifty-eight people. What followed for the next couple of months was massive communal violence in which most of the victims were Muslims. Though Hindutva forces painted this anti-Muslim violence, in which around a thousand people were killed, as a reaction to Godhra, documented evidence points to four crucial features of this violence which challenge the 'riots-as-post-Godhra-reaction' thesis. First, there was an active state complicity—through police inaction (see Human Rights Watch 2002); frequent police participation in anti-Muslim violence; hate speeches by members of the state government and the BJP; active participation of local and state leaders in fomenting violence; and availability of lists of Muslim establishments (data privy to the government) to the Hindu mobs. Second, there was a conscious and well-orchestrated pre-planning for communal violence through activities of various Hindutva organizations. Third, organizations such as VHP used the train incident as an excuse to 'teach Muslims a lesson' through vicious use of brutality. Fourth, the ruling party, BJP, used this to buttress its political position—a strategy that succeeded with the BJP coming to power with a greater majority in a snap election. In a few months time, the violence subsided but the hatred and its legacy remain as the struggle for rebuilding lives and securing justice continues.

What make the spectacle of anti-Muslim violence in Gujarat 2002 extraordinary is its banality and its 'participative' nature. Class, gender, age, or caste were not a barrier either for the willing participants or for the unwilling victims. It is not sufficient to explain this phenomenon in instrumental terms alone. While interests did play an important role (for instance, looting, grabbing of land, occupying houses, and settling scores), it was not the sole determining factor. For the majority who did not benefit in instrumental terms but still accepted Hindutva versions of the violence and voted with their feet by re-electing BJP in assembly polls, it was the imagined subjectivity of the victims (dangerous, fanatic, violent, and hence to be blamed for provoking Hindus) that was the important factor. It is these dehumanized representations of the Other as a danger that offer us a good handle to understand the normalization of abnormal violence and the construction of a secure Hindu identity through the humiliation and extermination of other identities.

The approving statements of a Hindu man (a non-participant middle-class professional man), quoted by Cohn (2003), reflect a sentiment that is widespread (both in the real and the virtual world; see Note 4): 'Muslim boys, even married ones, try to have friendships with Hindu girls. I tell you, most Muslim guys are very good looking, and Hindu girls are very innocent—once they give you their heart, it's easily broken ... I personally feel they're spoiling the lives of these Hindu girls. Our blood gets hot.... It's time that the Hindus fight violence with violence'.

The need to secure Hindu female body against the danger of 'The Muslim' was therefore seen as one of the rationale for violence against Muslims (for a detailed treatment, see IIJ 2003). Gujarat 2002 was a lesson in masculinization showing, through the defeat and humiliation of Muslim men, who the 'real men' are. The slogan, '*Jis Hinduon ka khoon na khola, woh Hindu nahin, woh hijra hain*' (Those Hindus whose blood does not boil, are not Hindus, they are eunuchs), chanted by the student wing of BJP at a premier university in Delhi during a post-Godhra procession (see T. Sarkar 2002) illustrates this obsession with manhood. Various forms of display of violent sexuality were seen emphasizing Hindu manhood as the violent protector of Hindus revealing the impotency of 'The Muslim'. The reaction of Praveen Togadia, a leader of the VHP, in the aftermath of Godhra is significant: 'Hindu Society will avenge the Godhra killings. Muslims should accept the fact that Hindus are not wearing bangles. We will respond vigorously to all such incidents' (*Labour File* 2002). Pamphlets exhorting Hindu men not to feel guilty about raping Muslim women; regional Gujarati newspapers sensationalizing false stories about Hindu girls being raped; Hindutva ideologues hammering on about the historic rape of Hindu women and nation at the hands of Muslims; distribution of bangles (an ornamental marker of femininity) to Hindu men who did not participate; punishing (through killing, boycott, and hate campaigns) of Hindu men and women who were seen as helping Muslims—all these show that the macabre display of 'tolerance', 'passion', and 'reaction' (these were the self-serving terms used by various proponents of Hindutva to characterize the anti-Muslim violence) was anything but spontaneous (for detailed reports, see *Communalism Combat* 2002). It shows the construction of a particular form of masculinity through acts of violence, a masculinity that declares itself the protector of the security of Hindu bodies as well as the Hindu body politic.

A majority of the people in the affected areas of Gujarat did not participate directly in violence. However, neither was there any strong protest against the violence. Many non-governmental organizations and citizens groups did not speak out in strong terms condemning the violence. 'All sides should calm down' is seen as implying that no one is responsible. The silent majority's inaction in Gujarat 2002 was an action loaded in favour of those perpetrating anti-Muslim violence. The BJP state leadership, which was clearly identified as complicit with the Gujarat 2002 killing machinery, was confident of gaining electorally after the riot, and the fact that this confidence paid off is an indictment of the silent majority. This electoral victory in the state assembly elections of December 2002, the best performance ever by BJP on its own in any state in India, challenged most factors that are seen as important in the electoral democracy in India (for example, anti-incumbency factor, lack of development, and strength of the opposition) and showed that violence against Muslims paid off. This cannot be explained by the instrumental interests of the Hindu majority alone but by the lack of compassion for the Muslim victims. There was a curious reversal of responsibility as many Hindus blamed Muslims for the violence and saw themselves as the victims whose security was threatened by 'The Muslim'.

DOES SECURITY KILL?

The chapter answers in the affirmative. Security is not a response to a pre-existing danger but is constitutive of it. This constitution of danger and insecurity is productive of violence. Security masks violence in the name of counter-violence, killing in the name of protection. As the case of Hindutva in India illustrates, violence against minorities is normalized in the name of personal, communal, national, and even international security. The will to secure the Self has as its corollary the will to insecure the Other, the desire to control and use violence. An engaged scholarship that recognizes the violence of security is a step in the direction of interrogating the theory and praxis of security that underpins the violent world we live in today.

NOTES

1. The Hindu Right in India is seen as subscribing to Hindu nationalism (Hindutva). While the main political party espousing this is the Bharatiya Janata Party (BJP), there are various other political and cultural organizations and movements, including the Rashtriya Swayamsevak Sangh (RSS), Vishva Hindu Parishad (VHP), Bajrang Dal, Durga Vahini, and so on, that are together seen as belonging to the Sangh Parivar (the Sangh family, where the Sangh, that is, the RSS, is seen as the parent organization).

2. India has a federal set-up and Gujarat is a state in western India. In 2002, the ruling party in Gujarat was the BJP under the chief ministership of Narendra Modi. As anti-Muslim riots spread through Gujarat in the first half of 2002, the national media reported of clear complicity of Modi administration in the violence. Yet the federal government at that time, consisting of the BJP in a coalition, ignored and downplayed the severity of riots. After violence abated with slightly less than a thousand Muslims killed and tens of thousands of people (mostly Muslim, but quite a few Hindus too) displaced, BJP in Gujarat was confident of gaining electorally and called for an early election for the state assembly. In this chapter, I am primarily interested in why such collective communal violence against minorities pays electorally. Why would Hindus who would not otherwise vote for BJP in the election, go out and vote for it even though the majority of the victims of violence are Muslims?

3. It would be simplistic to see this shift solely in terms of rise of Hindu nationalism. The changing global environment—the emergence of the United States as the sole superpower, dissipating of non-alignment movement, neoliberal globalization as the dominant regime—has led to liberalization, privatization, and marketization. The establishment of neoliberal orthodoxy in India has been an important part of this shift to the Right (see Ahmad 2004).

4. The sample is distilled from anecdotal evidence, discussions with those with Hindu chauvinist leanings, academic literature on the Hindutva, and most importantly, from pro-Hindutva websites, including http://www.hindu-unity.org/, http://www.hindutva.org/, http://www.freeindia.org/, http://www.organiser.org/, and http://www.swordoftruth.com/.

5. In this chapter, I do not examine two issues that are related to the questions about Hindutva and masculinity. One is the Hindutva image of women in general, and Muslim women in particular. The second is the role of Hindu women in Hindutva organizations and during communal riots. For various perspectives, see Bacchetta (2004), Jayawardena and Alwis (1998), and Sarkar and Butalia (1995).

6. The Hindutva forces have been agitating over building of a temple at the supposed birthplace of Lord Rama in Ayodhya, a town in north India. This town became infamous in 1992 when Babri Mosque (which allegedly was built by the Mughal ruler Babur, in sixteenth century, over a Hindu temple) was demolished. The demolition was followed by serious anti-Muslim riots in various parts of India. The Ram Janmabhoomi campaign to build a temple at the site of the demolished mosque has been deployed by Hindutva forces, especially the VHP, in an attempt to mobilize Hindus. At the start of 2002, VHP had restarted the campaign despite the warnings that this would incite communal hatred. For analyses of the movement, see Brass (1997), Ludden (1996b), and Pandey (1993).

REFERENCES

Ahmad, Aijaz. 2004, *On Communalism and Globalization: Offensives of the Far Right*, New Delhi: Three Essays Collective.

Anand, Dibyesh. 2011, *Hindu Nationalism in India and Politics of Fear*, New York: Palgrave Macmillan.

Bacchetta, Paola. 2004, *Gender in the Hindu Nation: RSS Women as Ideologues*, New Delhi: Women Unlimited.

Basu, Tapan, Pradip Datta, Sumit Sarkar, Tanika Sarkar, and Sambuddha Sen. 1993, *Khaki Shorts, Saffron Flags*, New Delhi: Orient Longman.

Bhargava, Rajeev (ed.). 1998, *Secularism and Its Critics*, New Delhi: Oxford University Press.

Brass, Paul. 1997, *Theft of an Idol: Text and Context in the Representation of Collective Violence*, Princeton: Princeton University Press.

————. 2003, *The Production of Hindu–Muslim Violence in Contemporary India*, New Delhi: Oxford University Press.

Brass, Paul and Achin Vanaik (eds). 2002, *Competing Nationalism in South Asia*, New Delhi: Orient Longman.

Butalia, Urvashi. 1995, 'Muslims and Hindus, Men and Women: Communal Stereotypes and the Partition of India', in T. Sarkar and U. Butalia (eds),

Women and Right-Wing Movements: Indian Experiences, London: Zed, pp. 58–81.

Campbell, David. 1998, *Writing Security: United States Foreign Policy and the Politics of Identity*, revised edition, Minneapolis: University of Minnesota Press.

Chitkara, M.G. 2003, *Hindutva Parivar*, New Delhi: APH Publishing Corporation.

Cohn, Martin R. 2003, 'India's "Lab" for Divisive Politics', *Toronto Star*, 26 October, available at http://stopfundinghate.org/resources/news/ 102603 TorontoStar.htm (accessed 12 February 2011).

Communalism Combat. 2002, 'Genocide Gujarat 2002', *Communalism Combat*, 8(76), available at http://www.sabrang.com/cc/archive/2002/marapril/index. html (accessed 10 January 2005).

Das, Veena. 1990, 'Our Work to Cry: Your Work to Listen', in V. Das (ed.), *Mirrors of Violence*, New Delhi: Oxford University Press, pp. 345–95.

Datta, Pradip Kumar. 1993, '"Dying Hindus": Production of Hindu Communal Common Sense in Early 20th Century Bengal', *Economic and Political Weekly*, 28(25): 1305–19.

Dayal, John. 2004, 'Indian Census: After Xenophobia, the Report Card of the Communities', *Countercurrents*, 12 December, available at http://www. countercurrents.org/comm-dayal120904.htm (accessed 1 May 2010).

Dillon, Michael. 1996, *Politics of Security: Towards a Political Philosophy of Continental Thought*, London: Routledge.

Elst, Koenraad. 1997, *The Demographic Siege*, New Delhi: Voice of India, available at http://www.bharatvani.org/books/demogislam/part1.html (accessed 12 January 2011).

Foucault, Michel. 1977, *Discipline and Punish: The Birth of the Prison*, trans Alan Sheridan, London: Penguin.

—————. 1988, *Madness and Civilization: A History of Insanity in the Age of Reason*, London: Vintage.

Gandhi, Rajmohan. 2003, 'Blah, Blah, Blood', *Hindustan Times*, 4 July, available at http://www.countercurrents.org/comm-gandhi040703.htm (accessed 10 February 2005).

Gupta, Charu. 2001, *Sexuality, Obscenity, Community: Women, Muslims, and the Hindu Public in Colonial India*, New Delhi: Permanent Black.

Hansen, Thomas Blom. 1999, *The Saffron Wave: Democracy and Hindu Nationalism in Modern India*, Princeton: Princeton University Press.

Hingle, G.S. 1999, *Hindutva Reawakened*, New Delhi: Vikas Publishing House.

Human Rights Watch. 2002, 'We Have No Orders to Save You', 14(3, April), available at http://www.hrw.org/reports/2002/india/ (accessed 14 December 2004).

Huntington, Samuel P. 1993, 'The Clash of Civilization', *Foreign Affairs*, 72(3): 22–49, available at http://www.alamut.com/subj/economics/misc/clash.html (accessed 5 January 2005).

International Initiative for Justice (IIJ). 2003, 'Threatened Existence: A Feminist Analysis of the Genocide in Gujarat', Report, available at http://www.onlinevolunteers.org/gujarat/reports/iijg/2003/ (accessed 15 January 2005).

Jaffrelot, Christopher. 1999, *The Hindu Nationalist Movement: 1925 to the 1990s*, New Delhi: Penguin.

Jayawardena, Kumari and Malathi De Alwis (eds). 1998, *Embodied Violence: Communalising Women's Sexuality in South Asia*, London: Zed.

Kabbani, Rana. 1986, *Imperial Fictions: Europe's Myths of Orient*, London: Pandora.

Kakar, Sudhir. 1996, *The Colors of Violence: Cultural Identities, Religion, and Conflict*, Chicago: University of Chicago Press.

Khalidi, Omar. 2003, *Khaki and the Ethnic Violence in India*, New Delhi: Three Essays Collective.

Krause, Keith and Michael Williams (eds). 1997, *Critical Security Studies*, Boulder, CO: Lynne Rienner.

Labour File. 2002, 'Gujarat Carnage 2002: A Report to the Nation', An Independent Fact Finding Mission, available at http://www.labourfile.org/cec1/labourfile/News%20Update2/Gujarat%20carnage%20II%20-%20fact%20finding.htm (accessed 10 January 2005).

Lessons from Gujarat. 2003, Mumbai: Vikas Adhyayan Kendra.

Lewis, Reina. 1996, *Gendering Orientalism: Race, Feminity and Representation*, London: Routledge.

Lipschutz, Ronnie D. 1995, *On Security*, New York: Columbia University Press.

Ludden, David (ed.). 1996a, 'Introduction. Ayodhya: A Window on the World', in *Making India Hindu: Religion, Community, and the Politics of Democracy in India*, New Delhi: Oxford University Press, pp. 1–27.

————. (ed.). 1996b, *Making India Hindu: Religion, Community, and the Politics of Democracy in India*, New Delhi: Oxford University Press.

Mander, Harsh, 2002, *Cry, the Beloved Country: Reflections on the Gujarat Massacre*, available http://www.sabrang.com/gujarat/statement/nv2.htm (accessed 10 November 2004).

Misra, Amalendu. 2004, *Identity and Religion: Foundations of Anti-Islamism in India*, New Delhi: Sage Publications.

Nandy, Ashis. 1988, 'The Politics of Secularism and the Recovery of Religious Tolerance', *Alternatives*, 13(2): 177–94.

Noorani, A.G. 2002, *Savarkar and Hindutva*, New Delhi: Leftword.

Paliwal, K.V. 2003, *Challenges before the Hindus (From Islam, Christianity and Pseudo-Secularism)*, Delhi: Hindu Writers Forum.

Pandey, Gyanendra. 1990, 'The Colonial Construction of "Communalism": British Writings on Banaras in the Nineteenth Century', in V. Das (ed.), *Mirrors of Violence*, New Delhi: Oxford University Press, pp. 94–134.

————. (ed.). 1993, *Hindus and Others: The Question of Identity in India Today*, New Delhi: Viking.

Rajalakshmi, T.K. 2004, 'The Population Bogey', *Frontline*, 21(20), available at http://www.frontlineonnet.com/fl2120/stories/20041008006101600.htm (accessed 15 February 2005).

Rashtriya Swayamsevak Sangh (RSS). 2003, 'Mission & Vision', available at http://www.rss.org/New_RSS/Mission_Vision/Why_RSS.jsp (accessed 10 November 2004).

Rediff.com. 2002, 'Muslims Don't Want to Live in Harmony, Says Vajpayee', Rediff.com, 12 April, available at http://www.rediff.com/news/2002/apr/12bhatt.htm (accessed 30 October 2004).

Said, Edward. 1978, *Orientalism: Western Conceptions of the Orient*, New York: Penguin.

Sarkar, Sumit. 2002, *Beyond Nationalist Frames: Relocating Postmodernism, Hindutva, History*, New Delhi: Permanent Black.

Sarkar, Tanika. 2002, 'Semiotics of Terror: Muslim Children and Women in Hindu Rashtra', *Economic and Political Weekly*, 37(28): 2872–6.

Sarkar, Tanika and Urvashi Butalia (eds). 1995, *Women and Right-Wing Movements: Indian Experiences*, London: Zed.

Savarkar, Vinayak Damodar. 1999, *Hindutva*, 7th edition, Mumbai: Pandit Bakhle.

Swordsoftruth.com. n.d., 'Hindus! Where Will You Go Now?' Swordsoftruth. com, available at http://www.swordoftruth.com/swordoftruth/archives/oldarchives/hindus.html (accessed 15 January 2004).

Varadarajan, Siddharth. 2002, *Gujarat: The Making of a Tragedy*, New Delhi: Penguin.

Varshney, Ashutosh. 2002, *Ethnic Conflict and Civic Life: Hindus and Muslims in India*, New Haven: Yale University Press.

Weldes, Jutta, Mark Laffey, Hugh Gusterson, and Raymond Duvall (eds). 1999, *Cultures of Insecurity: States, Communities, and the Production of Danger*, Minneapolis: University of Minnesota Press.

Zavos, John. 2000, *The Emergence of Hindu Nationalism in India*, New Delhi: Oxford University Press.

Contributors

DIBYESH ANAND is Reader (Associate Professor) in International Relations at the Centre for the Study of Democracy, Westminster University, London.

CHAD M. BAUMAN is Associate Professor of Religion at Butler University in Indianapolis, Indiana, USA.

NATASHA BEHL is Visiting Professor of Politics at Occidental College, Eagle Rock, California.

FARHANA IBRAHIM is Assistant Professor of Sociology and Social Anthropology at the Indian Institute of Technology Delhi, New Delhi.

MURZBAN JAL is Professor at the Indian Institute of Education, Pune.

LAURA DUDLEY JENKINS is Associate Professor of Political Science at the University of Cincinnati, Cincinnati, Ohio.

JOSEPH M.T. is Honorary Director of Institute of Indian Culture, Mumbai and Assistant Professor in Sociology at St. Xavier's College, Mumbai.

JOSEPH MARIANUS KUJUR is Assistant Research Director and Head of the Tribal Unit of the Indian Social Institute, New Delhi.

SIPRA MUKHERJEE is Associate Professor at the Department of English, West Bengal State University, West Bengal.

YOUSUF SAEED is an independent filmmaker and researcher based in New Delhi.

MICHEL SEYMOUR is full Professor of Philosophy at University of Montreal, Montreal, Quebec, Canada.

RINA VERMA WILLIAMS is Assistant Professor of Women's, Gender and Sexuality Studies and Political Science at the University of Cincinnati, Cincinnati, Ohio.

RICHARD F. YOUNG holds the Timby Chair in the History of Religions at Princeton Theological Seminary, Princeton, New Jersey.

Index